On September 28, 1978, while Pope John Paul I sat down to a frugal dinner in the third-floor dining room of the Apostolic Palace within Vatican City, other men in other places were deeply anxious about the activities of the newly elected pope. . . .

In the Vatican Bank, the lights still burned. Word had reached its head, Bishop Paul Marcinkus, that the new pope had quietly begun an investigation into the Vatican Bank and the methods Marcinkus used to run it. Paul Marcinkus was about to be removed. . . .

At his desk, Cardinal Jean Villot, Vatican Secretary of State, studied the list of appointments, resignations, transfers, that the pope had handed him one hour previously. In Villot's mind there could be no doubt that there was to be a dramatic change—one that would constitute a betrayal of Paul VI. . . .

In Buenos Aires, banker Roberto Calvi consulted his protector, Licio Gelli, the formidable head of the secret organization, P2, Calvi had been beset by problems even before the election of John Paul I. Now he faced total ruin. . . .

In New York, Sicilian banker Michele Sindona was fighting extradition to Italy. If John Paul I continued to dig into the web of corruption at the Vatican Bank, the trail would lead back to Michele Sindona. . . .

In Chicago, Cardinal John Cody received a phone call from Rome: the pope had decided that Cardinal Cody was to be replaced. . . .

Sometime during the late evening of September 28, 1978 and the early morning of September 29, 1978, thirty-three days after his election, John Paul I died. Time of death: Unknown. Cause of death: Unknown.

On September 28, 1978 these six men—Marcinkus, Villot, Calvi, Gelli, Sindona, Cody—had a great deal to fear if the papacy of John Paul I continued. One of these six men applied the Italian Solution: The pope must die!

—from the Prologue

IN GOD'S NAME

*An Investigation into
the Murder of
Pope John Paul I*

DAVID A. YALLOP

BANTAM BOOKS
TORONTO • NEW YORK • LONDON • SYDNEY • AUCKLAND

The author and publishers wish to thank the following for permis
sion to reproduce black and white photographs (numbers refer to
key references on the photo pages):

Agenzia Ansa: 1, 2, 3, 4, 6, 24, 26, 29, 34, 36, 47, 51, 52, 54, and 60;
Associated Press: 7, 10, 15, 21, 25, 32, 33, 35, 37, 39, 43, 45, 48,
49, 50, 57, 58, 61, 63, and 64; Camera Press (photo by Michelle
Noon), 62; Chicago Sunday Times, 11; Dufoto, 5, 8, 9, 14, 16, 19,
20, 22, 23, 46, 53, 55, and 65; Bruno Ferrario, 12, 13, 17, 18, and
38; Fotoattualita, 28; Liverani Foto Notizie d'Attualita per La
Stampa (photo by Gianni di Mango), 56; L'Osservatore Romano
Citta del Vaticano Servizio Fotografico (photos by Arturo Mari),
27, 30, 31, and 44; Press Association, 66; Private Collections, 40
and 59; Philip Willan, 42; Foto Felici, 41.

IN GOD'S NAME

Bantam Hardcover edition / June 1984
Bantam rack-size edition / May 1985

ISBN 0-553-24855-3

*Bantam Books are published by Bantam Books, Inc. Its trademark,
consisting of the words "Bantam Books" and the portrayal of a rooster,
is Registered in the United States Patent and Trademark Office and in
other countries. Marca Registrada. Bantam Books, Inc., 666 Fifth
Avenue, New York, New York 10103.*

PRINTED IN THE UNITED STATES OF AMERICA

H   0 9 8 7 6 5 4 3 2 1

To the memory of my mother,
Una Norah Stanton,
for the years that have gone—
and to Fletcher and Lucy,
love children of the middle years.

To the memory of my mother,
Una Norah Stanton,
for the years that have gone—
and to Fletcher and Lucy,
love children of the middle years.

CONTENTS

PREFACE

This book, the product of nearly three years' intensive research, would not exist without the active help and cooperation of many people and many organizations. Very many of these agreed to help only on the strict understanding that they remained publicly unidentified. As with previous books I have written under similar conditions, I respect my sources' wishes. On this occasion there is an even greater need to protect their identity. As will become clear to the reader, murder is a frequent accompaniment to the events recorded here. A considerable number of the murders committed remain officially unsolved. No one should doubt that the individuals responsible for those deaths have the capacity to murder again. To reveal the names of men and women who provided me with crucial help and who are now at risk would be an act of criminal irresponsibility. To them I owe a particular debt. Their reasons for divulging a wide range of information were many and varied, but again and again I heard the remark, "The truth must be told. If you are prepared to tell it, then so be it." I am deeply grateful to all of them and to the following, who with the greatest respect I classify as the tip of the iceberg:

Professor Amedeo Alexandre, Professor Leonardo Ancona, William Aronwald, Linda Attwell, Josephine Ayres, Alan Bailey, Dr. Shamus Banim, Dr. Derek Barrowcliff, Pia Basso, Father Aldo Belli, Cardinal Giovanni Benelli, Marco Borsa, Vittore Branca, David Buckley, Father Roberto Busa, Dr. Renato Buzzonetti, Roberto Calvi, Emilio Cavaterra, Cardinal Mario Ciappi, Brother Clemente, Joseph Coffey, Annaloa Copps, Rupert Cornwell, Monsignor Ausilio Da Rif, Dr. Antonio Da Ros, Maurizio De Luca, Daniele Doglio, Monsignor Mafeo Ducoli, Father François Evain, Cardinal Pericle Felici, Father Mario Ferrarese, Professor Luigi Fontana, Mario di Francesco, Dr. Carlo Frizziero, Professor Piero Fucci, Father Giovanni Gennari, Monsignor Mario Ghizzo, Father Carlo Gonzalez, Father Andrew Greeley, Diane Hall, Doctor John Henry, Father Thomas Hunt, William Jackson, John J. Kenney, Peter Lemos, Dr. David Levison, Father Diego Lorenzi, Eduardo Luciani, William Lynch, Ann McDiarmid, Father John Magee, Sandro Magister, Alexander Manson, Professor Vincenzo Masini, Father Francis Murphy, Monsignor Giulio Nicolini, Anna Nogara, Father Gerry O'Collins, Father Romeo Panciroli, Father Gianni Pastro, Lena Petri, Nina Petri, Professor Pier Luigi Prati, Professor Giovanni Rama, Roberto Rosone, Professor Fausto Rovelli, Professor Vincenzo Rulli, Ann Ellen Rutherford, Monsignor Tiziano Scalzotto, Monsignor Mario Senigaglia, Arnaldo Signoracci, Ernesto Signoracci, Father Bartolmeo Sorg, Lorana Sullivan, Father Francesco Taffarel, Sister Vincenza, Professor Thomas Whitehead, Phillip Willan. I am also grateful to the following organizations: the Augustinian Residence, Rome, Banco San Marco, the Bank of England, the Bank of International Settlements, Basle, the Bank of Italy, Catholic Central Library, Catholic Truth Society, City of London Police, the Department of Trade, Statistics and Market Intelligence Library, the English College, Rome, the Federal Bureau of Investigation, the Gregorian University, Rome, New Cross Hospital Poisons Unit, Opus Dei, the Pharmaceutical Society of Great Britain, the Tribunal of the Ward of Luxembourg, U.S. Department of State, U.S. District Court Southern District of New York, Vatican Press Office, and Vatican Radio.

Among those I cannot thank publicly are the people resident within Vatican City who contacted me and initiated my investigation of the events surrounding the death of Pope John Paul I, Albino Luciani. The fact that men and women living within the heart of the Roman Catholic Church cannot speak openly and be identified is an eloquent comment on the state of affairs within the Vatican.

Doubtless this book will be attacked by some and dismissed by others. It will be seen by some as an assault on the Roman Catholic faith in particular and on Christianity in general. It is neither of these. To a degree it is an indictment of specifically named men who were born Roman Catholics but who have never become Christians.

This book is not an attack on the faith practiced by the Church's devout millions of followers. What they hold sacred is too important to be left in the hands of men who have conspired to drag the message of Christ into the muddy marketplace—a conspiracy that has met with frightening success.

As already indicated, I confront an insurmountable difficulty when it comes to the task of naming specific sources within the text, as many of my sources must remain secret. I can assure the reader that all the information, all the details, all the facts have been checked and double-checked to the extent that multiple sources were available. I take the responsibility for putting the evidence together and for the conclusions reached.

I am sure that the fact that I recount conversations between men dead before my investigation began will be cause for comment. How, for example, could I know what passed between Pope John Paul I and Cardinal Villot on the day they discussed the issue of artificial birth control? Within the Vatican there is no such thing as a private audience that remains completely private. Quite simply, both men subsequently talked to others of what had transpired. These secondary sources, sometimes with deeply differing personal opinions on the issue discussed by the Pope and his secretary of state, provided the words attributed. Therefore, while the dialogue within this book is reconstructed, it is not fabricated.

May 1984   DAVID A. YALLOP

PROLOGUE

T he spiritual leader of nearly one-fifth of the world's
population wields immense
power. Yet any uninformed observer of Albino Luciani
at the beginning of his reign as Pope John Paul I would
have found it difficult to believe that this man truly
embodied such power. The diffidence and humility emanating from this small, quiet, sixty-five-year-old Italian
had led many to conclude that his papacy would not be
particularly noteworthy. The well informed, however,
knew differently: Albino Luciani had embarked on a
revolution.

On September 28, 1978, he had been pope for thirty-
three days. In little more than a month he had initiated
various courses of action that, had they been completed,
would have had a direct and dynamic effect on us all.
The majority in this world would have applauded his
decisions, a minority would have been appalled. The
man who had quickly been labeled "the smiling pope"
intended to remove the smiles from a number of faces
on the following day.

That evening Luciani sat down to dinner in the
third-floor dining room of the Apostolic Palace within
Vatican City. With him were his two secretaries, Father
Diego Lorenzi, who had worked closely with him in
Venice for more than two years when, as a cardinal,
Luciani had been patriarch there, and Father John Magee,

newly acquired since the papal election. As the nuns
who worked in the papal apartments hovered anxiously,
Albino Luciani ate a frugal meal of clear soup, veal,
fresh beans, and a little salad. He sipped occasionally
from a glass of water and considered the events of the
day and the decisions he had made. He had not wanted
the job. He had not sought or canvassed for the papacy.
Now as head of state the awesome responsibilities were
his.

While Sisters Vincenza, Assunta, Clorinda, and
Gabriella quietly served the three men as they watched
on television the events that preoccupied Italy that
evening, other men in other places were being caused
deep anxiety by the activities of Albino Luciani.

One floor below the papal apartments the lights
were still on in the Vatican Bank. Its head, Bishop Paul
Marcinkus, had other more pressing problems on his
mind than his evening meal. Chicago-born Marcinkus
had learned about survival on the streets of Cicero,
Illinois. During his meteoric rise to power, he had survived many moments of crisis. Now he was confronted
with the most serious challenge he had ever faced. In
the past thirty-three days his colleagues in the bank had
noticed a remarkable change in the man who controlled
the Vatican's millions. The 6-foot, 3-inch, 224-pound
extrovert had become moody and introspective. He was
visibly losing weight, and his face had acquired a gray
pallor. Vatican City in many respects is a village, and
secrets are hard to keep in a village. Word had reached
Marcinkus that the new pope had quietly begun a personal investigation of the Vatican Bank and specifically
of the methods Marcinkus was using to run that bank.
Countless times since the arrival of the new pope,
Marcinkus had regretted that business in 1972 concerning the Banca Cattolica del Veneto. . . .

The Vatican secretary of state, Cardinal Jean Villot,
was another who was still at his desk on that September evening. He studied the list of appointments, resignations to be asked for, and transfers the pope had
handed him one hour previously. He had advised, argued,

and remonstrated, but to no avail. Luciani had been adamant.

It was by any standards a dramatic reshuffle. It would set the Church in new directions—directions that Villot, and the others on the list who were about to be replaced, considered highly dangerous. When these changes were announced there would be millions of words written and uttered by the world's media, analyzing, dissecting, prophesying, explaining. The real explanation, however, would not be discussed, would not be given a public airing. There was one common denominator, one fact that linked each of the men about to be replaced. Villot was aware of it. More important, so was the pope. It had been one of the factors that had caused him to act, to strip these men of real power and put them into relatively harmless positions. It was Freemasonry.

The evidence the pope had acquired indicated that within the Vatican City State there were over one hundred Masons, ranging from cardinals to priests. This despite the fact that Canon Law stated that to be a Freemason ensured automatic excommunication. Luciani was further preoccupied with an illegal Masonic lodge that had penetrated far beyond Italy in its search for wealth and power. It called itself P2. The fact that it had penetrated the Vatican walls and formed links with priests, bishops, and even cardinals made P2 anathema to Albino Luciani.

Villot had already become deeply concerned about the new papacy before this latest bombshell. He was one of the very few who was aware of the dialogue taking place between the pope and the State Department in Washington. He knew that on October 23 the Vatican would be receiving a congressional delegation and that on October 24 the delegation would be having a private audience with the pope. The subject: artificial birth control.

Villot had looked carefully at the Vatican dossier on Albino Luciani. He had also read the secret memorandum that Luciani, then bishop of Vittorio Veneto, had sent to Paul VI before the papal announcement of the encyclical *Humanae Vitae*, an encyclical that prohibited Catholics from using any artificial form of birth control. His own discussions with Luciani had left him in no doubt where the new pope stood on this issue. Equally, in Villot's mind, there was no doubt what Paul's successor was now planning to do. There was to be a dramatic change of position. In Villot's view such a change would constitute a betrayal of Paul VI. . . .

In Buenos Aires, another banker, Roberto Calvi, had Pope John Paul I on his mind as September 1978 drew to a close. In the preceding weeks he had discussed the problems posed by the new pope with his protectors, Licio Gelli and Umberto Ortolani, two men who could list among their many assets their complete control of Calvi, chairman of Banco Ambrosiano. Calvi had been beset with problems even before the election that placed Albino Luciani upon St. Peter's throne. The Bank of Italy had been secretly investigating Calvi's Milan bank since April. It was an investigation prompted by a mysterious poster campaign against Calvi that had erupted in late 1977. The posters had given details of some of Calvi's criminal activities and hinted at a worldwide range of criminal acts.

Calvi was aware of exactly what progress the Bank of Italy was making with its investigation. His close friendship with Licio Gelli ensured a day-by-day account of it. He was equally aware of the papal investigation into the Vatican Bank. Like Marcinkus, he knew it was only a matter of time before the two independent investigations realized that to probe one of these financial empires was to probe both. He was doing everything within his considerable power to thwart the Bank of Italy and protect his financial empire, from which he was in the process of stealing over $1 billion.

Careful analysis of Roberto Calvi's position in September 1978 makes it abundantly clear that if Pope Paul had been succeeded by an honest man, then Calvi faced total ruin, the collapse of his bank, and certain imprisonment. There is no doubt whatever that Albino Luciani was just such a man. . . .

In New York, Sicilian banker Michele Sindona had also been anxiously monitoring Pope John Paul's activities. For over three years Sindona had been fighting the Italian government's attempts to have him extradited.

The Italian government wanted him brought to Milan to face charges involving fraudulent diversion of $225 million. Earlier that year, in May, it appeared that Sindona had finally lost the long battle. A federal judge had ruled that the extradition request should be granted.

Sindona remained free on a $3 million bail while his lawyers prepared to play one last card. They demanded that the United States government prove that there was well-founded evidence to justify extradition. Sindona asserted that the charges brought against him by the Italian government were the work of Communist and other left-wing politicians. His lawyers also asserted that the Milan prosecutor had concealed evidence that would clear Sindona and that if their client were returned to Italy he would almost certainly be assassinated. The hearing was scheduled for November.

That summer, in New York, others were equally active on behalf of Michele Sindona. One Mafia member, Luigi Ronsisvalle, a professional killer, was threatening the life of witness Nicola Biase, who had earlier given evidence against Sindona in the extradition proceedings. The Mafia also had a contract out on the life of Assistant U.S. Attorney John Kenney, who was chief prosecutor in the extradition proceedings. The fee being offered for the murder of the government attorney was $100,000.

If Pope John Paul I continued to dig into the affairs of the Vatican Bank, then no amount of Mafia contracts would help Sindona in his fight against being returned to Italy. The web of corruption at the Vatican Bank, which included the laundering of Mafia money through that bank, went back beyond Calvi, back to Michele Sindona. . . .

In Chicago another prince of the Catholic Church worried and fretted about events in the Vatican—Cardinal John Cody, head of one of the richest archdioceses in the world. Cody ruled over 2½ million Catholics and nearly 3,000 priests, over 450 parishes with an annual income that he refused to reveal in its entirety to anyone. It was, in fact, in excess of $250 million. Fiscal secrecy was only one of the problems that whirled around Cody. By 1978 he had ruled Chicago for thirteen years, and the demands for his replacement had reached extraordinary proportions. Priests, nuns, lay workers, and people from many secular professions had petitioned Rome in the thousands for the removal of the man they regarded as a despot.

Pope Paul had agonized for years about removing Cody. The pope had on at least one occasion actually steeled himself and made the decision, only to revoke the order at the last moment. The complex, tortured personality of Paul was only part of the reason for the vacillation. Paul knew that other, secret allegations had been made against Cody, with a substantial amount of evidence that indicated the urgent need to replace the cardinal of Chicago.

During late September, Cody received a phone call from Rome. The Vatican City village had leaked another piece of information—information well paid for over the years by Cardinal Cody. The caller told the cardinal that where Pope Paul had agonized, his successor, John Paul, had acted. The pope had decided that Cardinal John Cody was to be replaced. . . .

Over at least three of these men lurked the shadow of another, Licio Gelli. Men called him "Il Burattinaio"—the puppetmaster. The puppets were many and were placed in numerous countries. He controlled P2, and through it he controlled Italy. In Buenos Aires, the city where he discussed the problem of the new pope with Calvi, the puppetmaster had organized the triumphant return to power of Juan Perón—a fact that Perón subsequently acknowledged by kneeling at Gelli's feet. If Marcinkus, Sindona, or Calvi were threatened by the various courses of action planned by Albino Luciani, it was in Licio Gelli's direct interests that the threat be removed. . . .

It was abundantly clear that on September 28, 1978, these six men—Marcinkus, Villot, Calvi, Cody, Sindona, and Gelli—had a great deal to fear if the papacy of John Paul I continued. It is equally clear that all of them stood to gain in a variety of ways if Pope John Paul I should suddenly die.

He did.

Sometime during the late evening of September 28,

1978, and the early morning of September 29, 1978, thirty-three days after his election, Albino Luciani died.

Time of death: unknown. Cause of death: unknown.

I am convinced that the full facts and the complete circumstances merely outlined in the preceding pages hold the key to the truth of the death of Albino Luciani. I am equally convinced that one of these six men had, by the early evening of September 28, 1978, already initiated a course of action to resolve the problems that Albino Luciani's papacy was posing. One of these men was at the very heart of a conspiracy that applied a uniquely Italian "solution."

Albino Luciani had been elected pope on August 26, 1978. Emerging from the conclave, the English Cardinal Basil Hume said to the press, "The decision was unexpected. But once it had happened, it seemed totally and entirely right. The feeling he was just what we want was so general that he was unmistakably God's candidate."

Thirty-three days later, "God's candidate" died.

What follows is the product of three years' continuous and intensive investigation into that death. I have evolved a number of rules for an investigation of this nature. Rule One: begin at the beginning. Ascertain the nature and personality of the dead subject. What manner of man was Albino Luciani?

THE ROAD TO
ROME

The Luciani family lived in the small mountain village of Canale d'Agordo,* over three thousand feet above sea level and approximately seventy-five miles north of Venice.

At the time of Albino's birth on October 17, 1912, his parents, Giovanni and Bortola, were already caring for two daughters from the father's first marriage. As a young widower with two daughters and lacking a regular job, Giovanni would not have been every young woman's dream come true. Bortola had been contemplating the life of a convent nun. Now she was mother to three children. The birth had been long and arduous, and Bortola, displaying an overanxiety that would become a feature of the boy's early life, feared that the child was about to die. He was promptly baptized, with the name Albino, in memory of a close friend of his father who had been killed in a blast-furnace accident while working alongside Giovanni in Germany. The boy came into a world that within two years would be at war, after Archduke Francis Ferdinand and his wife had been assassinated.

*At the time of Albino Luciani's birth the village had been renamed Forno di Canale. It was changed back to Canale d'Agordo in 1964 at the instigation of Luciani's brother, Edoardo.

9

The first fourteen years of this century are considered by many Europeans to have been a golden age.
Countless writers have described the stability, the general feeling of well-being, the widespread increase in
mass culture, the satisfying spiritual life, the broadening of horizons, and the reduction of social inequalities.
They extol the freedom of thought and the quality of life
as if describing an early-twentieth-century Garden of
Eden. Doubtless all this existed, but so did appalling
poverty, mass unemployment, social inequality, hunger,
illness, and early death. Much of the world was divided
by these two realities. Italy was no exception.

Naples was besieged by thousands of people who
wanted to immigrate to the United States, or England,
or anywhere. Already the United States had written
some small print under the heroic declaration "Give me
your tired, your poor. Your huddled masses yearning to
breathe free." The "wretched refuse" now discovered
that disease, insufficient funds, contract labor, criminality, and physical deformity were a few of the grounds
for rejection from admission to the United States.

In Rome, within sight of St. Peter's, thousands lived
on a permanent basis in huts of straw and brushwood.
In the summer many moved to the caves in the surrounding hills. Some did dawn-to-dusk work in vine-
yards for pennies a day. On farms others worked the
same hours and received no money at all. Payment was
usually in rotten maize, one of the reasons that so many
agricultural laborers suffered from a skin disease called
pellagra. Standing waist deep in the rice fields of Pavia
ensured that many contracted malaria from the frequent mosquito bites. Illiteracy was over 50 percent.
While pope after pope yearned for the return of the
Papal States (lost since 1870), these conditions were the
reality of life for many who lived in this united Italy.

The village of Canale was dominated by children,
women, and old men. The majority of men of working
age were forced to seek work farther afield. Giovanni
Luciani would travel to Switzerland, Austria, Germany,
and France, leaving in the spring and returning in the
autumn.

The Luciani home, partly converted from an old
barn, had one source of heating, an old wood-burning

stove, which heated the room where Albino was born. There was no garden—such items are considered luxuries by the mountain people. The scenery more than compensated: pine forests and, soaring directly above the village, the stark, snowcapped mountains; the River Bioi cascaded down close to the village square.

Albino Luciani's parents were an odd match. The deeply religious Bortola spent as much time in the church as she did in her small home, worrying over her increasingly large family. She was the kind of mother who at the slightest cough would overanxiously rush any of her children to the nearby medical officers. Devout, with aspirations to martyrdom, she was prone to tell the children frequently of the many sacrifices she was obliged to make on their behalf. The father, Giovanni, wandered a Europe at war seeking work that ranged from bricklaying and engineering to being an electrician and a mechanic. As a committed Socialist he was regarded by devout Catholics as a priest-eating, crucifix-burning devil. The combination produced inevitable frictions. The memory of his mother's reaction when she saw her husband's name on posters plastered all over the village announcing that he was running in a local election as a Socialist stayed with the young Albino for the rest of his life.

Albino was followed by another son, Edoardo, and then a girl, Antonia. Bortola added to their small income by writing letters for the illiterate and working as a scullery maid.

The family diet consisted of polenta (cornmeal), barley, macaroni, and any handy vegetables. On special occasions there might be a dessert of carfoni, pastry full of ground poppy seeds. Meat was a rarity. In Canale if a man was wealthy enough to afford the luxury of killing a pig it would be salted and last his family for a year.

Albino's vocation for the priesthood came early and was actively encouraged by his mother and the local parish priest, Father Filippo Carli. Yet if any single person deserves credit for ensuring that Albino Luciani took his first steps toward the priesthood it is the irreligious Socialist, Giovanni. If Albino was to attend the minor seminary at nearby Feltre it was going to cost the Luciani family a considerable sum. Mother and son

discussed this shortly before the boy's eleventh birthday.
Eventually Bortola told her son to sit down and write to
his father, then working in France. Albino was later to
say it was one of the most important letters of his life.
His father received the letter and thought the problem
over for a while before replying. Then he gave his permission and accepted the added burden with the words,
"Well, we must make this sacrifice."

So in 1923, the eleven-year-old Luciani went off to
the seminary—to the internal war that was raging within
the Roman Catholic Church. This was a Church where
books such as Antonio Rosmini's *The Five Wounds of the
Church* were banned. Rosmini, an Italian theologian
and priest, had written in 1848 that the Church faced a
crisis of five evils: social remoteness of the clergy from
the people; the low standard of education of the priests;
disunity and acrimony among the bishops; the dependence of lay appointments on secular authorities; and
Church ownership of property and enslavement to wealth.
Rosmini had hoped for liberalizing reform. What he
got, largely as a result of Jesuit intrigue, was the condemnation of his book and the withdrawal of the cardinal's
hat that Pius IX had offered him.

Only forty-eight years before Luciani's birth the
Vatican had proclaimed the *Syllabus of Errors* and an
accompanying encyclical, *Quanta Cura*. In these the papacy denounced unrestricted freedom of speech and of
the press. The concept of equal status for all religions
was totally rejected. The pope responsible for these measures was Pius IX. He also made it clear that he disliked
intensely the concept of democratic government and
that his preference was for absolute monarchies. He
further denounced "the proponents of freedom of conscience and freedom of religion" as well as "all of those
who assert that the Church may not use force."

In 1870, this same pope, having summoned Vatican
Council I, indicated to the assembled bishops that the
main item on the agenda was papal infallibility. *His*
infallibility. After much intensive lobbying and some
very unchristianlike pressure, the pope suffered a major moral defeat when, out of over 1,000 bishops entitled to take part in the Council, only 451 voted for
infallibility. But by a strategy of politicking and threat-

ening all but two of the dissenters left Rome before a
final vote was taken. At the last meeting of the council,
on July 18, 1870, it was decided by 533 votes to 2 that
the pope was infallible when defining a doctrine concerning faith or morals.

Until they were liberated by Italian troops in 1870,
the Jews in Rome had been locked in a ghetto by the
pope who became infallible. He was similarly intoler-
ant of Protestants and recommended the introduction
of prison sentences for non-Catholics who were preaching in Tuscany. At the time of this writing considerable
efforts are being made to have Pius IX canonized
(declared a saint).

After Pius IX came Leo XIII, considered by many
historians to have been an enlightened and humane
man. He was followed by Pius X, thought by many of
the same historians to have been a total disaster. Pius X
reigned until 1914, and the damage he did was still very
evident when Albino Luciani entered the Feltre seminary.

The index of books that no Roman Catholic was
allowed to read grew ever longer. Publishers, editors,
and authors were excommunicated. When critical books
were published anonymously, the authors, whoever they
were, were excommunicated. Pius X coined a word to
encapsulate all that he was attempting to destroy:
"modernism." Any who questioned the current teachings of the Church were anathema. With the pope's
blessing and financial help, an Italian prelate, Umberto
Benigni, created a network of informers. The purpose
was to hunt and destroy all modernists. Thus in the
twentieth century the Inquisition was reborn.

With the diminution of his worldly powers through
the loss of the Papal States, the self-proclaimed "prisoner
in the Vatican" was not in a position to order any
burnings at the stake. But a nudge here, a wink there,
anonymous and unsupported allegations about a colleague or possible rival were enough to destroy many
careers within the Church. The mother was eating her
own children. The majority of those whom Pius and the
men around him destroyed were loyal and faithful members of the Roman Catholic Church.

Seminaries were closed. Those that were allowed to
remain open to teach the next generation of priests

were carefully monitored. In one encyclical the pope declared that everyone who preached or taught in an official capacity had to take a special oath abjuring all errors of modernism. He further declared a general prohibition against the reading of newspapers by all seminarians and theological students, specifically adding that his rule also applied to the very best journals.

Every year Father Benigni, the man in charge of the spy ring that eventually reached through every single diocese in Italy and right across Europe, received a subsidy of 1,000 lire (what would be about $5,000 today) directly from the pope. This secret organization of spies was not disbanded until 1921. Father Benigni then became an informant and spy for Mussolini.

Pius X died on August 20, 1914. He was canonized in 1954.

So, at Feltre, Luciani found it was a crime to read a newspaper or many periodicals. He was in an austere world where the teachers were as vulnerable as the pupils. A word or comment that did not meet with the entire approval of a colleague might result in a teaching priest losing the right to teach because of Father Benigni's spy ring. Although officially disbanded in 1921, two years before Luciani entered Feltre, its influence was still prevalent throughout his entire period of training for the priesthood. Critical questioning of what was being taught would have been anathema. The system was designed to give answers, not to encourage questions. The teachers who had been marked and scarred by the purge would in turn mark and scar the next generation.

Albino Luciani's generation of priests had to cope with the full force of the *Syllabus of Errors* and the antimodernist mentality. Luciani himself might easily have become, under such dominant influences, yet another priest with a closed mind. A variety of factors saved him from that fate. Not the least was a simple but great gift, a thirst for knowledge.

Although his mother's concern about his early health was exaggerated, her overprotectiveness yielded one considerable bonus. By refusing to let the boy enjoy the rough-and-tumble of his friends and by replacing the ball with a book, she opened the entire world to her son. He began to read voraciously at an early age—the complete works of Dickens and Jules Verne. Mark Twain, for example, he read at the age of seven, unusual in a country where still nearly half the adults could not read at all at that time.

At Feltre he absorbed every book they had. More significantly, he remembered virtually everything he read. He was endowed with an astonishing memory. And though provocative questions might be frowned upon, Luciani would from time to time have the temerity to ask them. Consequently, his teachers considered him diligent but "too lively."

In the summers the young seminarian would return home and, dressed in his long black cassock, work in the fields. When not helping with the harvest he could be found "reorganizing" Father Filippo's library. The school terms would be enlivened every now and then by a visit from Albino's father. The first act performed by Giovanni on returning home in the autumn was always a visit to the seminary. He would then spend the winter campaigning on behalf of the Socialists.

From Feltre, Luciani graduated to the major seminary at Belluno. One of his contemporaries described to me the regime at Belluno and his recollections of Luciani:

> We were woken up at 5:30 A.M. No heating; indeed, the water would often be solid ice. I used to lose my vocation every morning for five minutes. We had thirty minutes to get washed and make our beds.
>
> I met Luciani there in September 1929. He was then sixteen. He was always amiable, quiet, serene—unless you stated something that was inaccurate—then he was like a spring. I learned that in front of him one had to speak carefully. Any muddled thinking and you were in danger with him.

Among the books Luciani read were a number of works by Antonio Rosmini. Conspicuous by its absence from the seminary library was *The Five Wounds of the Church*. In 1930 it still remained on the index of forbidden books. Aware by now of the furor the book had caused, Luciani quietly acquired his own copy. It was to have a deep and lasting influence on his life.

To Luciani's teachers the *Syllabus of Errors* proclaimed in 1864 by Pius IX was to be considered in the 1930s as the ultimate truth. The toleration of a non-Catholic opinion in any country where Catholics were in a majority was inconceivable. Mussolini's version of fascism was not the only one being taught in Italy in the years immediately preceding the Second World War. Error has no rights. The exception apparently was if it was the teacher who was in error; then its rights were absolute.

Luciani's vision, far from being expanded by his teachers, began, in certain respects, to shrink. Fortunately, he was subjected to influences other than his teachers. Another former classmate at Belluno recalled:

> He read Goldoni's dramas. He read French novelists of the nineteenth century. He bought a collection of the writings of the seventeenth-century French Jesuit Pierre Couwase and read them from cover to cover.

So strongly did the writings of Couwase influence him that Luciani began to think seriously of becoming a Jesuit. He watched as first one, then a second, of his close friends went to the rector, Bishop Giousé Cattarossi, and asked for permission to join the Jesuit order. In both instances the permission was granted. Luciani went and asked for permission. The bishop considered the request, then responded, "No, three is one too many. You had better stay here."

At the age of twenty-three he was ordained a priest, on July 7, 1935, in San Pietro, Belluno. The following day he celebrated his first Mass in his hometown. His delight at being appointed curate in Forno di Canale was total. The fact that this was the humblest clerical position within the Church was of no consequence to him. In the congregation of friends, relations, local priests, and family was a very proud Giovanni Luciani, who now had a permanent job relatively close to home as a glass-blower on the island of Murano near Venice.

In 1937 Luciani was appointed vice-rector at his

old seminary in Belluno. If the content of his teaching at this time differed little from that of his own tutors, his manner certainly did. He lifted what was often dull and tedious theology to something fresh and memorable.

After four years he felt the need to expand. He wanted to earn a doctorate in theology. This would mean moving to Rome and studying at Gregorian University. His superiors in Belluno wanted him to continue teaching there while he studied for his doctorate. Luciani was agreeable, but Gregorian University insisted on at least one year's obligatory attendance in Rome. After the intervention of Angelo Santin, the director at Belluno, and Father Felice Capello, a renowned expert on canon law who taught at Gregorian and happened to be related to Luciani, Pope Pius XII personally granted a dispensation in a letter signed by Cardinal Maglione and dated March 27, 1941. (The fact that the Second World War was in full flood at the time is not apparent from the Vatican correspondence.) Luciani chose for his thesis, "The origin of the human soul according to Antonio Rosmini."

His experiences during the war were an extraordinary mixture of the sacred and the profane. They included improving his German as he listened to the confessions of soldiers from the Third Reich. They also included meticulous study of Rosmini's works, or that part of them that was not banned. Later, when Luciani became pope, it would be said that his thesis was "brilliant." That, at least, was the view of the Vatican newspaper *L' Osservatore Romano*—which it had not expressed in its preconclave biographies. It is not a view shared by teachers at Gregorian University. One described it to me as "a competent piece of work." Another said, "In my opinion it is worthless. It shows extreme conservatism and also lacks scholarly method."

Many would say that Luciani's interest in and involvement with the works of Rosmini were clear indications of his liberal thinking. The Albino Luciani of the 1940s was far from being a liberal. His thesis attempts to refute Rosmini on each point. He attacks the nineteenth-century theologian for using secondhand and incorrect quotations, for his superficiality, for "ingenious

cleverness." It is a scathing demolition job and a clear
indication of a reactionary mind.

In between establishing that Rosmini had misquoted
St. Thomas Aquinas, Albino Luciani trod a delicate path
when teaching his students at Belluno. He told them
not to intervene when they saw German troops rounding
up local resistance groups. Privately, he was in sympathy with the resistance, but he was aware that among
the trainee priests in the classroom were many who
were profascist. He was equally aware that the resistance movement was provoking reprisals by the Germans against the civilian population. Houses were
destroyed; men were taken out and hanged on trees.
Later in the war, however, Luciani's seminary became a
haven for members of the resistance. Discovery by the
German troops would have resulted in certain death,
not only for the resistance fighters but also for Luciani
and his colleagues.

On November 23, 1946, Luciani defended his thesis.
It was finally published on April 4, 1950. He became a
doctor of theology, receiving his degree *magna cum laude*.

In 1947, the bishop of Belluno, Girolamo Bortignon,
made Luciani pro-vicar-general of the diocese and asked
him to organize the approaching synod and interdiocesan
meeting of Feltre and Belluno. The increase in responsibility coincided with a broadening outlook. While still
unable to come to terms with Rosmini's "origins of the
soul," Luciani had begun to appreciate and agree with
Rosmini's view of what ailed the Church. The fact that
the same problems still obtained a hundred years later
made the factors of social remoteness, an uneducated
priesthood, disunion among bishops, the unhealthy in-
terlocking of power between church and state, and most
of all, the Church's preoccupation with material wealth,
even more pertinent.

In 1949, Luciani was made responsible for catechetics
in preparation for the eucharistic congress that was
taking place that year in Belluno. This plus his own
experiences of teaching prompted his first venture in
authorship, a small book embodying his views and entitled *Catechesi in Briciole* (Crumbs from the Catechism).

Catechism classes—possibly these are the earliest
memories of most adult Catholics. Many theologians

would dismiss them, but it is precisely this stage of growth that the Jesuits refer to when they talk of "catching a child for life." Albino Luciani was one of the best teachers of this subject the Church has had in this century. He had the simplicity of thought that comes only to the highly intelligent, and added to this was a genuine, deep humility.

By 1958, Don Albino, as he was known by all, had a settled life. His mother and father were both dead. He paid frequent visits to his brother, Edoardo, now married and living in the family home, and to his sister, Antonia, also married and living in Trento. As pro-vicar-general of Belluno he had more than enough work to occupy him. For leisure there were his books. He had little interest in food, eating whatever was put in front of him. His main forms of exercise were cycling around his diocese or climbing the nearby mountains.

This small, quiet man succeeded, apparently without trying, in having an extraordinary and lasting effect on people. Again and again as I talked to those who knew him I could see a remarkable change happen within the person recalling Albino Luciani. Their faces would soften, quite literally relax. They would smile. They smiled a great deal as they recalled the man. They grew gentler before my eyes. He clearly touched something very deep within them. Catholics would call it the soul. Happily oblivious, Albino Luciani was already leaving a unique legacy as he cycled around Belluno.

In the Vatican there was a new pope, John XXIII, a man born at nearby Bergamo, which was also the birthplace of the man from whom Albino acquired his Christian name. John was busy shuffling episcopal appointments. Urbani to Venice to replace himself, Carraro to Verona. In Vittorio Veneto there was a vacancy for a bishop. The pope asked Bishop Bortignon for a name. The response made him smile. "I know him. I know him. He will do me fine."

Luciani, with that disarming humility that so many would later totally fail to comprehend, declared after his appointment as bishop of Vittorio Veneto, "Well, I have taken a couple of train journeys with him, but he did most of the talking. I said so little he could not have gotten to know me."

The forty-six-year-old Luciani was ordained bishop by Pope John in St. Peter's Basilica two days after Christmas 1958.

The pope was fully aware of the pastoral activities of the young man from the North, and he praised him warmly. Picking up a copy of *The Imitation of Christ* by Thomas à Kempis, Pope John read aloud Chapter 23. In it the four elements that bring peace and personal liberty are quoted:

> My son, try to do another's will rather than your own. Always choose to have less rather than more. Always choose the lowest place and to be less than everyone else. Always long and pray that the Will of God may be fully realized in your life. You will find that the man who does all this walks in the land of peace and quietness.

Before his ordination as bishop, Luciani had written of the coming event in a letter to Monsignor Capovilla, the pope's private secretary. One phrase Luciani used demonstrates strikingly how closely he was already attempting to lead a life that embraced the ideals of Thomas à Kempis: "Sometimes the Lord writes his works in dust. . . ."

The first time the congregation gathered to hear their new bishop in Vittorio Veneto, he elaborated on this theme:

> With me the Lord uses yet again his old system. He takes the small ones from the mud of the streets. He takes the people of the fields. He takes others away from their nets in the sea or the lake, and he makes them Apostles. It's his old system.
>
> As soon as I became consecrated a priest I started to receive from my superiors tasks of responsibility and I have understood what it is for a man to be in authority. It is like a ball that is pumped up. If you watch the children

who play on the grass outside this cathedral, when their ball is punctured they don't even bother to look at it. It can stay with tranquillity in a corner. But when it is pumped up the children jump out from all sides and every one believes that they have the right to kick it. This is what happens to men when they move up. Do not therefore be envious.

Later he talked to the four hundred priests who were now answerable to him. A number of them had offered him gifts, food, money. He declined these. When they were all gathered he attempted to explain the reason: "I come without five lire. I want to leave without five lire."
He continued:

My dear priests. My dear faithful. I would be a very unfortunate bishop if I didn't love you. I assure you that I do, and that I want to be at your service and put at your disposal all of my poor energies, the little that I have and the little that I am.

He had the choice of living in a luxurious apartment in the city, or a more Spartan life in the castle of San Martino. He chose the castle.
Many bishops lead a relatively remote life. There is an automatic gulf between them and their flock, accepted by both. The bishop is an elusive figure, seen only on special occasions. Albino Luciani took a different view of his role in Vittorio Veneto. He dressed as a simple priest and took the gospel to his people. With his priests he practiced a form of democracy that was at that time extremely rare within the Church. His presbyterial council, for example, was elected entirely without nominations from the bishop.
When that same council recommended the closure of a particular minor seminary, despite the fact that he did not agree with the recommendation, he went to all his parishes and quietly talked over the issue with the parish priests. As soon as it became clear to him that the majority favored the closure, he authorized it. The

pupils were sent on the instructions of this former seminarian to state schools. He later stated publicly that the majority view had been right and his own wrong.

No priest of the diocese ever had to make an appointment to see this bishop. If one came, he was seen. Some considered his democracy a weakness. Others saw it differently and compared him to the man who had made him bishop.

> It was like having your own personal pope. It was as if Papa Roncalli [John XXIII] was here in this diocese working alongside us. His table usually had two or three priests at it. He simply could not stop giving of himself. One moment he would be visiting the sick or the handicapped. They never knew at the hospitals when he was coming. He would just turn up on a bike or in his old car, leaving his secretary to read outside while he wandered the wards. The next moment he would turn up in one of the mountain villages to discuss a particular problem with the local priest.

In the second week of January 1959, less than three weeks after he had ordained Bishop Luciani, Pope John was discussing world affairs with his pro-secretary of state, Cardinal Domenico Tardini. They discussed the implications of what a young man named Fidel Castro was doing to the Batista regime in Cuba; of the fact that France had a new president, General Charles de Gaulle; of the Soviet demonstration of advanced technology in sending a new rocket into orbit around the moon. They discussed the revolt in Algeria, the appalling poverty in many Latin American countries, the changing face of Africa, with a new nation emerging seemingly each week. It seemed to John that the Roman Catholic Church was not coming to terms with the problems of the mid-twentieth century. It was a crucial point in history, with a significant part of the world turning to things material and away from things spiritual. Unlike many in the Vatican, the pope thought that reform, like charity, should begin at home. Suddenly John had an idea. He was later to say it was an inspiration of the Holy Spirit.

Wherever it came from, it was an excellent one: "a council."

Thus did the idea for the Second Vatican Ecumenical Council emerge. The first, in 1870, had resulted in giving the Church an infallible pope. The effects of the second, many years after its conclusion, are still reverberating around the world.

On October 11, 1962, there were 2,381 bishops gathered in Rome for the opening ceremony of this Second Vatican Council. Among them was Albino Luciani. As the council meetings progressed, Luciani made friendships that would endure for the rest of his life. Suenens of Belgium. Wojtyla and Wyszynski of Poland. Marty of France. Thiandoum of Dakar. Luciani also experienced during the council his own road to Damascus. It was the council's declaration *On Religious Freedom.*

Others were less impressed with this new way of looking at an old problem. Men like Cardinal Alfredo Ottaviani, who controlled the Holy Office (now called the Sacred Congregation for the Doctrine of the Faith), were determined to wreck the concept of tolerance that was implicit in *On Religious Freedom;* more generally, they were fighting a bitter rearguard action against anything that smacked of what Pius X at the beginning of the century had termed "modernism." This was the generation that had taught Luciani in the Belluno seminary that religious freedom was confined to Roman Catholics: "Error has no rights." Luciani, in turn, had taught his own pupils this same appalling doctrine. Now at the Second Vatican Council he listened with growing wonder as bishop after bishop challenged the concept.

When Luciani considered the arguments for and against he was over fifty years of age. His response was typical of this prudent man of the mountains. He discussed the problem with others, he withdrew into thought, and he concluded that the "error" had been in the concept he had been taught.

It was also typical of the man that he subsequently published an article explaining how and why he had changed his mind. He began with a recommendation to his readers:

> If you come across error, rather than uprooting
> it or knocking it down, see if you can trim it
> patiently, allowing the light to shine upon the
> nucleus of goodness and truth that usually is
> not missing even in erroneous opinions.

Other aspects of the various debates caused him
less difficulty. When the principle of the poor Church—a
Church lacking political, economic, and ideological
power—was extolled, the Council was merely seeking
something in which Luciani already believed.

Before the council opened, Luciani had issued a
pastoral letter, "Notes on the Council," to prepare his
congregations. Now, with the council still in session,
the changes he had already introduced into the Vittorio
Veneto diocese were accelerated. He urged his seminary
teachers to read the new theological reviews and dis-
card manuals that still looked back lovingly to the nineteenth century. He sent his teachers on courses to the
principal theological universities of Europe. Not only
the teachers but also the pupils could now be found at
his dinner table. He wrote weekly to all his priests,
sharing his ideas and plans with them.

In August 1962, a few months before the opening of
the Second Vatican Council, Luciani was confronted
with an example of error of quite another kind. Two
priests in the diocese had become involved with a
smooth-talking sales representative who also speculated
in property. One of them came to Luciani, confessing
that the amount of money missing, much of it belonging to small-savers, was in excess of 2 billion lire.

Albino Luciani had very set ideas about wealth and
money, particularly Church wealth. Some of his ideas
stemmed from Rosmini; many came directly from his
own personal experience. He believed in a Roman Catholic Church of the poor, for the poor. The enforced
absences of his father, the hunger and the cold, the
wooden clogs with the extra nails banged into the soles
so that they would not wear out, cutting grass on the
mountainsides to augment the family dinners, the long
spells in the seminary without seeing a mother who
could not afford to visit him—these experiences produced in Luciani a deep compassion for the poor, a

total indifference to the acquisition of personal wealth, and a belief that the Church, his Church, should not only be materially poor but also should be seen to be so.

Conscious of the damage the scandal would do, he went directly to the editor of the Venice newspaper *Il Gazzettino*. He asked the editor not to treat the story in a lurid manner with sensational headlines.

Back in his diocese he called together his four hundred priests. Normal practice would have been to have claimed ecclesiastical immunity. To do so would ensure that the Church would not pay a penny. Speaking quietly, Luciani told his priests:

> It is true that two of us have done wrong. I believe the diocese must pay. I also believe that the law must run its due course. We must not hide behind any immunity. In this scandal there is a lesson for us all. It is that we must be a poor Church. I intend to sell ecclesiastical treasure. I further intend to sell one of our buildings. The money will be used to repay every single lira that these priests owe. I ask for your agreement.

Albino Luciani obtained their agreement. His morality prevailed. Some who were present at that meeting admired the man and his morality. Some rather ruefully observed that they considered Luciani too moral in such matters. The property speculator who had involved the two priests was obviously one who considered the bishop "too moral." Before his trial he committed suicide. One of the priests served a one-year prison sentence, and the other was acquitted.

Others among the priesthood by no means embraced the spirit of the Second Vatican Council. Like Luciani their thinking had been shaped in the early, more repressive years. Unlike him they were not prepared to have that thinking reshaped. This reshaping was, however, to characterize Luciani's work during the remainder of his time at Vittorio Veneto. With the same hunger with which he had read book after book in his youth, he now, in the words of Monsignor Ghizzo, who worked with him, "totally absorbed Vatican Council II. He had

the council in his blood. He knew the documents by
heart. Further, he implemented the documents."

He twinned Vittorio Veneto with Kiremba, a small
township in Burundi, formerly part of German East
Africa. In the mid-1960s when he visited Kiremba he
was brought face to face with the Third World. Nearly
70 percent of the country's 3¼ million people were
Roman Catholics. The faith was flourishing, but so were
poverty, disease, a high infant-mortality rate, and civil
war. Churches were full, bellies were empty. It was
realities like this that had inspired Pope John to summon the Second Vatican Council, as an attempt to drag
the Church into the twentieth century. While the old
curial palace guard in Rome were being blinded by the
Second Vatican Council, Luciani and others like him
were being illuminated by it.

John XXIII literally gave his life to ensure that the
council he had conceived would not be stillborn. Advised that he was seriously ill, he declined the operation
his specialists were insisting on. They told him that
such an operation would prolong his life. He retorted
that to leave the Second Vatican Council at the mercy
of the reactionary element within the Vatican during
the early delicate stages would be to ensure a theological disaster. He preferred to remain in the Vatican,
helping the child he had created to grow. In doing so he
calmly and with extraordinary courage signed his own
death warrant. When he died on June 3, 1963, the Roman Catholic Church, through the Second Vatican Ecumenical Council, was finally attempting to come to terms
with the world as it was rather than as it would like it
to be.

Under John's successor, Pope Paul VI, the Church
inched its way nearer to one specific reality, to one
particular decision, the most important the Roman Catholic Church has made in this century. In the 1960s this
question was being asked with increasing urgency: What
is the Church's position on artificial birth control?

In 1962 Pope John had set up the Pontifical Commission on the Family. Birth control was one of the
major issues it was directed to study. Pope Paul enlarged the commission until its membership reached

sixty-eight. He then appointed a considerable number of consultants to advise and monitor the commission. While hundreds of millions of Roman Catholics around the world waited and wondered, speculation that a change in the Church's position was imminent grew ever larger. Many Catholics began using the Pill or other forms of artificial contraception. While the experts in Rome debated the significance of Genesis 38:7–10 and a man called Onan, everyday life had to go on.

Ironically, the confusion that prevailed in the Catholic world on this issue was exactly mirrored by the pope's thinking on the problem. He did not know what to do.

During the first week of October 1965, Pope Paul granted a unique interview to Italian journalist Alberto Cavallari. They discussed many problems facing the Church. Cavallari later observed that he did not raise the issue of artificial birth control because he was aware of the potential embarrassment. His fears were unfounded. Paul raised the subject himself. It should be remembered that this was an era when the papacy still clung to royal illusions; personal pronouns were not Paul's style.

> Take birth control, for example. The world asks what we think and we find ourselves trying to give an answer. But what answer? We can't keep silent. And yet to speak is a real problem. The Church hasn't had to deal with such things for centuries. And it is a somewhat foreign and even humanly embarrassing subject for men of the Church. So the commissions meet, the reports pile up, the studies are published. Oh, they study a lot, you know. But then we still have to make the final decisions. And in deciding, we are all alone. Deciding is not as easy as studying. We have to say something. But what? God will simply have to enlighten us.

While Pope Paul waited for God's enlightenment on sexual intercourse, his commission on the family toiled on. While the sixty-eight labored, their efforts were closely watched by a smaller commission of approximately

twenty cardinals and bishops. For any liberalizing recommendation from the group of sixty-eight to reach the
pope it had to pass through this smaller group, which
was headed by a man who was the epitome of the
reactionary element within the Church, Cardinal Ottaviani. Many considered him the leader of that element.

A crucial moment in the commission's history came
on April 23, 1966. By that date the commission had
conducted an exhaustive and exhausting examination
of the artificial-birth-control issue. Those who had maintained their opposition to a change in the Church's
position were by now reduced to four priests, who stated
that they were irreversibly committed to maintaining a
position forbidding any form of artificial birth control.
Pushed by the other members of the commission, the
four admitted that they could not prove the correctness
of their position on the grounds of natural law. Neither
could they cite Scripture or divine revelation to justify
their view. They simply argued that various papal utterances over the years had all condemned artificial
contraception. Their reasoning would appear to be "once
in error, always in error."

Yet in October 1951, John's predecessor, Pius XII,
had softened somewhat the Church's austere position
on birth control. During an audience with Italian mid-
wives he gave his approval to the use of the rhythm
method by all Catholics with serious reasons for wishing to avoid procreation. In view of the notorious
unreliability of what became known as "Vatican roulette"
it is not surprising that Pius XII also called for further
research into the rhythm method. Nevertheless, Pius
had moved the Church away from its previous position
that procreation was the sole purpose of sexual intercourse.

After Pius XII came not only a new pope but also
the invention of the progesterone pill. Infallibility had
been claimed for certain papal opinions, but no one had
yet claimed papal clairvoyance. A new situation required a new look at the problem, but the four dissenting priests on the commission insisted that the new
situation was covered by old answers.

Finally the commission wrote its report. In essence
it advised the pope that consensus had been reached by

an overwhelming majority of its members (64 to 4), as well as by theologians, legal experts, historians, sociologists, doctors, obstetricians, and married couples, that a change in the Catholic Church's stand on artificial birth control was both possible and advisable.

The report was submitted in mid-1966 to a smaller commission of cardinals and bishops. These churchmen reacted with some perplexity. Obliged to record their own views on the report, six of the prelates abstained, eight voted in favor of recommending the report to the pope, and six voted against it.

Within the Roman Curia, that central administrative body of civil servants who control and dominate the Catholic Church, there was a wide range of reactions. Some applauded the recommendation for change, others saw it as part of the mischievous wickedness that Vatican Council II had generated. In this latter category was Cardinal Ottaviani, secretary of the Supreme Sacred Congregation of the Holy Office. The motto on his coat of arms read *Semper Idem* (Always the Same).

By 1966, Alfredo Ottaviani was, next to the pope, the most powerful person in the entire Roman Catholic Church. An ex-pupil of the Roman Seminary, he was a man who passed his whole career in the Secretariat of State and the Curia without ever being assigned outside Rome.

He had fought a bitter and often successful battle against the liberalizing effects of Vatican Council II. His forehead permanently furrowed, his skull curved back dramatically as if he were constantly avoiding a direct question, his neckline hidden by bulging jowls, Ottaviani had about him an air of sphinxlike immobility. He was a man not merely born old but also born out of his time. He exemplified that section of the Curia that has the courage of its prejudices.

He saw himself as defender of a faith that did not accommodate the here and now. To Ottaviani the hereafter was reached by embracing values that were old in medieval times. He was not about to budge on the issue of artificial birth control; more important, he was determined that Pope Paul VI was not going to budge.

Ottaviani contacted the four dissenting priests from the pontifical commission. Their views had already been

fully incorporated within the commission's report. He
persuaded them to enlarge their dissenting conclusions
in a special report. Thus the Jesuit Marcellino Zalba,
the Redemptorist Jan Visser, the Franciscan Ermenegildo
Lio, and the American Jesuit John Ford created a second document.

No matter that in doing so they acted in an unethi-
cal manner; the object of the exercise was to give
Ottaviani a weapon to brandish at the pope. The four
men bear an awesome responsibility for what was to
follow. The amount of misery and suffering that directly resulted from the final papal decision can to a
large degree be laid directly at their feet. An indication
of the thought processes applied by these four can be
gauged from one of their number, the American Jesuit,
John Ford. He believed he was in direct contact with
the Holy Spirit with regard to this issue and that this
divine guidance had led him to the ultimate truth. If
the majority view prevailed, Ford declared, he would
have to leave the Roman Catholic Church.

This minority report represents the epitome of
arrogance. It was submitted to Pope Paul along with
the official commission report. What followed was a
classic illustration of the ability of a minority of the
Roman Curia to control situations, to manipulate events.
By the time the two reports were submitted to Paul,
most of the sixty-eight members of the commission were
scattered to the corners of the earth.

Convinced that this difficult problem had finally
been resolved with a liberalizing conclusion, the majority of the commission members waited in their various
countries for the papal announcement approving artificial birth control. Some of them began to prepare a
paper that could serve as an introduction or preface to
the impending papal ruling, in which they provided
justification for the change in the Church's position.

Throughout 1967 and continuing into early 1968,
Ottaviani capitalized on the absence from Rome of the
majority of the commission. Those who were still in the
city were exercising great restraint in not bringing further pressure on Paul. By doing so they played straight
into Ottaviani's hands. He marshaled members of the
old guard who shared his views. Cardinals Cicognani,

Browne, Parente, and Samore met daily with the pope. Daily they told him that to approve artificial birth control would be to betray the Church's heritage. They reminded him of the Church's canon law and the three criteria that were applied to all Catholics seeking to marry; that without these three physiological essentials the marriage is invalid in the eyes of the Church: erection, ejaculation and the possibility of conception. To legalize oral contraception, they argued, would be to destroy that particular Church law.

Many, including his predecessor, John XXIII, have compared Pope Paul VI to the doubt-racked Hamlet. Every Hamlet has need of an Elsinore Castle in which to brood. Eventually the pope decided that he, and he alone, would make the final decision. He summoned Monsignor Agostino Casaroli and advised him that the problem of artificial birth control would be removed from the jurisdiction of the Congregation of the Holy Office. Then he retired to Castel Gandolfo, his summer residence, to work on the encyclical.

On the pope's desk at Castel Gandolfo, amid the various reports, recommendations, and studies on the issue of artificial birth control was one from Albino Luciani.

While his commissions, consultants, and curial cardinals were dissecting the problem, the pope had also asked for the opinions of various regions in Italy. One of these was the Vittorio Veneto diocese. The patriarch of Venice, Cardinal Urbani, had called a meeting of all the bishops within the region. After a day's debate it was decided that Luciani should draw up the report.

The decision to give Luciani the task was largely based on his knowledge of the problem. It was a subject he had been studying for a number of years. He had talked and written about it, he had consulted doctors, sociologists, theologians, and not least, that group who had personal, practical experience with the problem, married couples.

This last group included his own brother, Edoardo, who was struggling to earn enough to support an ever-growing family that eventually numbered ten children. Luciani saw firsthand the problems posed by a continuing ban on artificial birth control. He had grown up surrounded by poverty. Now, in the late 1960s, there appeared to him to be as much poverty and deprivation as in the days of his youth. When those one cares for are in despair because of their inability to provide for an increasing number of children, one is inclined to view the problem of artificial birth control in a different light from Jesuits who are in direct contact with the Holy Spirit.

The men in the Vatican could quote Genesis until the Day of Judgment, but it would not put bread on the table. To Albino Luciani, Vatican Council II had intended to relate the Gospels and the Church to the twentieth century, and to deny men and women the right of artificial birth control was to plunge the Church back into the Dark Ages. Much of this he said quietly and privately as he prepared his report. Publicly he was acutely aware of his obedience to the pope. In this Luciani remained an excellent example of his time. When the pope decreed, then the faithful agreed. Yet even in his public utterances there are clear clues to his thinking on the issue of birth control.

By April 1968, after much further consultation, Luciani's report had been written and submitted. It had met with the approval of the bishops of the Vittorio Veneto region, and Cardinal Urbani had duly signed the report and sent it directly to Pope Paul. Subsequently, Urbani saw the document on the pope's desk at Castel Gandolfo. Paul advised Urbani that he valued the report greatly. So highly did he praise it that when Urbani returned to Venice he went by way of Vittorio Veneto to convey directly to Luciani the pleasure the report had given.

The central thrust of the report was to recommend to the pope that the Roman Catholic Church should approve the use of the anovulant pill developed by Professor Pincus. *That it should become the Catholic birth-control pill.*

On April 13, Luciani talked to the people of Vittorio Veneto about the problems the issue was causing. With the delicacy that had by now become a Luciani hallmark, he called the subject "conjugal ethics." Having observed that priests in speaking and in hearing confessions "must abide by the directives given on several occasions by

the pope until the latter makes a pronouncement,"
Luciani went on to make three observations:

1. It is easier today, given the confusion caused
by the press, to find married persons who do
not believe that they are sinning. If this should
happen it may be opportune, under the usual
conditions, not to disturb them.

2. Toward the penitent onanist, who shows
himself to be both penitent and discouraged, it
is opportune to use encouraging kindness, within
the limits of pastoral prudence.

3. Let us pray that the Lord may help the
pope to resolve this question. There has never
perhaps been such a difficult question for the
Church—both for the intrinsic difficulties and
for the numerous implications affecting other
problems, and for the acute way in which it is
felt by the vast mass of the people.

Humanae Vitae was published on July 25, 1968.
Pope Paul had Monsignor Lambruschini of Lateran University explain its significance to the press, in itself a
rather superfluous exercise. More significantly, it was
stressed that this was not an infallible document. It
became for millions of Catholics a historic moment, like
the assassination of President John F. Kennedy. Years
later they knew exactly what they were doing and where
they were when the news reached them.

On a disaster scale for the Roman Catholic Church
it measures higher than the treatment of Galileo in the
seventeenth century or the declaration of papal infallibility in the nineteenth. This document, which was intended to strengthen papal authority, had precisely the
opposite effect.

Pope Paul, after having expanded the commission
that was advising him on the problem of birth control,
had proceeded to ignore its advice. He declared that the
only methods of birth control that the Church considered acceptable were abstinence and the rhythm method:
". . . in any use whatever of marriage there must be no
impairment of its natural capacity to procreate human
life."

Millions ignored the pope and continued to practice their faith and use the Pill or whatever other method they found most suitable. Millions lost patience and faith. Others shopped around for a different priest to whom to confess their sins. Still others tried to follow the encyclical and discovered they had avoided one Catholic concept of sin only to experience another, divorce. The encyclical totally divided the Church.

"I cannot believe that salvation is based on contraception by temperature and damnation is based on rubber," declared Dr. André Hellegers, an obstetrician and member of the ignored pontifical commission. One surprising line of the Vatican's defense came from Cardinal Felici: "The possible mistake of the superior [the pope] does not authorize the disobedience of subjects."

Albino Luciani read the encyclical with growing dismay. He knew the uproar that would now engulf the Church. He went to his church in Vittorio Veneto and prayed. There was no question in his mind but that he must obey the papal ruling; but deep as his allegiance to the pope was, he could not, would not, merely sing praise to *Humanae Vitae*. He knew a little of what the document must have cost the pope; he knew a great deal of what it was going to cost the faithful who would have to attempt to apply it to their everyday lives.

Within hours of reading the encyclical, Luciani had written his response to the diocese of Vittorio Veneto. In ten years' time, when he became pope, the Vatican would assert that Luciani's response was, "Rome has spoken. The case is closed." Nothing approaching that sentiment appears in his actual words. He began by reminding the diocese of his comments in April, then continued:

> I confess that, although not revealing it in what I wrote, I privately hoped that the very grave difficulties that exist could be overcome and the response of the Teacher, who speaks with special charisma and in the name of the Lord, might coincide, at least in part, with the hopes of many married couples after the setting up of a relevant pontifical commission to examine the question.

He acknowledged the amount of care and consideration the pope had given to the problem and said that the pope knew "he is about to cause bitterness in many," but he continued, "The old doctrine, presented in a new framework of encouraging and positive ideas about marriage and conjugal love, better guarantees the true good of man and family." Luciani faced some of the problems that would inevitably flow from *Humanae Vitae:*

> The thoughts of the pope, and mine, go especially to the sometimes grave difficulties of married couples. May they not lose heart, for goodness sake. May they remember that for everyone the door is narrow and narrow the road that leads to life (cf. Matt. 7:14). That the hope of the future life must illuminate the path of Christian couples. That God does not fail to help those who pray to Him with perseverance. May they make the effort to live with wisdom, justice and piety in the present time, knowing that the fashion of this world passes away (cf. I Cor. 7:31). . . . "And if sin should still have a hold on them, may they not be discouraged, but have recourse with humble perseverance to God's mercy through the sacrament of penance."

This last quotation, direct from *Humanae Vitae,* had been one of the few crumbs of comfort for men like Luciani who had hoped for a change. Trusting that he had his flock with him in a "sincere adhesion to the teaching of the pope," Luciani gave them his blessing.

Other priests in other countries took a more openly hostile line. Many left the priesthood. Luciani steered a more subtle course.

In January 1969 he returned yet again to this subject that the Vatican would have him make a one line, dogmatic pronouncement on. He was aware that some of his priests were denying absolution to married couples using the Pill and that other priests were readily absolving what Pope Paul had deemed a sin. Dealing with this problem, Luciani quoted the response of the Italian bishops' conference to *Humanae Vitae.* It was a response he had helped to draft. In it priests were advised to show "evangelical kindness" toward all married people, but especially, as Luciani pointed out, toward those "whose failings derive ... from the sometimes very serious difficulties in which they find themselves. In that case the behavior of the spouses, although not in conformity with Christian norms, is certainly not to be judged with the same gravity as when it derives from motives corrupted by selfishness and hedonism." Luciani also admonished his troubled people not to feel "an anguished, disturbing guilt complex."

Throughout this entire period the Vatican continued to benefit from the profits derived from one of the many companies it owned, the Istituto Farmacologico Sereno. One of Sereno's best-selling products was an oral contraceptive called Luteolas.

The loyalty Albino Luciani had demonstrated in Vittorio Veneto was not lost on the holy father in Rome. Better than most, the pope knew that such loyalty had been achieved at great personal cost. The document on his desk that bore Cardinal Urbani's signature, but was in essence Luciani's position on birth control, was mute testimony to that cost.

Deeply impressed, Pope Paul VI observed to his under secretary of state, Giovanni Benelli, "In Vittorio Veneto there is a little bishop who seems well suited to me." The astute Benelli went out of his way to establish a friendship with Luciani. It was to prove a friendship with far-reaching consequences.

Cardinal Urbani, patriarch of Venice, died on September 17, 1969. The pope remembered his little bishop. To Paul's surprise, Luciani politely declined what many saw as a glittering promotion. Entirely without ambition, he was happy and content with his work in Vittorio Veneto.

Pope Paul cast his net farther. Cardinal Antonio Samore, as reactionary as his mentor Ottaviani, became a strong contender. Murmurings of discontent from members of the Venetian laity, to the effect that they would be happier if Samore remained in Rome, reached the pope's ears.

Pope Paul then gave yet another demonstration of the papal dance he had invented since ascending to the throne of Peter: one step forward, one step back—Luciani, Samore, Luciani.

Luciani began to feel the pressure from Rome. Eventually he succumbed. It was a decision he regretted within hours. Unaware that its new patriarch had fought against accepting the position, Venice celebrated the fact that "local man" Albino Luciani was appointed on December 15, 1969.

Before leaving Vittorio Veneto, Luciani was presented with a donation of 1 million lire (approximately $16,000 at the time*). He quietly declined the gift and after suggesting that the people should donate it to their own personal charities reminded them what he had told his priests when he had arrived in the diocese eleven years earlier: "I came without five lire. I want to leave without five lire." Albino Luciani took with him to Venice a small pile of linen, a few sticks of furniture, and his books.

On February 8, 1970, the new patriarch, now Archbishop Luciani, entered Venice. Tradition decreed that the entry of a new patriarch be a splendid excuse for a gaily bedecked procession of gondolas, brass bands, parades, and countless speeches. Luciani had always had an intense dislike of such pomp and ceremony. He canceled the ritual welcome and confined himself to a speech, during which he referred not only to the historic aspects of the city but also acknowledged that his archdiocese contained industrial areas such as Mestre and Marghera. "This was the other Venice," Luciani observed, "with few monuments but so many factories, houses, spiritual problems, souls. And it is to this many-faceted city that Providence now sends me. Signor Mayor, the first Venetian coins, minted as long ago as A.D. 850, had the motto 'Christ, save Venice.' I make this my own with all my heart and turn it into a prayer, 'Christ, bless Venice.'"

The pagan city was in dire need of Christ's blessing. It was bulging with monuments and churches that proclaimed the former glories of an imperial republic; yet, as Albino Luciani rapidly learned, the majority of the

---

*Here and throughout the book, all monetary figures are expressed in values at the time in question.

churches within the 127 parishes were almost always nearly empty. If one discounted the tourists, the very young, and the very old, then church attendance was appallingly low. Venice is a city that has sold its soul to tourism.

The day after his arrival, accompanied by his new secretary, Father Mario Senigaglia, he was at work. Declining invitations to attend various soirees, cocktail parties, and receptions, he visited instead the local seminary, the women's prison of Giudecca, and the men's prison of Santa Maria Maggiore, and then celebrated Mass in the Church of San Simeone.

It was customary for the patriarch of Venice to have his own boat. Luciani had neither the personal wealth nor the inclination for what seemed to him an unnecessary extravagance. When he wanted to move through the canals, he and Father Mario would catch a water bus. If it was an urgent appointment, Luciani would telephone the local fire brigade, the *carabinieri*, or the finance police (the Guardia di Finanza, the equivalent of American customs agents) and beg the loan of one of their boats. Eventually the three organizations worked out a roster to oblige the unusual priest.

During a national gasoline crisis the patriarch took to a bicycle when visiting the mainland. Venetian high society shook its head and muttered disapprovingly. Many upper-class Venetians enjoyed the pomp and ceremony they associated with the patriarchate. To them a patriarch was an important person to be treated in an important manner. When Albino Luciani and Father Mario appeared unannounced at a hospital to visit the sick, they would immediately be surrounded by the administrators, doctors, monks, and nuns. Father Senigaglia recalled for me such an occasion:

"I don't want to take up your precious time. I can go around on my own."

"Not a bit of it, Your Excellency, it's an honor for us."

Thus a large procession would begin to make its way through the wards with an increasingly discomfited Luciani. Eventually he would say, "Well, perhaps it's better if I come back another time, it's already late."

He would effect several false exits in an attempt to shake off the entourage, but without success.

"Don't worry, Your Eminence. It's our duty."

Outside, he would turn to Father Senigaglia and say, "But are they always like this? It's a shame. I am used to something different. Either we shall have to make them understand or I shall lose a good habit."

Slowly some of the message got across, but it was never the same as at Vittorio Veneto.

His fresh approach was not confined to his technique for visiting the sick. A considerable number of monsignors and priests whose behavior did not accord with Luciani's view that "the real treasures of the Church are the poor, the weak who should not be helped with occasional charity but in such a way that they can really benefit" found themselves parish priests in a far province.

One such priest, a property owner, received from Luciani a personal lesson in social justice that left him bemused. The priest, having increased the rent on one of his houses, discovered that the tenant, an unemployed schoolteacher, could not afford the increase. He promptly served an eviction notice. Luciani, hearing of the incident through his secretary, remonstrated in vain with the priest, who shrugged his shoulders at this whimsical patriarch who quoted Christ to him: "My kingdom is not of this earth." He proceeded with the eviction of the schoolteacher and his family. Luciani immediately wrote out a check enabling the family to live in a pensione until they found a permanent residence. Today the teacher has a photocopy of the check framed and hanging in his living room.

On another occasion Senigaglia inadvertently interrupted a visit Luciani was making to a sick priest. Senigaglia discovered Luciani emptying his wallet on the priest's bed. Later the secretary gently remonstrated with the patriarch. "You can't do this." Albino Luciani's response sums up much of the man: "But it was all I had on me at the time."

Senigaglia explained that the Curia had a special fund so that the patriarch could help his priests in silence. This, Senigaglia explained, was how the previous patriarch had performed these various acts of charity. Luciani listened, then told his secretary to make the same arrangement with the Curia.

He discovered that as patriarch he had unwittingly acquired a house at San Pietro di Fileto. He attempted to give it to the unfortunate schoolteacher, but the Vatican objected. After a battle, it was finally conceded that Luciani could allow the retired Bishop Muccin to live there.

Within a short time of becoming patriarch, Luciani's offices were continuously overflowing with the poor. "The door of the patriarch is always open; ask Don Mario, and whatever I can do for you I will always willingly do it." The crowd murmured their thanks.

Don Mario spoke to his superior, gritting his teeth, "Your Excellency, you are ruining me, they will never leave me in peace."

Luciani smiled and replied, "Someone will help us."

The offices of the patriarch were frequently filled with ex-prisoners, alcoholics, poor people, abandoned people, tramps, and women who could no longer work as prostitutes. One of these people still wears the pajamas Luciani gave him and writes "thank you" letters to a man no longer here to read them.

During his first year in the city Luciani showed his concern for those who lived in what he had described on his first day as "the other Venice." When strikes and violent demonstrations erupted in Mestre and Marghera, he urged workers and management to seek a middle position. In 1971, when 270 workers were laid off at La Sava factory, he reminded the bosses of the paramount need to remember personal human dignity. Certain sections of the traditional Catholic establishment in Venice could be heard expressing the wish for a patriarch who would content himself with sermons to uncomprehending tourists. Pope Paul VI, however, was clearly delighted with Luciani. In 1971, the pope nominated him to attend the World Synod of Bishops. Items on the agenda were priestly ministry and justice in the world. One suggestion of Luciani's at the synod showed the shape of things to come:

> I suggest, as an example of concrete help to the poor countries, that the more fortunate churches should tax themselves and pay one percent of

their income to the Vatican aid organizations.
This one percent should be called the "brothers'
share" and should not be given as charity, but
as something that is owed, to compensate for
the injustices being committed by our consumer
world against the developing world, and to make
up in some way for social sin, of which we
should all be aware.

One of the injustices that Luciani continuously
worked to eliminate in Venice concerned a widely prevalent attitude toward the mentally retarded and the
handicapped. Not only did the mayor and city officials
show indifference, but Luciani also found the same prejudice among some of his parish priests. When he went to
give first communion to a large group of handicapped
people at St. Pius X Church in Marghera he had to cope
with a delegation of protesting priests, who argued that
he should not do such a thing. "These creatures do not
understand." He instructed the group that he was personally ordering them to attend the first communion.

After the Mass he picked up a young girl suffering
from spina bifida. The congregation was completely
silent.

"Do you know whom you have received today?" he
asked the little girl.

"Yes. Jesus."

"And are you pleased?"

"Very."

Luciani turned slowly and looked at the group of
protesting priests. "You see, they are better than we
adults."

Because of the reluctance of the city council to
contribute to special work centers for the handicapped,
Luciani was obliged initially to rely on diocesan funds
and the bank known as "the priests' bank," Banca
Cattolica del Veneto. In 1972, after he had been made
patriarch, he became aware that it was no longer the
priests' bank. Joining the regular crowd in his outer
office who required help, he now found bishops, monsignors, and priests.

In the past the bank had always loaned money to

the clergy at low interest rates. It had been founded so that the diocese could contribute to the vital work for that section of society which Luciani described in the following words: "They have no political weight. They cannot be counted on for votes. For those reasons we must all show our sense of honor as men and Christians toward these handicapped people."

By mid-1972, however, the low-interest loans had stopped. The Venetian clergy were advised that in the future they would have to pay the full rate of interest no matter how laudable the work. The priests complained to their bishops. The bishops made a number of discreet inquiries.

Since 1946 the Istituto per le Opere di Religione, the IOR, usually referred to as the Vatican Bank, had held a majority share in Banca Cattolica del Veneto. The various dioceses in the Veneto region also had small shareholdings in the bank, amounting to less than 5 percent of the bank's stock.

In the normal commercial world this would make the minority shareholder vulnerable, but this was not the normal commercial world. A clear understanding existed between Venice and the Vatican that the IOR's vast shareholding (by 1972 it was 51 percent) was insurance against any potential takeover by a third party. Despite the very low interest rates charged to the Veneto clergy, the bank was one of the wealthiest in the country. Where the priest banks, the parishioner will follow. (A significant amount of the bank's wealth was derived from real-estate holdings in northern Italy.) This happy arrangement had now been abruptly terminated. The bank that the bishops believed they owned, at least morally, had been sold over their heads without the patriarch or any person in the Veneto region having been consulted. The man who had done the selling was the Vatican Bank's president, Paul Marcinkus. The man who had done the buying was Roberto Calvi of Banco Ambrosiano, Milan.

The bishops of the region descended en masse on the patriarch's office in St. Mark's Square. He listened quietly as they outlined what had happened. They told him how in the past when they had wished to raise capital they had turned to the Vatican Bank, which had loaned them money, holding their shares in Banca Cattolica as security. Now these shares, along with a large stake independently acquired by the Vatican Bank, had been sold at a huge profit to Calvi.

The enraged bishops pointed out to Luciani that had they been given the opportunity they could have raised the necessary money to repay the Vatican Bank and thereby reacquire their shares. What was more pertinent in their eyes was the appalling breach of trust perpetrated by Marcinkus, acting on behalf of the Vatican, which claimed to be the moral leader in the world; he had at the very least displayed a total lack of morals. The fact that he had kept the entire profit on the transaction for the Vatican Bank may also have caused some of their anger.

The bishops urged Luciani to go directly to Rome. They wanted papal intervention. If that intervention took the form of firing Paul Marcinkus, it was clear that in the Veneto region, at least, not many tears would be shed. Luciani calmly weighed the problem. Ever a prudent man, he felt he needed more facts before taking such a problem to Pope Paul.

Luciani began to probe quietly. He learned a great deal about Roberto Calvi and also about a man named Michele Sindona. What he learned appalled him. It also alerted him to the dangers of complaining directly to the pope. Based on the information he had obtained, it was clear that Calvi and Sindona were highly favored sons of the Church and were held in high esteem by Paul VI. The man Albino Luciani turned to was one who had become a close friend over the previous five years, the undersecretary of state, Monsignor Giovanni Benelli.

Though Benelli was number two in the Secretariat of State, under Cardinal Villot, to all intents and purposes Benelli ran the department. And as Pope Paul's troubleshooter Benelli not only knew where all the bodies were buried, he was also responsible for the placement of quite a number of them.

Benelli listened while the patriarch of Venice told his story. As the monsignor gave His Eminence another cup of coffee, Luciani uttered a qualification.

"I have not, of course, seen any documentary evidence."

"I have," responded Benelli. "Calvi is now the major shareholder in the Banca Cattolica del Veneto. Marcinkus sold him thirty-seven percent on March thirty."

Benelli was a man who enjoyed reeling out facts and figures. He told the wide-eyed Luciani that Calvi had paid 27 billion lire (approximately $45 million) to Marcinkus and that the sale was the result of a scheme hatched jointly by Calvi, Sindona, and Marcinkus. He went on to tell of a company called Pacchetti, which had been purchased by Calvi from Sindona after its price had been grossly and criminally inflated on the Milan stock exchange, and of how Marcinkus had assisted Calvi in masking the nature of this and other operations from the eyes of Bank of Italy officials by putting the Vatican Bank facilities at the disposal of Calvi and Sindona.

Luciani was bewildered. "What does all this mean?" he asked.

"Tax evasion, illegal movement of shares. I also believe that Marcinkus sold the shares in your Venice bank at a deliberately low price and Calvi paid the balance via a separate thirty-one billion lire deal on another bank."

Luciani became angry. "What has all this to do with the Church of the poor? In the name of God . . ."

Benelli held up a hand to silence him. "No, Albino, in the name of profit."

"Does the holy father know these things?"

Benelli nodded.

"So?"

"So you must remember who put Paul Marcinkus in charge of our bank."

"The holy father."

"Precisely. And I must confess I fully approved. I've had cause to regret that many times."

"Then what are we to do? What am I to tell my priests and bishops?"

"You must tell them to be patient. To wait. Eventually Marcinkus will overreach himself. His Achilles' heel is his greed for papal praise."

"But what does he want to do with all this money?"

"He wants to make more money."

"For what purpose?"

"To make more money."

"And in the meantime should my priests get out begging bowls and tramp through the Veneto?"

"In the meantime you must counsel patience. I know you have it. Teach it to your priests. I'm having to apply it."

Albino Luciani returned to Venice and called his fellow bishops to his office. He told them some of what had transpired in Rome, enough to make it abundantly clear that the Banca Cattolica del Veneto was now forever lost to the diocese. Later some of them talked about it. They concluded that this would never have happened in the days of Cardinal Urbani. They felt that Luciani's innate goodness had proved a useless weapon against the IOR. Most of them, including Luciani, sold what remaining shares they held in the bank to express their disapproval of the Vatican's conduct. In Milan, Roberto Calvi was gratified to note that his brokers had acquired on his behalf another small piece of the priests' bank in Venice.

Albino Luciani and many others in Venice closed their accounts at the Banca Cattolica. For the patriarch of Venice to move the official diocesan accounts to the small Banco San Marco was an extraordinary step. He confided to one colleague, "Calvi's money is tainted. The man is tainted. After what I have learned of Roberto Calvi I would not leave the accounts in his bank if the loans they granted to the diocese were totally free of interest."

Luciani then attempted to get the directors of Banca Cattolica to change the name of the bank. He insisted that for the word "Catholic" to appear in their title was an outrage and a libel against all Catholics.

In Rome, Pope Paul VI was made fully aware of the added burden that had been placed on the Veneto region by the sale of the Banca Cattolica. Giovanni Benelli urged the holy father to intervene, but by then the sale to Calvi was already a reality. When Benelli argued for the removal of Marcinkus, the pope responded with an agonized, helpless shrug of the shoulders, but the fact that Luciani had not led an open rebellion left a deep impression on Paul. At the slightest opportunity he would proclaim the goodness of the man he had appointed patriarch of Venice. In an audience with Venetian priest Mario Ferrarese he declared three times, "Tell the priests of Venice that they should love their patriarch because he is a good, holy, wise, learned man."

In September 1972, Pope Paul stayed at the patriarch's palace on his way to a eucharistic congress in Udine. In a packed St. Mark's Square the pope removed his stole and placed it over the shoulders of a blushing Luciani. The crowd went wild. Paul was not a man to make insignificant public gestures.

When the two men were being served coffee in the palace he made a more private one. He indicated to Luciani that "the little local difficulty over finance" had reached his ears. He had also heard that Luciani was trying to raise money for the creation of a work center for the retarded at Marghera. He told Luciani how much he approved of such work and said that he would like to make a personal donation. Between Italians, that most voluble of peoples, much is often unsaid but understood.

Six months later, during March 1973, the pope made Albino Luciani a cardinal. Whatever his deep misgivings about the fiscal policies of the IOR, Luciani considered that he owed the pope, his pope, complete and unswerving loyalty. Italian bishops are in a unique position with regard to their relationship to the Vatican. Control of their actions is tighter. Retribution for any failure, real or imagined, is quicker.

When Luciani was made cardinal he was aware that Ottaviani and other curial reactionaries, far from demonstrating total obedience, were in fact involved in a long, acrimonious dispute with the pope. They were quite simply trying to destroy any good that had flowed from the historic Vatican Council II series of meetings. Called on to make a speech in front of not only the other new cardinals and the pope but also Ottaviani and his clique, Albino Luciani observed, "Vatican Council I has many followers and so has Vatican Council II. Vatican Council II, however, has far too few."

Two months later, in May, Luciani found himself playing host yet again to a visitor from Rome, Giovanni

Benelli. In general, Benelli had come to assure him that the problems they had discussed the previous year had not been forgotten. In particular, he had an extraordinary story to tell. It concerned the American Mafia, nearly $1 billion worth of counterfeit securities, and Bishop Paul Marcinkus.

On April 25, 1973, Benelli had received some very unusual guests in his offices at the Secretariat of State in Vatican City: William Lynch, chief of the organized crime and racketeering section of the U.S. Department of Justice, and William Aronwald, assistant chief of the strike force in the Southern District of New York. Two members of the FBI had acccompanied them.

"Having met these gentlemen from the United States," Benelli later told me in an interview, "I made my apologies and left them in the capable hands of three of my staff. They, of course, subsequently reported to me exactly what had taken place."

The secret FBI report that I acquired many months after my conversation with Cardinal Benelli confirmed that his account was very accurate. It also told a story that reads like an outline for a Hollywood movie.

Monsignors Edward Martinez, Carl Rauber, and Justin Rigali listened while William Lynch told of a police investigation that had begun in the world of the New York Mafia and had led inexorably to the Vatican. He told the priests that a package of $14.5 million of American counterfeit bonds had been carefully and painstakingly created by a network of members of the Mafia in the United States. The package had been delivered to Rome in July 1971, and there was substantial evidence to establish that the ultimate destination of those bonds was the Vatican Bank.

Lynch advised them that much of the evidence, from separate sources, also indicated that someone with financial authority within the Vatican had ordered the fake bonds. He pointed out that other evidence strongly indicated the $14.5 million was merely a down payment and that the counterfeit bonds ordered were in fact worth a total of $950 million.

The attorney then revealed the name of the "someone with financial authority" who had masterminded the illegal transaction. On the basis of the evidence in Lynch's hands, it was Bishop Paul Marcinkus.

Displaying remarkable self-control, the three priests listened as the two U.S. attorneys outlined the evidence.

At this stage of the investigation a number of the conspirators had already been arrested. One of them who had felt the desire to unburden himself was Mario Foligni, self-styled "count of San Francisco" with an honorary doctorate in theology. A first-class con man, Foligni had on more than one occasion narrowly avoided prison. When he was suspected of having manipulated the fraudulent bankruptcy of a company he controlled, a magistrate in Rome had issued a search warrant to the finance police. Opening Foligni's safe, the police had discovered a signed blessing from Pope Paul VI. They had apologized for the intrusion and departed.

Subsequently others had been equally impressed with Foligni's Vatican connections. He had opened the Vatican doors to an Austrian named Leopold Ledl. It was Ledl who had put the Vatican deal together—the purchase of $950 million of counterfeit bonds, with a purchase price of $635 million. A "commission" of $150 million would be paid back by the gang to the Vatican, leaving the Mafia with $485 million and the Vatican with bonds that had a face value of nearly $1 billion.

The American Mafia had been skeptical about the deal until Ledl produced a letter from the Vatican. Written under the letterhead of the Sacra Congregazione Dei Religiosi, it was confirmation that the Vatican wished to "buy the complete stock of the merchandise up to the sum of $950 million."

Foligni had told the American investigators that Marcinkus, ever prudent, had requested that a trial deposit of $1.5 million of the bonds be made at Handelsbank in Zurich. According to Foligni, Marcinkus had wanted to satisfy himself that the bonds would pass as genuine. Late in July 1971 the trial deposit was duly made by Foligni. He nominated Vatican cleric Monsignor Mario Fornasari as the beneficiary of the account he opened.

A second trial deposit of $2.5 million of the bonds had been made at the Banco di Roma in September 1971. On both occasions the bonds had passed bank scrutiny, a tribute to Mafia skill. Regrettably for the conspirators, however, both banks had sent samples to New York for physical examination. The Bankers Association in New York ascertained that the bonds were false. Hence the unusual presence of American attorneys and men from the FBI within the Vatican walls.

Apart from a desire to recover the balance of $10 million of the initial delivery, Lynch and his colleagues were anxious to bring all the participants in the crime to justice.

Foligni had told the investigators that the reason the Vatican required the fake bonds was to enable Marcinkus and Italian banker and businessman Michele Sindona to buy Bastogi, a giant Italian company with wide interests including property, mining, and chemicals. Bastogi's headquarters were in Milan; so were Sindona's. It was in this city that the then Archbishop Montini, later Pope Paul VI, had met Sindona. When Montini had become pope, the Vatican gained a new heir to Peter and the Vatican Bank gained a new lay financial adviser, Michele Sindona.

William Lynch, himself a devout Catholic, continued his story. Mario Foligni, it transpired, had fired a series of accusations at Bishop Marcinkus during the U.S. Department of Justice interrogations. Apart from the allegation that Sindona and Marcinkus had planned to buy Bastogi with fake bonds, Foligni also asserted that with Sindona's assistance, the bishop had established several secret numbered bank accounts in the Bahamas for his personal use.

Under interrogation Mario Foligni had claimed that he had been working personally with Benelli's office, the Secretariat of State, and that as a direct result of his cooperation "the secretary of state had caused stringent administrative action to be taken against Bishop Marcinkus, which severely restricted the bishop's enormous financial power within the Vatican." Foligni had insisted that he had told the Secretariat of State of the trial deposits he had made in Switzerland and Rome and that this information was used by Benelli's office against Marcinkus. Foligni had also advised the Justice Department that he was under orders from the secretary of state's office not to give the investigators any further details concerning the swindle.

Having put this evidence forward, the Americans sat back and waited for a response. As William Lynch and William Aronwald made clear when I interviewed them, this first meeting at the Vatican was not seen by either side as an interrogation. It was informal, an opportunity to lay before members of the Vatican's Secretariat of State some very serious allegations.

The Justice Department was aware that the central thrust of the allegations stemmed from two expert con men, but there was also powerful internal evidence to support the validity of the statements of Foligni and Ledl.

It was because of that evidence that William Aronwald had contacted Cardinal Cooke of New York via the U.S. attorney for the Southern District of New York. The cardinal had been most cooperative, and through the papal delegation in Washington this extraordinary meeting had been arranged. Its real object was not merely to lay down the information, but ultimately to confront Marcinkus.

While more coffee was served, the three monsignors remained silent but thoughtful. Eventually Monsignor Martinez, assessor of the cardinal secretary of state's office, responded. He assured the Americans that he and Monsignor Rauber had complete knowledge of all the affairs of Archbishop Benelli and categorically denied that Foligni had turned over any evidence to Benelli's office. As for the counterfeit bonds and the trial deposits, this was the first time that anyone in the Secretariat of State had heard about the affair. Taking a classic curial position, he remarked, "It is not the intention of the Vatican to collaborate with the United States officials in their investigation at this point, since this is considered to be an informal meeting, and our purpose at the present time is only to listen."

What Lynch and his colleagues were confronted with was a mentality that had defeated many minds better than theirs—that of the Curia, a body of men that gives absolutely nothing away, a government machine that holds the Roman Catholic Church in a viselike grip. Lynch reminded the monsignors that to date only

$4 million of the fake bonds had been recovered and continued, "Since all evidence strongly indicates that the eventual destination for all of the bonds was the Vatican Bank and in view of the fact that the total amount ordered is worth nine hundred fifty million dollars, perhaps I can give you a list of the types of bonds?"

Martinez merely swayed out of the path of that punch. Lynch persisted. "That way the records of the Istituto per le Opere di Religione can be checked to determine if any of the counterfeit stocks have been 'inadvertently' received on deposit at that bank."

The style of Martinez in the ring was really most impressive.

"I, of course, have no idea if any of these American counterfeit bonds have been received by our bank. I cannot, however, take a list from you to check. That would be the function of Bishop Marcinkus. He handles such matters. Perhaps if you have difficulty in contacting the bishop you might send a list with a formal letter to the papal nuncio in Washington."

It was obviously time for a change of tactics.

The U.S. attorneys produced a document they had taken from Leopold Ledl after his arrest. The Vatican seal was on the letterhead, below which was printed "Sacra Congregazione Dei Religiosi." It was the Vatican order for nearly $1 billion worth of counterfeit securities. It had convinced the Mafia. The monsignors examined it carefully. There was much staring and holding up to the light.

Martinez rubbed his chin thoughtfully. The Americans leaned forward eagerly. Perhaps they had finally gotten one past the redoubtable Martinez.

"The letterhead appears to be identical to the letterhead of one of our sacred congregations that is located here in the Vatican."

There was pause. Just time for the Americans to savor the moment. Then Martinez continued, "However, I would note that while the letterhead appears to be legitimate, that particular congregation changed its name in 1968, and that as of the date of this letter, June twenty-ninth, 1971, the name shown on the letterhead would be incorrect. The new name is Sacra Congregazione per i Religiosi e gli Istituti Secolari."

The American investigators had, however, succeeded in their main objective. It was agreed that they could see Bishop Paul Marcinkus face to face the following day. This in itself was an extraordinary achievement, for Vatican City fiercely guards its independent statehood.

During my interview with Cardinal Benelli he confirmed that he had indeed received information about the whole affair from Mario Foligni before the Vatican visit of the American investigators. It had seemed to the cardinal to be a self-serving effort by Foligni, who by that time knew the game was up. As to the validity of the information, Benelli confined himself to the observation that he found the information "very interesting and useful."

On the morning of April 26, 1973, the two American attorneys and the two FBI men were shown into the private office of Bishop Paul Marcinkus. Lynch and Aronwald repeated the story they had told the previous day, while Marcinkus puffed on a large cigar. In the light of some of his subsequent evasions, his initial remark is of particular interest:

"I am very disturbed by the seriousness of the allegations. In view of them I'll answer each and every question to the best of my ability."

He began with Michele Sindona.

"Michele and I are very good friends. We've known each other for several years. My financial dealings with him, however, have only been very limited. He is, you know, one of the wealthiest industrialists in Italy. He is well ahead of his time as far as financial matters are concerned."

He extolled the virtues and talents of Michele Sindona at some considerable length. Then, placing the Vatican Bank on a par with the confessional, Marcinkus remarked:

"I would prefer to withhold names in many of the instances I intend to give, because although the charges that Foligni makes against me are extremely serious, they are so wild that I do not believe it necessary to break banking secrecy laws in order to defend myself."

While the previous day's meeting had been largely

of an informal nature, this confrontation with Marcinkus
was an interrogation. On the evidence that the U.S.
Department of Justice had carefully and painstakingly
acquired over more than two years, Lynch and Aronwald
and FBI agents Biamonte and Tammaro had before
them the man who had masterminded one of the world's
greatest swindles. If the evidence was correct, then the
claim for world notoriety of the Chicago suburb of Cicero would in the future be shared by Al Capone and
Paul Marcinkus.

William Lynch raised the temperature a little.

"If it becomes necessary at some future date, will
you make yourself available for a face-to-face confrontation with Mario Foligni?"

"Yes, I will."

"If it becomes necessary, are you also prepared to
testify in a United States court?"

"Well, yes, if it's absolutely necessary. I hope it
won't be, though."

"Why?"

"Well, the only people who would gain anything if I
appeared in court would be the Italian press."

"How's that?"

"They frequently relish the opportunity to write
inflammatory material concerning the Vatican, whether
it's true or not."

Lynch and Aronwald showed a total lack of concern
for the Vatican's sensitivity toward the Italian press.

"Do you have a private numbered account in the
Bahamas?"

"No."

"Do you have an ordinary account in the Bahamas?"

"No, I don't."

"Are you quite certain, Bishop?"

"The Vatican does have a financial interest in the
Bahamas, but it's strictly a business transaction similar
to many controlled by the Vatican. It's not for any one
person's private financial gain."

"No, we are interested in personal accounts that
you have."

"I don't have any private or public account in the
Bahamas or anywhere else."

How Marcinkus constantly carried his salary and

expenses around in cash was not explored. It would have made him the first president of a bank in the world's history without a personal bank account. Neither did Marcinkus reveal that he was in fact on the board of directors of Banco Ambrosiano Overseas in Nassau and had been since 1971. He had been invited onto the board by the two men who had set up this Bahamas operation, Michele Sindona and Roberto Calvi. Both men used the bishop's name frequently in their business deals. Sindona put it bluntly to Marcinkus on one occasion: "I've put you on the board because your name helps me to raise money."

Sindona and Calvi showed their gratitude by giving Marcinkus and the Vatican Bank 2.5 percent of the Nassau bank's stock. This figure eventually rose to 8 percent. Marcinkus frequently attended board meetings and took holidays in the Bahamas.

At this point in the interrogation Bishop Marcinkus observed, "You know my position within the Vatican is unique."

One of the world's great understatements was followed by: "I'm in charge of what many people commonly refer to as the Vatican Bank. As such I have complete control of Vatican financial affairs. One of the things that makes my position completely unique is that I am answerable only to the pope as to how I handle those financial affairs. In theory my operations are directed by a group of cardinals who meet from time to time and generally act as overseers to the bank. In reality, however, I virtually have a sole hand in directing the financial affairs of the Vatican."

The personal testimony did not impress the bishop's listeners.

"What's the point you're trying to make?"

"Well, this position that I hold has led to, shall we say, certain hard feelings by other men in responsible positions within the Vatican."

"Really?"

"Oh, yes. It's just part of the job, I'm afraid. I am the first American ever to have risen to such a position of power within the Vatican, and I'm sure that this has also caused a certain amount of hard feelings."

Whether or not he was guilty of being the mastermind behind this enormous swindle, Paul Marcinkus undoubtedly spoke the truth when he talked about "certain hard feelings" held by other senior men within the Vatican, and not only there. In Venice, Cardinal Albino Luciani's feelings toward Marcinkus grew somewhat more than "hard" as Benelli told him of this latest episode in the Marcinkus saga. Ironically, what Benelli did not know was that during that private interview with the American investigators, Paul Marcinkus had attempted to entangle him in the swindle.

To read the statement Marcinkus made, it is clear that in his eyes everyone but himself merited investigation. Of Father Mario Fornasari, who was allegedly deeply involved in the affair, Marcinkus noted:

"Some of the people who work for me at the bank have pointed Fornasari out to me as an individual to avoid. I'm sure you know that Fornasari was denounced some time ago for writing libelous letters."

"Really? What happened?"

"I believe the charges were dropped."

Marcinkus conceded that he had been involved with Mario Foligni, without doubt one of the principal figures in the billion-dollar swindle, on at least two business ventures. The first concerned a $100 million investment scheme that did not come to fruition. The second was a $300 million deal involving Foligni and Italian industrialist Carlo Pesenti. That, too, had aborted, but as Marcinkus told his convoluted tale he was at pains to drag in Benelli's name. Apart from inadvertently demonstrating that his ego had been bruised because Benelli had asked Pope Paul to consider the $300 million deal and Marcinkus clearly believed that no one but he should talk to the pope about money, Marcinkus attempted to link Benelli and Foligni, presumably working on the law of guilt by association. In view of the subsequent activities of Michele Sindona and Roberto Calvi, both close friends of Marcinkus, it would be interesting to know if Marcinkus still holds to this dubious tenet.

What Marcinkus neglected to explain, perhaps because he was not asked to, was why he was even prepared to consider the $300 million deal involving Foligni some eight months after Foligni had unloaded $1.5 mil-

lion of fake securities in a Swiss bank and some six
months after he had unloaded $2.5 million of phony
bonds in the Banco di Roma. It is inconceivable that
Marcinkus did not know of these criminal activities; all
banks were alerted.

At the end of a long interrogation, Marcinkus maintained total innocence and disclaimed all knowledge.
He happily accepted a list of the counterfeit bonds and
said he would keep his eyes open for them.

A variety of people were eventually found guilty of
involvement in the billion-dollar swindle. With regard
to the allegations that Bishop Paul Marcinkus was
involved, Attorney William Aronwald told me:

> The most that could be said is that we were
> satisfied that the investigation had not disclosed
> sufficiently credible evidence to prove or dis-
> prove the allegation. Consequently, since we
> were not morally satisfied ourselves that there
> was anything wrong, or that Marcinkus or any-
> one else in the Vatican had done anything wrong,
> it would have been improper of us to try to
> grab some headlines.

It is abundantly clear that what seriously restricted
this investigation was not the lack of will of the United
States investigators. They tried hard, very hard. It would
later be alleged that they were themselves part of a
giant cover-up,* that they had merely gone through the
motions of an inquiry. This is nonsense and shows insen-
sitivity to the very real problems that are posed when
an investigation that begins in one country has to be
continued inside another. Vatican City is an independent state. That Lynch and Aronwald and the men from
the FBI got inside the Vatican gates at all is a tribute to
their tenacity. One cannot go rushing over the Tiber
like a TV cop, armed with a .45 gun, search warrants,
authority to hold and question witnesses, and the many
other legal devices that can be used within the United
States.

*Richard Hamer, *The Vatican Connection* (New York: Holt,
Rinehart & Winston), 1982.

If Vatican City were part of the United States, then doubtless all members of the Curia working in the Sacra Congregazione Dei Religiosi would have been interrogated in depth. Fingerprints would have been taken. Forensic tests on all typewriters within the congregation would have been made. If all that could have been done, the question of Bishop Marcinkus's guilt or innocence might have been resolved. The fact that the United States government took the evidence seriously enough to risk a very delicate political situation is illuminating in itself. As William Aronwald said to me, "We were not about to waste that amount of taxpayers' money unless we took the evidence very seriously indeed. . . . At the end of the investigation the case against Marcinkus had to be filed for lack of evidence that might have convinced a jury."

The question therefore remains unanswered. Who was the customer who ordered the counterfeit bonds? Based on all the available official evidence, it is possible to draw only two conclusions. Each is bizarre. One is that Leopold Ledl and Mario Foligni were planning to steal from the American Mafia a huge fortune in counterfeit bonds, having first conned the Mafia into going to the very considerable expense of creating the bonds. This particular section of the Mafia had a number of members who killed or maimed people whom they merely imagined had insulted them. If this is the real reason, then Ledl and Foligni were seeking an unusual form of suicide. The other conclusion is that the $950 million of counterfeit bonds were destined for the Vatican.

In Venice, Albino Luciani continued, literally, to wear the robes that had been left by his predecessor, Cardinal Urbani. Throughout the entire period of his patriarchate he refused to buy new ones, preferring instead to have the nuns who looked after him mend and remend. Indeed, he wore the robes of cardinal and patriarch rarely, preferring his simple priest's cassock.

His personal humility often created interesting situations. Driving through Germany in 1975 with Father Senigaglia, the cardinal arrived at the town of Aachen. Luciani particularly wanted to pray at a very

ancient altar in the main church. Senigaglia watched as
Luciani was told in rather a peremptory manner by the
church officials that the altar was closed and he should
return another day. Back in the car Luciani translated
the conversation he had had for Senigaglia's benefit.
Enraged, Senigaglia erupted from the car, ran to the
church, and gave the dignitaries a burst of Italian. They
understood enough to know that he was declaring that
the little priest they had turned away was the patriarch
of Venice. It was now Luciani's turn to get angry
with his secretary as he was almost dragged from the
car by the German priests. As Luciani entered the
church one of the still apologetic priests murmured to
him, "Eminence, a little bit of red, at least, could be
useful."

On another occasion in Venice, Luciani was attending a conference on ecology. He became deeply involved
in conversation with one of the participants. Wishing to
continue the dialogue, he invited the ecologist to call on
him at his home. "Where do you live?" asked the
ecologist. "Just next door to St. Mark's," responded
Luciani. "Do you mean the patriarch's palace?" "Yes."
"And whom do I ask for?" "Ask for the patriarch."

Underneath his humility and gentleness was a man
who, by his environment and his vocation, was excep-
tionally strong. Neither to the left nor the right—he
refused to become involved with the warring factions in
Rome. The power plays inside the Vatican left Luciani
on occasions puzzled as to why some of these men had
become priests at all. In an Easter sermon in 1976 he
observed:

> Some are in the Church only as troublemakers.
> They are like the employee who first moved
> heaven and earth to get into the firm but once
> he had the job was perpetually restless and
> became a pestilential hair shirt on the skin of
> his colleagues and his superiors. Yes, some peo-
> ple seem only to look at the sun in order to find
> stains on it.

His desire to achieve a new synthesis by taking what in
his view was right from both sides led him into consid-

erable conflict in Venice. The issue of divorce is an
example.

In Italy in the mid-1970s divorce was legal in the
eyes of the state but unacceptable in the eyes of the
Church. A move began to test the issue through a
referendum. Luciani was deeply opposed to the referendum, simply because he was convinced it would split
the Church and result in a majority committing themselves at the polling booths to a decision that the divorce laws should remain unchanged. If that happened,
it would be an official defeat for the Roman Catholic
Church in the country it traditionally claimed as its
own.

Benelli took the opposite view. He was convinced
that the Church would win if there was a referendum.

The debate not only within the Church but also
throughout Italy reached an intense level. Shortly before the referendum took place, a student group, FUCI,
organized by a priest in Venice, sent a forty-page
document to every bishop in the Veneto region. In it
was a powerful argument supporting the prodivorce
position. Albino Luciani read the document carefully,
considered for a while, then made national headlines
by apparently disbanding the student group. In the
Church, it was seen by many as an act of courage. In
the country, commentators seized upon Luciani's action
as yet another example of the bigotry of the Catholic
hierarchy.

What had outraged Luciani was not the prodivorce
statements but the fact that to buttress their arguments
the group had quoted extensively from a wide variety of
Church authorities, leading theologians, and a number
of Vatican Council II documents. To use these documents in such a way was to Luciani a perversion
of Church teaching. He had been there at the birth
of *Lumen Gentium*, *Gaudium et Spes*, and *Dignitatis
Humanae*. Error might well have rights in the modern
Church, but in Venice in 1974 for Luciani there was still
a limitation to those rights. In the document a quote
from *Dignitatis Humanae* that extolled the rights of the
individual

... Protecting and promoting the inviolable
rights of man is the essential duty of every civil
power. The civil power must therefore guarantee to every citizen, through just laws and
through other suitable means, the effective protection of religious liberty.

was followed by this statement:

On other occasions the Church has found itself
confronted by serious situations in society
against which the only reasonable possibility
was obviously not the use of repressive methods but the adoption of moral criteria and juridi-
cal methods which favored the only good which
was then historically possible: the lesser evil.
Thus Christian morality adopted the theory of
the just war; thus the Church allowed the legal-
ization of prostitution (even in the Papal States),
while obviously it remained forbidden on a
moral level. And so also for divorce. . . .

To see statements such as these juxtaposed in a
plea that the Church take a liberal view on divorce for
expediency's sake was unacceptable to Luciani. Obviously his beloved Vatican Council II teachings, like the
Bible, could be taken to prove and justify any position.
Luciani was aware that as he was head of the bishops'
council for the Veneto region, the Italian public would
consider the statement official policy and then be faced
with the dilemma of whether to follow the bishops
of the Veneto region or the bishops of the rest of
Italy. In fact, he did not disband the student group,
as is generally thought. He used a technique that was
central to his philosophy. He firmly believed that
you could radically alter power groups by identifying
the precise center of power and removing it. So he
simply removed the priest who was advising the student
group.
    In reality, as Father Mario Senigaglia confirmed to
me, Luciani's personal view on divorce would have surprised his critics:

It was more enlightened than popular comment would have it. He could and did accept divorcées. He also easily accepted others who were living in what the Church calls "sin."

As Luciani had prophesied, the referendum resulted in a majority for the prodivorce lobby. It left a split Church, a pope who publicly expressed his amazement and incredulity at the result, and a dilemma for those who had to reconcile the differences between Church and state.

Luciani's own dilemma was that he was committed to an unswerving obedience to the papacy. Often the pope would take a different position from that held by the patriarch of Venice. When that position became public, Luciani felt it his duty publicly to support it. What he did on a one-to-one basis with members of his diocese frequently bore no resemblance to the Vatican line. By the mid-1970s he had moved even farther toward a liberal position on artificial birth control. This man, who on the announcement of *Humanae Vitae* had allegedly declared, "Rome has spoken. The case is closed," clearly felt that the case was far from closed.

When his young secretary Father Mario Senigaglia discussed with Luciani, with whom he had developed an almost father-son relationship, different moral cases involving parishioners, Luciani always approved the liberal view that Senigaglia took. Senigaglia said to me, "He was a very understanding man. Very many times I would hear him say to couples, 'We have made of sex the only sin, when in fact it is linked to human weakness and frailty and is therefore perhaps the least of sins.'"

It is clear that Albino Luciani did not want for critics in Venice. Some felt that he revealed a nostalgia for the past rather than a desire for change. Some labeled him as being to the right, others as being to the left. Yet others saw his humility and gentleness as mere weakness. Perhaps posterity should judge the man on what he actually said rather than on what others thought he should have said.

On violence:

Strip God away from the hearts of men, tell children that sin is only a fairy tale invented by their grandparents to make them good, publish elementary school texts that ignore God and scoff at authority, and then don't be surprised at what is happening. Education alone is not enough! Victor Hugo wrote that one more school means one less prison. Would that that were so today!

On Israel:

The Church must also think of the Christian minorities who live in Arab countries. She cannot abandon them to fortune ... for me personally, there is no doubt that a special tie exists between the people of Israel and Palestine. But the holy father, even if he wanted to, could not say that Palestine belongs to the Jews, since this would be to make a political judgment.

On nuclear weapons:

People say that nuclear weapons are too powerful and to use them would mean the end of the world. They are manufactured and accumulated, but only to 'dissuade' the enemy from attacking and to keep the international situation stable.

Look around. Is it true or not that for thirty years there has not been a world war?

Is it true or not that serious crises between the two great powers, the U.S.A. and the U.S.S.R., have been avoided?

Let's be happy over this partial result. . . . A gradual, controlled, and universal disarmament is possible only if an international organization with more efficient powers and possibilities for sanctions than the present United Nations comes into being and if education for peace becomes sincere.

On racism in the United States:

> In the United States, despite the laws, Negroes are in practice on the edge of society. The descendants of the Indians have seen their situation bettered significantly only in recent years.

To call such a man a reactionary nostalgic may have validity. He yearned for a world that was not largely ruled by Communist philosophies, a world where abortion was not an every-minute event. But if he was a reactionary he had some remarkably progressive ideas.

Early in 1976 Luciani attended yet another Italian bishops' conference in Rome. One of the subjects openly discussed was the serious economic crisis Italy was then facing. Linked with this subject was another the bishops discussed privately: the Vatican's role in that economic crisis and the role of that good friend of Bishop Marcinkus, Michele Sindona. His empire had crashed in spectacular fashion. Banks were collapsing in Italy, Switzerland, Germany, and the United States. Sindona was wanted by the Italian authorities on a range of charges and was fighting his extradition from the United States. The Italian press had asserted that the Vatican had lost over $100 million. The Vatican had denied this but admitted that it had sustained some loss. In June 1975 the Italian authorities, while continuing their fight to bring Sindona to justice, had sentenced him *in absentia* to a prison term of 3½ years, the maximum they could give for the offenses. Many bishops felt that Pope Paul VI should have moved Marcinkus from the Vatican Bank when the Sindona bubble burst in 1974. Now, two years later, Sindona's friend was still controlling the Vatican Bank.

Albino Luciani left Rome, a city buzzing with speculation about how many millions the Vatican had lost in the Sindona affair, left a bishops' conference where the talk had been of how much the Vatican Bank owned of Banca Privata, of how many shares the bank had in this conglomerate or that company. He returned to Venice, where the Don Orione school for the handicapped did not have enough money for school books.

Luciani went to his typewriter and wrote a letter

that was published in the next edition of the archdiocesan magazine. The letter was entitled "A Loaf of Bread for the Love of God." He began by appealing for money to help the victims of a recent earthquake disaster in Guatemala, stating that he was authorizing a collection in all churches on Sunday, February 29. He then commented on the state of economic affairs in Italy, advising his readers that the Italian bishops and their ecclesiastical communities were committed to showing practical signs of understanding and help. He went on to deplore

> . . . the situation of so many young people who are looking for work and cannot find it. Of those families who are experiencing the drama or prospect of losing their jobs. Those who have sought security by emigrating far away and who now find themselves confronted by the prospect of an unhappy return. Those who are old and sick and because of the insufficiency of government pensions suffer worst the consequences of this crisis. . . .
>
> I wish priests to remember and frequently to refer in any way they like, to the situation of the workers. We complain sometimes that workers go and seek bad advice from the left and the right. But in reality how much have we done to ensure that the social teaching of the Church can be habitually included in our Catechism, in the hearts of Christians?
>
> Pope John asserted that workers must be given the power to influence their own destiny at all levels, even the highest. Have we always taught that with courage? Pius XII while on the one hand warning of the dangers of Marxism, on the other hand reproves those priests who remain uncertain in face of that economic system which is known as capitalism, the grave consequences of which the Church has not failed to denounce. Have we always listened to this?

Albino Luciani then gave an extraordinary demonstration of his own abhorrence of a wealthy, materialistic Church. He exhorted and authorized all his parish priests and rectors of sanctuaries to sell their gold, necklaces, and precious objects. The proceeds were to go to the Don Orione center for handicapped people. He advised his readers that he intended to sell the bejeweled cross and gold chain that had belonged to Pius XII and that Pope John had given to Luciani when he had made him a bishop.

> It is very little in terms of the money it will produce, but it is perhaps something if it helps people to understand that the true treasures of the Church are, as Saint Lorenzo said, the poor, the weak who must be helped not with occasional charity but in such a way that they can be raised a little at a time to that standard of life and that level of culture to which they have a right.

He also announced that he intended to sell to the highest bidder a valuable pectoral cross with gold chain and the ring of Pope John. These items had been given to Venice by Pope Paul during his visit in September of 1972.

Later in the same letter Luciani quoted two Indians. First he quoted Gandhi: "I admire Christ but not Christians." Then Luciani expressed the wish that the words of Sandhu Singh would perhaps one day no longer be true:

> One day I was sitting on the banks of a river. I took from the water a round stone and I broke it. Inside it was perfectly dry. That stone had been lying in the water for a very long time but the water had not penetrated it. Then I thought that the same thing happened to men in Europe. For centuries they have been surrounded by Christianity but Christianity has not penetrated, does not live within them.

The response to Luciani's letter was mixed. Some of the Venetian priests had grown attached to the precious jewels they had in their churches. Luciani also came under attack from some of the traditionalists of the city, those who were fond of recalling the glory and power that was interwoven in the title of patriarch, the last vestige of the splendor of a time when Venice was a world power. This man who was pledged to seeking out and living the essential, eternal truth of the Gospel met a deputation of such citizens in his office. Having listened to them, he said:

> I am first a bishop among bishops, a shepherd among shepherds, who must have as his first duty the spreading of the Good News and the safety of his lambs. Here in Venice I can only repeat what I said at Canale, at Belluno, and at Vittorio Veneto.

Then he phoned the fire brigade, borrowed a boat, and went to visit the sick in a nearby hospital.

As already recorded, one of the methods this particular shepherd employed to communicate with his flock was the pen. On more than one occasion Luciani told his secretary that if he had not become a priest he would probably have become a journalist. To judge by his writings he would have been an asset to the profession. In the early 1970s he devised an interesting technique to make a variety of moral points to the readers of the diocesan magazine: a series of letters to a variety of literary and historical characters. The articles caught the eye of the editor of a local newspaper, who persuaded Luciani to widen his audience through the paper. Luciani reasoned that he had more chance of spreading the "Good News" through the press than he did preaching to half-empty churches. Eventually a collection of the letters was published in book form, *Illustrissimi*—the most illustrious ones.

The book is a delight. Apart from providing an invaluable insight into the mind of Albino Luciani, each letter comments on aspects of modern life. Luciani's unique ability to communicate—unique, at least, for an Italian cardinal—is demonstrated again and again. The letters are also clear proof of just how widely read Luciani was. Chesterton and Walter Scott receive a letter from the patriarch, as do Goethe, Alessandro Manzoni,

Christopher Marlowe, and many others. There is even one addressed to Christ, which begins in typical Luciani fashion:

Dear Jesus,

I have been criticized. "He's a bishop, he's a cardinal," people have said, "he's been writing letters to all kinds of people: to Mark Twain, to Peguy, to Casella, to Penelope, to Dickens, to Marlowe, to Goldoni, and heaven knows how many others. And not a line to Jesus Christ!"

His letter to Saint Bernard grew into a dialogue, with the saint giving sage advice, including an example of how fickle public opinion could be:

In 1815 the official French newspaper, *Le Moniteur*, showed its readers how to follow Napoleon's progress: "The *brigand* flees from the island of Elba"; "The *usurper* arrives at Grenoble"; "*Napoleon* enters Lyons"; "The *Emperor* reaches Paris this evening."

Into each letter is woven advice to his flock on prudence, responsibility, humility, fidelity, charity. As a piece of work designed to communicate the Christian message it is worth twenty papal encyclicals.

Spreading the "Good News" was one aspect of Luciani's years in Venice. Another was the recalcitrance constantly demonstrated by some of his priests. Apart from those who spent their time evicting tenants or complaining about having to sell Church treasures, there were others who embraced Marxism as wholeheartedly as yet others were preoccupied with capitalism. One priest wrote in red paint across the walls of his church, "Jesus was the first socialist"; another climbed into his pulpit in nearby Mestre and declared to his astonished congregation, "I shall do no more work for the patriarch until he gives me a salary increase."

Albino Luciani, a man with a highly developed sense of humor, was not amused at such antics. In July 1978, from the pulpit of the Church of the Redemptor in

Venice, he talked to his congregation of clerical error: "It is true that the pope, bishops, and priests do not cease to be poor men subject to errors and often we make errors."

At this point he lifted his head from his manuscript, and looking directly at the people said with complete sincerity: "I am convinced that when Pope Paul VI destined me to the see of Venice he committed an error."

Within days of that comment Pope Paul VI died, at 9:40 P.M. on Sunday, August 6, 1978. The throne was empty.

THE EMPTY THRONE

Within twenty-four hours of Paul's death, with his body unburied and his papacy unevaluated, Ladbrokes, the London bookmakers, had opened a book on the papal election. *The Catholic Herald*, while carrying a front-page article criticizing the action, took care to let its readers know the current odds.

Cardinal Pignedoli was the favorite at 5–2. Cardinals Baggio and Poletti were joint second favorites at 7–2, followed by Cardinal Benelli at 4–1. Also strongly fancied was Cardinal Willebrands at 8–1. Cardinal Koenig was quoted at 16–1. England's Cardinal Hume was 25–1. These surprisingly long odds on the Englishman could perhaps be attributed to a statement Hume had made to the effect that he did not have the qualities for the job. Odds on any American cardinal were at better than 100–1. Longest odds were quoted for Cardinal Suenens. Albino Luciani did not appear in the list of papal runners.

Condemned by some for displaying lack of taste, Ladbrokes defended itself by pointing out that with regard to the empty throne the "newspapers are full of speculation about front-runners, contenders and outsiders."

Indeed, the speculation had begun even before Pope Paul's death. Peter Hebblethwaite, an ex-Jesuit priest converted to Vatican-watching, had asked in the *Spectator*

on July 29, "Who is running for pope?" He picked out
three favorites to follow—Pignedoli, Baggio, and Pironio.
Whether Pope Paul had in his last few days read
Hebblethwaite's comment that he "cannot be expected
to live very much longer" is not known.

The Italian media were a little slower off the mark.
On the day after the pope's death the radio gave out
nothing but Beethoven. On day two they relaxed a little
with continuous Mozart. On day three there was a diet
of light orchestral music. On day four the solemnity
eased a little more with vocal renditions of "Moonlight
Serenade" and "Stardust." Italian television for the first
few days gave its viewers a variety of movies entirely
peopled with nuns, popes, and cardinals.

Careful analysis of the English-speaking press covering the first few weeks of August 1978 indicates that if
the 111 cardinals eligible to vote were as perplexed as
the Vaticanologists, then the Church was in for a long,
confusing conclave.

Followers of Hebblethwaite's writings must have
had a particularly hard time backing the winner. In *The
Sunday Times* of London on August 13, Cardinals Felici,
Villot, Willebrands, Pellegrino, and Benelli were added
to his list of tips. The following Sunday he told his
readers, "The new pope: it could be Bertoli." The Sunday after that even Luciani got a mention. It was reminiscent of a racing correspondent reviewing the form for
the Kentucky Derby. If he mentioned every horse, then
after the race his paper could quote his comment about
the winner.

A fish-seller in Naples had better luck. Using the
numbers derived from the date of Pope Paul's death, he
won the national lottery.

Despite the pomp and ceremony, the funeral of the
pontiff was a curiously unemotional affair. It was as if
his papacy had ended long ago. After *Humanae Vitae*
there had been no more papal encyclicals and, apart
from his courageous comments when his close friend,
the former Prime Minister Aldo Moro, had been first
kidnapped then murdered, there had been little from
Paul over the past decade to inspire an outpouring of
grief at his death: a man to respect, not one to love.
There were many long and learned articles analyzing

his papacy in depth, but if he is remembered at all by posterity it will be as the man who banned the Pill. It may be a cruel epitaph, an unfair encapsulation of a sometimes brilliant and often tortured mind, but what transpires in the marital bed is of more import to ordinary people than the fact that Paul flew in many airplanes, went to many countries, waved at many people, and suffered agonies of mind.

In October 1975, Pope Paul had issued a number of new rules that were to apply upon his death. One of these was that all cardinals in charge of departments of the Roman Curia would automatically relinquish their offices. This ensured that the pope's successor would have a completely free hand to make appointments. It also ensured during the period of *sede vacante*, between death and election, a considerable amount of nervous agitation. One of the few exceptions to this rule of automatic dismissal was the *camerlengo*, or chamberlain. This office was held by the secretary of state, Cardinal Jean Villot. Until the throne was filled, Villot became the keeper of the keys of Peter. During the vacancy the government of the Church was entrusted to the Sacred College of Cardinals, who were obliged to hold daily meetings or "general congregations."

Another of the late pope's rules quickly became the subject of furious debate during the early general congregations. Paul had specifically excluded from the conclave that would elect his successor all cardinals over the age of eighty. Ottaviani mounted an angry attack on this rule. Supported by the eighty-five-year-old Cardinal Confalonieri and the other over-eighties, they attempted to reverse it. Paul had fought many battles with this group. In death he won the last one. The cardinals voted to adhere to the rules. The general congregations continued, on one occasion discussing for over an hour whether ballot papers should be folded once or twice.

Rome was beginning to fill, but not with Italians—most of them were at the beaches. Apart from tourists, the city was swarming with pressure groups, Vaticanologists, foreign correspondents, and the lunatic fringe. Part of this last group went around the city putting up posters that proclaimed, "Elect a Catholic Pope."

One of the "experts" breathlessly informed *Time* magazine, "I don't know of one Italian cardinal who would feel happy voting for a foreigner." He obviously did not know many Italian cardinals, certainly not the one who was patriarch of Venice. Before leaving for Rome, Luciani had made it clear to former secretary Monsignor Mario Senigaglia, now officiating at the Church of Santo Stefano, "I think the time is right for a pope from the Third World."

He also left no doubt whom he had in mind: Cardinal Aloisio Lorscheider, archbishop of Fortaleza, Brazil. Lorscheider was widely regarded as a man possessed of one of the best minds in the modern Church. During Luciani's years in Venice, he had come to know him well, and as Luciani confided to Senigaglia, "He is a man of faith and culture. Further than that, he has a good knowledge of Italy and of Italian. Most important of all, his heart and mind are with the poor."

Apart from their meetings in Italy, Luciani had spent a month with Lorscheider in Brazil in 1975. They had conversed in a variety of languages and discovered they had much in common. What was unknown to Luciani was the high regard that Lorscheider had for him. Lorscheider was later to observe of that month in Brazil, "On that occasion many people hazarded the guess that one day the patriarch of Venice could become pope."

Driven to Rome by Father Diego Lorenzi, the man who had replaced Senigaglia as secretary to the patriarch two years previously, Luciani stayed at the Augustinian residence near St. Peter's Square. Apart from his attendance at the daily general congregations he kept very much to himself, preferring to walk in the Augustinian gardens, quietly contemplating. Many of his colleagues led more strenuous lives: Ladbrokes' favorite, for example, Cardinal Pignedoli.

Cardinal Sergio Pignedoli had been a close friend of the late pope. Some Italian commentators cruelly observed he was the only friend Paul had. Certainly he appeared to be the only one to address him by the intimate "Don Battista." In support of Pignedoli, Cardinal Rossi of Brazil was at pains to remind the other cardinals of the tradition of popes indicating who their successor should be and insisted that Pignedoli was "Paul's best-loved son." Pignedoli was one of the most progressive of the curial cardinals and hence was disliked by most of the other curial cardinals. He was cultured, well-traveled, and perhaps most important for his candidacy, he had influenced either directly or indirectly the appointments of at least twenty-eight of his brother cardinals.

Straightforward, overt running for the Vatican throne is considered bad form in the higher reaches of the Roman Catholic Church. Candidates are not encouraged to stand up and announce publicly what their program or platform will be. In theory there are no canvassing, lobbying, or pressure groups. In practice there is all of this and much more. In theory the cardinals gather in secret conclave and wait for the Holy Spirit to inspire them. As the hot August days went by, phone calls, secret meetings, and preelection promises ensured that the Holy Spirit was being given considerable worldly assistance.

One standard technique is for a candidate to state that he really does not think he measures up to the job. In this election that was said by a number with total sincerity—for example, Cardinal Basil Hume. Others made similar statements and would have been distressed if they had found their colleagues accepting them at their face value.

Attending afternoon tea on August 17, Pignedoli declared to a gathering of Italian cardinals that went across the entire spectrum of right, center, and left that in spite of all the urgings and promptings he did not feel he was suited for the papacy. He suggested to his colleagues that they should vote instead for Cardinal Gantin. It was an imaginative suggestion.

Cardinal Bernardin Gantin, the cardinal of Benin, was fifty-six years of age. In view of his relative youth, there was very little chance of his election. The ideal age was felt to be somewhere in the late sixties. Pignedoli was sixty-eight. Further, Gantin was black. Racism is not confined to one side of the Tiber. Putting forward Gantin's name could well attract votes for Pignedoli from the Third World, whose cardinals held a vital thirty-five votes.

Pignedoli remarked that whoever was elected it should be done with all possible speed. Voting in the conclave was to begin on the morning of August 26, a Saturday. Pignedoli felt that it would be fitting if the new pope was elected by the morning of Sunday, August 27, so he could address the crowds at midday in a packed St. Peter's Square.

If there was a widespread desire among the cardinals for a quick resolution of the conclave, this would, of course, work greatly to the advantage of the candidate who entered with the largest following. Cardinals are just as susceptible to bandwagons as lesser mortals are. To attain the papacy, Pignedoli knew that he had to look to the noncurial cardinals to give him the seventy-five votes (two thirds plus one) essential for election. When the Curia had finished its internal fighting, it would eventually focus on a specific candidate, preferably one of its own group. Like demented jugglers the pundits tossed a variety of curial candidates into the air—Bertoli, Baggio, Felici.

In a curious maneuver to assist his own candidacy, Baggio contacted Paul Marcinkus and assured him that he would be confirmed in his post as head of the Vatican Bank if Baggio were elected. Bishop Marcinkus, unlike the cardinals who had been dispossessed by the late pope's rules, was still running the bank. There was no public indication that he would not continue to do so. The gesture by Baggio mystified Italian observers. If they had been able to persuade any of the cardinals present during the private general congregations to talk, the move by Baggio would have taken on a deeper significance.

These meetings were giving very serious consideration to the problems facing the Church and to the possible solutions. In this manner papal candidates emerge who are considered to have the abilities to implement the solutions. The August meetings were inevitably far-ranging. The concerns that surfaced included discipline within the Church, evangelization, ecumenism, collegiality, and world peace. There was another subject that occupied the minds of the cardinals: Church finances. Many were appalled that Marcinkus was still running the Vatican Bank after the Sindona scandal.

Others wanted a full-scale investigation into Vatican finances. Cardinal Villot, as secretary of state and *camerlengo*, was obliged to listen to a long list of complaints that all had one common denominator, the name of Bishop Paul Marcinkus. This had been the reason for Baggio's offer to keep him on in the job, an attempt to maintain the status quo and also a gambit to win the votes of such men as Cardinal Cody of Chicago, who would be perfectly content to let Marcinkus stay in his job.

The cardinal from Florence, Giovanni Benelli, was another who preoccupied observers. As Paul's troubleshooter he had made many enemies, but it was freely acknowledged that he could influence at least fifteen votes.

To confuse the oddsmakers even further, the fifteen very disgruntled old men who were about to be excluded from the actual conclave began to bring pressure to bear on their colleagues. Their group, which contained some of the most reactionary men in the Vatican, predictably began to push for the cardinal they felt most completely represented their collective point of view, the archbishop of Genoa, Cardinal Giuseppe Siri. Siri had led the fight against many of the Second Vatican Council reforms. He had been the principal right-wing candidate in the conclave that had elected Paul. Now a number of the overage cardinals considered that he was the ideal man for the chair of Peter. The octogenarians were not unanimous, however—at least one, Cardinal Carlo Confalonieri, was quietly singing the praises of Albino Luciani. Nevertheless, the group as a whole thought Siri should be the next pope.

Cardinal Siri claims that he is a much misunderstood man. During one sermon he had castigated women for wearing pants and exhorted them to return to dresses "so that they could remember their true function on this earth."

During the series of nine memorial Masses for Pope Paul, homilies were delivered by, among others, Cardinal Siri. The man who had blocked and obstructed Pope Paul at every turn pledged himself to the aims of the late pontiff. The campaign for Siri went largely unnoticed by the press. One of the arguments used by Siri's supporters was that the next pope must be an Italian. To insist that the next pope be homegrown, even though only 27 of the voting cardinals out of a total of 111 were Italian, was typical of an attitude that abounds throughout the Vatican.

The belief that only an Italian papacy can control not just the Vatican and the wider Church beyond but also Italy itself is deeply embedded in the thinking of the Vatican village. The last so-called foreign pope had been Adrian VI from Holland, in 1522. This highly talented and scrupulously honest man became fully aware of the many evils flourishing in Rome. In an attempt to halt the rising tide of Protestantism in Germany he wrote to his delegate in that country:

> You are also to say that we frankly acknowledge that . . . for many years things deserving of abhorrence have gathered around the Holy See. Sacred things have been misused, ordinances transgressed, so that in everything there has been a change for the worse. Thus it is not surprising that the malady has crept down from the Head to the members, from the Popes to the hierarchy. We all, prelates and clergy, have gone astray from the right way. . . . Therefore in our name give promises that we shall use all diligence to reform before all things, what is perhaps the source of all evil, the Roman Curia.

Within months of making that statement Pope Adrian was dead. Evidence suggests that he was poisoned by his doctor.

Now with Paul VI buried, the Roman Curia minority were yet again attempting to prevail over the majority. In one of the early general congregation meetings, with only 32 cardinals present, most of them Italian, it had been agreed that the 111 cardinals would not go into conclave until August 25 and that voting would not start until August 26. The delay of twenty days was just one day short of the longest permissible period laid down by the rules of the late pope. It was also the longest in modern history. In 1878, *sans* TWA and Pan Am, the cardinals had waited a mere ten days before going into the conclave that elected Leo XIII. The period of almost three weeks gave the Italian cardinals the maximum time to persuade the "foreigners" of the wisdom of electing an Italian successor to Paul VI. They met unexpected opposition. Albino Luciani was not alone in thinking the time had come for a pope from the Third World. Many from the Third World felt the same.

The majority of the cardinals from Latin America attended a secret meeting at the Brazilian College in Rome on August 20. No major candidate emerged, but it was agreed that the need was for a pastoral pope, for a man who clearly manifested holiness, who recognized the needs of the poor, a man in favor of power-sharing, of collegiality, a man who by his very nature and qualities would have worldwide appeal. The group was primarily concerned with what the new pope should represent rather than with which individual should be chosen, though the qualifications they specified reduced the field of possible winners dramatically.

In Florence,* Giovanni Benelli, wrongly thought by many observers to be running for the papacy, received the Latin American specification. He smiled as he considered the qualities the Latin Americans were seeking. It read like an accurate biography of exactly the man Benelli thought should be pope. Picking up the telephone, he dialed a number outside Florence and moments later was engaged in animated conversation with the Belgian cardinal, Suenens.

In Rome, Pignedoli continued to give lavish dinner parties, curial cardinals continued to lobby discreetly on behalf of Siri, and the Vatican press office maintained its policy of giving the world's commentators the minimum of cooperation as the date of what Peter Nichols of *The Times* of London called "The World's Most Secret Ballot" drew nearer.

---

*Giovanni Benelli had been maneuvered out of Rome in 1977. His continuing efforts to have Marcinkus removed from the Vatican Bank had resulted in a cabal (which included among its members Marcinkus and Paul's secretary, Monsignor Macchi) that had Benelli removed from the Secretariat of State's office. He had been made cardinal of Florence in compensation.

   The Latin American cardinals were not the only
group to formulate a document that amounted to a job
description. A week earlier, a group of Catholics calling
themselves CREP (Committee for the Responsible Election of the Pope) held a press conference in the Colum-
bus Hotel in Rome. The brave man chosen to field
questions from over four hundred reporters was Father
Andrew Greeley. Not himself a member of CREP, Greeley had, together with a group of theologians, drawn up
the job description on behalf of the committee.

   There were to be many critics of the document.
Much of the criticism was banal, much was dismissive.
Undoubtedly the signatories were looking for an extraordinary man. It is equally without doubt that the document showed a deep love for the Roman Catholic Church.
These men cared desperately about the nature and quality of the new papacy. To dismiss men of the quality of
Hans Küng, Yves Congar, and Edward Schillebeeck re-
quires a mentality bordering on spiritual sterility. Professor Küng, for example, is in the view of many who
are qualified to judge, the most brilliant Catholic theologian alive today. All the signatories of the press release
have impressive records.

HELP WANTED

A hopeful, holy man who can smile.

Interesting work, guaranteed income, residence
comes with position. Protection by proven security organization. Apply College of Cardinals,
Vatican City.

   Thus began the job description. It went on to de-
scribe the man they would like chosen by the secret
conclave. It did not matter, they stated, if he was curial
or noncurial; Italian or non-Italian; whether he was of
the First, Second, or Third World. It did not matter if
he was an intellectual or a nonintellectual, a diplomat
or a pastor, progressive or moderate, an efficient administrator or lacking in administrative experience. . . . What
was needed, the theologians said, at this present critical
time in history was "a man of holiness, a man of hope, a
man of joy. A holy man who can smile. A pope not for

all Catholics but for all peoples. A man totally free from the slightest taint of financial organizational wheeling and dealing." It went on to list other vital essentials. Reading the qualifications needed and comparing it with the list of leading candidates, the overriding impression is one of deep, urgent need bordering on desperation.

Greeley was given a rough ride, which got rougher when he had the temerity to suggest that perhaps a pope of the female gender might not be a bad idea. To suggest this in a room largely full of *macho* Italian reporters indicates either enormous courage or a desire to provoke. Eventually the meeting ended in some disorder, with a young Italian woman screaming at Father Greeley that he was evil and had sexual problems.

A few days later Professor Hans Küng indicated in an interview with the Italian news magazine *Panorama* that in his view the entire Roman Catholic Church had and would continue to have sexual problems until something was done about *Humanae Vitae*. He put birth control at the head of the problems facing the new pope. "It is a fundamental question for Europe and the United States but above all, for the Third World. . . . A revision of *Humanae Vitae* is necessary. Many theologians and also bishops would have no difficulty in consenting to birth control, even by artificial means, if the idea could be accepted that rules established in the past by popes could be corrected."

On August 21, Cardinal Lorscheider of Brazil made public through an interview exactly what was on the Latin Americans' "wanted" list. The Latin American cardinals sought a pope who was a man of hope with a positive attitude toward the world. They wanted a man who would not seek to impose Christian solutions on non-Christians; someone who was sensitive to social problems and open to dialogue, with a commitment to the search for unity; a good pastor, a good shepherd in the way that Jesus was; a man who sincerely believed that the bishops' conference should be an influencing factor on the papacy rather than a mere charade. He must be open to finding a new solution to birth control that, while it would not contradict *Humanae Vitae*, would go beyond it.

Cardinals Benelli and Suenens, still avoiding the heat of Rome, were quietly building the candidacy of a man who measured up to the desires of the Latin American cardinals, Father Greeley, and Professor Küng: Albino Luciani.

When Luciani's name surfaced in the Italian press during the preconclave period, his candidacy was dismissed as a gambit. One Italian Vatican expert, Sandro Magister, referred to "the uncolorful patriarch of Venice." Another, who should have known better, was Giancarlo Zizola. A few days before the conclave, Zizola—who had interviewed Albino Luciani in depth nine years earlier— wrote a dismissive little biography entitled "With the Poor (Not on the Left)." Zizola quoted an unnamed source who had observed, "the least you can say is that he is now the recognized leader of the ecclesiastical right, a Venetian replica of Cardinal Ottaviani."

Luciani, when questioned by the press about the spasmodic emergence of his name among the contenders, dismissed the suggestion with a laugh. "I am at best on the C list for pope." Content, the news media left him alone. His name was quickly forgotten.

Luciani remained aloof from the wheeling and dealing. Walking in the gardens of the Augustinian residence, which overlooks St. Peter's, he engaged Brother Clemente in conversation. Clemente was perspiring as he labored among the flower beds. Luciani recalled that when he was a boy he had worked in the fields. "Then I had calluses on my hands. Now I have calluses in my brain."

As the day of the conclave drew nearer, Albino Luciani had other concerns. His five-year-old Lancia 2000 had developed engine trouble. He told his secretary, Father Lorenzi, that he must get it repaired quickly. The voting in the conclave was due to start on Saturday, August 26. Luciani insisted that the car must be ready for their return journey to Venice on the following Tuesday. He wanted to make an early start. There was much to do on returning home.

On August 25, Luciani wrote to his niece, Pia:

Dear Pia,

I am writing to let you have the new stamps of the Sede Vacante and also to congratulate you for your first exam which went well. Let us hope the Lord will help you also for the rest. Today we finished the pre-Conclave with the last General Congregation. After which, having drawn lots for a cell, we went to see them. I've got number 60, a drawing room converted into a bedroom; it is like being in the seminary in Feltre in 1923. An iron bed, a mattress, a basin to wash in.

In 61 is Cardinal Tomasek of Prague. Further on, Cardinals Tarancon, Madrid; Medeiros, Boston; Sin, Manila; Malual, Kinshasa. The only one missing is Australia and we would have a concentration from the whole world. I don't know how long the Conclave will last, it is difficult to find the right person to confront so many problems which are very heavy crosses. Fortunately I am out of danger. It is already a very heavy responsibility to cast one's vote in these circumstances. I am sure that as a good Christian you will pray for the Church in these moments. Say "hello" to Francesco, Father, and Mother. I am not writing to these last two as I am rather busy at the moment. Your very affectionate

                                Albino Luciani

The following day, a few hours before the conclave, he wrote to his sister, Antonia:

Dear Sister,

I am writing to you shortly before going into the Conclave. These are heavy moments of responsibility, even if there is no danger for me, despite the gossip in the papers. Casting one's vote for a Pope in these moments is a heavy weight. Pray for the Church, and an affec-

tionate greeting also to Errere, Roberto, and
Gino.

                              Albino Luciani

Handing his letter to the Augustinians to be mailed,
he advised them that he had left most of his belongings
in his room. That morning he had celebrated a Mass
"for the election of a pope" with his brother cardinals.
Clemente had already taken an overnight bag for Luciani
to the Sistine Chapel. Now the cardinal joined his colleagues in the Pauline Chapel with its frescoes by
Michelangelo. Fussed over by Monsignor Virgilio Noé
the papal master of ceremonies, and preceded by the
Sistine Chapel choir singing a hymn to the Holy Spirit,
they walked through the Sala Ducale, beneath Bernini's
cherubs, and into the Sistine Chapel.

When Monsignor Noé called, *"Extra omnes"* (All
out), the choir, altar servers, television crews, and all
extraneous personnel departed. With Cardinal Villot
standing just inside and Noé just outside, the door slowly
closed on the 111 cardinals. It would not open until a
pope had been elected. The world's most secret ballot
would continue until puffs of white smoke told the waiting crowds in St. Peter's Square and the many millions
of observers worldwide that the Vatican throne had
been filled.

INSIDE THE CONCLAVE

Whatever Pope Paul's failings might have been, he certainly knew how to organize a conclave. He had left very clear instructions about the proceedings to elect his successor.

One of Paul's preoccupations had been secrecy. Two days before the conclave, the cardinals were obliged to swear a solemn oath. Under pain of excommunication they were forbidden subsequently to discuss the balloting "either by signs, word or writing, or in any other manner." To drive home the point, the cardinals also had to promise and swear "not to use devices designed in any way for taking pictures." Obviously Pope Paul did not entirely trust these princes of the Roman Catholic Church.

In case any of the cardinals might have suffered a memory lapse between taking the oath of secrecy and entering the conclave, they were obliged to take it again when those extraneous to the proceedings had left the Sistine Chapel.

To make triply sure, after the cardinals had gone to their assigned rooms (or "cells," as Paul preferred to call them), Cardinal Villot, helped by a number of colleagues and two technicians, made a search of the entire conclave area looking for anyone who had hidden himself hoping for the scoop of a lifetime. Then, in a manner reminiscent of San Quentin all the various personnel were physically checked and a roll call was taken in the chapel.

To ensure that nobody without was trying to get within, Paul had also instructed that a large retinue of Vatican personnel, including the Swiss Guard and Vatican architects, were to make a careful check outside the Sistine Chapel. Whether Paul was fearful that the banned octogenarians might attempt to climb the outer wall is not stated within the rules!

Villot and his assistants plus the two technicians certainly earned their lire during the conclave. Yet another of their tasks was to make random searches of the entire conclave area, looking for tape recorders, video equipment, and all forms of bugging devices.

With all this searching, body counting, and double-checking, the late pope clearly appreciated that there would be very little time on the first day to get down to the actual task of voting for a pope.

While Rome basked in a heat wave, the temperature within the Sistine Chapel must have been close to unbearable for those mainly elderly men. The late pope had not forgotten the windows. Under his instructions all of them had been sealed and boarded up. In this environment 111 cardinals would on the morrow make the most important decision of their lives.

If outside the walls the hopes, needs, and desires of millions concerning the new papacy were myriad, then they accurately mirrored the cross section of views contained within the conclave. The right wing was reflected in the aspirations of those who desired a return to the pre-Vatican Council II world, where ecclesiastical discipline of a rigid nature was the keystone. The left wing sought a pope who understood and related the Church to the poor, a pope who would rule in a democratic manner and acknowledge that his bishops should influence the direction in which the Church moved. They yearned for a John XXIII, while the right wing longed for a Pius XII. In the middle were men grappling with both points of view, attempting to go backward and forward simultaneously.

There was also Albino Luciani, a man with a simplicity that is rarely given to a person of such high intelligence—a simplicity that sprang from a sophisticated and complex mind. He saw his task as the need to acknowledge the unfulfilled aspirations of the Third World. Hence his decision to vote for the archbishop of Fortaleza, Brazil, Aloisio Lorscheider, a man with glittering intellectual gifts who knew all about the problems of the poor. To elect such a man as pope would be an inspired choice with or without the aid of the Holy Spirit.

Giovanni Benelli and Leo Josef Suenens had an equally inspired choice. Before the conclave Benelli had watched with wry amusement when media speculation identified him as a possible pope. He had remained silent when subjected to snide attacks by curial cardinals such as Pericle Felici, the administrator of the patrimony for the Holy See, who had said of him, "His vote will go only to himself."

Felici was soon to discover that Benelli had different plans for his vote and, more important, for the votes of others. When news of some of the quiet, discreet lobbying being done by Benelli and Suenens reached the Curia, they were as dismissive of Albino Luciani as had been the men and women of the media. Of the many preconclave biographies issued by the Vatican, that on Luciani was the shortest. Clearly those in power agreed with his own assessment that he was no more than a C-list candidate. Like the world's press, the Curia did not know the man. Unfortunately for the Curia, other cardinals did. After the election, many members of the world's press and many Vatican experts would excuse their inability to pick the winner by stating that he was "unknown, had not traveled outside Italy, does not speak any languages." None of this was true.

Albino Luciani was fluent in German, French, Portuguese, and English, as well as in Latin and his native Italian. Apart from being well known by the noncurial Italian cardinals, he had a wide range of friendships among foreign cardinals. The Poles, Wojtyla and Wyszynski, had stayed with him in Venice. Wojtyla had shaped Luciani's thinking with regard to the problem of Marxism. Luciani had stayed with Lorscheider during a trip to Brazil in 1975. Cardinal Arns, also from Brazil, was another close friend. Suenens of Belgium, Willebrands of Holland, Marty of France, Cooke of New

York, Hoeffner and Volk of Germany, Manning of Los Angeles, and Medeiros of Boston were just a few of the cardinals who enjoyed friendships with Luciani. In addition to Brazil he had also been to Portugal, Germany, France, Yugoslavia, Switzerland, and Austria, as well as Africa, where he had created the link between Vittorio Veneto and Kiremba, a town in Burundi.

He had also formed friendships with many non-Catholics. The black Phillip Potter, secretary of the World Council of Churches, had been his house guest. Others included Jews, Anglicans, and Pentecostal Christians. He had exchanged books and letters with Hans Küng. If the Roman Curia had known that, alarms would have rung all over Vatican City.

This was the man who now merely wished to cast his vote, see a new pope elected, climb into his repaired Lancia, and go home to Venice. He had already considered the possibility that by some absurd twist of fate his name might emerge from the pack. When Mario Senigaglia had wished him luck and urged him to take some of his speeches "just in case," Luciani had dismissed the suggestion. "There is always a way out of it. You can always refuse."

In Rome Diego Lorenzi, Luciani's secretary since 1976, had also expressed the wish that this man, whom—like Senigaglia before him—he regarded as a father, should be the next pope. Again Luciani dismissed the suggestion. He reminded Lorenzi of the rules that the late pope had drawn up. He referred to that supreme moment when one of the cardinals has received two thirds plus one of the votes—in this case, 75. The cardinal in question is then approached and asked, "Do you accept?" Luciani smiled at his secretary. "And if they elect me, I will say, 'I'm sorry. I refuse.' "

On Saturday morning, August 26, after they had celebrated Mass and breakfasted, the cardinals walked to their allotted chairs in the Sistine Chapel. The rules urged that each cardinal disguise his handwriting on the voting card that was so designed that when folded in two it was reduced in size to about one inch. After scrutineers were appointed to check the votes, three more cardinals were appointed to scrutinize the scrutineers. The two thirds plus one rule was Pope Paul's safeguard against a cardinal voting for himself.

Eventually, with the temperature as well as the tension mounting, the first ballot began.*

After the ballot cards had been counted, checked, checked again, and then checked for a third time to ensure that no one had voted twice, they were then carefully threaded together, recounted, rechecked, and placed in a designated box for subsequent burning. The voting on the first ballot produced the following result:

Siri 25
Luciani. 23
Pignedoli 18
Lorscheider. 12
Baggio 9

The remaining twenty-four votes were scattered. Two Italians, Bertoli and Felici, received votes, as did Cardinals Pironio of Argentina, Wojtyla of Poland, Cordeiro of Pakistan, and Koenig of Austria.

Albino Luciani had listened with growing incredulity as the scrutineer called out his name twenty-three times. When a number of the cardinals sitting nearby had turned and smiled at him, he merely shook his head, bemused. How could it be that he had obtained so many votes?

Cardinals Benelli, Suenens, and Marty could have supplied the answer. They had created what they considered to be a successful base from which to promote Luciani. Like these three, the other cardinals voting for Luciani on the first ballot represented an international cross section: from France, Renard and Gouyon; from Holland, Willebrands and Alfrink; Koenig of Austria;

*The only official record of what transpired is buried deep in the Vatican archives. What follows is the result of evidence I have acquired from a variety of informed sources. The figures did not always agree, and consequently I fully acknowledge that there must be a margin of error. This also applies to the names of the cardinals who voted for Luciani on the first ballot. Though there will inevitably be variances, I am satisfied that the general shape and pattern of voting recorded here is accurate.

Volk and Hoeffner of Germany; Malula of Zaire; Nsubuga
of Uganda; Thiandoum of Dakar; Gantin from Benin;
Colombo of Milan; Pellegrino of Turin; Ursi of Naples;
Poma of Bologna; Cooke of New York; Lorscheider of
Brazil; Ekandem of Nigeria; Wojtyla of Cracow; Sin of
Manila.

Unaware of the identities of his supporters, Luciani
concluded that this aberration would correct itself in
the second ballot, and, reaching for another voting card,
he again wrote down the name of Aloisio Lorscheider.

The curial cardinals were eyeing Luciani with new
interest. Their first task had been to halt the Pignedoli
campaign for the papacy. The second ballot confirmed
they had achieved that objective.

Siri 35
Luciani 30
Pignedoli 15
Lorscheider 12

The remaining nineteen votes were again scattered.

The voting cards together with those from the first
ballot were stuffed into the antiquated stove, the *nero*
(Italian for black) handle was pulled, and black smoke,
instead of emerging outside on the roof, promptly filled
the Sistine Chapel. Despite the fact that the funeral of
Pope Paul and the conclave were costing the Church
several million dollars, some Vatican official decided to
save a few cents and had decreed that the chimney
should not be swept. The result, with all windows sealed,
threatened to bring the conclave to a sudden and dramatic end. The late pope had not foreseen the possibility of all 111 cardinals being suffocated to death, but he
had provided for several members of the Vatican fire
brigade to be locked in the area. They promptly ignored
the rules and opened several windows.

Eventually some of the black smoke made its way
out of the Sistine Chapel chimney, and Vatican Radio
confirmed that the morning had not produced a pope.
Many Vatican experts had predicted a long conclave,
reasoning that it would take a great deal of time for 111
men from around the world to arrive at any form of
relative unanimity. Seeing the black smoke, the pundits

nodded sagely and continued in their attempts to pry from the Vatican press office such vital details as the lunch menu in the conclave.

The biggest and most diverse conclave in the Church's entire history moved hastily out of the Sistine Chapel to the temporary canteen.

The third ballot would be crucial. Siri and Luciani were finely balanced. While a very troubled patriarch of Venice picked at his food, others were busy. Giovanni Benelli talked quietly to the cardinals from Latin America. They had made their point, he assured them, but clearly a pope from the Third World was not going to emerge during this conclave. Did they want a man like Siri, with his reactionary views, on the throne? Why not a man who, if not from the Third World, clearly loved it? It was no secret, Benelli told them, that Luciani was voting for their own Aloisio Lorscheider.

In fact Benelli was in danger of gilding the lily. The cardinals from Latin America had done their homework to a far greater degree than any other geographical group. Aware that their chances of electing Lorscheider were not great they had, before the conclave, prepared a short list of noncurial Italians. One of the men with whom they discussed the list was Father Bartolomeo Sorges, a Jesuit priest based in Rome. During a two-hour discussion Sorges pointed out the various arguments for and against each of the possibilities. The name that had emerged was Albino Luciani. Father Sorges recalled for me his final words of advice to the group of cardinals:

> If you want to elect a pope who will help to build up the Church in the world, then you should vote for Luciani. But remember he is not a man who is accustomed to governing; consequently he will need a good secretary of state.

As the quiet buzz of conversation continued, Cardinals Suenens, Marty, and Gantin, less flamboyantly but with equal effectiveness, spoke to others who were still wavering. Koenig of Vienna quietly remarked to those sitting near him that non-Italians should have no objection to another Italian as their spiritual leader.

The Curia members were also considering their options over lunch. It had been a good morning for them. They had stopped Pignedoli. Siri, their candidate that morning, had clearly reached his maximum position. Despite all the pressure they had exerted before the conclave it was now obvious to Felici and his clique that the left and the center could not be drawn in sufficient numbers to Siri. Luciani, the quiet man from Venice, would surely be easy to control in the Vatican. Those who yearned for a pre-Vatican II papacy were not convinced. They pointed out that Luciani more than any other Italian cardinal had put into practice the spirit of Pope John's Second Vatican Council.

In England everything stops for tea. In Italy the same state of suspended animation is achieved during siesta. While some lingered in the dining hall, talking quietly, others retired to their rooms to sleep. In cell 60, Albino Luciani knelt and prayed.

"You can't make *gnocchi* out of this dough," Luciani had remarked to several well-wishers before the conclave. It now appeared that a significant number of his fellow cardinals disagreed with this self-evaluation.

Through prayer he sought the answer, not to the ultimate result of the balloting, but to what he should do if elected. Luciani, who had never wanted to be anything other than a parish priest, stood on the threshold of the most powerful position in the Roman Catholic Church and went down on his knees earnestly to entreat his God to choose someone else.

Emerging from his cell at 4:00 P.M., Luciani was warmly embraced by Cardinal Joseph Malula from Zaire. Full of joy, Malula offered his congratulations.

Luciani shook his head sadly. "A great storm is troubling me," he said as the two men made their way back for the third ballot.

Luciani 68
Siri 15
Pignedoli 10

The remaining eighteen votes on the ballot were

scattered. Albino Luciani was now within seven votes of
the papacy. With a hand to his forehead he was heard
to murmur, "No. Please no."

It was Cardinals Willebrands and Ribeiro, seated
on either side of Luciani, who heard the entreaty. Both
men instinctively reached out and gripped Luciani.
Willebrands spoke quietly. "Courage. If the Lord gives
the burden, He also gives the strength to carry it."

Ribeiro nodded and then added, "The whole world
prays for the new pope."

There was no doubt whatsoever in the minds of
many present that the Holy Spirit was manifest on that
hot afternoon. Others, however, took a more cynical
view of what was inspiring the conclave. Taofinu'u of
Samoa was heard to murmur, "Power in the form of
man, or rather a cardinal of the Curia." His eyes were
fastened on Felici when he made this observation.

Felici, who had spent the morning voting for Siri,
now approached Albino Luciani. Felici handed him an
envelope with the remark, "A message for the new pope."
The piece of paper within contained the words "via
crucis," (the way of the cross).

There was great excitement in the conclave. Many
were now convinced that they were acting by divine
inspiration. Dispensing with the late pope's instructions
that each cardinal should swear a solemn oath each
time before voting, the fourth ballot began.

Luciani...................................... 99
Siri 11
Lorscheider .... 1 (that of Albino Luciani)

As the final vote was announced there was a tremen-
dous burst of applause from the gathering. The time
was 6:05 P.M. A clique of Siri supporters, members of the
intransigent right, had held out to the end. The doors of
the chapel opened and various masters of ceremonies
came, accompanying the *camerlengo*, Villot, to where
Albino Luciani sat. Villot spoke.

"Do you accept your canonical election as supreme
pontiff?"

All eyes were upon Luciani. Cardinal Ciappi described for me that moment. "He was sitting three rows

behind me. Even at the moment of his election he was hesitating. Cardinal Villot put the question to him and he continued to hesitate. Cardinals Willebrands and Ribeiro were clearly encouraging him.''

Luciani eventually responded. ''May God forgive you for what you have done in my regard.'' Then he added, ''I accept.''

''By what name do you wish to be called?'' asked Villot.

Luciani hesitated again. Then for the first time he smiled, and he said: ''John Paul the First.''

There were murmurs of delight from some of the listening cardinals. The name was an innovation, the first double name in the history of the papacy. Tradition holds that by the choice of name a pope gives an indication of the direction his reign may take. Hence the choice of Pius would have delighted the right wing, indicating perhaps a return to a preconciliar Church. What message Luciani was sending out with his choice of name depended on what message his listeners wanted to receive.

Why had Luciani, a man without ambition, accepted this position that for a number of other cardinals present would have been the realization of their life's ambition?

The answer, like much about this simple man, is complex. Research indicates that he was overwhelmed by the speed and size of the vote. Many spoke to me of this aspect. It is perhaps best summarized by a member of the Curia who had a close, twenty-year friendship with Albino Luciani:

> He was distressed by it. If he had not been so overwhelmed by the sheer quantity, if events had moved more slowly, taken the conclave into a second day, he would have had time to gather himself and refuse; and yet, if he had decided in that conclave that he was not the man to become pope, he would have refused. He was one of the strongest men I have known in thirty years in the Curia.

There is also the vital element of Luciani's personal

humility. Describing the acceptance of the papacy as an act of humility may appear to be contradictory. To equate the taking of supreme power with meekness is, in fact, entirely consistent if the last thing you want on earth is supreme power.

Inside the conclave, as the new pope was led to the sacristy, all was joy. Outside all was confusion. While the Gammarelli brothers, tailors to the Vatican, tried to find a papal white cassock that fitted, the cardinals were merrily burning their voting papers with the special chemical that was designed to ensure a white smoke for the watching world. The watching world saw first white smoke, then a short while later, puffs of black (indicating that the Church was still without a pope) emerge from the small chimney. The smoke had begun to emerge at 6:24 P.M. As it continued to belch out in a variety of hues, the Gammarelli brothers inside were not having any better luck with the white cassocks. Normally before a conclave they made three: small, medium, and large. This time, working from a list of twelve *papabile*, they had produced four, including an extra-large one. The slightly built Luciani obviously had not been featured on their short list of cardinals. Eventually, nearly drowning in his new cassock, he emerged from the sacristy and, sitting on a chair in front of the altar, received each cardinal who, having kissed Luciani's hand, was then warmly embraced by him.

Suenens, one of the cardinals largely responsible for this election, observed, "Holy Father, thank you for saying 'yes.'"

Luciani smiled broadly at him. "Perhaps it would have been better if I had said 'no.'"

The cardinals in charge of the stove were still happily throwing on voting cards and a large bundle of chemical candles that were supposed to produce the elusive white smoke. Vatican Radio manifestly knew less about what was going on than anyone else and uttered this remarkable statement: "We can now say with total certainty that the smoke is either black or white." In fact at that moment it was gray.

Vatican Radio telephoned the home and office of

the Gammarelli brothers and obtained no answer. The
brothers, meanwhile, were in the sacristy attempting to
fasten the blame on someone else for the fiasco of the
white cassocks. It was rapidly becoming one of those
operas that only Italians can stage.

Meanwhile, inside the Sistine Chapel, the cardinals
had started to sing the *Te Deum*, the hymn of thanksgiving.

Outside, Father Roberto Tucci, the Jesuit director
of Vatican Radio, was observed hurtling toward the
bronze door of the papal palace across the piazza. The
captain of the Swiss Guard, who was obliged to greet
the new pope with a loyal salute of his men, was interro-
gating the guard, who said there had been a burst of
clapping when, to his astonishment, he heard the *Te
Deum*. That meant but one thing—whoever he was, they
had a pope. The problem was he did not have a retinue
of guards ready.

Assuming the multicolored smoke indicated a dead-
locked conclave, the crowds in the square had largely
dispersed when a voice boomed out on the massive
loudspeakers.

"Attenzione."

People began to hurry back into the square. The
large door behind the balcony of St. Peter's swung open.
Figures could be seen emerging onto the balcony itself. . . .
It was now 7:18 P.M., over an hour since the election.
Senior Cardinal Deacon Felici appeared on the balcony,
and suddenly the crowd below was still.

Among that crowd was Luciani's secretary, Don
Diego Lorenzi. He was standing next to a family from
Sweden who had asked him what work he did. Young
Lorenzi remarked, "I am in Rome for a few days. I work
in Venice." Then he turned his gaze to the figure of
Felici on the balcony.

"Annuncio vobis gaudium magnum! Habemus papam
(I bring you news of great joy! We have a Pope)
—*Cardinalem Albinum Luciani."*

At the mention of the name "Albinum," Lorenzi
turned back to the Swedish family. Tears were running
down his face. He smiled, then said proudly, "I am the
secretary of the newly elected pope."

The roar from the crowd had almost drowned the

"Luciani." When Felici continued, "who has chosen the name John Paul the First," there was a bedlam of noise. Many—indeed, most—had never heard of Luciani, but what mattered was that they had a pope. The personal reaction came a short while later, when Albino Luciani stepped onto the balcony. The enduring memory is of that smile. It touched the very soul. The man exuded delight and joy. Whatever else this papacy was going to be, it was going to be exhilarating. After the gloom and agonizing of Paul, the contrast was an extraordinary shock. As the new pope intoned the blessing *Urbi et Orbi* (To the City and the World), the effect was similar to a burst of bright, dazzling sunlight after an eternity of dark days.

In a moment he was gone, only to return. The captain of the Swiss Guard had finally assembled a battalion. Albino Luciani waved and smiled. That smile reached out to everyone. The man from the mountains of northern Italy who as a small boy had wanted more than anything to be a parish priest, stood on St. Peter's balcony on the evening of Saturday, August 26, 1978, as Pope John Paul I.

Luciani kept the conclave in session that night. Having sat down to dinner in his previously assigned place, one of his first thoughts was for the overage, excluded cardinals. They had already been given the election result by telephone. Now Luciani invited them into the conclave for the following morning's Mass.

The Secretariat of State had already prepared a speech that in theory was intended to indicate the direction of the new papacy, any new papacy. Luciani took the speech and, retiring to cell 60, altered and amended what had initially been vague statements about love, peace, and war to a number of specifics.

The speech was delivered at the end of the Mass of thanksgiving celebrated the following morning. Luciani pledged his pontificate to the teachings of the Second Vatican Council. He placed a high value on collegiality, the sharing of power with his bishops. He declared that he intended to bring back into force the great discipline of the Church, and to this end he gave high priority to the revision of the two codes of canon law. Union with other denominations would be pursued without compromise to the Church's teachings but equally without hesitation.

The central thrust of the speech revealed that this man who described himself in Venice as "a poor man accustomed to small things and silence" had a dream: a revolutionary dream. He gave notice of his intention to pursue the pastoralization of the entire Church—indeed, of the entire world:

> The world awaits this today; it knows well that the sublime perfection it has attained by research and technology has already reached a peak, beyond which yawns the abyss, blinding the eyes with darkness. It is the temptation of substituting for God one's own decisions, decisions that would prescind from moral laws. The danger for modern man is that he would reduce the earth to a desert, the person to an automaton, brotherly love to planned collectivization, often introducing death where God wishes life.

With the text of *Lumen Gentium* (the Light of Nations), the Second Vatican Council's dogmatic constitution on the Church in his hand, Albino Luciani gave notice that he intended to put the Church back where it belonged: back to the world and the words of Christ; back to the simplicity and honesty of its origins. If Christ returned to earth, Luciani wanted him to find a Church he would recognize—one free of political interests, free of the big-business mentality that had corroded the original vision.

At noon the new pope appeared on the central balcony of the basilica. The square below was packed tight with some two hundred thousand people. Millions more around the world watched on television as Luciani's smile broadened in response to the thunderous applause. He had come out to say the *Angelus*, but before giving the midday prayer he had decided to give his listeners a glimpse into the secret conclave. When the applause and cheering had died down he promptly broke two papal precedents: the obsessive secrecy that Paul had sternly insisted on with respect to the conclave, and the use of the majestic "we" that for nearly two thousand years had demonstrated papal aspirations to territory. He smiled at the crowd and then began.

"Yesterday . . ." The word was followed by an almost imperceptible shrug of the shoulders, as if to say "a funny thing happened to me on my way to the conclave." The crowd roared with laughter. Luciani joined in the merriment, then began again.

"Yesterday morning I went to the Sistine Chapel to vote peacefully. Never could I have imagined what was about to take place. As soon as it began to be a danger for me, two of my colleagues who were sitting near me whispered words of encouragement." Simply and without a trace of pomposity he recalled the words of Willebrands and Ribeiro. He told the crowd why he had chosen his particular name:

My thoughts were like this. Pope John had wanted to consecrate me with his own hands here in the Basilica of St. Peter's. Then, though unworthy, I succeeded him in the Cathedral of St. Mark, in that Venice which is still filled with the spirit of Pope John. The gondoliers remember him, the sisters, everyone. On the other hand, Pope Paul not only made me a cardinal, but some months before that, on the wide footbridge in St. Mark's Square, he made me blush to the roots of my hair in front of twenty thousand people, because he took off his stole and placed it on my shoulders. I was never so red-faced. Furthermore, in the fifteen years of his pontificate, this pope showed not only me but the whole world how he loved the Church, how he served it, worked for it, and suffered for this Church of Christ. And so I took the name John Paul.

Be sure of this. I do not have the wisdom of heart of Pope John, nor do I have the preparation and culture of Pope Paul. However, I now stand in their place. I will seek to serve the Church and I hope that you will help me with your prayers.

With those simple, everyday words followed by the *Angelus* and his blessing, Pope John Paul I announced his arrival to the world. The warm, enthusiastic response of the crowd in Rome was an accurate reflection of the larger, watching world.

Vatican-watchers puzzled over the clues to the new papacy contained in the choice of names. Is he John or is he Paul? One of those who was asked was Cardinal Suenens: "He will be both in his own way. His manner is closer to John's but it is like mixing oxygen and hydrogen—you get water, two different elements producing a third substance."

His chosen *names* seemed to hint at a continuity. But the fact that John Paul had included the designation "the first"—a convention that is never applied until there is a second of the same name—should have told the Vatican-watchers something. What they and the rest of the Church were about to experience related to neither of the new pope's immediate predecessors. It was unique.

He had not spelled out to the listening world on this, his first day, exactly how he intended to make his dream of a poor Church a reality, but within hours he embarked on a course of action that was of vital importance if his vision was to be realized.

On the evening of Sunday, August 27, 1978, he had dinner with Cardinal Jean Villot and asked him to continue, at least for a while, as secretary of state. Villot accepted. The new pope also reconfirmed the various cardinals in charge of the departments of the Roman Curia. Having entered the conclave without any aspirations to become pope, it would have been extraordinary if he had emerged with a prepared list of new cabinet members.

On August 31, Italy's leading and highly respected economic periodical *Il Mondo* addressed a long open letter to Albino Luciani. The letter asked for papal intervention to impose "order and morality" on the Vatican's financial dealings, which included "speculation in unhealthy waters." The letter, entitled "Your Holiness, Is It Right?" made a series of slashing attacks on what it saw to be the state of affairs inside the Vatican's financial operations. Accompanying the open letter was a long analysis entitled "The Wealth of Peter."

Il Mondo asked Albino Luciani a number of highly relevant questions:

> Is it right for the Vatican to operate in markets like a speculator? Is it right for the Vatican to have a bank whose operations help the illegal transfer of capital from Italy to other countries? Is it right for that bank to assist Italians in evading tax?

Financial editor Paolo Panerai attacked the Vatican links with Michele Sindona. Panerai attacked Luigi Mennini (managing director) and Paul Marcinkus of the Vatican Bank and their relationships with "the most cynical financial dealers in the world, from Sindona to the bosses of the Continental Illinois Bank in Chicago (through which, as Your Holiness's advisers can tell you, all of the Church's investments in the United States are handled)."

Panerai asked:

> Why does the Church tolerate investments in companies, national and multinational, whose only aim is profit; companies which, when necessary, are ready to violate and trample on the human rights of millions of the poor, especially in that Third World which is so close to Your Holiness's heart?

Of Marcinkus the open letter observed:

> He is, however, the only bishop who is on the board of a lay bank, which incidentally has a branch in one of the great tax havens of the capitalistic world. We mean the Cisalpine Overseas Bank at Nassau in the Bahamas.* Using tax havens is permitted by earthly law, and no

*Cisalpine Overseas Bank became Banco Ambrosiano Overseas in a subsequent reorganization.

lay banker can be hauled into court for taking
advantage of that situation (they all do); but
perhaps it is not licit under God's law, which
should mark every act of the Church. The Church
preaches equality but it does not seem to us
that the best way to ensure equality is by evading taxes, which constitute the means by which
the lay state tries to promote the same equality.

There was no official reaction from the Vatican, but
inside Vatican City the responses ranged from quiet
satisfaction felt by those who objected to the activities
of the Vatican Bank and the Extraordinary Section of
the Administration of the Patrimony of the Holy See
(APSA), to anger and resentment from those who considered that the only problem with the Vatican's financial
speculations was that they should make even bigger
profits.

The Italian newspaper *La Stampa* weighed in with
another piece, entitled "The Wealth and Powers of the
Vatican." Journalist Lamberto Furno took a largely sympathetic look at Vatican finances and discounted some
of the accusations that had been published over the
years alleging massive Vatican wealth. But Furno did
see a number of pressing problems facing the new pope,
including verification that the Church reforms to achieve
a state of poverty, which in Furno's mind had been
implemented by Pope John and continued by Pope Paul,
had become a reality. This could be achieved only by
"publishing the Vatican budgets."

Furno concluded:

The Church does not have riches or resources
that exceed its needs. But it is necessary to give
proof of this. Bernanos has his country curate
observing, "on sacks of money our Lord has
written in his own hand, 'Danger of death.' "

The new pope read these articles with interest. They
confirmed in his mind the wisdom of a course he had
already embarked on.

Before his election, Luciani had been aware of the
many complaints about Vatican finances that had been

aired to Cardinal Villot: complaints about the way that
Bishop Marcinkus ran the Vatican Bank; complaints
about his involvement with Michele Sindona; complaints
about the links between the APSA and Sindona. Luciani
had personal experience of the manner in which Marcinkus operated the Vatican Bank—experience dating from
1972, when Marcinkus had sold the controlling interest
in Banca Cattolica del Veneto to Roberto Calvi without
consulting the patriarch of Venice.

He had known as early as 1972 that there was
something terribly wrong with the whole structure and
philosophy of Vatican finance, but he had been powerless.
Now he had the power. On Sunday, August 27, 1978, as
he sat eating dinner with Cardinal Villot, the new pope
instructed his newly confirmed secretary of state to
initiate an investigation immediately. There was to be a
review of the entire financial operation of the Vatican, a
detailed analysis of every aspect. "No department, no
congregation, no section is to be excluded," Luciani
told Villot.

Luciani made it clear that he was particularly concerned with the operation of the Istituto per le Opere di
Religione (IOR), the Institute for Religious Works, generally known as the Vatican Bank. The financial review
was to be done discreetly, quickly, and thoroughly. The
new pope advised his secretary of state that once he had
considered the report he would decide on appropriate
courses of action.

Clearly Luciani was a firm believer in practicing
what he preached. In one of his "letters" to Saint Bernard he had discussed the virtue of prudence:

> I agree that prudence should be dynamic and
> urge people to action. But there are three stages
> to consider: deliberation, decision, and execu-
> tion.
>
> Deliberation means seeking the means that
> lead to the end. It is made on the basis of
> reflection, of advice that has been asked for, of
> careful examination.
>
> Decision means, after examining the vari-
> ous possible methods, make up your mind to
> choose one of them. . . . Prudence isn't an ever-

lasting seesaw, suspending everything and tear-
ing the mind apart with uncertainty; nor is it
waiting in order to decide for the best. It is said
that politics is the art of the possible, and in a
way that is right.

Execution is the most important of the
three: prudence, linked with strength, prevents
discouragement in the face of difficulties and
impediments. This is the time when a man is
shown to be a leader and guide.

Thus Albino Luciani, a man totally committed to
the belief that the Roman Catholic Church should be
the Church of the poor, set in motion an inquiry into
the wealth of the Vatican. He would deliberate, decide,
then execute.

VATICAN INCORPORATED

When Albino Luciani became head of the Roman Catholic Church in August 1978 he was in command of a truly unique organization. Over eight hundred million people, nearly one fifth of the world's population, looked to Luciani as their spiritual leader. Nearer at hand, within Vatican City, was the structure that controlled not only the faith but also the fiscal policy of the Church.

"Vatican Incorporated" is a vital part of this structure. It exists in bricks and mortar. It exists within certain philosophies. Paul Marcinkus of the Vatican Bank is credited with the observation that "you can't run the Church on Hail Marys." Obviously the power of prayer has been devalued along with many of the world's currencies in recent years.

Marcinkus should not be condemned for what might appear to be a materialistic observation. The Church plays many roles in many countries. It needs money. How much money is a different question. What it should be doing with that money is another. That it does much good is beyond doubt. That it does much that is highly questionable is also beyond doubt. A large quantity of published works give details of the many charities financed by the Church, of the aid it gives to famine relief, of aid to alleviate suffering of every kind. Education, medicine, food, shelter—these are some of the ben-

efits that derive from the work of the Church. What is
lacking is information on how much is acquired and how
it is acquired. On these matters the Vatican is and always
has been very secretive. That secrecy has inevitably
given rise to one of the world's great unsolved mysteries.
How much is the Roman Catholic Church worth?

In mid-1970, commenting on a Swiss newspaper
article that declared, "the productive capital of the Vatican can be reckoned at between 50 and 55 billion Swiss
francs" (a figure approaching $13 billion), the Vatican
newspaper *L'Osservatore Romano* said: "It is a simply
fantastic figure. In reality, the productive capital of the
Holy See, including both deposits and investments,
placed both in Italy and outside Italy, is far from reaching one hundredth of this sum." That would place a
ceiling figure on Vatican wealth on July 22, 1970, of
$111 million.

The first falsehood contained in the Vatican newspaper's statement is the exclusion of the assets of the
Vatican Bank. It is comparable to asking IBM or Du
Pont for complete disclosure and being told the total in
the petty-cash box. Even excluding the annual profits of
the Vatican Bank, the figure quoted by the Vatican is
outrageous. It was a lie that over the years was to be
heard again. In April 1975 Lamberto Furno of *La Stampa*
asked Cardinal Vagnozzi: "If I were to put forward the
sum of 300 billion lire ($452 million) for the productive
patrimony of the five administrations,* would I be close
to the mark?"

Furno had deliberately excluded the Vatican Bank
in stating his question. He drew from Vagnozzi the
assertion, "I tell you, the productive patrimony of the
Holy See, in Italy and in the world, is less than a
quarter of the sum you mention."

If that were true it would follow that on April 1,

---

*(1) The Ordinary Section of the Administration of the Patri-
mony of the Holy See (APSA) and the Extraordinary Section of
the Administration of the Patrimony of the Holy See, again
usually abbreviated to APSA, (2) the Governorship of the Vatican City State, (3) the Prefecture for Economic Affairs, (4) St.
Peter's Workshop, and (5) Propaganda Fide.

1975, the productive wealth* of the Holy See, excluding the Vatican Bank, was a figure lower than 75 billion lire, or approximately $113 million. One single administration, the Extraordinary Section of the Administration of the Patrimony of the Holy See, or the APSA, is treated as a central bank by the World Bank, the International Monetary Fund, and the Bank for International Settlements at Basel. Every year the staff at Basel publish annual figures that show what the world's central banks have deposited or borrowed from other banks in the Group of Ten. Their figures for 1975 indicate that the Vatican had $120 million on deposit in foreign banks and that, uniquely, the Vatican was debtless, the only bank in the entire world to be in such a position. This was just one administration within the Vatican, and to ascertain the entire actual wealth of just that one section, a great many other tangible assets must be added.

Like Rome itself, Vatican wealth was not built in a day. The problem of a wealthy Church—and all who aspire to follow the teachings of Jesus Christ must regard that wealth as a problem—has its roots as early as the fourth century. When the Roman emperor Constantine converted to Christianity and gave colossal wealth to Pope Silvester I, he created the first rich pope. Dante ends the *Inferno* with these lines:

Alas! Constantine, how much misfortune you caused,
Not by becoming Christian, but by the dowry
Which the first rich Father accepted from you.

The Catholic faith's claim to uniqueness is valid. It is the only religious organization in the world that has as its headquarters an independent state, Vatican City, which is a law unto itself. At 108.7 acres it is smaller than many of the world's golf courses, is the size of St. James's Park in London, and is approximately one eighth the size of Central Park in New York City. A leisurely

*I.e., income-producing assets. The Vatican makes a distinction between productive wealth and nonproductive wealth, an example of the latter being the Vatican art treasures.

stroll around Vatican City takes something over an hour.
To count the wealth of the Vatican would take far longer.

The modern wealth of the Vatican is based on the
generosity of Benito Mussolini. The Lateran Treaty, which
his government concluded with the Vatican in 1929,
gave the Roman Catholic·Church a variety of guarantees and measures of protection.

The Holy See obtained recognition of itself as a
sovereign state. It was exempted from paying taxes both
for its properties and its citizens, exempted from paying
duty on imported goods; it had diplomatic immunity
and accompanying privileges for its own diplomats and
those accredited to it by foreign powers. Mussolini guaranteed the introduction of Catholic religious teaching in
all public high schools in Italy, and the entire institution of marriage was placed under canon law, which
ruled out divorce. The benefits for the Vatican were
many, not least the fiscal ones.

> Article one. Italy undertakes to pay the Holy
> See, on the ratification of the Treaty, the sum
> of 750 million lire and to hand over at the same
> time Consolidated 5 percent State Bonds to the
> bearer for the nominal value of 1 billion lire.

At the 1929 rate of exchange this package represented $81 million. A 1984 equivalent figure is approxi-
mately $500 million. Vatican Incorporated was in
business. It has never looked back.

To handle the windfall, Pope Pius XI created on
June 7, 1929, the Special Administration. Appointed to
run it was a layman, Bernardino Nogara. Apart from
having many millions of dollars to work with, Nogara
had another very important asset. One hundred years
earlier, the Roman Catholic Church had completely reversed its position on money-lending. Indeed, the Church
can rightfully claim to have changed the meaning of the
word "usury."

In the classic sense usury means *all* gains from
money-lending. For over eighteen hundred years, the
Roman Catholic Church had dogmatically stated that
the charging of any interest on a loan was absolutely
forbidden as being contrary to divine law. The prohibi-

tion was restated in various Church councils: Arles (A.D. 314), Nicea (325), Carthage (345), Aix (789), Lateran (1139)—at this council, usurers were condemned to excommunication. So, although the laws of many states made the practice legal, it was still heresy—that is, until 1830, when the Church reversed its position. Thus, by courtesy of the Roman Catholic Church, usury now means lending money at *exorbitant* rates of interest.

Self-interest produced a total reversal on the Church's teaching with regard to money-lending. Perhaps if celibacy was no longer the rule for priests it might move the Roman Catholic Church's teaching on artificial birth control.

Bernardino Nogara was a member of a devout Roman Catholic family; many of its members made, in a variety of ways, significant contributions to the Church. Three of his brothers became priests, another became director of the Vatican Museum, but Bernardino Nogara's contribution was by any standard the most profound.

Born in Bellano, near Lake Como, in 1870, he achieved early success as a mineralogist working in Turkey. In October 1912 he played a leading role in the peace treaty of Ouchy between Italy and Turkey. In 1919 he was a member of the Italian delegation that negotiated the peace treaty between Italy, France, Britain, and Germany. He subsequently worked on behalf of the Italian government as a delegate to the Banca Commerciale in Istanbul. When Pope Pius XI was seeking a man capable of administering the fruits of the Lateran Treaty, his close friend and confidant Monsignor Nogara suggested his brother Bernardino. With that selection Pius XI struck pure gold.

Nogara was reluctant to accept the job and did so only when Pope Pius XI agreed to certain conditions. Nogara did not wish to be trammeled by any traditional views the Church might still hold about making money. The ground rules Nogara insisted on included the following:

1. His decisions on what investments to make would be totally and completely free of any religious or doctrinal considerations.
2. He would be free to invest Vatican funds anywhere in the world.

The pope agreed and opened the doors to currency speculation and to playing the market in stock exchanges, including the buying of shares in companies whose products were inconsistent with Roman Catholic teaching. Items such as bombs, tanks, guns, and contraceptives might be condemned in the pulpit, but the shares Nogara bought for the Vatican in companies that manufactured these items helped to fill the coffers in St. Peter's.

Nogara played the gold market and the futures market. He bought Italgas, sole supplier of gas in many of Italy's cities, placing on the board, on behalf of the Vatican, Francesco Pacelli. Pacelli's brother became, in time, the next pope (Pius XII), and the nepotism that stemmed from that papacy was manifest throughout Italy. If there was a Pacelli on the board, six-to-four the company belonged to the Vatican.

Among the banks that came under Vatican influence or control through Nogara's purchases were Banco di Roma, Banco di Santo Spirito, and Cassa di Risparmio di Roma. The man clearly not only had a way with money but was also fairly gifted in the art of persuasion. When Banco di Roma was floundering and threatening to take with it a large amount of Vatican money, Nogara persuaded Mussolini to take over the bank's largely worthless securities and transfer them to a government holding company, Institute for Industrial Reconstruction (IRI). Mussolini also agreed that the Vatican should be reimbursed, not at the current market value of the securities, which was virtually nil, but at their original purchase price. IRI paid Banco di Roma over $630 million. The loss was written off by the Italian treasury, which is another way of saying the ordinary people picked up the bill, just as they had been doing for the clerics since the Middle Ages.

Much of the speculation Nogara indulged in on behalf of the Vatican certainly contravened canon law and probably civil law, but as his client was the pope, who was not asking questions, Nogara remained untroubled by such niceties.

Using Vatican capital, Nogara acquired significant and often controlling shares in company after company. Having acquired a company he rarely sat on the board, preferring to nominate one of the trusted Vatican elite to look after the Church's interests.

The three nephews of Pius XII—Princes Carlo, Marcantonio, and Giulio Pacelli—were three of the inner elite whose names began to appear as directors on an ever-growing list of companies. These were the Church's *uomini di fiducia* (men of trust).

Textiles. Telephone communications. Railways. Cement. Electricity. Water. Bernardino Nogara was everywhere. When Mussolini needed armaments for his invasion of Ethiopia in 1935, a substantial proportion was supplied by a munitions plant Nogara had acquired on behalf of the Vatican.

Realizing, before many, the inevitability of the Second World War, Nogara moved part of the assets then at his disposal into gold. He bought from the United States $26.8 million worth of gold at $35 per ounce. Later, he sold about 20% of it on the open market at a profit so substantial that the original purchases were covered in their entirety. His speculations in gold continued throughout his time at the head of Vatican Incorporated. Between 1945 and 1951 he purchased more than 450,000 ounces; during the following two years he sold more than 70,000 ounces. My research indicates that nearly 500,000 ounces are on deposit at the Federal Reserve Bank of New York; this single holding of the Vatican—purchased originally for less than $20 million—is now worth some $200 million.

In 1933 "Vatican Incorporated" again demonstrated its ability to negotiate successfully with Fascist governments. The concordat of 1929 with Mussolini was followed with a concordat between the Holy See and Hitler's Third Reich. Solicitor Francesco Pacelli had been one of the key figures in the Mussolini agreement; his brother Cardinal Eugenio Pacelli, the future Pius XII, had a leading negotiating role as the Vatican's secretary of state in concluding a treaty with Nazi Germany.

Hitler saw many potential benefits in the treaty, not least the fact that Pacelli, a man already displaying marked pro-Nazi attitudes, might prove a useful ally in the approaching world war. History was to prove that Hitler's assessment was accurate. Despite a great deal of world pressure, Pope Pius XII declined to excommuni-

cate either Hitler or Mussolini. Perhaps his refusal was
based on an awareness of just how politically irrelevant
he was. His was a papacy that affected neutrality, which
talked to the German episcopate about "just wars" and
did precisely the same with the French bishops. This
resulted in the French bishops supporting France and
the German bishops supporting Germany. His was a
papacy that declined to condemn the Nazi invasion of
Poland because, he said, "We cannot forget that there
are forty million Catholics in the Reich. What would
they be exposed to after such an act by the Holy See?"

For the Vatican, one of the major advantages to
emerge from the very lucrative deal with Hitler was
confirmation of the *Kirchensteuer* (church tax). This is a
state tax that is still deducted at source from all wage-
earners in Germany. One can opt out by renouncing
one's religion. In practice few choose to. This tax represents between 8 and 10 percent on income tax collected
by the German government. The money is handed over
to the Protestant and Catholic churches. Substantial
amounts derived from the *Kirchensteuer* began to flow
to the Vatican in the years immediately preceding the
Second World War. The flow continued throughout that
war ($100 million in 1943, for example). In the Vatican
Nogara put the German revenue to work alongside the
other currencies that were pouring in.

On June 27, 1942, Pope Pius XII decided to bring
another part of the Vatican into the modern world and
into the ambit of Bernardino Nogara. He changed the
name of the Administration of Religious Works to the
Institute for Religious Works. The change did not cap-
ture the front pages of the world's newspapers; but by
that act the IOR, or the Vatican Bank as it is known by
all but the Vatican, was born. Vatican Incorporated had
sired a bastard child. The original function of the
administration, set up by Pope Leo XIII in 1887, had
been to gather and administer funds for religious works;
it was in no sense a bank. Under Pius, its function
became "the custody and administration of monies (in
bonds and cash) and properties transferred or entrusted
to the institute itself by fiscal or legal persons for the
purposes of religious works, and works of Christian
piety." It was and is in every sense a bank.

Nogara took to reading the terms of the Lateran Treaty very closely, particularly Clauses 29, 30, and 31. These dealt with tax exemptions and the formation of new, tax-exempt "ecclesiastical corporations" over which the Italian state would have no control. Interesting discussions began about the meaning of the phrase "ecclesiastical corporations." Doubtless distracted by other events of the time, Mussolini took a liberal view. In 1942, the Finance Ministry of the Italian government issued a circular stating that the Holy See was exempt from paying the tax on stock dividends. It was signed by the director general of the ministry, whose name, quite appropriately, was Buoncristiano (good Christian). The circular specified the various organizations within the Holy See that were exempt from the tax. The list was long and included the Special Administration and the Vatican Bank.

The man whom Nogara selected to control the Vatican Bank was Father (later Cardinal) Alberto di Jorio. Already functioning as Nogara's assistant in the Special Administration, he kept a foot in both sections by retaining that position and assuming the role of first secretary, then president, of the Vatican Bank. Apart from the controlling interests in many banks that Nogara acquired outside the Vatican walls, he now had two in-house banks to work with.

Nogara, applying his mind to the task of increasing the Vatican's funds, went from strength to strength. The tentacles of Vatican Incorporated spread worldwide. Close links were forged with an array of banks. Rothschilds of Paris and London had been doing business with the Vatican since the early nineteenth century. With Nogara at the Vatican's helm the business increased dramatically: Crédit Suisse, Hambros, Morgan Guaranty, Bankers Trust (useful when Nogara wanted to buy and sell stock on Wall Street), Chase Manhattan, and Continental Illinois, among others, became Vatican partners.

Evidently Nogara was not a man with whom to play Monopoly. Apart from banks, he acquired for the Vatican controlling interests in companies in the fields of insurance, steel, financing, flour and spaghetti, mechanical industry, cement, and real estate. With regard to the last-named his purchase of at least 15 percent of

the Italian giant Immobiliare gave the Church a share
of an astonishing array of property. Società Generale
Immobiliare is Italy's oldest construction company.
Through its ownership of the building firm Sogene,
Immobiliare—and therefore to a significant degree the
Vatican after its 15 percent acquisition—owned the Rome
Hilton, Italo Americana Nuovi Alberghi, Alberghi Am-
brosiani (Milan), Compagnia Italiana Alberghi Cavalieri,
and Società Italiani Alberghi Moderni. These are just
the major hotels in Italy. The list of major buildings
and industrial companies owned by Immobiliare is twice
as long.

In France it built a huge block of offices and shops
at 90 Avenue des Champs Elysées, another at 61 Rue de
Ponthieu, and another at 6 Rue de Berry.

In Canada it owned one of the world's tallest skyscrapers (the Stock Exchange Tower, situated in Montreal), the Port Royal Tower, a 224-apartment block, a
huge residential area in Greensdale, Montreal. . . .

In the United States it had five huge apartment
blocks in Washington, D.C., including the Watergate
Hotel, and in New York, a residential area of 277 acres
at Oyster Bay.

In Mexico it owned an entire satellite city of Mexico
City called Lomas Verdes.

This list of properties is by no means exhaustive.

Nogara also bought into General Motors, Shell, Gulf
Oil, General Electric, Bethlehem Steel, IBM, and TWA.
If the shares moved, and moved upward, men like Nogara
created the movement.

Although Nogara retired in 1954, he continued to
give the Vatican his unique brand of financial advice
until his death in 1958. Scant mention was made of the
man's passing by the press, as the majority of his activities on behalf of the Roman Catholic Church had been
cloaked in secrecy. This one man who demonstrated
that, wherever Christ's kingdom might be, that of the
Catholic Church was most assuredly of this world, was
given a memorable epitaph by Cardinal Spellman of
New York: "Next to Jesus Christ the greatest thing that
has happened to the Catholic Church is Bernardino
Nogara."

Starting with $80 million, less the $30 million that

Pius XI and his successor, Pius XII, held back (to spend on regional seminaries and parish houses in southern Italy, the building of Santa Maria in Trastevere, and the massive building projects in Rome, including the setting up of the Vatican library and art gallery), Nogara had created Vatican Incorporated. Between 1929 and 1939 he also had access to the annual worldwide collection of Peter's pence. With the "pennies" of the faithful plus the lire from Mussolini and the Deutsche marks from Hitler, Nogara was able to pass on to his successors a complex array of financial interests worth, at a very conservative estimate, $500 million controlled by the Special Administration, $650 million controlled by the Ordinary Section of the APSA, and assets in the Vatican Bank in excess of $940 million, with an annual profit from the bank averaging $40 million going directly to the pope. In capitalistic terms, Nogara's service in the cause of the Roman Catholic Church was an incredible success. Viewed in the light of the message contained in the Gospels, it was an unmitigated disaster. The vicar of Christ had acquired a new unofficial title—chairman of the board.

Four years after Nogara's death in 1958 the Vatican had urgent need of the kind of expertise Nogara had provided. The Italian government had raised the specter of taxing stock dividends again. What followed has a direct bearing on a sequence of disasters for the Vatican including Mafia involvement, financial mayhem, and murder, that would begin in 1968.

In any list of years purporting to be the worst in the Church's history, 1968 should feature very near the top. It was the year of *Humanae Vitae*. It was also the year when "the Gorilla" and "the Shark," as they were known, were let loose on the two Vatican banks. The Gorilla is Paul Marcinkus; the Shark, Michele Sindona, and the events that led to their control of Vatican finances make salutory reading.

Benjamin Franklin memorably observed, "But in this world, nothing can be said to be certain except death and taxes." Not many have chosen to argue with that statement. Among the few who have are the men who control the Vatican's finances. They have made strenuous attempts to eliminate taxes.

In December 1962 the Italian government passed legislation taxing the profits on dividends. Initially the tax was set at 15 percent. Then it went the way of all taxes and was doubled.

The Vatican at first raised no objection to paying the tax, at least not publicly. Privately, through diplomatic channels, it advised the Italian government: "In the spirit of our concordat and considering the law of 1942, it would be desirable that a favorable treatment be granted to the Holy See." Negotiations had begun.

The secret letter from the Vatican secretary of state, Cardinal Cicognani, to the Italian ambassador to the Holy See, Bartolomeo Mignone, goes on to detail exactly what the "favorable treatment" should be: tax exemption for a list of departments as long as a cardinal's arm, including, of course, the two Vatican banks—the Special Administration and the IOR.

The Vatican wanted to play the market but not to pay for the privilege. The minority Vatican-backed Christian Democrat government of the day touched its forelock, kissed the papal ring, and agreed to the Vatican's request. Neither Parliament nor public opinion was consulted. When the minority government fell, to be replaced by Christian Democrat Aldo Moro with a coalition of Christian Democrats and Socialists, the post of finance minister went to Socialist Roberto Tremelloni. He was disinclined to approve what was clearly an illegal agreement made by his predecessor, made, furthermore, without being ratified by Parliament and, even more important, made eight days after the government had resigned.

Aldo Moro, confronted with a finance minister threatening to resign on the one hand and an intransigent Vatican on the other, sought a compromise. He asked the Vatican to submit a statement of its holdings as a prelude to obtaining exemption. Not unreasonably, the prime minister felt that the Italian nation should know just how much money they were being deprived of. The Vatican refused to reveal the details and talked loudly about being a sovereign state. Apparently it is perfectly permissible to exploit the stock market of another sovereign state and make profits from the exploitation, but the exploited state is not allowed to know by just how much it is being exploited.

Various governments came and went. The issue was discussed from time to time in the Italian Parliament. At one point in 1964 the Vatican indicated just how far it had gone in abandoning Christ's dictum "my kingdom is not of this earth" and embracing instead the teachings of Bernardino Nogara: "Increase the size of your company because fiscal controls on the part of government become advantageously difficult." The "company" to which Nogara was referring was Vatican Incorporated, the "government" those unfortunates across the Tiber, who were obliged to deal with an offshore tax haven in the middle of Rome.

In June 1964, with Aldo Moro again in power, the Church of the poor threatened to bring down the entire Italian economy. During negotiations Vatican officials told the Italian government that if they did not get their way they would throw onto the market every single share they held in Italy. They picked their moment well. The Italian stock market was going through a particularly bad period, with shares dropping daily. Suddenly to dump on the market the enormous holdings of the Vatican would have destroyed the entire Italian economy. The Italian government, faced with this reality, capitulated. In October 1964 a draft bill was prepared that would ratify the illegal agreement.

The draft bill was never put before Parliament, mainly because governments were collapsing more quickly than the various finance ministers could discover what was in their in-boxes. Meanwhile the Vatican continued to enjoy tax exemption. It had not paid tax on its shares since April 1963. In 1967 the Italian press, specifically the left-wing press, went on the attack. They wanted to know why. They also wanted to know how much. They also wanted to know how many shares the Vatican held in their country. Figures began to fly. They ranged from estimates that put the worth of the Vatican investment on the Italian stock exchange at $160 million, to others that put it at $2.4 billion.

In March 1967, the Italian finance minister, Luigi Preti, in response to questions in the Italian Senate, threw some official light on the Vatican's holdings in

Italy. His breakdown showed that by far the biggest Vatican investor was the IOR, followed by the Special Administration. Various other Vatican departments, with high-sounding names such as the Fabric of St. Peter's, the Pontifical Society for St. Peter Apostle, the Administration of the Holy See Patrimony, and Propaganda Fide, were also revealed as players of the stock market. Finance Minister Preti stated that the Vatican owned shares worth approximately 100 billion lire ($104.4 million at the 1967 rate of exchange).

The actual total figure was undoubtedly much higher. Preti's figures did not take into account the large Vatican investment in government bonds and debentures that are completely exempt from any form of taxation. He was dealing only with shares that were taxable. Nor did Preti concern himself with the fact that under Italian stock exchange regulations, the holder of shares is allowed to leave the dividends uncollected for five years. Evidence indicates that the Vatican investments covered by these two aspects were, at the very least, as great as those that had come under the minister's province. The real value, therefore, of the Vatican investment in 1968 in Italian shares alone was at the very minimum $202.2 million. To that must be added the value of the Vatican's real-estate holdings, particularly in Rome and the surrounding districts, as well as all non-Italian investments.

Eventually Italy decided to call the Vatican's bluff: the Roman Catholic Church should, at least in Italy, render unto Caesar what was Caesar's. In January 1968 yet another transitory government, led by Giovanni Leone, declared that at the end of the year the Vatican would have to pay up. With considerable ill grace and comments about its investments being a wonderful stimulus for the Italian economy, the Vatican agreed—but in typical Vatican fashion. Like a defendant found guilty, it asked for time to pay in easy installments.

The whole affair had a number of unfortunate results for the Vatican. Whatever the actual total, everyone in Italy was now aware that the Church of the poor had very large investments producing millions of dollars of annual profit. Further, the six-year-old dispute had resulted in many companies being identified as

2. The 11-year-old Albino Luciani at Feltre Seminary. (*Numbers refer to photo credits on copyright page.*)

3. (*Below, left*) Giovanni and Bortola with Pia: the photograph that accompanied Luciani everywhere.

4. (*Below, right*) Luciani, the newly ordained priest, July 7, 1935.

5. Cardinal Ottaviani (*above, left*) led those who were against reform of the Church's position on birth control.

6. (*Above, right*) Luciani, shown here with his brother, Edoardo, sister-in-law, and their ten children, took the opposing view.

7. Vatican City State.

8. The Patriarch of Venice with some of his priests, including (*second, right*) his secretary, Father (now Monsignor) Senigaglia.

9. Pope Paul VI and Albino Luciani in St. Mark's Square, Venice.

10. Pope Paul VI with Secretary of State Cardinal Villot.

11. Cardinal Cody of Chicago (*foreground, left*); behind Pope Paul VI (*to the left*) is Helen Wilson.

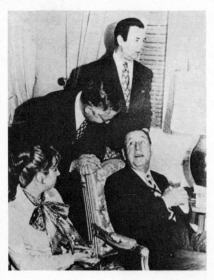 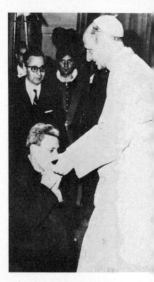

12. The puppetmaster, Licio Gelli, leaning forward in conversation with General Juan Peron, and (*right,* 13) waiting to be received by Pope Paul VI.

14. (*Below*) President Richard Nixon with Pope Paul VI and Monsignor Macchi, one of the members of "the Milan Mafia."

15. John Volpe, then U.S. Ambassador to Italy, congratulates Michele Sindona (*right*) on being named "Man of the Year" by the American Club.

16. President Lyndon Johnson meets Pope Paul VI, with Paul Marcinkus (*second, left*) acting as interpreter.

17. The two leaders of P2 in the company of President Giovanni Leone: second and fourth from the president's left are Licio Gelli and Umberto Ortolani.

18. Gelli with Prime Minister Giulio Andreotti.

Some contenders for the empty throne: (*above, left,* 19) Cardinals Siri and Felici; (*above, right,* 20) Cardinal Pignedoli in conversation with Cardinal Gantin;

(*below, left to right*) Luciani's choice, Cardinal Lorscheider (21); Cardinal Bertoli, a good friend of Gelli's (22); and Cardinal Baggio (23).

24. "We have a pope!"

25. Cardinal Felici places the woollen pallium over the shoulders of the new pope.

Luciani's impact was immediate with young and old alike
(*top*, 26; *below* 27).

28. (*Above, left*) Between the pope and his secretary, Father Diego Lorenzi, sits a member of the curial old guard, Monsignor Martin.

29. (*Above, right*) Luciani exchanges greetings with the Communist mayor of Rome, Giulio Argan, during his only visit outside the Vatican as Pope John Paul I.

30. (*Below*) Members of the Curia attempted to monitor the pope's every movement.

31. The Swiss Guard acknowledges the arrival of Paul Marcinkus at the Vatican.

Like Marcinkus, all of these men stood to gain by the death of Luciani: (*opposite, above,* 32) Cardinal Jean Villot, (*opposite, below,* 33) Robert Calvi, (*above,* 34) Cardinal John Cody, (*above, right,* 35) Umberto Ortolani, and (*right,* 36) Michele Sindona.

37. Licio Gelli stood to lose his grip on a whole empire through Luciani's proposed reforms.

Vatican-owned or -controlled. The wide portfolio might indicate shrewd capitalism, but it was bad public relations to let the man who complained that his phone/water/electricity/gas were not working, know that he had the Church to thank for it. Then, most important of all, if the Vatican maintained its heavy investments in Italy, it was going to face very large tax bills. Pope Paul VI had a problem. The men he turned to for the solution were "the Gorilla" and "the Shark."

If Sigmund Freud's conclusion that a person's entire personality is formed in the first five years of life is correct, then Paul Marcinkus merits particularly close study by the experts. And even those who dispute Freud's conclusion acknowledge that environment is a major influence in the formative years.

Marcinkus was born into a city ruled by the Mafia, where gang-style murders were everyday occurrences, where corruption reached from the mayor to the pre-pubescent youth. It was a city riddled with every conceivable type of crime, in which, between 1919 and 1960, 976 gang-style murders were committed and only two of the murderers convicted. It was a city where in the autumn of 1928 the president of the crime commission appealed to one man to ensure that the forthcoming November elections were conducted in an honest, democratic manner. The man in question was Al Capone. The city: Chicago. Capone boasted, "I own the police." A more accurate statement would have been, "I own the city." Capone responded to the plea for fair elections. He told the police of America's second-largest city what to do, and the police obeyed. The president of the crime commission later observed: "It turned out to be the squarest and the most successful election day in forty years. There was not one complaint, not one election fraud, and no threat of trouble all day."

Paul Marcinkus was born in the suburb of Cicero on January 15, 1922. The following year Al Capone, confronted with the extraordinary spectacle of an honest mayor and an equally honest chief of police in Chicago, moved his headquarters to Cicero. The population of some sixty thousand, mainly first- and second-generation Poles, Bohemians, and Lithuanians, became accustomed to the sight of the Mafia in their midst. Capone set up headquarters at the Hawthorne Inn at 4833 Twenty-second Street. Along with Capone came such gentlemen as Jake "Greasy Thumb" Guzik, Tony "Mops" Volpi, Frank "the Enforcer" Nitti, and Frankie "the Million-aire Newsboy" Pope.

This was the Cicero in which Paul Casimir Marcinkus grew up. His parents were Lithuanian immigrants. His father earned a living cleaning windows, and his mother worked in a bakery. Their grasp of the English language was poor. In the classic manner of many of the poor immigrants who sought a better life in the land of the free, they determined that their children through hon-est endeavor and hard work should have better lives. Marcinkus, the youngest of their five children, succeeded beyond their wildest dreams. His is the story of "Local Boy Makes God's Banker."

Guided by his parish priest, Marcinkus developed a vocation for the priesthood. He was ordained in 1947, the year Al Capone died. Monsignor William Gorman, who officiated at the Catholic burial of America's all-time Public Enemy Number One, explained to reporters: "The Church never condones evil, nor the evil in any man's life. This very brief ceremony is to recognize his [Capone's] penitence and the fact that he died fortified by the sacraments of the Church."

Marcinkus went to Rome and studied at the same Catholic university, Gregorian, at which Albino Luciani had obtained his degree. Marcinkus was equally success-ful and obtained his doctorate in canon law. During his high school days he had used his 6 feet 3 inches of height and his 224 pounds of brawn with considerable success on the football field. When he went for the ball during a game, he usually came up with it. His physical strength was to prove a decided asset in his rise to the top. Clearly some of the lessons learned on the streets of Cicero paid off.

Returning to Chicago, he worked as a parish priest and then became a member of the ecclesiastical court of the diocese. One of the first to be impressed with Marcinkus was the then head of the archdiocese of Chicago, Cardinal Samuel Stritch. After a recommenda-tion from the cardinal, Marcinkus was transferred to the English section of the Vatican secretary of state's office in 1952. Tours of duty attached to the papal nuncios of Bolivia and Canada followed; then, in 1959, he returned to Rome and the secretary of state's department. His fluency in Spanish and Italian ensured his constant employment as an interpreter.

In 1963 the cardinal of New York, Francis Spellman, during one of his frequent trips to Rome, advised Pope Paul that Marcinkus was a priest with an excellent potential. In view of the fact that Spellman headed one of the wealthiest dioceses in the world at that time and was frequently referred to as "Cardinal Moneybags"— a tribute to his financial genius—the pope began quietly to monitor Paul Marcinkus.

In 1964, during a visit to downtown Rome, the pope was in danger of being trampled by the overenthusiastic crowds. Suddenly Marcinkus appeared. Using shoulders, elbows, and hands, he physically cleared a path through the crowds for the frightened Paul. The following day the pope summoned him for personal thanks. From then on he became the unofficial bodyguard to the pope, and his nickname, the Gorilla, was born.

In December 1964, he accompanied Pope Paul to India; the following year he went with him to the United Nations. By now Marcinkus had taken over the duties of security adviser on such trips. Personal bodyguard. Personal security adviser. Personal translator. The boy from Cicero had come far. He was by now a close friend of the pope's personal secretary, Father Pasquale Macchi. Macchi was a key member of the papal entourage, which the Roman Curia referred to as "the Milan Mafia." When the archbishop of Milan, Montini, was elected pope in 1963, he had brought with him a whole train of advisers, financiers, and clerics. Macchi was one of the entourage. All roads may lead to Rome; a number go via Milan. The dependence that the pope placed on men like Macchi was out of all proportion to their official positions. Macchi would berate the pope when he considered him morbid or depressed. He would tell him when to go to bed, who should be promoted, who should be punished with an uncomfortable transfer. After having bid His Holiness good night, Macchi could invariably be found in an excellent restaurant just off the Piazza Gregorio Settimo. His usual companion for dinner was Marcinkus.

Further trips abroad with "the pilgrim pope," to Portugal in May 1967 and to Turkey in July of the same year, cemented Marcinkus's friendship with Pope Paul. Later that year Pope Paul created a department called the Prefecture of the Economic Affairs of the Holy See. A more comprehensible title would have been the General Accounting Office. What the pope sought was a department that would be able to produce an annual summary of the exact state of Vatican wealth and the progress of all assets and liabilities of every administration of the Holy See, with a view to obtaining figures in black and white that would give a final balance or estimate for each year. From its creation the department has struggled under two very serious handicaps. First, on Pope Paul's express instructions the Vatican Bank was specifically excluded from the economic exercise. Second, there was Vatican paranoia.

After the department had been established by a trio of cardinals, the man subsequently appointed to run it was Cardinal Egidio Vagnozzi. In theory he should have been able after a maximum of one year in the job to inform the pope of the exact state of Vatican finances. In practice Vagnozzi found that the inordinate desire for financial secrecy that the various Vatican departments frequently demonstrate to inquiring journalists was extended to him. The Congregation of the Clergy wanted to keep its figures to itself. So did the APSA. So did they all. In 1969 Cardinal Vagnozzi observed to a colleague: "It would take a combination of the KGB, the CIA, and Interpol to obtain just an inkling of how much and where the monies are."

To assist the eighty-four-year-old Cardinal Alberto di Jorio, who having been appointed by Bernardino Nogara, was still functioning as head of the Vatican Bank, Pope Paul consecrated as bishop, Paul Marcinkus. The morning after Marcinkus had prostrated himself at the feet of the pope he took over as the Vatican Bank's secretary. For all practical purposes he was now running the bank. Interpreting for President Johnson when he talked to the pope had been relatively easy but, as

Marcinkus freely admitted, "I have no banking experience." From being an obscure priest in Cicero, Paul Marcinkus had risen higher and farther in terms of real power in the Church than any American before him.

One of the men who had assisted the rise of Paul Marcinkus was Giovanni Benelli. His initial assessment to Pope Paul of the golf-playing, cigar-chewing extrovert from Cicero was that Marcinkus would be a valuable asset to the Vatican Bank. Within two years Benelli concluded that he had made a disastrous misjudgment and that Marcinkus should be removed immediately. He soon discovered, however, that in that brief period Marcinkus had built himself a power base stronger than his own. When the final showdown came in 1977, it was Benelli who left the Vatican.

The extraordinary promotion of Marcinkus was part of a carefully planned change of Vatican policy. Paying large amounts of tax on share profits and having a high profile as an owner of countless Italian companies was now decidedly passé for Vatican Incorporated, particularly when those companies made embarrassing little items such as the contraceptive pill, on which Pope Paul had just invoked the wrath of God. The pope and his advisers had decided to reduce their commitments in the Italian money markets and transfer the bulk of Vatican wealth to the foreign markets, particularly the United States. They also wished to move into the highly lucrative world of Eurodollar blue chips and offshore profits.

Marcinkus was selected as an essential component in this strategy. Another essential component was drawn from the pope's "Milan Mafia." This man was in reality not from Milan, which was merely his adopted city, but he actually was Mafia. "The Shark" had been born in Patti, near Messina, Sicily. His name—Michele Sindona.

Like Albino Luciani, Michele Sindona knew poverty as a child, and like Luciani he was deeply affected and influenced by that environment. While the former grew to manhood determined to relieve the poverty of others, the latter resolved to relieve others of their wealth.

Born on May 8, 1920, and educated by the Jesuits, Sindona demonstrated early in life a marked proclivity for mathematics and economics. Having graduated from

Messina University with an excellent law degree, in 1942 he avoided conscription in Mussolini's armed forces with the aid of a distant relation of his fiancée who worked in the Vatican Secretariat of State, one Monsignor Amleto Tondini.

During the last three years of the Second World War, Sindona put his law degree to one side and earned a very lucrative living doing what he would ultimately become world-famous for: buying and selling. He bought food on the black market in Palermo and smuggled it with the aid of the Mafia to Messina, where it was sold to the starving population.

After June 1943 and the Allied landings, Sindona turned to the American forces for his supplies. As business expanded, so did his Mafia connections. In 1946 he left Sicily for Milan, taking with him his young wife, Rina; invaluable lessons in the law of supply and demand; and a number of even more invaluable letters of introduction from the archbishop of Messina, whose friendship Sindona had carefully cultivated.

In Milan he lived in the suburbs at Affori and worked for a business consultancy and accounting firm. Sindona's speciality, as American capital began to flow into Italy, was to show would-be investors how to dance their way through Italy's complex tax laws. His Mafia associates were suitably impressed with his progress. He was talented, ambitious, and, more important in the eyes of the Mafia, he was also ruthless, totally corruptible, and one of their own. He knew the importance of Mafia traditions such as *omerta*, the rule of silence. He was Sicilian.

The Mafia family Gambino were particularly taken with the young Sindona and his dexterity at placing dollar investments without bothering with tiresome tax regulations. The Gambino family has global interests, but its two main power centers are New York and Palermo. The former is controlled by the Gambinos, the latter by their Sicilian cousins the Inzerillos. On November 2, 1957, there was a "family" reunion in the Grand Hotel des Palmes, Palermo. Also invited to enjoy the wine and food was Michele Sindona.

The Gambino family made Sindona an offer he accepted with enthusiasm. They wanted him to manage the family's reinvestment of the huge profits just beginning to accrue from the sales of heroin. They needed a laundryman. Sindona, with his proven ability at moving amounts of money in and out of Italy without disturbing the tranquillity of the government's taxation departments, was an ideal choice. Added to this ability was the fact that he was by the time of this Mafia summit conference already a director of an increasing number of companies. He frequently said to grateful clients, "No, I'll take payment in some shares in your company." He had also begun to perfect the technique of acquiring troubled companies, dividing them up, selling off pieces, merging other pieces, shuffling everything sideways, and then selling at a large profit. It was dazzling to behold, particularly if you were not paying the conjurer.

Within seventeen months of the Mafia summit conference Sindona bought his first bank, aided by Mafia funding. Sindona had already discovered one of the cardinal rules of theft: the best way to steal from a bank is to buy one.

Sindona created a Liechtenstein holding company, Fasco AG. Shortly afterward, Fasco acquired a bank in Milan, the Banca Privata Finanziaria, usually called BPF. Founded in 1930 by a Fascist ideologist, the BPF was a small, very private, exclusive institution that served as a conduit for the illegal transfer of funds from Italy on behalf of a favored few. It was doubtless this proud heritage that won Sindona's heart. Though disdaining to fight for Mussolini, Michele Sindona was a natural Fascist. It would have appealed to him to acquire such a bank.

In 1959, the same year in which he acquired BPF, Sindona made another very shrewd investment. The archbishop of Milan was trying to raise money for an old people's home. Sindona stepped in and raised the entire amount: $2.4 million. When Cardinal Giovanni Battista Montini opened the Casa della Madonnina, Sindona was by his side. The two men became firm friends, with Montini relying more and more on Sindona's advice on problems other than diocesan investments.

What Cardinal Montini may not have known is that

the $2.4 million were supplied to Sindona very largely from two sources: the Mafia and the CIA. Former CIA agent Victor Marchetti has revealed:

> In the 1950s and the 1960s the CIA gave economic support to many activities promoted by the Catholic Church, from orphanages to the missions. Millions of dollars each year were given to a great number of bishops and monsignors. One of them was Cardinal Giovanni Battista Montini. It is possible that Cardinal Montini did not know where the money was coming from. He may have thought it was coming from friends.

"Friends"—as part of their determination to stop Italy from voting into power a Communist government they not only poured many millions of dollars into the country but also were prepared to smile benignly on men like Michele Sindona. He might well be a criminal of growing significance, but at least he was a right-wing criminal.

The Shark began to swim faster. The Milanese, who as a group are inclined to be dismissive about the Romans, let alone the Sicilians, had initially disregarded this quiet-spoken, polite man from the South. After a while the financial circles of the city, which is the financial capital of Italy, conceded that Sindona was a fairly bright tax consultant. When he began to acquire a company here and there they put it down to beginner's luck. By the time he had become a bank owner and confidant of the man many were predicting would become the next pope, it was too late to stop him. His progress was irresistible. Again through his holding company, Fasco, he acquired the Banca di Messina. This move particularly pleased the Mafia families Gambino and Inzerillo, giving them, as it did, unlimited access to a bank in Sicily, in Sindona's own home region.

Sindona forged close links with Massimo Spada, one of the Vatican's trusted men, administrative secretary of the Vatican Bank and sitting on the board of twenty-four companies, including Banca Cattolica del Veneto on behalf of the Vatican. Luigi Mennini, another top Vatican Bank official, also became a close friend; Father Macchi, Montini's secretary, yet another. Banca Privata began to flower. In March 1965, Sindona sold 22 percent to Hambros Bank of London. Hambros, with its long-standing close links with Vatican finances, considered Sindona's direction of the funds flowing into BPF "brilliant." So did the Gambino and Inzerillo families. So did Continental Illinois, which also bought 22 percent of the bank from Sindona. Continental Illinois was by now the major conduit for all U.S. investment by the Vatican. The bonds Sindona was placing around himself and the various Vatican elements were now multilayered. He became a close friend of Monsignor Sergio Guerri. Guerri had taken over the responsibility of running Nogara's monolithic creation, the Special Administration.

In 1964, Sindona had acquired yet another bank, this time in Switzerland, the Banque de Financement (Finabank) in Geneva. Largely owned by the Vatican, it was, like Sindona's first bank, little more than an illegal conduit for the flight of money from Italy. After Sindona's purchase of the controlling block of shares, the Vatican still retained a 29 percent share of the bank. Hambros of London and Continental Illinois in Chicago also had a stake in Finabank.

For three such august institutions as Vatican Incorporated, Hambros, and Continental Illinois to be involved so closely with Sindona must surely indicate that Sindona ran his banks in an exemplary manner. Or does it?

Carlo Bordoni discovered a different reality. Bordoni first met Sindona in the latter half of November 1964 at Studio Sindona, Via Turati 29, Milan. Previously Bordoni had worked as manager of the Milan branch of Citibank. Shortly before his meeting with Sindona, Bordoni had been fired by Citibank for exceeding his limits on foreign-exchange deals. Sindona could be counted on to look kindly at such a man. He offered Bordoni the opportunity of handling the foreign exchange of BPF. In view of the fact that the bank's entire deposits were less than 15 billion lire (approximately $15 million), Bordoni declined. Compared with the billion-dollar turnover at Citibank, this was small change. Further, at that stage, the BPF

was not even an agent bank and therefore was not even
authorized to deal in foreign currency. It was unknown
internationally, with, in Bordoni's view, "no possibility
of inserting itself in the noble club of international
banks."

Bordoni had a better idea. Why not create an international brokerage company? With hard work and
Bordoni's excellent contacts, such a company could earn
large commissions. It would, again in Bordoni's words,
"increase the luster of the then modest Sindona group
and after a while there would be the near certainty of
consistent foreign-currency credits in favor of BPF and
Finabank."

As Bordoni recalled later in a sworn deposition to
the Milan magistrates when he turned state's evidence
against his former boss, Sindona became visibly excited
and gave his approval for the project without hesitation.
It is easy to understand Sindona's delight. The aptly
named Moneyrex went into operation on February 5,
1965. Initially run in an ethical manner, it made significant profits. By 1967 it was dealing in a volume of $40
billion per year with net profits in excess of $2 million—
profits that in Sindona's hands promptly disappeared
before the tax authorities had time to blink. But Sindona
wanted more than honest profit. He urged Bordoni to
channel the maximum possible amount of foreign currency toward his two banks. Bordoni pointed out that
several very serious difficulties made the idea impractical.
The Shark began to get angry and shouted that Bordoni
should remember his "force of conviction" and his
"power." Bordoni shouted back that these were precisely the difficulties he had been talking about. In case
Sindona was in any doubt, Bordoni elaborated: "Your
'force' is the Mafia and your 'power' is Freemasonry. I
don't intend to risk my good name and the success of
Moneyrex just because a Mafioso asks me to."

Eventually Bordoni's discretion overcame his valor,
and he agreed to look over the banking operations of
BPF and Finabank. What he found tells as much about
the Vatican, Hambros, and Continental Illinois as it
does about Sindona. Twelve years later, in his sworn
affidavit from a prison hospital in Caracas to the Milan
magistrates, he recalled his discoveries:

When I started to go to BPF during the summer of 1966, I was deeply affected by the chaos which reigned in the various sectors. It was a tiny bank which was able to survive only thanks to the margins that emanated, duly masked, of course, from a myriad of "black operations" which BPF effected on behalf of Credito Italiano, Banca Commerciale Italiana, and other important national banks. These foreign-currency black operations, a vast illegal export of capital, took place daily and large figures were involved. The technique was really the most coarse and criminal which can be imagined.

He found numerous overdrawn accounts without any real guarantees and for amounts far in excess of the legal limit of a fifth of capital and reserves. He also found massive theft. The staff was transferring large amounts of money from the accounts of depositors without their knowledge. These sums were then moved to the account held by the Vatican Bank. The Vatican Bank then transferred the amounts, less a 15 percent commission, to Sindona's account at Finabank in Geneva. The account name in Finabank was MANI. MA stood for Marco, NI for Nino: the names of Sindona's sons. The amount of 15 percent commission paid to the Vatican was a variable figure, depending on the current exchange rate operating for black-market money.

If a client of BPF Milan remonstrated that a check he had made out in good faith had bounced or that his account should contain more than was shown, he was initially told to take his business elsewhere. If he persisted, then the manager would appear, and full of Milanese sincerity, would apologize and offer the explanation, "It is all a big accounting error—you know—these modern computers."

Bordoni's discoveries at Finabank in Geneva were as bad. The managing director, one Mario Olivero, knew nothing about banking. The general manager spent all day playing the stock, commodity, and currency markets. If he lost, the loss was transferred to a client's account. If he won, the profit was his. The heads of the various divisions followed the example of the general manager, as did the Vatican Bank.

The IOR, apart from being part owner of the bank, also had a number of accounts there. Bordoni discovered that these accounts "reflected exclusively gigantic speculative operations that resulted in colossal losses." These losses, like everyone else's, were financed by a shell company called Liberfinco (Liberian Financial Company). At the time of Bordoni's inspection, this shell company was showing a loss of $30 million. By the time Swiss bank inspectors appeared on the scene in 1973, the loss this phantom company was showing had grown to $45 million. The Swiss told Sindona, the Vatican, Continental Illinois, and Hambros they had forty-eight hours to close Liberfinco or they would declare Finabank bankrupt. Another Sindona aide, Gian Luigi Clerici di Cavenago, then demonstrated he had as many bright ideas as names. By means of a counter account for $45 million, a device that did not use any actual cash, he closed Liberfinco and opened another company, Aran Investment of Panama, with an immediate deficit of $45 million.

When Sindona had asked Bordoni to look into Finabank, Sindona had observed in one of the great understatements of all time, "Strange things are happening there." When Bordoni told him just how strange these things were, Sindona insulted him and threw him out of his office. Business continued as usual at both banks. Bordoni tried to extricate himself; Sindona used one of his classic techniques: blackmail. Bordoni, too, had transgressed in his foreign speculations. His transgressions would be reported to the president of the Bank of Italy. Bordoni stayed.

Carlo Bordoni should have seen the writing on the wall before he put his hand in the till. During one of their initial confrontations, Sindona had shouted at him, "You will never be a real banker because not only are you unable to lie, you are also a man with principles. You would never know how to use the valid weapon of blackmail!"

Sindona's respect for his colleague might have increased immeasurably if he had known that Bordoni had begun to siphon off money into secret accounts in

Switzerland. Before the end, Bordoni would relieve Sindona of over $45 million. It was hardly on a par with Sindona's own criminal activities, but then, he lacked Sindona's schooling.

Sindona was a master when it came to blackmail. Apart from an innate ability in this direction, he had his Mafia training and he also had available to him the talents of the most skilled blackmailer then practicing the art in Italy, Licio Gelli. When Bordoni had contemptuously thrown Sindona's Mafia and Masonic connections in his face, he was playing with double fire. Sindona was not a member of a Masonic lodge that could claim to trace its origins back to the stonemasons of Solomon. His was no lodge inspired by the Italian patriot Garibaldi. There was no Duke of Kent as the grand master. The lodge was "Propaganda Due," or P2, and its grand master was Licio Gelli.

Gelli was born in Pistoia, in central Italy, on April 21, 1919. His formal education ceased when he was expelled from school in his midteens. A story from Gelli's school days indicates that a peculiar kind of cunning came early to him. There was a youth in one particular class attended by Gelli who was bigger and stronger than the rest. He was admired by many and feared by all. One day Gelli stole the youth's lunch and during the ensuing uproar said to him, "I know who stole your food, but I have no wish to get the boy into trouble. You'll find it hidden under the third bench." The youth became Gelli's friend and protector from that day, and Gelli had learned the art of manipulation. By the age of seventeen he had already acquired a hatred of communism comparable to King Herod's attitude toward the firstborn. As members of the Italian Black Shirt Division, Gelli and his brother fought alongside Franco's army against the Communists in Spain. Of this period in his life Gelli observes: "Only I returned alive."

During the early stages of the Second World War, Gelli fought in Albania. Subsequently he obtained the rank of *Oberleutnant* in the SS in Italy and worked for the Nazis as a "liaison officer." His work involved spying on the partisans and betraying them to his German masters. Some of his early wealth was derived from his presence in the Italian town of Cattaro, where, during the war, the national treasures of Yugoslavia were hidden. A significant proportion of those treasures have never been returned to Yugoslavia but were stolen by Gelli. Gelli's early devotion to a hatred of all things Communist lessened in direct proportion to the defeats suffered by the Axis powers as the war progressed. He began to collaborate with the Italian partisans, who were very largely Communists. Thus he would locate a partisan hideout, dutifully tell the Germans, then advise the partisans to move before the raid.

He continued to play both ends against the middle throughout the remainder of the war and was one of the last of the Fascists to surrender in northern Italy, close to where a young priest, Albino Luciani, had been hiding partisans in Belluno.

Gelli's agreement to continue to spy for the Communists after the war was instrumental in saving his life when he faced an anti-Fascist commission sitting in Florence. The evidence that he had tortured and murdered patriots was deemed, after discreet intervention by the Communists, to be insufficient.

Having been cleared of these charges, he immediately organized a "rat line" for Nazis wishing to flee to South America. His fee was 40 percent of their money. Another organizing member of the "rat line" was a Catholic priest from Croatia, Father Krujoslav Dragonovic. Among the men who escaped was Gestapo chief Klaus Barbie, usually referred to as the Butcher of Lyons. Barbie was not obliged to pay either Father Dragonovic or Gelli. The cost was borne by the U.S. Counterintelligence Corps, which employed Barbie in espionage work until February 1951.

While continuing to assist Vatican officials and U.S. intelligence, Gelli also continued spying for the Communists until 1956. The termination of his espionage work for the Communists coincided with the commencement of his work for the Italian secret service. Part of his fee for spying for his own country was the closure of the file that the secret service had on him. This also occurred in 1956. Two years earlier he had followed the same path on which he had sent so many members of the Third Reich to South America, aligning himself with extreme right-wing elements in Argentina, where he became a close friend and confidant of General Juan Perón. When Perón was excommunicated by the Catholic Church, Gelli experienced one of his few failures in attempting to intercede with the Vatican. Perón's anticlerical campaign, which had led to his excommunication, weighed more heavily with the Church than Gelli's assurances that the general was a greatly misunderstood genius. When Perón left the country after a military coup in 1956, Licio Gelli promptly set about befriending the incoming junta. Slowly and carefully Gelli set about building a power base that began to stretch through much of South America.

It was always the rich and powerful, or the potentially rich and powerful, whom Gelli courted. In terms of political philosophies or ideals, Gelli was a whore. If you could afford him, he would perform for you. While helping the right-wing junta of Argentina, he simultaneously recommenced spying on behalf of the Soviet Union, through his links with Romania. He carried a recommendation from the Communists of Italy that had saved his life after the war and the phone numbers of the CIA contacts to whom he also sold information. In addition he continued to work for SID, the Italian Army intelligence.

While Sindona was moving upward through the financial jungles of postwar Milan, Gelli was ascending the complex power structure of South American politics. A general here, an admiral there, politicians, senior civil servants—while Sindona cultivated contacts in the belief that power lay in money, Gelli, through his new friends, aspired to the source of real power: knowledge. Information, the personal file on this banker, the secret dossier on that politician—his network spread from Argentina into Paraguay, into Brazil, Bolivia, Colombia, Venezuela, and Nicaragua. In Argentina he acquired dual nationality and became that country's economic adviser to Italy in 1972. One of his principal tasks was to negotiate and arrange the purchase of large quantities of arms for Argentina. These included tanks, planes, ships, radar installations, and ultimately the deadly Exocet missile. Before that he held less exalted positions. In Italy they included the post of general manager to

Permaflex, a company making mattresses, and a spell as manager of Remington Rand in Tuscany. Among the directors listed at that time on the board of Remington Rand was Michele Sindona.

Ever anxious to increase his circle of power and influence, Gelli saw the rehabilitated Masonic movement as the perfect vehicle. Ironically it had been his beloved leader Mussolini who had banned the Freemasons. Mussolini had considered them "a state within a state." It was equally ironic that the democratic Italian government Gelli held in such total contempt restored the freedom of Masons, though they retained an aspect of the Fascist law that made it a punishable offense to create a secret organization. Consequently the reformed Masons were obliged to deposit lists of their members with the government.

Gelli joined a conventional Masonic lodge in November 1963. He rapidly rose to third-degree membership, which made him eligible to lead a lodge. The then grand master, Giordano Gamberini, urged Gelli to form a circle of important people, some of whom might eventually become Masons but all of whom could be useful to the growth of legitimate Freemasonry. Gelli leaped at the opportunity. What he in fact conceived was an illegal secret organization. This group was given the name "Raggruppamento Gelli—P2." The "P" stood for "Propaganda," the name of a historic lodge of the nineteenth century. Initially he brought into it retired senior members of the armed forces. Through them he obtained access to active service heads. The web he spun was gradually to cover the entire power structure of Italy. The ideals and aspirations of genuine Freemasonry were rapidly abandoned, though not officially. Gelli's aim was somewhat different: extreme right-wing control of Italy. Such control would function as a secret state within a state, unless the unthinkable happened and the Communists were elected to power. If that happened then there would be a coup. The right wing would take over. Gelli was confident that the Western powers would accept the situation. Indeed, from the very early days of P2, he had the active support and encouragement of the CIA operating in Italy. It may

sound like the scenario of a madman, doomed to the
fate of all such schemes, but it should be noted that
within the membership of P2 in Italy alone (there were,
and still are, powerful branches in other countries) were
the armed forces commander, Giovanni Torrisi; the Secret Service chiefs, Generals Giuseppe Santovito and
Giulio Grassini; the head of Italy's financial police, Orazio
Giannini; cabinet ministers and politicians of every political shade (except, of course, the Communists); thirty
generals; eight admirals; newspaper editors; television
executives; top businessmen; and bankers, including Roberto Calvi and Michele Sindona. Unlike conventional
Freemasonry, the list of members of P2 was secret; only
Gelli knew all the names.

Gelli used a variety of techniques to obtain new
members and increase the power of P2. One of them
was the innocuous method of personal contact and introduction from an already existing member. Others
were less tasteful. Blackmail was the most prevalent.
When a "target" joined P2, he was obliged to demonstrate loyalty by placing at Gelli's disposal documents
that would compromise not only himself but also other
possible targets. Confronted with the evidence of their
own misdeeds, these new targets also joined P2. This
technique was used, for example, on the president of
ENI (Ente Nazionale Idrocarburi, the state oil company),
Giorgio Mazzanti. Shown the evidence of his own corruption concerning proposed huge bribes and payoffs
on a pending Saudi oil deal, Mazzanti caved in and
joined P2, bringing to Gelli even more compromising
information.

Another technique Gelli used to obtain a new member was to ascertain from already corrupted sources the
short list of candidates for important jobs. He would
then telephone these candidates, announcing to each
that he intended to fix it for him. Naturally, one of the
candidates would be hired, and Gelli would then have a
very grateful new member of P2.

On the surface P2 was and still is a fanatical insurance policy against potential Communist governments.
Excluding Italy, there are still branches functioning in
Argentina, Venezuela, Paraguay, Bolivia, France, Portugal, and Nicaragua. Members are even active in Swit-

zerland and the United States. Moreover, P2 interlocks with the Mafia in Italy, Cuba, and the United States. It interlocks with a number of the military regimes of Latin America and with a variety of groups of neo-Fascists. It also interlocks very closely with the CIA. It reaches right into the heart of the Vatican. Apparently the central common interest of all these elements is a hatred and fear of communism.

In fact, P2 is not a world conspiracy with the aim of preventing the spread of Marxism or its many variations. It is an international group with a number of diverse aims. It combines an attitude of mind with a community of self-interest, its main goals being not the destruction of a particular ideology but the acquisition of unlimited power and wealth and the furtherance of self. These goals hide behind the acceptable face of "defenders of the free world." In the world of P2, however, nothing is free. Everything has a price.

Licio Gelli's contacts and associates eventually spread far and wide. They included Stefano delle Chiaie, Pierluigi Pagliai, and Joachim Fiebelkorn, all members of the private army set up in Bolivia by ex-Gestapo chief Klaus Barbie. The group took the name "Fiancés of Death." Political assassinations were performed to order, including that of Bolivian Socialist leader Marcelo Quiroga Cruz. The "Fiancés of Death" were also instrumental in bringing to power in Bolivia in 1980 General García Meza. Klaus Barbie put his Nazi training to good use as "security adviser" to Colonel Luís Gómez, a man with a great deal of Bolivian blood on his hands.

The group that Barbie controlled with the blessing of the Bolivian junta expanded its activities after the coup of 1980. The murders of political opponents, investigating journalists, labor leaders, and students increased. Added to this work was the task of "regulating" the cocaine industry—destroying the small dealers to ensure that the big drug traffickers could flourish with the junta's protection. And from 1965 on, Barbie's activities in Bolivia had included arms deals not only on behalf of Bolivia but also for other right-wing South American regimes and, incredibly, Israel.

It was through such arms deals that Klaus Barbie, an unrepentant member of the SS, and Licio Gelli became business partners: Barbie, the man who between May 1940 and April 1942 was responsible for the liquidation of all known Freemasons in Amsterdam, and Licio Gelli, the grand master of Masonic Lodge P2. The two men had much in common, including the high regard in which they held men such as Stefeno delle Chiaie. The Italian delle Chiaie has been involved in at least two attempted coups in his own country. When a civilian government returned to office in Bolivia in October 1982, delle Chiaie fled to Argentina. There he was given comfort and aid by P2 member José López Rega, the creator of the notorious Triple-A death squads as well as of a large cocaine-smuggling connection between Argentina and the United States.

Clearly, Licio Gelli is as skillful at selling his particular vision of the world as he once was selling mattresses. To have a range of close friends and associates that includes a man such as José López Rega as well as Klaus Barbie and the enigmatic Cardinal Paolo Bertoli is a considerable achievement. Like Gelli, the cardinal is a Tuscan. His career includes forty years in the Vatican diplomatic service. Bertoli was not without support in the conclave that elected Albino Luciani.

Cardinal Bertoli was only one of the many "doors" to Gelli's entry into the Vatican. Gelli dined with Bishop Paul Marcinkus. He had a number of audiences with Pope Paul. Many a cardinal, archbishop, bishop, monsignor, and priest who today would deny all knowledge of Licio Gelli was only too pleased to be seen in his company in the 1960s and the 1970s.

One of Gelli's closest P2 associates was Italian lawyer and businessman Umberto Ortolani. Like "the Puppetmaster," Ortolani learned early in life the value of secret information. During the Second World War he became head of two large operational units of SISMI, the military intelligence service in Italy. His specialty was counterespionage. A Roman Catholic, he appreciated while still a young man that one of the real centers of power was across the Tiber within Vatican City. His penetration of the Vatican and its corridors of influence was total.

Vatican dignitaries were frequent dinner guests at Ortolani's Rome house on Via Archimede. An indication of how far back Ortolani's excellent Vatican contacts reached can be gauged from the fact that he was first introduced to Cardinal Giacomo Lercaro in 1953. Lercaro had immense influence within the Church and was destined to become one of the four "moderators" of the Second Vatican Council. He was widely regarded as one of the liberal enlightened influences that helped to ensure that many of the reforms flowing from the council became realities. Ortolani was generally known as the cardinal's cousin, a misconception he actively encouraged.

In the prelude to the conclave that elected Paul VI, the central issue was whether the work of Pope John XXIII would continue or whether the papacy should revert to the reactionary ethos of Pius XII. The "liberals" needed a safe house to debate strategy. Lercaro, one of the liberal front-runners, asked Ortolani to host the meeting. It was held at Ortolani's villa in Grottaferata, near Rome, a few days before the conclave. A large number of cardinals attended, including Suenens of Brussels, Doepfner of Munich, Koenig of Vienna, Alfrink of Holland, and, of course, "Cousin" Lercaro.

This highly secret meeting was the single most important factor in what subsequently occurred in the conclave. It was agreed that if Lercaro's very considerable support should prove insufficient, then his votes should swing to Giovanni Battista Montini. Thus on the third ballot Montini suddenly found himself twenty additional votes nearer to the papacy he eventually acquired.

Within months the new pope bestowed on Umberto Ortolani the Vatican award of "Gentleman of His Holiness." He subsequently received many more Vatican honors and awards. He even succeeded in affiliating Licio Gelli, a non-Catholic, to the Knights of Malta and the Holy Sepulcher. A close friend of Casaroli, the man usually referred to as the Vatican's Kissinger because of his major involvement in foreign policy, lawyer Ortolani provided his P2 master with an unrivaled entrée into any part of the Vatican. Like his master, Ortolani is a man who (on paper, at least) is a citizen of many countries. Born in Viterbo in Italy, he has since become a Brazilian national. A useful by-product of that arrangement is that no extradition treaty exists between Italy and Brazil.

*   *   *

The list of P2 members grew ever larger. In 1981, when a huge quantity of Gelli's secret documents were seized in Tuscany, they revealed that the secret society had nearly a thousand members in Italy alone. But those thousand are merely the tip of the iceberg. The SISMI, Italy's military intelligence agency, puts Italian membership at nearly two thousand. Gelli himself puts the figure at twenty-four hundred. In either event a number of Europe's intelligence agencies agree that the identity of the majority of P2 members has yet to be revealed and that within their ranks are nearly three hundred of the most powerful men in what it pleases the twentieth century to call the free world.

When the Italian exposure of nearly a thousand members of this illegal secret society occurred in 1981, one P2 member, Senator Fabrizio Cicchitto, stated a fundamental truth: "If you wanted to make it to the top in Italy in the 1970s the best way was Gelli and P2."

The close relationship between P2 and the Vatican was, like all relationships formed by Gelli, self-serving to both parties. Gelli played on the almost paranoid fear of communism within the Vatican. He was particularly given to quoting pre–Second World War statements that had justified fascism, including one by Cardinal Hinsley of Westminster, who had told Catholics in 1935, "If fascism goes under, God's cause goes under with it."

The most bizarre factor in the close and continuous contacts that existed between P2 and the Vatican is that various cardinals, bishops, and priests could smile so benevolently on this bastard child of orthodox Masonry. For hundreds of years the Roman Catholic Church has viewed Freemasons as sons of evil.

The true origins of Freemasonry are to be found in the medieval guilds of stonemasons that, ironically, built many of Europe's great Roman Catholic cathedrals. (Some tenacious but fanciful Masonic historians claim that its beginnings go back to the building of Solomon's Temple!) The legacy of its original association with the building trades can be seen today in the paraphernalia of its rituals, which include the tools of the mason's trade.

As Freemasonry developed, it took on a more speculative quality and absorbed theologies and symbols from
Christianity, from ancient religions, and, to an extent,
from Islam, at least as it was interpreted by the knights
returning from the Crusades.

In the seventeenth century Freemasonry became
associated with "free thinking" and various revolutionary movements and, in many cases, took on a markedly
anti-Catholic character.

The organization has been repeatedly condemned
and has inspired at least six papal bulls that have been
specifically directed against it, the earliest being *In
Eminenti* from Pope Clement XII in 1738.

The Church regards this secret society of self-interest
as an alternative religion controlled by the godless. It
considers that one of Freemasonry's principal aims is
the destruction of the Catholic Church. Consequently,
any Catholic discovered to be a member has been subjected to automatic excommunication from the Church.

There can be little doubt that many historical revolutionary movements used Freemasonry in their quar-
rels with the Church. A classic example is the Italian
patriot Garibaldi, who forged the Masons of the country
into a force that aroused the general populace, over-
threw papal domination, and resulted in a unified Italy.

Today Freemasonry means different things in different countries. All Masons contend that it is a force for
good. Non-Masons view this self-serving, secret society
with varying degrees of hostility and suspicion. But
until very recently, the Roman Catholic Church has
maintained an entirely consistent position—Freemasonry
is a profound evil, and all who belong to it are anathema in the eyes of the Church. If this was the thinking
of the Church on conventional Freemasonry, then it
makes the close ties between P2 and the Vatican even
more extraordinary—one of the smallest but most powerful states on earth embracing a state within a state.
The overwhelming majority of P2 members were and
are practicing Roman Catholics.

Though the Italian lodge of P2 never met in its
entirety (they would have needed to hire La Scala for
that), there were numerous meetings of selected groups.
Discussions were not confined merely to lamenting the

evils of communism. Active steps were planned to combat and contain what Gelli and his friends saw as the ultimate disaster, a Communist government democratically elected to power.

There have been over the past two decades a number of bombing outrages in Italy that remain unsolved. If the Italian authorities ever catch Gelli they will be in a position, if he chooses to talk and tell the truth, to solve some of those mysterious attacks. These include: Milan 1969, the Piazza Fontana bomb attack—16 people killed; Bologna 1974, bomb attack on the Rome–Munich express, the *Italicus*, near Bologna—12 people killed; Bologna 1980, train station bombing—85 people killed, 182 injured. According to the sworn testimony of a disenchanted follower of Gelli, a neo-Fascist called Elio Ciolini, this last outrage was planned at a P2 meeting held in Monte Carlo on April 11, 1980. Licio Gelli was the grand master at that meeting. Again according to the testimony of Ciolini, three of the men responsible for the train station bombing are Stefano delle Chiaie, Pierluigi Pagliai, and Joachim Fiebelkorn.

The purpose of this series of appalling attacks was to direct public outrage toward Italian Communists by making it appear that they were responsible.

In July 1976 Italian magistrate Vittorio Occorsio was in the middle of an investigation into the links between a neo-Fascist movement called National Vanguard and P2. On July 10 the magistrate was murdered by an extended burst of machine-gun fire. The neo-Nazi group New Order subsequently claimed responsibility. New Order, National Vanguard—the names become academic. What mattered was that Vittorio Occorsio, a man who could not be bought, lay dead, and the investigation into P2 had been halted.

By the late 1960s Michele Sindona was a member of P2 and also a close friend of Licio Gelli. Sindona had much in common with Gelli, not least the close attention they were both paid by the CIA and Interpol. The functions of these two organizations do not always run in tandem. Interpol's investigation of Sindona is a perfect illustration of this. In November 1967 Interpol,

Washington, telexed the following message to the Rome
police headquarters:

> Recently we have received unverified informa-
> tion that the following individuals are involved
> in the illicit movement of depressant, stimulant,
> and hallucinogenic drugs between Italy, the
> United States, and possibly other European
> countries.

Leading off the list of four names was Michele
Sindona. The Italian police replied that they had no
evidence to link Sindona with the drug trade. A copy of
the Interpol request and the response were in Sindona's
hands the same week. A similar request by Interpol,
Washington, to the CIA operating out of the embassy in
Rome and the legation in Milan, if answered honestly,
would have produced confirmation that the information Interpol had was entirely correct.

The CIA file on Sindona was by this time extensive.
It details Sindona's link with the New York Gambino
Mafia family, with its 253 members and its 1,147
"associates." It tells how the five New York Mafia
families—Colombo, Bonanno, Gambino, Lucchese, and
Genovese—were interlocked in a range of crimes that
include drug refining, smuggling, and dealing, the drugs
in question being heroin, cocaine, and marijuana. Further criminal activities of these Mafia families that are
annotated in the CIA files include prostitution, gambling,
pornography, usury, protection, racketeering, fraud, and
large-scale thefts from banks and pension funds.

The files are full of details of how the Sicilian Mafia
families Inzerillo and Spatola moved the refined heroin
from Sicily to their colleagues in New York; of their
infiltration of the Italian airline Alitalia; and of how
$50,000 contracts were awarded by the New York fami-
lies to "associates" to collect unaccompanied baggage
from Palermo—baggage containing heroin that had been
refined at one of the five Inzerillo narcotics laboratories
in Sicily. By the late 1960s the profits from heroin sales
to these two Sicilian families were over $500 million
per year.

The files detail the journeys of the nearly thirty

ships per year that until very recently left Lebanese ports with cargoes of both unrefined and refined heroin, destined for a variety of ports in southern Italy.

The most serious question this information raises is why did such incriminating evidence lie dormant and unused throughout the 1960s and the 1970s? The CIA never initiates policy; it merely implements or attempts to implement presidential instructions. Did a succession of presidents take the view that the Mafia's activities were to be tolerated if they helped to ensure that NATO member Italy did not fall to the Communists through the polling booths?

The Mafia families themselves desperately needed men like Michele Sindona. The extraordinary growth of bank deposits and the array of new banks and branches in Sicily, one of the poorest regions in the country, is mute testimony to the size of the Mafia's problem. Enter Michele Sindona. On one occasion Sindona was asked where he obtained the money for his grandiose schemes. He replied, "Ninety-five percent of it is other people's money." It was a response that was 95 percent true.

Michele Sindona was the man chosen by Pope Paul VI to act as a financial adviser to the Vatican; the man chosen, after a long friendship with the pope, to relieve the Church of its high-profile business position in Italy. The plan was to sell Sindona some of the major assets acquired under Nogara. Vatican Incorporated was about to distance itself from the unacceptable face of capitalism. *Theoretically* it was going to embrace the philosophy contained in the message Pope Paul VI gave the world in his 1967 encyclical *Populorum Progressio:*

> God has destined the earth and all it contains for the use of all men and of all peoples, so that the goods of creation must flow in just proportion into the hands of everybody, according to the rule of justice, which is inseparable from charity. All other rights, of whatever kind, including those of private property and of free trade, must be subordinated to it: they must not obstruct, but on the contrary foster its achievement, and it is a grave and urgent social duty to restore them to their original aims.

Pope Paul in the same encyclical quoted Saint Ambrose, "You never give to the poor what is yours; you merely return to them what belongs to them. For what you have appropriated was given for the common use of everybody. The land is given to everybody, and not only to the rich."

When that statement was uttered, the Vatican was the biggest owner of private real estate in the world. *Populorum Progressio* also contained the memorable observation that even when entire populations are suffering massive injustice, revolutionary insurrection is not the answer. "One cannot fight a real evil at the cost of a greater evil."

Confronted with the problem of the evil of a wealthy Roman Catholic Church when he apparently desired a poor Church for the poor, the pope and his advisers decided to liquidate a sizable proportion of the Vatican's Italian assets and reinvest in other countries. Thus they would avoid heavy taxation, and the yield on the investment would be better. When Pope Paul proclaimed the magnificent aspirations of *Populorum Progressio* in 1967, Vatican Incorporated had already for a number of years been a close working partner of Michele Sindona. Through the illegal flight of currency from Sindona's Italian banks via the Vatican Bank to the Swiss bank that they jointly owned, Sindona and the Vatican, if not, perhaps, making the goods of creation flow to the poor, were certainly making them flow out of Italy. By early 1968 another Vatican-controlled bank, the Banca Unione, was in trouble. The Vatican Bank owned approximately 20 percent. It was represented on the board of directors by Massimo Spada and Luigi Mennini. At that point, Sindona came in and bought control. Two years later, with the Vatican still substantial part owners, the bank became, in theory, an astonishing success. Because it was now aiming at the small saver and offering higher interest rates, the bank saw its deposits rise from $35 million to over $150 million. That was the theory.

In practice during the same period, the bank was robbed of over $250 million by Sindona and his associates. Most of this fortune was poured through yet another Sindona bank, the Amincor Bank of Zurich. Much was lost in wild speculation on the silver market. One of the men who was deeply impressed with Sindona at this time was David Kennedy, chairman of Continental Illinois, soon to be appointed treasury secretary in the Nixon cabinet.

By 1969 it was clear to Vatican Incorporated that it had lost the long battle with the Italian government over taxation of dividends. Realizing that to unload its entire stock on the market would result in the possible collapse of the Italian economy, it occurred to the Vatican that such an action would also be self-defeating. A collapse of that magnitude would result in staggering Vatican losses.

The pope, in conjunction with the now Cardinal Sergio Guerri, head of the Special Administration of the APSA, decided to unload from the Italian portfolio a major asset, the Vatican's share in the giant Società Generale Immobiliare. With assets of over half a billion dollars scattered around the world, that was certainly highly visible wealth. They again sent for the Shark.

The shares of Società Generale Immobiliare were selling at about 350 lire. The Vatican held directly and indirectly some 25 percent of the 143 million shares. Would Sindona like to buy? The question was put by Cardinal Guerri. Sindona's response was immediate and positive. He would take the lot—at 700 lire each . . . double the market price. Guerri and Pope Paul were delighted. The agreement between Sindona and Guerri was signed at a secret midnight meeting in the Vatican, in the spring of 1969.

For the Vatican this was a particularly good meeting. It also wished to unload its majority share of Condotte d'Acqua, Rome's water company, and its controlling share of Ceramica Pozzi, a chemical and porcelain company that was losing money. The Shark smiled, agreed on a price, and snapped up both holdings.

Precisely who had conceived this entire transaction? Who was the man who collected a handsome commission from Sindona and high praise from Pope Paul VI and Cardinal Guerri? The answer is powerful evidence of not only how far P2 had penetrated the Vatican but also how the interests of P2, the Mafia, and the Vatican often were identical. Licio Gelli's number two, Umberto Ortolani, was the man responsible for arranging the mammoth transaction. All Sindona had to do now was pay for it.

It is easy to purchase massive companies if you are using other people's money. Sindona's initial payment was made entirely with money illegally converted from the deposits of Banca Privata Finanziaria. In the last week of May 1969 Sindona transferred $5 million to a small Zurich bank, Privat Kredit Bank. The Zurich bank was instructed to send the money back to BPF for the account of Mabusi Beteiligung. Mabusi resided in a post office box in the Liechtenstein capital of Vaduz and was a company controlled by Sindona. From there it was transferred again to another Sindona-controlled company, Mabusi Italiana. From there the $5 million were paid to the Vatican. Further money was raised to pay for the huge acquisitions by bringing in Hambros and the American giant Gulf + Western.

Sindona obviously has a highly developed sense of humor. One of the companies owned by Gulf + Western is Paramount, and one of their most successful films of the period was the adaptation of Mario Puzo's book *The Godfather*. Thus a film taking a highly glamorous and amoral look at the world of the Mafia produced enormous profits, some of which went to sustain Michele Sindona, financial adviser to the Mafia families Gambino and Inzerillo. They in turn were channeling the multi-million-dollar profits acquired largely from heroin dealing into Sindona's banks. The circle was complete. Life was imitating art.

By the early 1970s the massive illegal flight of money from Italy was having a serious effect on the economy. Sindona and Marcinkus might be making significant profits through their efforts at diverting this money out of Italy, but the effect on the lira was devastating. Unemployment rose. The cost of living increased. Uncaring, Sindona and his associates continued to play the markets. By pushing up the price of shares to a much inflated level, the Sindona banks went through millions of dollars of other people's money.

Sindona and his close friend since 1968, Roberto Calvi of Banco Ambrosiano, openly boasted that they controlled the Milan Stock Exchange at this time. It was a control they criminally exploited again and again. Shares went up and down like yo-yos. Games were played with companies for the amusement and financial benefit of Sindona and his associates. The manipulation of a company called Pacchetti gives an example of the everyday activities of these men.

Pacchetti began life as a small, insignificant, leather-tanning company. Sindona acquired it in 1969 and decided to transform it into a conglomerate. He took as his model Gulf + Western, whose widespread interests range from Paramount studios through publishing to airlines and whose chairman, Charles Bluhdorn, served on the board of Immobiliare. Sindona's acquisitions for Pacchetti were more modest. In fact, it became a commercial garbage can containing interests in unprofitable steelworks and commercially unsuccessful household cleaners. There was, however, one jewel in it—he had acquired from Bishop Marcinkus an option to purchase Banca Cattolica del Veneto. Doubtless the fact that the president of Pacchetti, Massimo Spada, was also the managing director of the Vatican Bank helped Marcinkus forget the prior claims of the Veneto clergy and Patriarch Luciani.

Roberto Calvi, who was a party to the Veneto negotiations, agreed to buy on a specified date a Sindona company called Zitropo. The way was now paved for yet another illegal manipulation of the Milan Stock Exchange.

The book value of the Pacchetti shares was about 250 lire per share. Sindona instructed the stock exchange department of the Banca Unione to purchase Pacchetti shares. By using nominees the shares were then illegally parked in Sindona-owned companies. The price of the shares began to surge dramatically, eventually reaching 1,600 lire on the exchange. In March 1972 the day for Calvi's purchase of Zitropo duly arrived. Simultaneously all the Sindona companies dumped their Pacchetti shares into Zitropo. The effect was to inflate artificially the value of Zitropo. Calvi paid an astronomically higher price than the company was worth. Sindona, having funded the entire operation with fictitious guarantees, made a huge illegal profit. An indication of

just how much profit he made on this one operation
emerges from the fact that in 1978 a government-
appointed liquidator, Giorgio Ambrosoli, discovered powerful evidence that Sindona had paid a kickback to
Calvi of $6.5 million, which Calvi shared fifty-fifty with
Bishop Paul Marcinkus.

Why would Calvi pay so much over the market
value for Zitropo? There are three reasons. First, he
used money belonging to others to effect the purchase.
Second, there was a $3.25 million profit for him. Third,
at the conclusion of the Pacchetti/Zitropo deal he acquired an option to buy Banca Cattolica del Veneto, the
option that Sindona had earlier acquired from Marcinkus.
The fact that no one had consulted Albino Luciani, the
patriarch of Venice, or the members of his diocese who
had lodged their shares with the Vatican Bank, was
considered irrelevant by Bishop Marcinkus.

Sindona and Calvi became very adept at this form
of robbery. Never in the history of banking has so much
been paid for so little. In 1972 Calvi pocketed a further
$5 million from Sindona when Bastogi shares changed
hands, and an additional 540 million Swiss francs (about
$140 million) when Sindona sold him 7,200 shares in
Finabank. Each time Sindona paid the kickback to Calvi
through his MANI account in Finabank. These huge
amounts were paid into Calvi's secret Swiss accounts,
which he held jointly with his wife. At the Union de
Banques Suisses and Credit Bank of Zurich the Calvis
held four secret accounts: account number 618934; account number 619112; account number Ralrov/G21; and
account Ehrenkranz. The very minimum that Sindona
himself would have made on each deal was equivalent
to the amount he was kicking back to Calvi.

Roberto Calvi developed an insatiable appetite for
this particular game and on occasions played it as a
solo performer. Hence he obliged one of his own banks,
Centrale, to buy a large block of Toro Assicurazioni
shares in 1976 for 25 billion lire (close to $30 million)
more than they were worth. The 25 billion ended up in
one of the Swiss accounts previously noted. So did a
further 20 billion lire after Calvi played the game again
with over one million shares in Centrale. These huge
sums were not just items on a balance sheet. The money

physically moved from a variety of shareholders' pockets directly into the pockets of the Calvis and Sindona.

The shares in the Banca Cattolica were also subjected to this treatment. Sindona was aware that Calvi was negotiating with Marcinkus to acquire control of the bank—hence the share push. At the end of that exercise everyone except the Veneto diocese was immeasurably richer.

Calvi had been introduced to Marcinkus by Sindona in 1971. Thus Bishop Marcinkus, the man who on his own admission "knew nothing about banking," had two excellent tutors. Meanwhile, Marcinkus had been promoted by Pope Paul and was now president of the Vatican Bank.

The various Vatican departments continued to unload a wide variety of companies on Sindona and then on Calvi. In 1970, for example, they finally sold Sereno, a pharmaceutical company that featured among its more successful lines an oral contraceptive pill.

An additional source of profit for the Sindona/Vatican-owned Finabank was another part of the cause of Italy's faltering economy: double invoicing. As Bordoni observed: "It was less succulent than the kickbacks earned through the illegal exportation of black money but it still reached a high figure."

Exports would be invoiced at costs that were much lower than the real ones. Thus the doctored invoice would be officially paid via the Bank of Italy, which, of course, would pass the information on to the Taxation Department. The exporter would be taxed on this low figure.

The balance was paid by the receiver of the goods abroad direct to Finabank. In many instances Italian exporters actually showed a loss, which was converted into tax credits by the government.

The large number of Sindona-owned exporting companies showed such losses. Sindona would bribe various politicians to allow this situation to continue. He would also argue that by doing so the government was helping to keep down unemployment.

A similar crime was worked on imports. Then the invoice would be for a much higher figure than the actual cost of the goods. When the goods passed through

customs, payment of the artificially high figure would
be made by the company to the foreign supplier. The
foreign supplier in turn would assign the balance to a
numbered account at Finabank or, occasionally, one of
the other Swiss banks.

Pope Paul's poor Church for the poor grew instead
immeasurably richer. The Vatican divestment of Italian
wealth had resulted in men such as Sindona and Calvi
robbing the world to pay St. Peter and an apparently
oblivious Pope Paul.

Finabank was also part of a giant laundry for
Mafia/P2/criminal money. With the Vatican retaining a
5 percent share of Società Generale Immobiliare, it
owned part of that laundry. With the further use by the
Mafia of the Vatican Bank to move money both into and
out of Italy, the Vatican ultimately owned the entire
laundry. Use by Sindona and his staff of the Vatican
Bank's accounts at BPF has already been explained.
That was one of the methods of getting dirty money out
of the country and cleaning it at Finabank, but this was
a two-way operation. Dirty money from the Mafia operating in Mexico, Canada, and the United States was
also being cleaned as it flowed into Italy. The operation
was very simple. To quote again from Carlo Bordoni's
deposition to the Milan magistrates:

> These companies in Canada and Mexico were
> used to bring into the U.S.A. over the Canadian
> and Mexican borders dollars from the Mafia,
> from the Freemasons, and from numerous il-
> legal and criminal operations; the money ar-
> rived in suitcases and was then invested in U.S.
> state bonds. There were then sent to Finabank.
> Clean and easily negotiable.

The American Mafia obviously had no problems
with borders. Their money was converted to bonds directly by Edilcentro of Washington (a subsidiary of
Immobiliare that, among other things, built the Watergate apartment complex); then the bonds also found
their way to Finabank. If the Mafia wished to bring
some of their clean money into Italy they used Vatican
Bank channels.

In the early 1970s Sindona extolled his own virtues to Bordoni. "My operating philosophy is based on my personality, which is unique in the world, on well-told lies, and on the efficient weapon of blackmail."

Part of the blackmail technique was to bribe. A bribe in Sindona's view was "merely an investment. It gave you a hold over the individual bribed." Thus he unofficially "financed" the ruling Italian political party, the Christian Democrats: 2 billion lire to ensure the promotion of party nominee Mario Barone to the position of managing director of Banca di Roma; 11 billion lire to finance the party's campaign against the divorce referendum. He arranged for the Christian Democrats to "earn" billions of dollars. He opened an account for the party at Finabank, account SIDC. Throughout the early 1970s $750,000 was regularly transferred to this account. Sindona, the self-proclaimed hero of anticommunism, was also a man to hedge his bets. He opened another account at Finabank, for the Italian Communist Party. Into this he also poured $750,000 per month of other people's money, account SICO.

He speculated against the lira, the dollar, the German mark, and the Swiss franc. With regard to his massive speculation against the lira (a $650 million operation entirely created by Sindona), he told Prime Minister Andreotti of Italy that he was aware of the existence of heavy speculation against the lira and that in order to learn more about the size of the operation and the source, he had instructed Bordoni through Moneyrex to join in in a "symbolic" manner. Having reaped enormous profits by attacking the lira, he was hailed by Andreotti as "the Savior of the Lira." It was during this period that he received a citation presented by the American ambassador to Rome, John Volpe: "Man of the Year for 1973."

A year earlier, at a reception given to celebrate his purchase of the Rome *Daily American*, Sindona had announced that he intended to expand his interests and move a further $100 million into the United States. Among those listening to his speech was his close friend Bishop Paul Marcinkus. In reality, by purchasing the *Daily American* Sindona was already expanding his U.S. interests. The paper had been backed by the CIA. The

U.S. Congress was pressing the CIA to make precise disclosures of exactly what it did with the millions allocated to it. Like Pope Paul, the CIA thought the moment seemed propitious to jettison a few embarrassing investments. Sindona insists that he bought the paper at the specific request of then Ambassador Graham Martin of the United States; Martin feared that it would "fall into the hands of the leftists." Martin in decidedly undiplomatic language has denied this. He called Sindona "a liar."

Whoever asked him, there is no doubt that the paper had been previously subsidized by the CIA. There is also no doubt that this was not the first favor Sindona did for "the Company." In 1970 the CIA had asked him to buy a $2 million bond issue from the National Bank of Yugoslavia. Sindona obliged. The CIA placed the bonds in Yugoslavia in what they considered "friendly hands." Sindona also moved money on behalf of the CIA into the hands of right-wing groups in Greece and Italy.

Thwarted in his attempt to take over Bastogi, the large Milan-based holding company, by the Italian establishment, who were motivated partly by fear of an increasingly powerful Sindona and partly by prejudice against a Sicilian, the Shark turned his attention to the United States. There this man, who already owned more banks than many men do shirts, bought another bank, the Franklin National Bank in New York.

Franklin National was the twentieth-largest bank in the country. Sindona paid $40 million for one million shares in it, representing a 21.6 percent interest. He paid $40 per share at a time when the share price was $32. More important, this time he had bought a very sick bank. Unbeknownst to Sidona, Franklin National was tottering on the very edge of bankruptcy.

The true megalomania of Sindona can be gauged from the fact that, when he realized what he had acquired, he didn't give a damn. To him dealing with tottering banks was an everyday event as long as huge deposits could be kept whirling around on paper—as long as the telex machine was there to transfer A to B and then to C and then back to A again.

Within twenty-four hours of his purchase and before he had even had an opportunity to try out the

boardroom for size, Franklin National announced its
trading figures for the second quarter of 1972. These
showed a 28 percent drop from the same period for
1971. Sindona the Shark, the savior of the lira, and the
man Marcinkus considered to "be well ahead of his
time as far as banking matters are concerned" took the
news in a typical Sindona fashion. "I have important
connections in all important financial centers. Those
who do business with Michele Sindona will do business
with Franklin National." The previous owners, meanwhile, were laughing all the way to another bank.

As to the "important connections," no one could
deny the truth of that. These connections ranged from
the Mafia families Gambino and Inzerillo in New York
and Sicily to Pope Paul VI, Cardinals Guerri and Caprio,
and Bishop Marcinkus in the Vatican. They included
Andreotti and Fanfani in Rome and President Nixon
and Treasury Secretary David Kennedy in Washington.
They included intimate banking relationships with some
of the most powerful institutions in the world—the Vatican Bank, Hambros of London, Continental Illinois, and
Rothschilds of Paris. Through Gelli's P2 he had forged
close links with the men who ruled in Argentina,
Paraguay, Uruguay, Venezuela, and Nicaragua. Of the
Nicaraguan dictator Somoza, he told a Rome lawyer:

> I prefer to deal with men like Somoza. Doing
> business with a one-man dictatorship is much
> easier than doing business with democratically
> elected governments. They have too many com-
> mittees, too many controls. They also aspire to
> honesty; that's bad for the banking business.

This is a perfect illustration of the P2 philosophy as
expressed by its founder, Licio Gelli: "The doors to all
bank vaults open to the right." While Sindona was
doing business with Somoza, Gelli had not been idle in
Argentina. Sensing the nation's disenchantment with
the ruling junta, he began to plot the return of General
Perón from exile. In 1971 he convinced Lanusse, who
was then president, that the only way Argentina could
regain political stability was through the return of Perón.
The general returned in triumph. One of his first ac-

tions was to kneel in gratitude at the feet of Licio Gelli, a gesture witnessed by, among others, Prime Minister Andreotti of Italy. By September 1973, Perón had again become president of Argentina.

While Gelli was busy making one president, Sindona, having surveyed the political arena in the United States, focused on the man who, to his mind, was closest to the political ideals of Somoza and Perón, Richard Milhous Nixon.

To further his connections, Sindona arranged a meeting with Maurice Stans, Nixon's chief fund raiser in the 1972 presidential campaign. He took with him to the meeting a large suitcase. It contained $1 million in cash. Sindona offered it to Stans for the Nixon campaign fund to "show his faith in America." He insisted, however, that the gift must remain a secret. According to later statements, Stans declined the gift because under a new federal law anonymous election gifts were no longer allowed.

At about the time that Bishop Marcinkus was extolling the banking brilliance of the Shark to the U.S. attorneys investigating the billion-dollar counterfeit securities operation, he was also writing out a check for $307,000. It was the amount Sindona had cost the Vatican as a result of illegal dealings on the American Stock Exchange in the shares of a company called Vetco Industries. In violation of Securities and Exchange Commission regulations, a Los Angeles investment broker had acquired on behalf of Sindona and Marcinkus some 27 percent of Vetco. The Vatican paid the fine, then sold its shares at a profit.

By mid-1973 the hole in Sindona's banks had reached enormous proportions. It is one thing to move large amounts of money on paper from bank to bank, contravening all kinds of laws and committing countless offenses (provided the bribes are placed in the right hands, it is an endless game). It is something else when you siphon off capital in large amounts to third parties. A hole begins to appear. It fills up with the declaration of false and nonexistent profits, but that is only on paper. The hard cash, meanwhile, is continuing to pour out to the third parties. The hole grows bigger and the false and nonexistent profits needed to fill it have to be proportionally greater. Sindona was pouring out other people's money in a variety of directions. The Christian Democrats, the Vatican, P2, right-wing juntas in Latin America—these were just a few of the major beneficiaries. Many of his staff were creating their own personal fortunes, too.

Appropriately, the Shark sat at his desk practicing the Japanese art of origami. The executive suite in his office on Avenue of the Americas in New York was littered with countless examples of his paper-folding expertise—just like so many of his companies, empty little boxes piled one on top of another. The Shark was now involved in a wild, intercontinental juggling act— the merging of this company with that finance house, the transfer of those shares for that company. Merge. Divide. Remerge.

Il Crack Sindona, the Italians called it. When it came, the collapse of the monument to greed and corruption that Sindona had erected was not unimpressive. He had talked grandly of not knowing what his personal wealth was, but he claimed it was in the neighborhood of $500 million. Sindona was a bit confused. The reality was somewhat different. But then a grasp of reality had never been one of the Shark's strong points. His self-delusions had been fed by the illusions of others, as the meteoric pattern of his career shows:

September 1973: At the Waldorf-Astoria in New York the prime minister of Italy, Giulio Andreotti, rises to his feet at a luncheon and, delivering a speech in praise of the Shark, hails him as "the Savior of the Lira."

January 1974: At the Grand Hotel in Rome, U.S. ambassador John Volpe names the Shark "Man of the Year for 1973."

March 1974: Prices on the Milan Stock Exchange are flying high, as is the exchange rate against the dollar at 825 lire. If Sindona were to close down the huge currency operations now he would emerge with a profit of at least 100 billion lire. Anna Bonomi, a rival in the Milan financial world, makes an excellent offer for Sindona's holding in Immobiliare. Sindona refuses to sell.

April 1974: The stock market goes into decline and

the exchange rate falls dramatically. This is the beginning of Il Crack Sindona. The Franklin National Bank in New York announces a net operating income for the first quarter of 2 cents per share compared with the previous year's 68 cents per share for the first quarter. Even this is a falsified figure. The reality is that the bank had suffered a $40 million loss.

May 1974: Franklin has the brakes put on its massive currency speculation. National Westminster of London objects to the volume of Franklin's sterling clearings through its account. In the previous week they have averaged £50 million per day. Franklin now announces that it will not declare a quarterly dividend, the first time since the Depression that a major American bank has been forced to omit a payment to shareholders. The Shark tells the board of Società Generale Immobiliare that the balance sheet is the best in the company's history.

July 1974: The holes are showing both in Italy and in the United States. In an attempt to fill the Italian hole, the Shark merges Banca Unione and Banca Privata Finanziaria. He calls the new creation Banca Privata. Instead of two medium-sized sick banks, he now has one very large sick bank. Instead of two large holes, one gigantic hole is revealed: a 200 billion lire hole.

August 1974: It is time for the establishment to rally round. In Italy, Banca di Roma, having taken a large part of the Sindona empire as collateral, sinks $128 million into Banca Privata in an attempt to fill the hole. In the United States the government, fearing that the collapse of Franklin National could have serious repercussions, gives Franklin National unlimited access to federal funds. Over $2 billion flows from the Federal Reserve into the Franklin.

September 1974: Banca Privata goes into compulsory liquidation. Estimated losses are over $300 million. This includes $27 million of Vatican money plus their share of the bank.

October 3: Licio Gelli repays a little of the huge investment that Sindona has made in P2. By courtesy of P2 members in the judiciary and the police force, Gelli is advised that Sindona will be arrested the following day. Gelli tips off Sindona.

October 4: An arrest warrant for Michele Sindona is issued. Sindona has fled the country. Ever a man of vision, he has previously changed his nationality. He is now a citizen of Switzerland. The boy from Sicily flies to his homeland in Geneva.

October 8: The Franklin National collapses. Losses to the Federal Deposit Insurance Corporation—$2 billion. It is the biggest bank failure in American history.

October 1974–January 1975: Europe resounds to the noise of crashing banks that are Sindona-controlled or -linked—Bankhaus Wolff A. G. of Hamburg, Bankhaus I. K. Herstatt of Cologne, Amincor Bank of Zurich, and Finabank of Geneva. With regard to Finabank, Swiss banking sources estimate Vatican losses at $240 million. The Finabank's losses on foreign-exchange dealings alone are a minimum of $82 million.

The Italian authorities, or rather those of them not controlled by P2, were by now attempting to take active measures. Sindona, having eventually surfaced in the United States, showed a marked disinclination to return to Italy. October 1974 was the beginning of a long battle to extradite him. This battle was destined to have a direct influence on the ultimate fate of the then patriarch of Venice who at that time was preoccupied trying to raise money to help a group of mentally handicapped people. It would be difficult to find a greater contrast between two men than the values that separated Albino Luciani from the Shark.

Sindona's presence may have been urgently required in Italy, but inside the Vatican he had become *persona non grata*. As the secretary of state, Cardinal Villot, brought Pope Paul news of each new aspect of "the Crack," His Holiness grew more distressed. It has been said that Pope Paul aspired to be the first poor pope in modern times. This is a fallacy. The divestment, under Pope Paul, of the majority of the Vatican's Italian holdings had but one aim: more profit. Prompted by the desire to avoid Italian taxes and obtain a lower profile in Italy, Vatican Incorporated had been seduced by Sindona and his clan with the prospect of greater wealth through investment in the United States, Switzerland, Germany, and other countries.

The story that the Vatican would have one believe today is that Pope Paul alone was responsible for the Vatican's deep, nearly decade-long involvement with Michele Sindona. This is yet another Vatican fallacy. Significantly, it is one that never surfaced during Pope Paul's lifetime. Persuaded by his secretary, Monsignor Pasquale Macchi; by his advisers Cardinal Guerri and Benedetto Argentieri from the Special Administration; by his secretary of state, Cardinal Villot; and by Umberto Ortolani that Sindona was the answer to the Vatican's prayers, the pope undoubtedly opened the bronze doors to the Shark and beckoned. Once inside, Sindona did not want for company. Indeed, the pope might have been alerted if his advisers had exercised elementary caution. Close study of the events already described leads unavoidably to the conclusion that many within the Vatican walls were ready, willing, and eager to join in the criminal activities of Michele Sindona.

Bishop Marcinkus was obliged to suffer the indignity of several sessions of intensive questioning by the Italian authorities about his personal and business relationship with Sindona. Marcinkus, who sat at the behest of Sindona and Roberto Calvi as a bank director in the tax haven of Nassau; Marcinkus, the close friend of Sindona.

In April 1973, when the U.S. investigators had asked Marcinkus about his dealings with Sindona, Marcinkus had said:

> Michele and I are very good friends. We've known each other for several years. My financial dealings with him, however, have only been very limited. He is, you know, one of the wealthiest industrialists in Italy. He is well ahead of his time as far as financial matters are concerned.

Less than two years later, in February 1975, Bishop Marcinkus was asked a similar question by the Italian magazine *L'Espresso*. This time his reply was, "The truth is that I don't even know Sindona. How can I have lost money because of him? The Vatican has not lost a cent, the rest is fantasy."

For a bank president, Bishop Marcinkus constantly displayed an alarmingly poor memory—with the U.S. investigators as well as with the Italian reporters. Far from being limited, his financial dealings with Sindona were large and continuous from the late 1960s until shortly before Il Crack Sindona in 1975. In 1971 Sindona had played a crucial role in Marcinkus's sale of Banca Cattolica to Roberto Calvi for $46.5 million and had made an illegal $6.5 million kickback to Calvi and Marcinkus. This, like the later losses inflicted on the Vatican by Sindona, was far from "fantasy."

Dr. Luigi Mennini, secretary inspector of the Vatican Bank, was arrested as a result of the Sindona crash, and his passport was withdrawn. Mennini, who worked directly under Marcinkus, denied everything and knew nothing. Possibly one of his sons, Alessandro, who held a high executive position in the foreign-affairs section of Banco Ambrosiano, the nerve center of much of the currency speculation, would have been equally mystified if questioned about the criminal activities of Sindona and Calvi.

Before Il Crack Sindona, Mennini speculated, on behalf of the Vatican Bank, in foreign currencies alongside Sindona's colleague Carlo Bordoni. Over the years Bordoni got to know him well:

> Despite the fact that he acted like a prelate he was a seasoned gambler. He tormented me in every sense of the word because he wanted to earn money in ever-increasing quantities. He speculated in Finabank, in shares, in commodities. I recall one day he gave me a short letter from Paul VI which gave me his benediction for my work as consultant to the Holy See. Mennini was virtually a slave to Sindona's blackmail. Sindona had often threatened to make public information about Mennini's illegal operations carried out with Finabank.

Massimo Spada, administrative secretary to the Vatican Bank, again directly under Bishop Marcinkus, although officially retired from the bank in 1964, had continued to represent a wide cross section of Vatican

interests. Like Mennini, Spada opened his front door
one morning to find the Italian finance police there
armed with search warrants. His personal bank accounts
were frozen by court order, his passport was withdrawn.
Three separate legal cases were started against him, all
alleging a wide range of banking law violations and
fraudulent bankruptcy.

Spada, who according to Carlo Bordoni's sworn
statement was another slave to Sindona's blackmail,
and who was fully acquainted with all of Sindona's
illegal operations, expressed the classic Vatican Bank
position when questioned by *L'Espresso* in February
1975: "Who would have thought that Sindona was a
madman?" Spada asked. This man, who was a director
of three of Sindona's banks, work for which he was very
highly paid, continued:

> In forty-five years I have never found myself in
> a situation of this kind. I have lived through
> the most difficult periods, but I have never seen
> anything like it. Raving lunatics started to buy
> billions of dollars with European currencies.
> All the losses come from that. Who could have
> known that every day Mr. Bordoni was selling
> 50 or 100 million dollars against Swiss francs
> or Dutch guilders?

At the time Spada made these observations he was
considered, at the age of seventy, to be so brilliant as a
businessman that he was still on the board of directors
of thirty-five companies.

And so it went on. No one in Vatican Incorporated
knew Sindona or anything about his criminal activities.
The trusting men of God had been "conned" by the devil.
Is it possible that they were indeed all honorable
men who were betrayed by Michele Sindona? Is it possible that Vatican representatives such as Mennini and
Spada could sit on the boards of Sindona's banks and
remain ignorant of the crimes Sindona and Bordoni
were perpetrating? Massimo Spada gave the game away
during his interview with *L'Espresso*. He was asked if it
was indeed only Sindona and Bordoni who were guilty
of currency speculation.

You must be joking. Using hundreds and hundreds of billions in currency operations has become a habit for the banks. When an average-sized dealer on the Milan market moves an average value of 25–30 billion lire and a small Milanese bank moves 10–20 billion a day in currency, one has to conclude that if the entire Italian banking system did not go up in smoke we have to thank Providence, God, Saint Ambrose, Saint George, and above all, Saint Januarius. I would say in this respect that they should have sent legal letters to all Italian banks warning them they were being investigated.

So, according to Spada, a man whose name was synonymous with Vatican Incorporated, a man who was born into the business dynasty of the Spada family—his great-grandfather banker to Prince Torlonia; his grandfather a director of the Bank of Italy; his father, Luigi, an exchange agent; he himself having worked for Vatican Incorporated since 1929—according to a man with that illustrious record, the entire Italian banking industry was up to its neck in criminal activity, yet he claimed to be ignorant of what was going on in the very banks where he sat as a director.

After the crash, estimates of the size of the Vatican losses were many and varied. They ranged from the Swiss banking estimate previously referred to of $240 million to Vatican Incorporated's own estimate: "We have not lost a cent." The true figure is probably somewhere around $50 million. When the multinational across the Tiber talked of not losing a cent it was no doubt figuring in the previous massive profits made through its association with the Shark, but a reduction of overall profit from $300 million to $250 million is a loss in any language, including Latin.

Added to that $50 million, Sindona-created loss was a further $35 million loss sustained by Vatican Incorporated in the curious affair of Banca di Roma per la Svizzera in Lugano (Svirobank). The Vatican Bank held the majority 51 percent share in the Swiss bank. The bank president was Prince Giulio Pacelli; the executive director, Luigi Mennini. Like other Vatican-linked banks,

Svirobank speculated with the funds it held on behalf of
the illegal exporters of lire and members of the Italian
Mafia. Gold and foreign-exchange speculation was an
everyday occurrence. In 1974 a hole began to appear.
The person blamed was Deputy Manager Mario Tronconi,
which is odd, since the deals were transacted by Franco
Ambrosio, another Svirobank employee.

In the autumn of 1974 Mario Tronconi was "suicided"—his body was found on the Lugano–Chiasso rail-
road line. In his pocket was a farewell letter to his wife.
Before his death, doubtless for the sake of tranquillity,
Pacelli, Mennini, and the other Svirobank directors had
obliged Tronconi to sign a confession in which he assumed full responsibility for the missing $35 million.
No one denounced Ambrosio; indeed, he was given the
task of recovering the loss. The truth came to light only
two years later, when Mario Barone, one of Banca di
Roma's joint chairmen of the board (Banca di Roma
held a 40 percent share of Svirobank), was arrested and
questioned in conjunction with Il Crack Sindona.

Clearly Italian banking has many attendant risks.
Mario Tronconi was by no means the only banker to be
"suicided." In the following decade the list would grow
alarmingly.

While Michele Sindona fought his extradition from
the United States and began to plot revenge against
real and imagined enemies, Vatican Incorporated was
already involved again in speculating, this time through
Roberto Calvi. Calvi was known in Milan business circles as "Il Cavaliere" (the Knight), a curious nickname
for the man who was paymaster to P2. He had acquired
the nickname in 1974 when Giovanni Leone, who was
then president of Italy, made him a Cavaliere del Lavoro
(Knight of Labor) for his services to the economy. Calvi
was to be Sindona's replacement as laundryman for the
Mafia, and the man who carried out the biggest theft in
the history of banking.

Roberto Calvi was born in Milan on April 13, 1920,
but his family roots are in the Valtellina, an Alpine
valley near the Swiss border and near the home of
Albino Luciani. After studying at the prestigious Bocconi
University, Calvi fought for Mussolini on the Russian
front in the Second World War. After the war, Calvi

followed his father into banking. In 1947 Calvi went to work for Banco Ambrosiano in Milan. Named after Saint Ambrose, the bank exuded religiosity. Like Banca Cattolica del Veneto, it was known as "the Priests' Bank"; among its customers was Cardinal Giovanni Montini. Baptismal certificates establishing that the holder was Catholic were required to open a bank account. Prayers thanking God for the annual figures were offered at the end of board meetings. In the early 1960s there was a greater air of reverence inside the bank than in a number of the nearby churches.

Roberto Calvi had plans for himself and for this sleepy diocesan bank that included among its customers the cardinal archbishop of Milan, Giovanni Montini. By the time Montini became Pope Paul VI in 1963, Calvi had been promoted to central manager. When Pope Paul decided to call Sindona into the Vatican to relieve the Church of its embarrassingly large Italian holdings, Sindona counted Calvi among his friends. In fact, the Shark and the Knight were already plotting to gain control of Banco Ambrosiano and transform it into a very special kind of international banking institution. In 1971, Calvi became managing director of Banco Ambrosiano. At fifty-one years of age he had risen far above his father's humble clerical position. The average man might have been content to rest on his laurels for a while and enjoy leading the prayers at the board meeting.

The only thing that was average about Roberto Calvi was his height. His ability to dream up crooked schemes for laundering Mafia money, exporting lire illegally, evading taxes, concealing the criminal acts of buying shares in his own bank, rigging the Milan Stock Exchange, for bribery, for corruption, for perverting the course of justice, arranging a wrongful arrest here, a murder there—his ability to do all of this and more puts the Knight in a very special criminal class. Calvi was prone to advise all and sundry that if they really wanted to understand the ways of the world, they should read Mario Puzo's novel *The Godfather*. He himself carried a copy everywhere, like a priest with his Bible.

Calvi was introduced to Bishop Marcinkus by Sindona in 1971 and instantly joined the very select Vatican clan of *uomini di fiducia* (men of trust), that

small elite group of laymen who worked with and for
Vatican Incorporated; men such as Sindona, Spada,
Mennini, and Bordoni; men chosen with the greatest
possible care.

In 1963 Calvi had formed a company in Luxembourg called Compendium (the name was later changed
to Banco Ambrosiano Holdings). This shell company
was crucial to Calvi's schemes. Millions of borrowed
Eurodollars were destined to flow through the Luxembourg holding company. Over 250 banks worldwide
would be conned into lending it money. And the amount
of money involved would total over $450 million.

Calvi's empire had grown rapidly. By the early 1960s
Banco Ambrosiano had acquired Banca del Gottardo in
Lugano, Switzerland. (Banca del Gottardo eventually
became the main conduit for laundering Mafia money,
after the collapse of Sindona's Amincor in Zurich.) Other
foreign assets followed. One of these was Banco Ambrosiano Overseas, Nassau. This branch was founded in
1971 and from the beginning had on its board of directors Bishop Paul Marcinkus. It was originally called
Cisalpine Overseas Bank to deflect any inquiries from
Italy's finance police.

The profits being channeled into the coffers of the
Vatican Bank grew proportionately with Calvi's empire.
To understand many of the very complicated and often
deliberately overcomplicated financial convolutions in
which Calvi indulged throughout the 1970s, one fact
has to be grasped: essentially, Banco Ambrosiano of
Milan and the Vatican Bank were interlocked. Many of
the crucial operations were joint operations. The reason
that Calvi was able to break the law again and again
was because of the ready assistance given to him by the
Vatican Bank.

Thus when on November 19, 1976, Calvi acquired
53.3 percent of Banco Mercantile of Florence, the purchase appeared to be on behalf of the Vatican Bank. On
December 17 the shares were in the hands of Milan
stockbroker Giammei and Company, which frequently
acted on behalf of the Vatican. By dexterous paperwork
the shares were "parked" on the same day at the Vatican Bank. The fact that the Vatican did not have adequate funds in a particular account to pay for the shares

was overcome by crediting on December 17 to the Vatican Bank, in a newly opened account (number 42801), 8 billion lire (about $9.6 million). The following summer, on June 29, 1977, Giammei bought the shares back from the Vatican Bank through Credito Commerciale of Milan. Calvi then bought them from Giammei. As the shares followed this snakelike path, they underwent—at least on paper—a dramatic price increase. The original purchase had been made at 14,000 lire per share. By the time the shares found their way back to Giammei again they were valued at 26,000 lire per share. On June 30 the shares were sold by Credito Commerciale to Immobiliare XX Settembre, which was controlled by Calvi. On paper the Vatican Bank had made a profit of 7,724,378,100 lire ($87,274) as the price of the shares was hiked. The reality was that Calvi paid the Vatican Bank 800 million lire (or about $900,000) for the privilege of using its name and facilities. The Vatican Bank, situated in the independent state of Vatican City, was beyond the reach of the Italian bank inspectors. By selling himself shares he already owned at twice the original purchase price, Calvi vastly increased the worth, on paper, of Banco Mercantile and stole 7,724,378,100 lire—less, of course, the kickback he gave to the Vatican Bank. Subsequently Calvi sold his shares to Milan business rival Anna Bonomi for 33 billion lire ($37 million).

With the close and continuous cooperation of the Vatican Bank, Calvi was able to dance an illegal and criminal path through the Italian laws again and again. Operations such as the one described here could not have taken place without the full knowledge and approval of Marcinkus.

The same is true of the scheme concerning Banca Cattolica del Veneto. All the available evidence points to a criminal conspiracy involving Sindona, Calvi, and Marcinkus.

Marcinkus wanted to keep the operation secret, even from Pope Paul VI. Some years afterward Calvi recalled the deal to friend and business associate Flavio Carboni:*

---

*Carboni secretly tape-recorded this and many other conversations with Calvi between October 1981 and May 1982.

Marcinkus, who is a rough type, born in a suburb of Chicago of poor parents, wanted to carry
out the operation without even telling the boss.
That is the pope. I had three meetings with
Marcinkus regarding Banca Cattolica del Veneto.
He wanted to sell it to me. I asked him: "Are
you sure? Is it available to you? Is the boss in
agreement with it?" It was I who insisted and
told him, "Go to the boss, tell him." Marcinkus
took my advice. Later Marcinkus told me, yes,
he had spoken with Paul VI and had his assent.
Sometime later Marcinkus got me an audience
with Paul VI, who thanked me because in the
meantime I had sorted out some problems of
the Ambrosiano Library. In reality I understood
he was thanking me for buying Banca Cattolica
del Veneto.

If anyone seeks confirmation that by the early 1970s
the pope had acquired the new title of "chairman of the
board," they can find it in Calvi's description. There the
holy father and vicar of Christ is reduced to "the boss."
Equally illuminating are Calvi's anxious questions to
Marcinkus. "Are you sure? Is it [the bank] available to
you?" The Milanese banker was obviously fully aware
of the close ties that bound the bank to the Venetian
clergy. The fact that Marcinkus wished to keep the pope
ignorant of the transaction is a further indication of just
how dubious the sale to Calvi was. Cardinal Benelli's
advice to Albino Luciani that the pope would not intercede on behalf of him, his bishops, and his priests is
demonstrated as being well-founded. There was not much
point in complaining about the sale to the man who
had given it his personal blessing. What Pope Paul VI,
with the aid of Calvi, Marcinkus, and Sindona had
created was a time bomb that would continue to tick
until September 1978.

The transaction took place in July 1971. Fearful of a
hostile reaction from Venice, Marcinkus and Calvi suppressed all news. On March 30, 1972, Calvi's group
finally announced that it had acquired 37.4 percent of
Banca Cattolica. The documentary evidence I have tells
another story.

On July 27, 1971, Calvi wrote to Marcinkus:

> With this letter we wish to inform you of our
> firm offer to buy up to 50 percent of the shares
> of the Banca Cattolica del Veneto, Vicenza, at a
> price of 1,600 lire each share with normal usu-
> fruct to take place through the following steps:
>   1. For 45 percent of the shares making up
> the aforesaid company, that is, 16,254,000 shares,
> with the application depending on your accep-
> tance of our firm offer and against a payment
> by us of $42 million.
>   2. For the remaining shares, that is, up to
> a further 5 percent of the capital, 1,806,000
> shares, to take effect from the date of the
> "declaration of intent" concerning the afore-
> mentioned Banca Cattolica del Veneto, to take
> place before October 31, 1971, and against a
> payment of $4,500,000 on October 29, 1971.

The Vatican Bank received $46.5 million, at the 1971
value. A comparable figure today would be $1.15 billion.
    Calvi, who was aware that, at his insistence, this offer
would be shown to the pope, continued in his letter:

> We inform you that we formally assume the
> responsibility of maintaining unchanged from
> the point of view of the high social, moral, and
> Catholic religious purposes the conduct of Banca
> Cattolica del Veneto's activities.

The Vatican copy of this letter is officially stamped
and signed by Marcinkus.
    The Banca Cattolica's "high social, moral, and Cath-
olic religious purposes" were so rapidly dispensed with
by Calvi that the entire clergy of the region had been up
in arms and besieging Luciani's residence in Venice by
mid-1972. Luciani had hurried to Rome, but 1972 was
clearly not the time for remedial action, with Paul VI
having given the deal his blessing. The time for action
was to be September 1978.
    During the intervening years a curious situation
obtained: the shares never left the Vatican Bank. On

October 29, 1971, the date on which the final 5 percent was sold to Calvi, the shares—which were still held in their entirety by the Vatican Bank—were reassigned to Zitropo, a company owned at that time by Sindona. Later Zitropo became first a Calvi-owned asset and subsequently a Vatican Bank asset. And the shares of Banca Cattolica continued to remain in the Vatican safe. It is little wonder that as late as March 1982 Paul Marcinkus, now archbishop, would talk of "our investments in Banca Cattolica, which are going very well."

When the Milan Stock Exchange began to fall in 1974, among those to be hurt was Banco Ambrosiano. Calvi was especially vulnerable. The main ingredient in international banking is confidence. It was known that he was a close associate of Sindona. When Il Crack occurred, the banking world began to take a more cautious view of the Knight. Credit limits to Ambrosiano were cut back. Loans on the international market became difficult to obtain and, most ominous of all, the demand by small investors for the bank's shares began to diminish, with a consequent drop in the price.

Magically, at what was fast becoming the eleventh hour for Ambrosiano, a company called Suprafin, with a registered office in Milan, entered the market. This finance house began to display supreme confidence in Signor Calvi. It bought shares in his bank daily and before there was time for the name Suprafin to be written on the list of shareholders, the shares were resold to companies in Liechtenstein and Panama. Confidence in Calvi began to return, and Suprafin kept on buying. In 1975, 1976, 1977, 1978, throughout all of these years, Suprafin continued to display massive faith in the future of Calvi's bank—$50 million worth of faith.

Suprafin clearly knew something that no one else did. Between 1974 and 1978 Ambrosiano shares continued to fall, yet Suprafin, acquired over 15 percent of the bank. "Officially," Suprafin was owned by two Liechtenstein companies, Teclefin and Imparfin, which were owned by the Vatican Bank. In practice, Suprafin was owned by Calvi. Consequently, with the complete knowledge of the Vatican Bank, he was supporting the market value of Ambrosiano shares by massive purchases—a totally illegal activity. The money to finance the fraud came from international loans made to a Luxembourg subsidiary and from the parent bank in Milan.

The Vatican Bank received huge annual payments for providing the facilities for the Knight to operate a gigantic international fraud. This money was paid in a variety of ways. All Vatican deposits with Ambrosiano banks received interest payments at least 1 percent higher than for other depositors. Another method was for Ambrosiano to "buy" shares from the Vatican. On paper the Vatican Bank would sell a block of shares to a Panamanian company at a price approaching 50 percent more than the shares were actually worth. The shares would never leave the Vatican portfolio, and the bank that Marcinkus controlled would be millions of dollars better off. The Panamanian company, usually with a capital of only a few thousand dollars, would borrow the millions from Banco Ambrosiano Overseas in Nassau, where Marcinkus was a director. The Nassau branch would have been loaned the money initially by the Luxembourg company, which in turn had borrowed the money from international banks.

Calvi was obviously hoping against hope that the price of Banco Ambrosiano shares would eventually pick up so he could unload them. By 1978 he was walking on a tightrope. As if this entire operation was not enough to keep the banker awake at nights, he was also contending with the problems of laundering Mafia money. And then there were the constant demands being made by P2 for funds. This involved further embezzlement. Calvi was already suffering from the aftereffects of a black-mail campaign by Sindona.

While the Knight was busy embezzling millions of dollars to maintain fraudulently the share price of Ambrosiano, the Shark had been far from inactive. Sindona is like a character from a Pirandello play where all expectations may prove to be illusions. The man exudes theater. A fiction writer, however, would balk at such a creation. Only real life could create Michele Sindona.

Licio Gelli continued to repay Sindona's commitment to P2. When the Milan public prosecutor's office applied for Sindona's extradition in January 1975, the American authorities made a routine request for more information, including a photograph, and asked that

the extradition papers be translated into English. The
Milan office completed a new, two-hundred-page-long
request and sent it to the Ministry of Justice in Rome,
to be translated and sent to Washington. The ministry,
however, eventually returned the request to Milan, claiming that it could not manage the translation. This was
despite the fact that it has one of the largest translation
departments in Italy. And the American embassy in
Rome declared that it had no knowledge of the extradition request. Licio Gelli had friends in many places.

Sindona, meanwhile, was living in his luxurious
Hotel Pierre apartment in New York. He retained the
Richard Nixon/John Mitchell law firm to help him fight
extradition. Questioned by reporters, Sindona claimed
the charges were part of a conspiracy:

> The governor of the Bank of Italy and other
> members of the Italian establishment are plot-
> ting against me. I have never done a single
> foreign-exchange contract in my life. My ene-
> mies in Italy have swindled me and I hope that
> one day justice will be done.

In September 1975, when photographs of a dinner-
jacketed Sindona shaking hands with New York's Mayor
Abraham Beame appeared in Italian newspapers, there
was a cry of outrage from at least some quarters. *Corriere
della Sera* observed:

> Sindona continues to release statements and
> interviews and continues, in his American exile-
> refuge, to frequent the jet set. The laws and
> mechanisms of extradition are not equal for all.
> Someone who steals apples can languish in
> prison for months, perhaps years. An emigrant
> working abroad who does not reply to his draft
> board is forced to come back and face the rig-
> ors of the military tribunal. For them, the twists
> and turns of the bureaucracy do not exist.

In Italy, small savers appointed lawyers in an attempt to salvage some of their money from the Sindona
wreckage, and the Vatican declared a "serious budget

deficit." In the United States, the Shark hired a public-relations man and went on the university lecture circuit.

While senior executives of the Franklin National were being arrested and charged with conspiring to misapply millions of dollars by speculating on the foreign exchange, Sindona was telling students at the Wharton School of Finance and Commerce:

> The aim, perhaps an ambitious one, of this brief talk is to contribute to restoring the faith of the United States in its economic, financial, and monetary sectors, and to remind it that the free world needs America.

While he was being sentenced in his absence by a Milan court to 3½ years' imprisonment, having been found guilty on 23 counts of misappropriating almost 14.5 billion lire (about $22.2 million), he was busy moralizing to students at Columbia University:

> When payments are made with the intent of evading the law in order to obtain unfair benefits, a public reaction is clearly called for. Both the corrupted and the corrupter should be punished.

While he was planning the blackmail of his fellow P2 member and close friend Roberto Calvi, Sindona painted a visionary image to students who yearned to emulate him:

> I hope in the not too distant future, when we will have been in contact with other planets and new worlds in our myriad galaxies, the students of this university will be able to suggest to the companies they represent that they expand to the cosmos creating "cosmo-corporations" which will bring the creative spirit of the private entrepreneur throughout the universe.

At about this same time, Sindona arranged a number of meetings between the American and Sicilian Mafias and attempted to persuade them and Licio Gelli that they should organize the secession of Sicily from Italy. He had earlier, in 1972, been a conspirator in the so-called White Coup—a plot to take over Italy. The Mafia was skeptical, and Gelli was contemptuous. He called the idea "mad" and told Sindona that secession of Sicily could take place only with the support of the military and political members of P2, and that the members were biding their time. He advised Sindona: "Put the plan in the 'pending' file."

In September 1976 the Italian authorities finally succeeded in having Sindona arrested in New York. It was the first significant breakthrough they had achieved in the long fight for his extradition. Sindona expressed surprise that "the United States chose now, some two years after these false charges were lodged against me in Italy, to begin these extradition proceedings. I want to emphasize that the charges were made in Italy on the basis of little or no investigation and, on their face, are false." He was released on $3 million bail, but by 1977 the net was finally beginning to close. A federal grand jury began investigating alleged violations by Sindona involving the collapse of the Franklin National.

Sindona used all the weapons at his disposal. Important people went to court to speak for the Shark as he fought extradition. Carmelo Spagnuolo, president of a division of the Supreme Court in Rome, swore in an affidavit that the charges against Sindona were a Communist plot. He also swore that Sindona was a great protector of the working class, that the people investigating Sindona in Italy were at best incompetent and were controlled by those with political motivations. For good measure he advised the grand jury that many members of the Italian judiciary were left-wing extremists and that if Sindona were returned to Italy he would be murdered. Carmelo Spagnuolo was a member of P2.

Licio Gelli also swore an affidavit on behalf of Sindona. Gelli noted that he himself had been accused of being a "CIA agent; the chief of the Argentine death squad; a representative of the Portuguese secret service; the coordinator of the Greek, Chilean, and West German secret services; the chief of the international movement of underground fascism, etc."

He made no attempt to deny these various allegations, and he offered no evidence that all or any of them were ill founded. He attributed them to "the rise of Communist power in Italy." On oath he then went on to make a few allegations of his own, including: "Communist influence has already reached certain sectors of the government, particularly the Ministry of Justice, where during the last five years there has been a political shift from the center toward the extreme left." Again he offered no evidence. Gelli asserted that because of "left-wing infiltration" Sindona would not receive a fair trial in Italy and probably would be murdered. He continued: "The Communists' hatred of Michele Sindona is due to the fact that he is an anti-Communist and that he has always been favorable to the free-enterprise system in a democratic Italy."

On November 13, 1977, Sindona gave a demonstration of his version of the free-enterprise system at work in democratic Italy. The planned blackmail of Calvi was activated, and posters and pamphlets began to appear all over Milan. They accused Calvi of fraud, exporting currency, falsifying accounts, embezzlement, and tax evasion. They quoted secret Swiss bank account numbers belonging to Calvi. They detailed illicit deals. They referred to his Mafia links. It became more interesting to read the walls of the city than *Corriere della Sera*. Sindona, who had orchestrated this public washing of Calvi's dirty laundry, had come to the conclusion that his fellow P2 member and former protégé Roberto Calvi was not taking a sufficiently active interest in his predicament. Sindona had appealed to Licio Gelli, who agreed that Calvi should make a "substantial contribution" to Sindona's war chest. Gelli offered to serve as an intermediary between his two Masonic friends. This ensured that they both paid him a commission.

Roberto Calvi dipped into his pocket yet again—or, more accurately, dipped into the pockets of those who banked with him. Half a million dollars were paid by Calvi into Banca del Gottardo, Lugano, in April 1978. It was placed in a Sindona account.

The man who had organized the poster and pamphlet campaign on behalf of Sindona, Luigi Cavallo, had gone about his task with enormous relish. Cavallo had operated for some time in Italy as a one-man smear

campaign unit that, like all professional whores, sold
itself to the highest bidder. The posters were followed on
November 24, 1977, with a letter to the director of the
Bank of Italy, Paolo Baffi. The letter listed all the accusations that had appeared on the walls of Milan. It also
referred to an earlier communication, which had included
photocopies of Calvi's Swiss bank accounts. Cavallo
concluded his letter to the director by threatening to
sue the Bank of Italy for failure to carry out its legal
duties unless it began to investigate Banco Ambrosiano.

This letter shows the fundamental difference between a top-notch criminal like Sindona and a third-
rate crook like Cavallo. The letter was Cavallo's idea.
He wrote it without consulting Sindona, who would
never have authorized such action. You may steal eggs
from the golden goose but you don't kill it—at least not
while it's still capable of laying.

The same week in April 1978 in which Sindona
received his $500,000 payoff, officials from the Bank of
Italy, who for a number of years had had their eyes on
Banco Ambrosiano and Roberto Calvi, moved into the
bank in force. Twelve investigators had been carefully
selected by Paolo Baffi and his senior colleague, Mario
Sarcinelli. The man chosen to head the investigation
was Giulio Padalino. Unfortunately for Calvi, Padalino
was incorruptible.

The poster and pamphlet attack by Sindona was
trivial compared to the problems Calvi now faced. News
of the massive investigation leaked and was soon known
throughout Milan's business world. The price of Ambrosiano shares plummeted further, forcing Calvi to divert
even more money to prop up the price. By now the
tangled empire he controlled had a branch in Nicaragua;
another was planned for Peru. There were Calvi companies in Canada, Belgium, and the United States.

The Achilles' heel was Suprafin. If the bank inspectors discovered the truth about Suprafin, then the collapse of Banco Ambrosiano and the arrest and imprisonment of Calvi were inevitable. And the extradition of
Sindona would suddenly become a much simpler matter.
Both men stood to lose everything, including their liberty,
if the inspectors could crack the Suprafin puzzle. In
Milan, Calvi became agitated. In New York, Sindona

stopped gloating about the $500,000 he had just extorted from Calvi. The one hope for both men was Bishop Paul Marcinkus. Marcinkus duly obliged. When the inspectors from the Bank of Italy asked Ambrosiano's general manager, Carlo Olgiati, who owned Suprafin, he told them it was owned by the Istituto per le Opere di Religione, the Vatican Bank.

Calmly the bank inspectors continued probing, working their way through the maze of share purchases, transfers, cross-transfers, buy-backs, and parkings. They were severely limited by Italian law, especially when it came to information involving foreign associates. If, for example, they had been able to obtain detailed information on Calvi's Luxembourg holding company and had realized that millions of dollars borrowed on the European market had been funneled to Nassau, where Marcinkus sat on the board with Calvi, and to Managua, Nicaragua, and that these two Ambrosiano-owned banks had then loaned millions to small Panamanian shell companies *without security*, the game would have been up then and there. But full information on the Luxembourg holding company was denied to the inspectors. Calvi stalled; he grew evasive, claiming he could not breach his foreign associates' rules on confidentiality. The bank inspectors continued to dig. They discovered that on May 6, 1975, Luigi Landra, a former chief executive of Banco Ambrosiano, and Livio Godeluppi, brother of Ambrosiano's chief accountant, had been made directors of Suprafin. How was it that these two men from Ambrosiano happened to be directors of a company owned by the Vatican Bank?

The inspectors also established that Suprafin had been created in Milan in November 1971 by two of Calvi's closest associates, Vahan Pasargiklian, who by the time of the 1978 investigation had become managing director of Banca Cattolica, and Gennaro Zanfagna. Suprafin had "owned by Calvi" written all over it.

The probe continued. Careful analysis of the current accounts held by Suprafin convinced the inspectors that the company was indeed owned by Banco Ambrosiano and not the Vatican. If Suprafin were owned by the Vatican, why would Ambrosiano buy La Centrale

shares from it at 13,864 lire as against a market price of
9,650 and then sell them back to it at 9,340? To obtain a
letter of thanks from Pope Paul? A pat on the back from
Marcinkus?

In July 1978 they again tackled Calvi's executive
colleague, Carlo Olgiati. Olgiati consulted Calvi. He returned bearing a letter. The letter was from the Vatican
Bank to Roberto Calvi and was dated January 20, 1975.
It read:

> This is to refer to the portfolio of shares as per
> December 31, 1974, held by the company Supra-
> fin SA, a company pertaining to our institute.
> You are herewith requested to manage and ad-
> minister the said portfolio in the most appropri-
> ate form and to arrange for all suitable invest-
> ment and divestment operations. Will you please
> keep us periodically up to date as regards the
> position of the above named portfolio and re-
> lated transactions.

The letter was signed by Luigi Mennini and by the
Vatican Bank's chief accountant, Pellegrino de Strobel.
It might well be dated January 1975, but the bank
inspectors strongly suspected that it had been written
after their investigation had begun in April 1978 and
written with the full approval of Bishop Marcinkus.

If Marcinkus and his colleagues at the Vatican Bank
were to be believed, then the Holy See had given a new
definition to the phrase "Christian charity." It now embraced entering the Milan stock market and spending
millions merely to defend the price of Banco Ambrosiano
shares. In any event, Calvi, by courtesy of Bishop
Marcinkus, was off the hook, at least temporarily. Here,
apparently, was the proof that Suprafin was indeed
owned by the Vatican Bank. The normally cold and
aloof Calvi suddenly became almost affable in the eyes
of some of his more senior colleagues at the Milan
headquarters. Confident that he had blocked the investigation in what was potentially his most vulnerable area,
he finalized the arrangements for a trip to South America with his wife, Clara. The trip was to be part business,
part pleasure. There was to be some sightseeing of po-

tential sites for branches on the South American continent plus the inevitable business meetings associated with such a development, and then some sightseeing of the more usual sort.

Once in South America, Calvi began to relax. Then Pope Paul VI died. The lines between Calvi's hotel suite in Buenos Aires and various parts of Italy became busy. When he heard the name of the new pope—Albino Luciani—Calvi was shocked. Virtually any of the other 110 cardinals would have been preferable.

Calvi was fully aware of the anger his takeover of the Banca Cattolica del Veneto had generated in Venice; aware that Luciani had gone to Rome in an attempt to regain diocesan control over the bank. He was equally aware that Luciani was a man with a formidable reputation for personal poverty and for intolerance of any shady dealings on the part of clergy. The episode of the two priests and the speculating salesman in Vittorio Veneto was legendary throughout northern Italy.

From Buenos Aires Calvi phoned instructions to sell some of the shares in the bank that Suprafin held. With bank inspectors looking over their shoulders, his staff had to move cautiously. Nevertheless, in the first three weeks of September 1978, they unloaded 350,000 shares. Then Calvi heard the news he had been dreading. Bishop Paul Marcinkus' days were numbered. If Marcinkus went, total exposure of the entire fraud was inevitable. He recalled what Marcinkus had told him over the phone shortly after Luciani's election: "Things are going to be very different from now on. This pope is quite a different man."

Albino Luciani represented a very serious threat to Sindona as well as Calvi. Subsequent events were to demonstrate powerfully what happened to people who represented serious threats to these two.

The new pope also clearly represented a major threat to Bishop Paul Marcinkus, president of the Vatican Bank. If Luciani investigated the bank there were likely to be quite a number of vacancies. Mennini and de Strobel, who had put their names to the Suprafin letter, were on borrowed time. Both had been involved over the years with the criminal activities of Sindona and Calvi. If Marcinkus had any doubts whatsoever about Luciani's

capacity to take vigorous, effective action, he had but to
confer with de Strobel, who had been a lawyer near
Venice and who was fully conversant with the affair of
the embezzling priests in Vittorio Veneto.

Bernardino Nogara may well have had a purely
capitalistic mentality, but compared with what came
after him in Vatican Incorporated, the man was a saint.
The company had come a long way since Mussolini
gave it its modern impetus in 1929.

Now, in September 1978, Albino Luciani, the man
who was dedicated to a poor Church for the poor, had a
task that was as supreme as his position. If his dream to
be the last "rich father" was to become a reality, then
Vatican Incorporated—that massive multinational corporation—would have to be dismantled. The Papal States
might have been lost forever, but in their place was an
extraordinary moneymaking machine.

There was the Administration of the Patrimony of
the Holy See (APSA), with its president, Cardinal Villot;
its secretary Monsignor Antonetti; and its Ordinary and
Extraordinary Sections. The Ordinary Section administered all the wealth of the various congregations,
tribunals, and offices. It specifically administered a great
deal of the real estate of the papacy. In Rome alone this
amounted to over five thousand rented apartments. In
1979, its gross assets were over $1 billion.

The Extraordinary Section, the Vatican's other bank,
was as active in its daily stock speculations as the IOR,
controlled by Marcinkus. It specialized in the currency
market and worked closely with Crédit Suisse and the
Société de Banque Suisse. Its gross assets in September
1978 were over $1.2 billion.

The Vatican Bank, which Marcinkus was running,
had gross assets of over $1 billion. Its annual profits by
1978 were over $120 million; 85 percent of this went
directly to the pope to use as he saw fit. Its current
accounts numbered over 11,000. Under the terms by
which the bank was created by Pius XII during the
Second World War, these accounts should have belonged
primarily to religious orders and religious institutes.
When Albino Luciani became pope only 1,047 accounts
belonged to religious orders and institutes, 312 to
parishes, and 290 to dioceses. The remaining 9,351 were

the property of diplomats, prelates, and "privileged citizens"; a significant number of this last category were not even Italian citizens. Those who were included: Sindona, Calvi, Gelli, and Ortolani. Other accounts were held by leading politicians of every stripe, and major businessmen. Many of the accountholders used the facility as a conduit through which to export currency out of Italy illegally. Deposits were not subjected to any taxation.

The two departments of APSA and the Vatican Bank were Albino Luciani's major problems that had to be overcome before the Church could revert to its early Christian origins. There were many others, not least the wealth that had been acquired over centuries. This took many forms, including a multitude of art treasures.

The Vatican's patronage is there for all to see: the Caravaggios, the Raphael tapestries, the Farnese gold altar cross and candlesticks by Gentile de Fabriano, the Belvedere Apollo, the Belvedere Torso, the paintings of Leonardo da Vinci, Bernini's sculptures. Would the words of Jesus Christ be heard less clearly in someplace more modest than the Sistine Chapel with its majestic "Last Judgment" by Michelangelo? The Vatican classifies all of these as nonproductive assets. What the founder of Christianity would classify them as can be gauged from his own comments about wealth and property.

What would Jesus Christ have felt if he had returned to earth in September 1978 and been allowed into the State of Vatican City?

What would the man who declared "My kingdom is not of this earth" have felt if he had wandered through the departments of APSA with its teams of clerical and lay stock analysts, each an expert in his own field, following the day-by-day and often minute-by-minute fluctuations of the shares, securities, and investments that APSA owns throughout the world? What would the carpenter's son have made of the IBM equipment that functioned both in APSA and the Vatican Bank? What would the man who compared the difficulty of a rich man entering the kingdom of Heaven with a camel passing through the eye of a needle have said about the latest stock market quotations from London, Wall Street,

Zurich, Milan, Montreal, and Tokyo that are heard end-
lessly in the Vatican?

What would the man who said "Blessed are the
poor" have said about the annual profit from the sale of
Vatican stamps—profit in excess of $1 million? What
would have been his opinion of the annual collection of
Peter's pence that went directly to the pope? (This annual collection, considered by many to be an accurate
barometer of the popularity of the pope, had under the
charismatic John XXIII produced between $15 million
and $20 million a year. Under Paul VI this figure had
dropped after *Humanae Vitae* to an annual average of
$4 million.)

What would the founder of the faith have felt about
these examples of how far his teaching had been
perverted? The question is, of course, rhetorical. If Jesus Christ had returned to earth in September 1978, or
if he came now and attempted to enter the Vatican, the
result would be the same. He would not get as far as the
doors of the Vatican Bank. He would be arrested at the
St. Anne Gate and handed over to the Italian authorities.
He would never have the opportunity to learn firsthand
about Vatican Incorporated, the multinational conglomerate that is fed from so many directions. He would not
hear, for example, how it derives vast sums from the
United States and also from West Germany, where in
1978, through the state tax of *Kirchensteuer*, the Roman
Catholic Church of West Germany received $1.9 billion,
a significant portion of which it then passed on to the
Vatican.

If Albino Luciani was to succeed with his dream of
a poor Church for the poor, it was going to be a Herculean
task. The modern monster created by Bernardino Nogara
had by 1978 become self-perpetuating. When the cardinals elected Albino Luciani to the papacy on that hot
August day in 1978, they set an honest, holy, totally
incorruptible pope on a collision course with Vatican
Incorporated. The powerful market forces of the Vatican
Bank, APSA, and the other moneymaking elements were
about to be met by the unyielding integrity of Albino
Luciani.

THE THIRTY-THREE DAYS

When Albino Luciani threw open the windows of the papal apartments within twenty-four hours of his election, that gesture epitomized his entire papacy. Fresh air and sunlight rushed into a Roman Catholic Church that had grown increasingly dark and somber during the last years of Paul VI.

Luciani, who during his Venice days had described himself as "just a poor man accustomed to small things and silence," now found himself obliged to confront the Vatican grandeur and the curial babble. The son of a bricklayer was now supreme head of a religion whose founder was the son of a carpenter.

Many of the Vatican experts, having failed even to consider the possibility of Luciani's election, now titled him "the unknown pope." He had been well enough known by ninety-nine cardinals, however, to be entrusted with the Church's future, this man without any diplomatic training or curial experience. The many curial cardinals had been rejected. In essence, the entire Curia had been rejected in favor of a quiet, humble man who promptly announced that he wished to be called pastor rather than pontiff. Luciani's aspirations quickly became clear: total revolution. He was intent on taking the Church back to its origins, back to the simplicity, honesty, ideals, and aspirations of Jesus Christ. Others

before him had had the same dream only to have the
reality of the world as perceived by their advisers im-
pinge on that dream. How could this small, unassuming
man accomplish even the beginnings of the transforma-
tions both material and spiritual that would be required?

In electing Albino Luciani, his fellow cardinals had
made a number of profound statements about what
they wanted and what they did not want. Clearly they
did not want a reactionary pope. Nor did they want a
pope whose concerns would be primarily abstract and
intellectual. It appears that what they sought was to
make an impact on the world by electing a man whose
goodness, wisdom, and exemplary humility would be
manifest to all. That was what they got—a shepherd
intent on pastoral care.

His new name was considered a bit of a mouthful
by the Romans. They quickly abbreviated "Giovanni
Paolo" to the more intimate "Gianpaolo," a corruption
the pope happily accepted and used to sign letters, only
to have them returned by Secretary of State Villot for
correction to the formal title. One such letter written in
his own hand was to thank the Augustinians for their
hospitality during his stay before the conclave. This
simple act was typical of the man. Two days after being
elected pope to over eight hundred million Catholics,
Luciani found time to thank his former hosts.

Another letter, written on the same day, struck a
more somber note. Writing to an Italian priest whose
work he admired, Luciani revealed his awareness of the
burden that was now uniquely his. "I don't know how I
could have accepted. The day after, I already regretted
it, but by then it was too late." One of his first acts on
entering the papal apartments had been to make several phone calls to his region in the North. He spoke to
an astonished Monsignor Ducoli, a longtime friend and
working associate, now bishop of Belluno. He told the
bishop he was "lonely for my people." Later he spoke to
his brother Edoardo: "Now look what's happened to
me." These acts were private; others of a more public
nature caught the world's imagination.

And it was not just his actions. Because to begin
with, there was his smile. It effectively caught the joy
that this man had discovered in Christianity, and in

turn it touched many. It was impossible not to warm to the man, and as one warmed, the feeling was good. Pope Paul's agonizing had turned people off by the millions. Albino Luciani dramatically reversed the trend. He recaptured world interest in the papacy. When the world listened to what was behind the smile, the interest quickened. What Luciani demonstrated in a manner and to a degree never before seen in a pope, any pope, was the ability to communicate, whether directly or through the media. It was an undreamed-of asset to the Roman Catholic Church.

Luciani was an object lesson in how to win the battle for mankind's heart, mind, and soul. For the first time in living memory a pope was talking to his people in a manner and a style they could understand. The sigh of relief from the faithful was almost audible. The murmurs of delight continued through the Indian summer of 1978. Luciani began to take the Church on the long walk back to the Gospel.

The public rapidly judged this charismatic man a huge success. Vatican observers simply did not know what to make of him. Many had given instant and learned opinions about his choice of a papal name, they had talked of "symbolic continuity." Luciani had unwittingly demolished all of that on the first Sunday with, "John made me a bishop, Paul made me a cardinal." Not much symbolic continuity there. The experts wrote speculative articles about what the new pope might or might not do on a range of issues. A large amount of that speculation was rendered superfluous in Pope John Paul's very first speech, when he referred to "the Second Vatican Council, to whose teachings I wish to commit my total ministry. . . ." There was no need to speculate; all that was necessary was to refer to the various conclusions of the council.

Luciani, speaking to a packed St. Peter's Square on Sunday, September 10, talked of God and said, "He is our father; even more, he is our mother." The Italian Vatican experts, in particular, were beside themselves. In a country notorious for its *machismo*, the suggestion that God was a woman was deemed by some as tantamount to the end of the world. There were many anxious debates about this fourth member of the Trinity until Luciani gently pointed out that he had been quoting Isaiah. The male-dominated Mother Church relaxed.

Earlier, on September 6, during a general audience, members of the papal entourage, fussing around the holy father like irritating flies around a horse, publicly displayed embarrassment as Luciani held over fifteen thousand people spellbound. Entering almost at a trot into the Nervi Hall, which was filled to capacity, he talked about the soul. There was nothing remarkable about that. What was remarkable was the manner and the style.

> Once a man went to buy a new motorcar from the agent. The salesman gave him some advice. "Look, it's an excellent car, make sure you treat it correctly. Premium gasoline in the tank, the best oil in the engine." The customer replied, "Oh, no, I can't stand the smell of gasoline or oil. Fill the tank with champagne, which I like very much, and I'll oil the joints with jam." The salesman shrugged. "Do what you like, but don't come and complain if you end up in a ditch with your car."
>
> The Lord did something similar with us: he gave us this body, animated by an intelligent soul, a good will. He said, "This machine is a good one, but treat it well."

While the Vatican elite shuddered at such secular allusions, Albino Luciani knew full well that his words were being carried around the world. Scatter enough seed, some will grow. He had been presented with the most powerful pulpit on earth. His use of the gift was deeply impressive. Many within the Church talk *ad nauseam* of the "Good News of the Gospel" while giving the impression that they are informing their listeners of unmitigated disasters. When Luciani talked of the "Good News," it was clear from his whole demeanor that the news was very good indeed.

Several times he brought a young boy out of the choir to share the microphone with him, to help him work not only the audience inside Nervi Hall but also the wider audience outside. Other world leaders were adept at picking up the young and kissing them. Here was a man who actually talked to them and even more remarkably listened and responded to what they had to say.

He quoted Mark Twain, Jules Verne, and the Italian poet Trilussa. He talked of Pinocchio. Having already compared the soul to a car, he now drew an analogy between prayer and soap. "Prayer well used would be a marvelous soap, capable of making us all saints. We are not all saints because we have not used this soap enough." The Curia, particularly certain bishops and cardinals, winced. The public listened.

A few days after his election he faced over one thousand members of the world's press and, gently chiding them for concentrating on the conclave trivia rather than on its true significance, he acknowledged that theirs was not a new problem by recalling the advice an Italian editor had given to his reporters: "Remember, the public does not want to know what Napoleon III said to William of Prussia. It wants to know whether he wore beige or red trousers and whether he smoked a cigar."

Luciani obviously felt at home with the reporters. More than once in his life he had remarked that had he not become a priest he would have become a journalist. The quality of his two books and numerous articles indicates that he could have held his own with many of the listening correspondents. Recalling the late Cardinal Mercier's observations that if the apostle Paul were alive today he would have been a journalist, the new pope showed a keen awareness of the respective importance of the various news media by enlarging on the apostle's possible modern role: "Not only a journalist. Possibly head of Reuters. Not only head of Reuters, I think he would have also asked for airtime on Italian television and NBC."

The correspondents loved it. The Curia was less amused. All the above remarks to the reporters were censored out of the official records of the speech. What remains for posterity is a drab, unctuous, prepared speech, written by Vatican officials—though in fact the pope had continually departed from it—grossly inadequate as testimony to the wit and personality of Albino

Luciani. This Vatican censorship of the pope became a
constant feature during September 1978.

Illustrissimi, the collection of his letters to the
famous, had been available in book form in Italy since
1976. It had proved to be highly successful. Now with
its author the leader of eight hundred million Roman
Catholics, the commercial potential was not lost on the
publishing world. High-powered executives began ap-
pearing at the office of *Il Messaggero di San Antonio* in
Padua. The Catholic monthly was sitting on the prover-
bial gold mine, less author's royalties. For the author,
the real payoff was that the ideas and observations
contained within the letters would be read by a worldwide audience. The fact that they would be read only
because he had become pope mattered not at all to
Luciani. More seed was being scattered. More would
grow.

It soon became apparent that as long as Luciani
was in charge, Vatican interpreters, watchers, experts,
and seers had all been rendered useless. Verbatim reporting was needed. Given that, the new pope's intentions were very clear.

On August 28, the beginning of his papal revolution
was announced. It took the form of a Vatican statement
that there was to be no coronation, that the new pope
refused to be crowned. There would be no *sedia gestatoria*,
the chair used to carry the pope, no tiara encrusted
with emeralds, rubies, sapphires, and diamonds. No
ostrich feathers, no six-hour ceremony. In short, the
ritual with which the Church demonstrated that it still
lusted after temporal power was abolished. Albino
Luciani had been obliged to engage in long, tedious
argument with the Vatican traditionalists before his
wishes prevailed. Luciani, who never once used the royal
"we," the monarchical first-person plural, was determined that the royal papacy with its appurtenances of
worldly grandeur should be replaced by a Church that
resembled the concepts of its founder. The "coronation"
became a simple Mass. The spectacle of a pontiff carried in a chair like a caliph from *Arabian Nights* was
supplanted by the sight of a supreme pastor quietly
walking up the steps of the altar. With that gesture
Luciani abolished a thousand years of history and moved

the Church a little farther back down the road toward Jesus Christ.

The triple-decked, beehive-shaped tiara was superseded by the pallium, a white woollen stole around the pope's shoulders. The monarch had made way for the shepherd. The era of the poor Church had officially begun.

Among the twelve heads of state and numerous other official representatives at the ceremony were men whom the pope had been anxious to avoid meeting. In particular he had asked his Secretariat of State not to invite the leaders of Argentina, Chile, and Paraguay to his inaugural Mass, but Cardinal Villot's department had already sent out the invitations before checking with Albino Luciani. The department had assumed there would be the traditional coronation, and the invitation list reflected that assumption.

Consequently, taking part in the Mass in St. Peter's Square were General Videla from Argentina, the Chilean foreign minister, and the son of the president of Paraguay—representatives from countries where human rights were not considered pressing priorities. Italian protesters demonstrated against their presence, and there were nearly three hundred arrests. Later Albino Luciani would be criticized for the presence of such men at the Mass. Those who criticized were unaware that the blame should have been laid at Cardinal Villot's door, and Villot said nothing to enlighten them.

At the private audience that followed the Mass, Luciani, the son of a Socialist who had abhorred all aspects of fascism, left General Videla in no doubt that he had inherited his father's views. He spoke particularly of his concern over *los desaparecidos*, the thousands of Argentinians who had "disappeared." By the end of the fifteen-minute audience, the general was probably wishing he had heeded the eleventh-hour attempts of Vatican officials to dissuade him from coming to Rome.

The audience with Vice President Mondale was a happier affair. Mondale gave the new pope a book containing the front pages of over fifty American newspapers reporting Luciani's election. A more thoughtful present was a first-edition copy of Mark Twain's *Life on the*

Mississippi. Someone in the State Department had evidently done his homework.

Thus the papacy of John Paul I began, a papacy with clear aims and aspirations. Immediately Luciani set cats among a variety of Vatican pigeons. Before the inaugural Mass Luciani had addressed the diplomatic corps accredited to the Vatican. His own diplomatic staff visibly blanched when he observed on behalf of the entire Roman Catholic Church:

> We have no temporal goods to exchange, no economic interests to discuss. Our possibilities for intervention are specific and limited and of a special character. They do not interfere with purely temporal, technical, and political affairs, which are matters for your governments.
> In this way, our diplomatic missions to your highest civil authorities, far from being a survival from the past, are a witness to our deepseated respect for lawful temporal power, and to our lively interest in the humane causes that the temporal power is intended to advance.

"We have no public goods to exchange...." Luciani had pronounced the death sentence on Vatican Incorporated. All that remained uncertain was the number of days and months during which it would continue to function. The men of the international money markets of Milan, London, Tokyo, and New York pondered Luciani's words with interest. If he really meant what he said, then clearly there were going to be changes. Those changes would not merely affect the personnel of the Vatican Bank and the APSA but also would inevitably mean the curtailment of a number of Vatican Incorporated's activities. For the men in the world's money markets there were billions to be made if they could correctly guess the direction this new Vatican philosophy would take. Albino Luciani wanted a poor Church for the poor. What did he plan to do with those who had created a wealthy Church? What did he plan to do with the wealth?

Luciani's humility gave rise to several misconceptions. Many observers concluded that this demonstrably holy man was a simple, uncomplicated person who lacked the culture and sophistication of his predecessor, Paul VI. The reality was that he had a far richer cultivation and a much deeper sophistication than Paul. It was precisely because he was so extraordinary that he could appear so simple. His was a simplicity acquired only by a very few, a simplicity stemming from a deep wisdom.

One of the peculiarities of this age is that humility and gentleness are inevitably taken to be indications of some form of weakness. Frequently they indicate precisely the opposite, great strength.

When the new pope remarked that he had been leafing through the Vatican's yearbook to find out who did what, many in the Curia smirked and concluded that he would be a pushover, a man they could control. There were others who knew better.

Men who had known Albino Luciani for many years watched and waited. They knew the steel within, the strength to make difficult or unpopular decisions. Monsignor Tiziano Scalzotto, Father Mario Senigaglia, Monsignor Da Rif, Father Bartolomeo Sorge, and Father Busa were among the many who spoke to me of the inner strength of Pope John Paul I. Father Busa observed:

> His mind was as strong, as hard, and as sharp as a diamond. That was where his real power was. He understood and had the ability to get to the center of a problem. He could not be overwhelmed. When everyone was applauding the smiling pope, I was waiting for him *tirare fuori le unghie* (to reveal his claws). He had tremendous power.

Without an entourage—no Venetian Mafia followed the Milan clique into the papal apartments—Albino Luciani would need every scrap of inner strength he could muster if he was to avoid becoming the prisoner of the Vatican Curia.

In the days following the conclave, the Vatican government machine had not been idle. On Sunday, August 27, after his noon speech to the crowds, Luciani lunched

with Cardinal Jean Villot. As Pope Paul's secretary of
state since April 1969, Villot had built a reputation for
quiet competence. During the period preceding the conclave Villot, as chamberlain, had virtually functioned
as a caretaker pope, aided by his committees of cardinals.
Luciani asked Villot to continue as secretary of state for
"a little while, until I have found my way." Villot, now
seventy-two years old, had been hoping that the moment had come when he could retire. Luciani reconfirmed all the curial heads in their previous positions,
but all were made aware that this was merely a temporary measure. Ever the prudent man of the mountains,
the new pope preferred to bide his time. "Deliberation.
Decision. Execution." If the Curia wanted to know how
their new pope would act, they had merely to read his
letter to Saint Bernard. A great many did. They also did
much deeper research on Pope John Paul I. What they
discovered caused consternation in many Vatican departments and a deep pleasure of anticipation in others.

The death of Pope Paul VI had brought to the surface many animosities that had existed within the Vatican village. The Roman Curia, the central administrative
body of the Church, had been engaging in internecine
warfare for many years; only through Paul's expertise
had most of the battles been kept from public view.
Now after the rebuff within the conclave, the curial
warfare reached the papal apartments. Albino Luciani
complained bitterly about the situation to a number of
friends who came to see him. "I want to learn quickly
the trade of pope but almost no one explains problems
and situations in a thorough and detached manner.
Most of the time I hear nothing but bad spoken about
everything and everyone." To another friend from the
North he observed, "I have noticed two things that
appear to be in very short supply in the Vatican. Honesty and a good cup of coffee."

There were as many Roman curial factions as choir-
boys in the Sistine Chapel choir. There was the Curia of
Pope Paul VI, totally committed to ensuring not only
that the memory of the late pope was constantly and
continually honored but also that there were no devia-
tions from his views, opinions, and pronouncements.

There was the Curia that favored Cardinal Giovanni

Benelli and the Curia that wished he was in Hell. Pope Paul VI had made Benelli his under secretary of state, number two to Cardinal Villot. Benelli rapidly became the pope's muscle, ensuring that policy was adhered to. Because of this, animosity toward him had grown to the point that in order to protect him Paul had promoted him and moved him to Florence. Now Benelli's protector was dead but the long knives remained sheathed. Luciani was pope *because* of men like Benelli.

There were curial factions that favored or opposed Cardinals Baggio, Felici, and Bertoli. There were curial factions wanting more central power and control, others wanting less.

Throughout his life Albino Luciani had avoided visits to the Vatican. He had kept his contact with the Roman Curia to a minimum. As a result, before his election, he probably had fewer curial enemies than any other cardinal. It was a situation that quickly changed. Here was a pope who considered "mere execution" as the basic function of the Curia. He believed in greater power-sharing with the bishops throughout the world and planned to decentralize the Vatican structure. By refusing to be crowned he had distressed the traditionalists. Another innovation hardly likely to endear Luciani to the more materially minded members of the Curia was his instruction that the extra month's salary paid automatically upon the election of a new pope should be cut by half.

Obviously there were many among the three thousand or so members of the Curia who would loyally serve and love the new pope; but the way of the world is to ensure that negative forces often predominate. As soon as the result of the election was known, the Curia, or certain sections of it, swung into action. Within hours a special edition of *L'Osservatore Romano* was on the streets with a full biography of the new pope. Vatican Radio was already broadcasting similar details.

As an example of how to influence the world's thinking about a previously unknown leader, *L'Osservatore Romano*'s treatment of Albino Luciani is definitive. Because of its deliberate distortions, this particular edition of *L'Osservatore Romano* is also an excellent example of why the Vatican's semiofficial newspaper has been compared unfavorably with *Pravda*. Using the "official facts" from the Vatican, many journalists fighting deadlines filed copy that portrayed a man who did not exist. *The Economist*, to take one of several hundred examples, said of the new pope, "He would not be much at home in the company of Dr. Hans Küng." Research would have established that Luciani and Hans Küng had exchanged very friendly letters as well as sending one another books. Further research would have revealed that Luciani had several times quoted Küng favorably in his sermons. Virtually every newspaper and magazine in the world that carried profiles of the new pope made similar totally erroneous assertions.

To read the special edition of *L'Osservatore Romano* is to read of a new pope who was even more conservative than Pope Paul VI. The distortion covered a wide range of Luciani's views, but one in particular is highly relevant when considering the life and death of Albino Luciani: artificial birth control.

The Vatican newspaper described a man who was an active and unquestioning supporter of *Humanae Vitae*. The discussion of the topic began:

> He made a meticulous study of the subject of responsible parenthood and engaged in consultations and talks with medical specialists and theologians. He warned of the grave responsibility of the Church (the ecclesiastical magisterium) in pronouncing on such a delicate and controversial question.

That was entirely accurate and truthful. What followed was completely inaccurate.

> With the publication of the encyclical *Humanae Vitae*, there could be no room for doubt, and the bishop of Vittorio Veneto was among the first to circulate it and to insist with those who were perplexed by the document that its teaching was beyond question.

When the Curia moves, it is a formidable machine. Its efficiency and speed would leave other civil services breathless. Men from the Roman Curia appeared at Gregorian College and removed all notes and papers that referred to Luciani's period of study for his degree. Other members of the Curia went to Venice, Vittorio Veneto, Belluno. Wherever Luciani had been, the Curia went. All copies of the Luciani document on artificial birth control were seized and immediately placed in the Vatican's secret archives along with his thesis on Rosmini and a large quantity of other writings. It could be said that the beatification process for Albino Luciani began the day he was elected pope. It would be equally accurate to observe that the curial cover-up of the real Albino Luciani began the same day.

What certain members of the Curia had realized much to their shock was that in electing Albino Luciani, the cardinals had given them a pope who would not let the issue of artificial birth control rest with *Humanae Vitae*. Careful study by members of the Curia of what Luciani had actually said, not only to his parishioners in public but also to his friends and colleagues in private, quickly established that the new pope favored artificial birth control. The inaccurate and false picture that *L'Osservatore Romano* painted of a man who rigorously applied the principles of *Humanae Vitae* was the opening shot in a counterattack designed to hem Albino Luciani inside the strictures of his predecessor's encyclical. It was quickly followed by another blast.

United Press International (UPI) discovered that Luciani had advocated a Vatican ruling in favor of artificial birth control. Italian newspapers also carried stories referring to the Luciani document sent to Pope Paul by Cardinal Urbani of Venice in which the strong recommendation in favor of the contraceptive pill had been made. The Curia speedily located Father Henri de Riedmatten, who had been secretary to the papal birth-control commission. Riedmatten characterized as "a fantasy" the reports that Luciani had been opposed to an encyclical condemning artificial birth control. He asserted that Luciani had never been a member of the commission, which was accurate. He then went on to deny that Pope Paul had ever received a letter or a report on the subject from Luciani.

This sort of denial is characteristic of the duplicity

that abounds in the Curia. The Luciani document went
to Rome via Cardinal Urbani and therefore bore the
cardinal's signature. To deny that there existed a document actually signed by Luciani was technically correct.
To deny that Luciani on behalf of his fellow bishops in
the Veneto region had forwarded such a document to
the pope via the cardinal was an iniquitous lie.

Within three weeks of his election, Albino Luciani
took the first significant steps toward reversing the Roman Catholic Church's position on artificial birth control.
While those steps were being taken, the world's press,
thanks to *L'Osservatore Romano*, Vatican Radio, and
off-the-record briefings by certain members of the Roman Curia, had already firmly established a completely
false image of Luciani's views on the topic.

During his papacy Luciani referred to and quoted
from a number of the pronouncements and encyclicals
that had come from Pope Paul VI. Notably absent was
any reference to *Humanae Vitae*. The defenders of that
encyclical had first been alerted to the new pope's views
when they learned with consternation that the draft
acceptance speech, which had been prepared for Paul's
successor by the Secretariat of State and contained glow-
ing references to *Humanae Vitae*, had had all such
references excised by Luciani. The anti-birth-control element within the Vatican then discovered that in May
1978, Albino Luciani had been invited to attend and
speak at an international congress being held in Milan
on June 21–22. The main purpose of the congress was to
celebrate the tenth anniversary of the encyclical *Humanae
Vitae*. Luciani had let it be known that he would not
speak at the congress and further that he would not
attend. Among those who did attend and speak in glow-
ing terms about *Humanae Vitae* was the Polish cardinal
Karol Wojtyla.

Now in September, while the world's press unques-
tioningly repeated the lies of *L'Osservatore Romano*, Albino Luciani was heard in the papal apartments talking
to his secretary of state, Cardinal Villot: "I will be
happy to talk to this United States delegation on the
issue. To my mind we cannot leave the situation as it
currently stands."

The "issue" was world population. The "situation"

was *Humanae Vitae*. As the conversation progressed, Villot heard Pope John Paul I express a view that many others, including his private secretary, Father Diego Lorenzi, had heard many times before. Father Lorenzi is only one of a number of people who have been able to quote to me Luciani's exact words:

> I am aware of the ovulation period in a woman with its range of fertility from twenty-four to thirty-six hours. Even if one allows a sperm life of forty-eight hours, the maximum time of possible conception is less than four days. In a regular cycle this means four days of fertility and twenty-four days of infertility. How on earth can it be a sin to say instead of twenty-four days, twenty-eight days?

What had prompted this truly historic conversation between Luciani and Villot had been a feeler put out to the Vatican by the American embassy in Rome. The American embassy had been contacted by the State Department in Washington and also by Congressman James Scheuer. The congressman headed a House select committee on population and was also vice-chairman of the UN fund for population activities, an interparliamentary working group. The story of the Luciani document to Pope Paul VI on artificial birth control had alerted Scheuer and his House committee to the possibility of change on the Church's position on artificial birth control. It seemed to Scheuer that it was unlikely that his group would obtain an audience with Luciani so soon in his papacy, but he still considered it worth making an attempt, through the State Department and also through the embassy in Rome. Scheuer was destined to hear some good news.

Villot, like many of the men who surrounded Luciani, was having considerable difficulty adjusting to the new papacy. He had developed over the years a close working relationship with Paul VI. He had grown to admire the Montini style. Now the world-weary eighty-one-year-old had been replaced by an optimistic and energetic sixty-five-year-old.

The relationship between Luciani and his secretary

of state was uneasy. The new pope found Villot cold and aloof, full of observations about what Paul VI would have said and done about this problem or that issue. Paul VI was dead, but it became apparent that Villot and a significant section of the Curia had not accepted that the Montinian approach to problems had died with him.

The speech that the new pope had delivered twenty-four hours after the conclave had been for the most part a generalized statement. His real program began to be formulated only during the early days of September 1978. He was fired with the inspiration of Pope John XXIII's first hundred days.

John had been elected pope on October 28, 1958. Within the first hundred days he had made a number of crucial senior appointments, including appointing as secretary of state, a position that had been vacant since 1944, Cardinal Domenico Tardini. Most significant of all had been his decision to call the Second Vatican Council. That decision was made public on January 25, 1959, eighty-nine days after his election.

Now that Albino Luciani was wearing the shoes of the Fisherman he determined to follow John's example of a revolutionary hundred days. At the top of his list of priorities of reform and change were altering radically the Vatican's relationship with capitalism and alleviating the suffering that had stemmed directly from *Humanae Vitae*.

According to Cardinal Benelli, Cardinal Felici, and other Vatican sources, the austere Villot listened askance as the new pope elaborated on the problems the encyclical had caused. It was clear from his attitude during my interviews with him that on this issue Felici was heavily in sympathy with Villot.

Only a few months earlier, Villot had been extolling the encyclical on the tenth anniversary of its publication. In a letter to Archbishop John Quinn of San Francisco, Villot reaffirmed Paul's opposition to artificial contraception. The secretary of state had stressed how important Paul considered this teaching to be, that it was "according to God's law."

There was much more in a similar vein. And yet now Villot was obliged to listen to Paul's successor taking a reverse position. The coffee grew cold as Luciani rose from his desk and began to pace his study, quietly talking about some of the effects *Humanae Vitae* had produced over the past decade.

The encyclical, which had been designed to strengthen papal authority by denying that there could be any change in the traditional teaching on artificial birth control, had had precisely the opposite effect. The evidence was irrefutable. In Belgium, Holland, Germany, Britain, the United States, and many other countries there had not only been marked opposition to the encyclical but also marked disobedience. The maxim had rapidly become that if one priest did not take a tolerant attitude within the confessional, the sinner shopped around for a more liberated priest. Luciani added that he was well aware that the maxim had applied in the Veneto region.

The theory of *Humanae Vitae* might well look like an ideal moral viewpoint when proclaimed from within the all-male preserve of the Vatican. The reality Luciani had observed in northern Italy and abroad clearly demonstrated the inhumanity of the edict. In the ten years since *Humanae Vitae*, world population had increased by over 750 million.

When Villot pointed out that Pope Paul had stressed the virtues of the natural method of contraception, Luciani merely smiled at him—not the full beaming grin that the public knew, but more of a sad half smile. "Eminence, what can we old celibates really know of the sexual desires of the married?"

This conversation, the first of a number the pope had with his secretary of state on the subject, took place in the pope's study in the papal apartments on Tuesday, September 19. They discussed the subject for nearly forty-five minutes. When the meeting ended and Villot was about to leave, Luciani walked to the door with him and said:

> Eminence, we have been discussing birth control for about forty-five minutes. If the information I have been given, the various statistics, if that information is accurate, then during the period of time we have been talking, over one

thousand children under the age of five have
died of malnutrition. During the next forty-five
minutes while you and I look forward with
anticipation to our next meal a further thousand children will die of malnutrition. By this
time tomorrow thirty thousand children who
at this moment are alive, will be dead—of
malnutrition. God does not always provide.

The secretary of state for the Vatican was apparently unable to find an adequate exit line.

All details of the possible audience with a United
States delegation on the subject of population were
kept a carefully guarded secret both by the Vatican and
the State Department. Such a meeting coming so early
in Luciani's papacy would rightly be seen as highly
significant if it became known publicly.

Even greater significance would have been attached
to this by world opinion if it became known that this
was one of the reasons why Pope John Paul I was not
going to attend the Puebla Conference in Mexico. This
conference was to be the follow-up to an extremely
important conference in Medellín, Colombia, in 1968.

At Medellín, the cardinals, bishops, and priests of
Latin America had injected new life into the Roman
Catholic Church in their part of the world. The "Medellín
Manifesto" included the statement that the central thrust
of their Church in the future would be to reach out and
relate to the poor, the neglected, and the impoverished.
It was a revolutionary change in a Church that had
previously been identified with the rich and the powerful.
The "theology of liberation" that came out of Medellín
put juntas and oppressive regimes on clear notice that
the Church intended to work toward ending financial
exploitation and social injustice. It had, in effect, been a
call to arms. Inevitably, resistance to this liberal philosophy came not only from repressive regimes but also
from the reactionary element within the Church. The
Puebla meeting, a decade later, promised to be crucial.
Would the Church continue farther down the same path,
or would there be a retreat to the old position? For the
new pope to decline the invitation to attend the conference underscores just how much importance he placed

on his meeting with Scheuer's delegation. He certainly knew the implications of the Puebla meeting.

In the conclave, less than an hour after he had been elected pope, Cardinals Baggio and Lorscheider, two key figures in organizing the conference in Mexico, had approached Luciani. Puebla had been postponed as a result of the death of Pope Paul VI. The cardinals were anxious to know if the new pope was prepared to sanction a new date for the Mexico meeting.

Thus Luciani had discussed the Puebla Conference less than an hour after his election. He agreed that the conference should take place, and the dates of October 12 to October 28 were decided on. During his discussion with Baggio and Lorscheider he astonished both cardinals with his knowledge and grasp of the central issues to be explored at Puebla. With regard to his own attendance, he declined to commit himself so early in his papacy.

When Villot advised him that Scheuer's delegation would like an audience on October 24 he told Baggio and Lorscheider that he would not be attending Puebla. He also told Villot to confirm the meeting with the U.S. delegation. In fact, the request had been for Luciani merely the final confirmation that for the next few weeks his place was in the Vatican. There were other very cogent reasons for the decision to stay in Rome. Pope John Paul I had concluded by mid-September that his first priority should be to put his own house in order. The problem of the Vatican Bank and its entire operating philosophy had become of paramount importance to him.

Luciani moved with an urgency that had been noticeably lacking in his predecessor's last years. He was determined that within his first hundred days the Church should at least begin to change direction, particularly with regard to Vatican Incorporated.

Within his first week he had given an indication of the shape of things to come. He "assented" to the desire of Cardinal Villot to be relieved of one of his many posts, the office of president of the pontifical council, "Cor Unum." The job went to Cardinal Bernardin Gantin. Cor Unum is one of the great funnels through which pass monies collected from all over the world to be distributed to the poorest nations.

To Luciani, Cor Unum was a vital element in his philosophy that Vatican finance, like every other factor, should be inspired by the Gospel. Villot was gently replaced, but replaced nonetheless, by Gantin, a man of great spirituality and transparent honesty.

The Vatican village buzzed with speculation and with defensive moves. Some proclaimed that they had never met Sindona or Calvi or any of the Milan Mafia who had infested the Vatican during Pope Paul's reign. Others in their individual bids for survival began to funnel information to the papal apartments.

A few days after the Gantin appointment the new pope found a copy of an Italian Office of Exchange Control (UIC) circular on his desk. There was no doubt that the circular was a direct response to *Il Mondo*'s long, open letter to the pope outlining an untenable situation for a man committed to personal poverty and a poor Church.

The circular, signed by Minister of Foreign Trade Rinaldo Ossola, had been sent to all Italian banks. It reminded them that the IOR, the Vatican Bank, is "to all effects a nonresidential banking institute," in other words, foreign. As such, relationships between the Vatican Bank and Italian credit institutes were governed by precisely the same rules that applied to all other foreign banks.

The minister was particularly concerned with currency abuses involving the illegal flight of money from Italy. His circular was a clear ministerial admission that these abuses were realities. It was seen in Italian financial circles as an attempt to curb at least one of the Vatican Bank's many dubious activities. In Vatican City it was generally regarded as further confirmation of the death knell for Bishop Paul Marcinkus's presidency of the bank.

A story I believe to be apocryphal but that many within the Vatican and within the Italian media believe to be true began to circulate around the Vatican village in early September 1978. According to the story, before the sale of Banca Cattolica del Veneto, Albino Luciani had gone to the Vatican in an attempt to stop the sale from going through. In reality Luciani had the meeting with Benelli after the sale, as recorded earlier in this book. The version that buzzed through the village introduced elegant Italian variations. Luciani had directly confronted Paul VI, who had responded, "Even you must make this sacrifice for the Church. Our finances have still not recovered from the damage caused by Sindona. But do explain your problem to Bishop Marcinkus." A short while later, the story goes, Luciani presented himself in Marcinkus's office and repeated the list of diocesan complaints concerning the bank sale. Marcinkus heard him out, then said, "Your Eminence, have you nothing better to do today? You do your job and I'll do mine." At which point Marcinkus showed Luciani the door.

Any who have seen Marcinkus in action will know that his manners match his nickname of the Gorilla. To the bishops, monsignors, priests, and nuns in Vatican City, the general feeling was that the confrontation had happened. Now out of the blue, the small, quiet man from Belluno could remove Marcinkus at a moment's notice. Members of the Curia organized a lottery. The object was to guess on which day Marcinkus would be formally removed from the bank.

In addition to the investigation being conducted on his behalf by Cardinal Villot, the pope, with his characteristic mountain shrewdness, opened up other lines of inquiry. He began to talk to Cardinal Felici about the Vatican Bank. He also telephoned Cardinal Benelli in Florence.

It was from Giovanni Benelli that the pope learned of the Bank of Italy investigation into Banco Ambrosiano. It was typical of the way the Roman Catholic Church operated. The cardinal in Florence told the pope in Rome what was happening in Milan.

The former number two in the Secretariat of State had built a strong network of contacts throughout the country. Licio Gelli of P2 would have been suitably impressed at the range and the quality of information to which Benelli had access. Benelli's contacts included very well-placed sources within the Bank of Italy. These were the sources that had informed him of the investigation taking place within Roberto Calvi's empire, an investigation that in September 1978 was moving to its climax. What particularly concerned Benelli, and subsequently Luciani, was the part of the investigation that was probing Calvi's links with the Vatican. The Bank of Italy contact was certain that the investigation would be followed by serious criminal charges against Roberto Calvi and possibly against some of his fellow directors. Equally certain was the fact that the Vatican Bank was deeply implicated in a considerable number of deals that broke various Italian laws. The men at the top of the investigating team's list of potential criminals inside the Vatican Bank were Paul Marcinkus, Luigi Menninni, and Pellegrino de Strobel.

Benelli had learned over nearly a decade that one did not influence Luciani by strenuously urging a particular course of action. He told me:

> With Pope Luciani, you laid out the facts, made your own recommendation, then gave him time and space to consider. Having absorbed all the available information, he would decide, and when Pope Luciani decided, nothing, and understand me on this, nothing would move him or shift him. Gentle, yes. Humble, yes. But when committed to a course of action, like a rock.

Benelli was not alone in having access to the thoughts of senior Bank of Italy officials. Members of P2 were feeding precisely the same information to Licio Gelli in Buenos Aires. He in turn was keeping his traveling companions Roberto Calvi and Umberto Ortolani fully briefed.

Other P2 members planted inside Milan's magistrates' offices advised Gelli that when the investigation into Banco Ambrosiano was completed, the papers would be passed to Judge Emilio Alessandrini. A few days after this information became available to Gelli, a left-wing terrorist group based in Milan, Prima Linea, received word from their contact within the magistrates' offices about the man whom the contact recommended as their next potential victim. The terrorist leader pinned a photograph of the target on his apartment wall: Judge Emilio Alessandrini.

In early September Albino Luciani found that in some mysterious way he had been added to the exclusive distribution list of an unusual news agency called *L'Osservatore Politico* (OP). It was run by journalist Mino Pecorelli and invariably carried scandalous stories that subsequently turned out to be highly accurate. Now, along with top politicians, journalists, pundits, and others with a need to know first, the pope read about what OP called "The Great Vatican Lodge." The article gave the names of 121 people who were alleged to be members of Masonic lodges. A number of laymen were included in the list, but it largely comprised cardinals, bishops, and high-ranking prelates. Pecorelli's motives for publishing the list were simple. He was involved in a struggle with his former grand master, Licio Gelli. Pecorelli was a member of P2, a disenchanted member.

He believed that the publication of lists of Vatican Masons would cause the Grand Master of P2 a great deal of embarrassment, especially since many of those on the list were good friends of Gelli and Ortolani.

If the information was authentic, then it meant Luciani was virtually surrounded by Masons. Recall that to be a Mason meant automatic excommunication from the Roman Catholic Church. Before the conclave there had been various murmurings that several of the leading *papabili* were Masons. Now on September 12, the new pope was presented with the entire list. With regard to the issue of Freemasonry, Luciani held the view that it was unthinkable for a priest to become a member. He was aware that a number of the lay Catholics he knew were members of various lodges—in much the same way that he had friends who were Communists. He had learned to live with *that* situation. But for a man of the cloth there was, in Luciani's view, a different criterion. The Roman Catholic Church had decreed long ago that it was implacably opposed to Freemasonry. The new pope was open to discussion on the issue, but a list of 121 men who were confirmed members hardly constituted discussion.

The secretary of state, Cardinal Villot, Masonic name Jeanni, lodge number 041/3, enrolled in a Zurich lodge on August 6, 1966. The foreign minister, Monsignor Agostino Casaroli. The cardinal vicar of Rome, Ugo

Poletti. Cardinal Baggio. Bishop Paul Marcinkus and Monsignor Donato de Bonis of the Vatican Bank. The disconcerted pope read a list that seemed like a Who's Who of Vatican City. Noting with relief that neither Benelli nor Cardinal Felici appeared on the list, which even included Pope Paul's secretary, Monsignor Pasquale Macchi, Albino Luciani promptly telephoned Felici and invited him over for coffee.

Felici advised the pope that a very similar list of names had been passed quietly around the Vatican in May 1976. Its reemergence now was obviously an attempt to influence the new pope's thinking on appointments, promotions, and demotions.

"Is the list genuine?" Luciani asked.

Felici told the pope that in his view it was a clever mix. Some on the list were Masons, others were not. He elaborated. "These lists appear to have emerged from the Lefebvre faction. . . . Not created by our rebel French brother but certainly used by him."

Bishop Lefebvre had been a thorn in the side of the Vatican and particularly of Pope Paul VI for a number of years. A traditionalist who considered the Second Vatican Council to be the ultimate heresy, he had largely ignored its conclusions. He had obtained worldwide notoriety by his insistence that the Mass should be celebrated only in Latin. His right-wing views on a variety of subjects had resulted in his public condemnation by Pope Paul VI. When Pope John Paul I had been elected, Lefebvre's supporters had initially stated that they would refuse to recognize him because the conclave had excluded cardinals over the age of eighty. They had subsequently bemoaned the choice of names as being "ominous."

Luciani considered for a moment. "You say lists like this one have been in existence for over two years?"

"Yes, Holiness."

"Has the press gotten hold of them?"

"Yes, Holiness. Although the full list has never been published; just a name here, a name there."

"And the Vatican's reaction?"

"The normal one. No reaction."

Luciani laughed. He liked Pericle Felici. Curial through and through, traditionalist in his thinking, he was nevertheless a witty, sophisticated man of considerable culture. Luciani now asked him, "Eminence, the revision of canon law that has preoccupied so much of your time, did Pope Paul envisage a change in the Church's position on Freemasonry?"

"There have been over the years various pressure groups. Certain interested parties who urged a more modern view. The Holy Father was still considering the arguments when he died."

Felici went on to indicate that among those who strongly favored a relaxation of the canon rule declaring that any Roman Catholic who became a Freemason was automatically excommunicated was Cardinal Jean Villot.

In the days that followed their discussion the pope took to looking carefully at a number of his visitors. The trouble was that Freemasons looked uncommonly like the rest of the human race. While Luciani considered the unforeseen problem of Freemasonry, several members of the Roman Curia who were strongly sympathetic to Licio Gelli's right-wing view of the world were channeling information out of the Vatican. The information eventually reached its destination, Roberto Calvi.

The news from the Vatican was grim. The Milanese banker was convinced that the pope was seeking revenge for the takeover of Banca Cattolica del Veneto. He could not imagine that Luciani's probe into the Vatican Bank was motivated by anything other than a desire to attack him personally. Calvi recalled the anger among the clergy in Venice and Luciani's protests, the closure of the many diocesan accounts and their transfer to a rival bank. What should he do? A substantial gift to the Vatican, perhaps? A lavish endowment for charitable works? Everything he had learned of Luciani, however, told Calvi that he was dealing with a type of man he had met only rarely in his business, someone who was completely incorruptible.

As the days of September ticked by, Calvi moved around the South American continent—Uruguay, Peru, Argentina. Near him at all times was either Gelli or Ortolani. If Marcinkus fell, a new man would soon discover the state of affairs and the true nature of the relationship between the Vatican Bank and Banco Ambrosiano. Mennini and de Strobel would be removed. The Bank of Italy would be informed, and Roberto Calvi would spend the rest of his life in prison.

He had covered every eventuality, considered every potential danger, closed up every loophole. What he had created was perfect: not *one* theft—not even one *big* theft. His was continuing theft on a scale never before dreamed of. By September 1978 Calvi had already stolen over $400 million. The secret concerns, the foreign associates, the dummy companies—most thieves would feel a sense of triumph at pulling off one bank robbery; Calvi was robbing banks by the dozen. The banks were lining up to be robbed, fighting each other for the privilege of lending money to Banco Ambrosiano.

Now in the midst of this unparalleled success, Calvi had to contend with officials from the Bank of Italy who could not be corrupted and who were every day moving closer to the conclusion of their investigation. Gelli had assured him that the problem could and would be handled, but how could even Gelli, with all his power and influence, handle a pope?

If by some miracle Albino Luciani were to drop dead before Marcinkus was removed, then Calvi would have time. Not much time, of course. But a lot can happen in the period between the death of one pope and the election of another. A lot could happen in the next conclave. Surely it would not produce another pope who wanted to reform Vatican finances? He turned as always to Gelli and confided his worst fears. As they conversed in several South American cities, Roberto Calvi began to feel relieved. Gelli had reassured him. The "problem" could and would be resolved.

Meanwhile, the daily routine within the papal apartments had fallen into a new pattern around Luciani. Maintaining the habit of a lifetime, Luciani rose very early. He had chosen to sleep in the bed used by John XXIII rather than that used by Paul VI. Father Magee had told Luciani that Paul had declined to sleep in John's bed "because of his respect for Pope John." Luciani had responded, "I will sleep in his bed because of my love for him."

Though his bedside alarm clock was set for 5:00 A.M. in case he overslept, the pope would be awakened by a knock on his bedroom door at 4:30 A.M. The knock informed him that Sister Vincenza had left a container of coffee outside. Even this simple act had been subjected to curial interference. In Venice the nun had been accustomed to knock on the door, call out "Good morning," and bring the coffee directly into Luciani's bedroom. The monsignors in the Vatican considered this innocent gesture to be a breach of some imaginary protocol. They remonstrated with a baffled Luciani, who agreed that the coffee could be left in his adjoining study. Luciani's habit of drinking coffee as soon as he woke up stemmed from a sinus operation he had had many years before. As a result of the operation, Luciani would wake up with an unpleasant taste in his mouth. When traveling, if coffee was not available, he would substitute candy.

Having drunk his coffee, he would shave and take a bath. From five to five-thirty he practiced his English with the aid of a cassette course. At five-thirty, Luciani would leave his bedroom and go to the small private chapel nearby. Until 7:00 A.M. he prayed, meditated, and said his breviary.

At seven he would be joined by the other members of the papal household, particularly secretaries Father Lorenzi and Father Magee. Lorenzi, like himself new to the Vatican, had asked the pope if Magee, who had been one of Pope Paul's secretaries, could stay on at his post. The pope, who had been particularly impressed with Father Magee's ability in procuring cups of coffee during the first two days of his papacy, readily agreed. The three men would be joined for Mass by the nuns from the Congregation of Maria Bambina whose duties were to clean and cook for the pope. The nuns, Mother Superior Elena and Sisters Margherita, Assunta, Gabriella, and Clorinda were augmented, at Father Lorenzi's suggestion, by Sister Vincenza from Venice.

Vincenza had worked for Luciani since his Vittorio Veneto days and she knew his ways, his habits. She had accompanied him to Venice and had been the mother superior of the community of four nuns who looked after the patriarch. In 1977 she suffered a heart attack

and had been hospitalized. The doctors told her she
must never engage in active work again, that she should
sit and merely give instructions to the other nuns. Ignoring this advice, she had continued to supervise Sister
Celestina's cooking and fuss over the patriarch, reminding him to take his medicine for his low blood pressure.

For Albino Luciani, Sister Vincenza and Father
Lorenzi represented his only link with his region of
northern Italy, a home he would now see but rarely and
never live in again. It is a sobering thought that when a
man is elected pope he immediately begins to live where
he will, in all probability, die and, in all certainty, be
buried. Premature residence in one's own cemetery.

Breakfast, consisting of *cafe latte*, a roll, and fruit,
followed the Mass. As Vincenza was to tell the other nuns,
feeding Albino Luciani was a considerable challenge.
He was usually oblivious to what he ate, and his appetite was like a canary's. Like many who had known
poverty, he abhorred waste. The leftovers from a special
dinner for guests would be served as one of his meals
the following day.

At breakfast, Luciani would read a variety of Italy's
morning papers. He had the Venice daily *Il Gazzettino*
added to the list. Between 8:00 A.M. and 10:00 A.M. the
pope would work quietly in his study preparing for the
first of his audiences. Between 10:00 A.M. and 12:30 P.M.,
with men such as Monsignor Jacques Martin, the prefect of the pontifical household, attempting to keep people moving in and out on time, the pope met visitors
and conversed with them on the second floor of the
Apostolic Palace.

Martin and other members of the Curia soon discovered that Luciani had a mind of his own. Despite muttered objections, the pope's conversations with his guests
had a habit of running over and throwing the schedule
into confusion. Men such as Monsignor Martin epito-
mize a very prevalent attitude within the Vatican—the
attitude that if it were not for the pope, they could all
get on with their jobs.

A lunch of minestrone or pasta, followed by whatever Vincenza had created for a second course, was
served at 12:30 P.M. Even this was cause for comment.
Pope Paul had always lunched at 1:30 P.M. That such a

trivial event could inspire excited comment within the Vatican is indicative of just how much of a village it is. An even greater cause for comment was the fact that the pope had introduced members of the female sex to his dinner table. Pia, his niece, and his sister-in-law probably made it into the Vatican record books.

Between 1:30 P.M. and 2:00 P.M., Luciani took a short siesta. This would be followed by a walk on the roof garden or in the Vatican gardens. Occasionally he was accompanied by Cardinal Villot; more frequently Luciani read. Apart from his breviary, he read authors as diverse as Mark Twain and Sir Walter Scott. Shortly after 4:00 P.M. he would be back at his office, studying the contents of a large envelope received from Monsignor Martin, containing a list of the following day's visitors with a full briefing.

At 4:30 P.M., while sipping a cup of camomile tea, the pope received in his office "the Tardella"—the various cardinals, archbishops, and secretaries of congregations that together formed his inner cabinet. These were the key meetings ensuring that the nuts and bolts of running the Roman Catholic Church were all in place.

The evening meal was at 7:45 P.M. At 8:00 P.M., while still eating, Luciani would watch the news on television. His dinner companions, unless there were also guests, were Fathers Lorenzi and Magee.

Dinner, like lunch, was an unsophisticated affair. On September 5, for example, Luciani entertained a Venetian priest, Father Mario Ferrarese. Luciani's excuse for inviting the priest to the papal apartments was that he wanted to repay the hospitality that Father Mario had shown him in Venice. The fact that the rich and the powerful of Italy were attempting to get Albino Luciani to their dinner tables was irrelevant; he preferred the company of an ordinary parish priest. That particular meal was served by two members of the papal staff, Guido and Gian Paolo Guzzo. The pope asked his guest for news of Venice, then quietly remarked, "Ask the people there to pray for me because it's not easy being a pope." Turning to the Guzzo brothers, the pope said, "As we have a guest, we must serve him dessert." After some delay bowls of ice cream arrived on the papal table. For others at the table wine was freely available. Luciani was content with mineral water.

After dinner there was further preparation for the audiences of the following day; then with the final part of the daily breviary said, the pope would retire for the night at approximately 9:30 P.M.

This was the daily routine of Pope John Paul I—a routine he took delight in occasionally disturbing. Without consulting anyone, he would go for walks in the Vatican gardens. A simple diversion, one might think, but an impromptu stroll threw Vatican protocol and the Swiss Guard into total confusion. He had already caused consternation among the senior officers of the guard by talking to men on sentry duty and by requesting that they refrain from kneeling at his every approach. He observed to Father Magee, "Who am I that they should kneel to me?"

Monsignor Virgilio Noè, the master of ceremonies, begged him not to talk to the members of the guard and to content himself with a mute nod. The pope asked why. Noè spread his hands wide in amazement. "Holy Father, it is not done. No pope has ever spoken to them."

Albino Luciani smiled and continued to talk to the guards. It was a far cry from the early days of Paul's reign, when priests and nuns would drop to their knees to converse with the pope even when they were carrying on a telephone conversation with him.

Luciani's attitude toward telephones also provoked alarm among many of the curial traditionalists. They now had to contend with a pope who considered himself capable of dialing numbers and answering phones. He phoned friends in Venice. He phoned several mothers superior, just for a chat. When he advised his friend Father Bartolomeo Sorge that he would like the Jesuit priest Father Dezza to hear his confession, Father Dezza phoned within the hour to arrange his visit. The voice on the telephone informed him, "I'm sorry the pope's secretary isn't here at the moment. Can I help?" Father Dezza replied, "Well, to whom am I speaking?"

"The pope."

It simply was not done this way. It never had been and perhaps never will be again. Both of the men who functioned as Luciani's secretaries strenuously deny it ever happened. It was unthinkable. Yet it definitely happened.

Luciani began to explore the Vatican with its 10,000 rooms and halls and its 997 stairways, 30 of which were secret. He would suddenly take off from the papal apartments either alone or with Father Lorenzi for company. Equally suddenly he would appear in one of the curial offices. "Just finding my way around the place," he explained on one occasion to a startled Archbishop Caprio, the deputy head of the Secretariat of State.

They did not like it. They did not like it at all. The Curia was accustomed to a pope who knew his place, one who worked through the bureaucratic channels. This one was everywhere, into everything, and what was worse, he wanted to make changes. The battle over the wretched *sedia gestatoria*, the chair on which previous popes had always been carried during public appearances, began to assume extraordinary proportions. Luciani had banished it to the attic. The traditionalists began a fight to have it brought back. That issues so petty should take up a pope's time is an illuminating comment on the values and perspectives of certain elements in the Roman Curia.

Luciani attempted to reason with men such as Monsignor Noè as one does with a child. Their world was not his, and he was clearly not about to join theirs. He explained to Noè and to others that he walked in public because he felt he was no better than any other man. He detested the chair and what it symbolized. "Ah, but the crowds cannot see you," the Curia said. "They are demanding its return. All should be able to see the Holy Father." Luciani doggedly pointed out that he was frequently on television, that he came to the balcony every Sunday for the *Angelus*. He also said how much he detested the idea of being carried on the backs of other men.

"But Holiness," the Curia said, "if you seek an even deeper humility than you already clearly have, what could be more humiliating than to be carried in this chair which you detest so much?" Faced with this argument, the pope conceded defeat. At his second public audience he was carried into Nervi Hall on the *sedia gestatoria*.

Although some of Luciani's time was taken up by
Curia trivia, most of his waking hours were devoted to
more serious problems. He had told the diplomatic corps
that the Vatican renounced all claims to temporal power.
Notwithstanding, the new pope rapidly discovered that
virtually every major world problem passed through
his in-box. The Roman Catholic Church, with over 18
percent of the world's population owing spiritual allegiance to it, represents a potent force; as such it is
obliged to take a position and have an attitude on a
wide range of problems.

Apart from his attitude toward Argentina's General
Videla, what would be Albino Luciani's response to the
plethora of dictators who presided over large Catholic
populations? What would be his response to the Marcos
clique in the Philippines, with its forty-three million
Catholics? To the dictator Pinochet in Chile, with its
over 80 percent Catholic population? To General Somoza
of Nicaragua, the dictator so much admired by Vatican
financial adviser Michele Sindona? How would Luciani
restore the Roman Catholic Church as a home for the
poor and underprivileged in a country such as Uganda,
where Idi Amin was arranging fatal accidents for priests
as an almost daily event? What would be his response
to the Catholics of El Salvador, where some members of
the ruling junta considered that to be a Catholic was to
be the "enemy"? This, in a country with a 96 percent
Catholic population, promised to be a problem slightly
more serious than the Vatican debate about the pope's
chair.

How would the man who had uttered harsh words
about communism from his pulpit in Venice speak to
the Communist world from St. Peter's balcony? Would
the cardinal who had approved of a "balance of terror"
with regard to nuclear weapons hold to the same position when the world's unilateral disarmers came seeking an audience?

Within his own realm were a multitude of problems inherited from Pope Paul. Various groups were
calling for changes. Many priests were urging the end of
the vow of celibacy. There was pressure to allow women
into the priesthood. There were groups urging reform of
the canon laws covering divorce, abortion, homosexuality,

and a dozen other issues—all reaching up to one man, demanding, pleading, urging.

The new pope very quickly demonstrated, in the words of Monsignor Loris Capovilla, the former secretary of Pope John XXIII, that "there was more in his shop than he put in the window." When the foreign minister, Monsignor Agostino Casaroli, came to the pope with seven questions concerning the Church's relationship with various Eastern European countries, Albino Luciani promptly gave him answers on five of them and asked for a little time to consider the other two.

A dazed Casaroli returned to his office and told a colleague what had occurred. The priest inquired: "Were they the correct solutions?"

"In my view, totally. It would have taken me a year to get those responses from Paul."

Another of the problems tossed into the new pope's lap concerned Ireland and the Church's attitude toward the IRA. Many felt that the Catholic Church had been insufficiently emphatic in its condemnation of the continuing carnage occurring in Northern Ireland. A few weeks before Luciani's election, Irish Archbishop Tomás O'Fiaich had made the headlines with his denunciation of the conditions in Maze prison at Long Kesh. O'Fiaich had visited the prison and later talked of his "shock at the stench and filth in some of the cells, with the remains of rotten food and human excreta spattered around the walls." There was much more in a similar vein. Nowhere in his very long statement, released to the news media with considerable professionalism, did the archbishop acknowledge that these conditions were created by the prisoners themselves.

Ireland was without a cardinal; a great deal of pressure was exerted by a variety of people attempting to influence Luciani. Some elements were for O'Fiaich; others felt his previous promotion to the archdiocese of Armagh had proved an unmitigated disaster.

Albino Luciani returned the dossier on O'Fiaich to his secretary of state with a shake of the head and a one-line epitaph: "I think Ireland deserves better." The search for a cardinal went on.*

*The search ended when Luciani's successor presented O'Fiaich with the cardinal's red hat after all.

In September 1978 the troubles in Lebanon did not
seem to rank particularly high on the list of the world's
major problems. For two years there had been a kind of
peace, interspersed with sporadic fighting between Syr-
ian troops and Lebanese Christians. Long before any
other head of state, the quiet little priest from the Veneto
saw Lebanon as a potential slaughterhouse. He discussed the problem at considerable length with Casaroli
and told him that he wished to visit Beirut before Christmas 1978.

On September 15, one of the men whom Luciani
saw during his morning audiences was Cardinal Gabriel-
Marie Garrone, prefect of the Sacred Congregation for
Catholic Education. This particular audience exemplifies
just how remarkable Luciani's talents were. Garrone had
come to discuss a document called *Sapientia Christiana*,
which dealt with the apostolic constitution and with
the directives and rules governing all Catholic faculties
throughout the world.

Back in the early 1960s, Vatican Council II had
revised the guidelines for seminarians. After two years
of internal discussion the Roman Curia had sent its
proposals to the world's bishops for their recommendations. All the relevant documents had then been submitted to two more curial meetings attended by noncurial
consultants. The results were then examined by at least
six curial departments, and the final document had
been handed to Pope Paul VI in April 1978, sixteen
years after the proposed reforms had first been discussed.
Paul had wanted to issue the document on June 29, the
feast day of St. Peter and St. Paul, but a document with
a gestation period of some sixteen years could not be
rushed so quickly through the Curia's translation section.
By the time they had the document prepared, Pope Paul
was dead.

Any initiative unproclaimed at the time of a pope's
death falls unless his successor approves it. Consequently,
Cardinal Garrone went into his audience with the new
pope with considerable trepidation. Sixteen years of
long, hard work could be tossed in the wastebasket if
Luciani rejected the document. The former seminary
teacher from Belluno told Garrone that he had spent
most of the previous day studying the document. Then,

without even looking at a copy of it, he began to discuss it at length and in great detail. Garrone sat astonished at the pope's grasp and understanding of such a highly complex document. At the end of the audience, Luciani told him that the document had his approval and that it was to be published on December 15.

Like Casaroli, Baggio, Lorscheider, and a number of other men, Garrone left his discussion with Luciani in complete awe. Returning to his office, he chanced to meet Monsignor Scalzotto of Propaganda Fide and remarked: "I have just met a great pope."

The "great pope" meanwhile continued to work his way through the mountain of problems left by Paul. One such was Cardinal John Cody, head of one of the world's wealthiest and most powerful archdioceses, Chicago.

For a cardinal, any cardinal, to be considered a major problem by the Vatican was unusual, but then Cody was a very unusual man. The allegations made about Cardinal Cody in the ten years before Luciani's papacy began were extraordinary. If even 5 percent of them were true, then Cody had no business being a priest, let alone cardinal of Chicago.

Before his promotion to the Chicago archdiocese in 1965 he had run the diocese of New Orleans. Many of the priests who attempted to work with him in New Orleans still have the scars to prove it. One recalled: "When that son-of-a-bitch was given Chicago, we threw a party and sang the *Te Deum* [a hymn of thanksgiving]. As far as we were concerned, our gain was Chicago's loss."

When I discussed the cardinal's subsequent career in Chicago with Father Andrew Greeley, a noted Catholic sociologist, author, and long a critic of Cody, I observed that another Chicago priest had compared Cardinal Cody with Captain Queeg, the paranoid, despotic naval captain in *The Caine Mutiny*. Father Greeley's response was: "I think that's unfair to Captain Queeg."

In the years that followed Cardinal Cody's appointment to Chicago it became fashionable in the Windy City to compare him with Mayor Richard Daley, a man whose practices in running the city were democratic only by accident. There was one basic difference. Every four years Daley was, at least in theory, answerable to the electorate. If they could overcome his political machine, they could vote him out of office. Cody had not been elected. Short of very dramatic action from Rome, he was there for life. Cody was fond of observing: "I am answerable to no one except Rome and God." Events were to prove that Cody declined to be answerable to Rome. That left God.

When Cody arrived in Chicago he had the reputation of being an excellent manager of finances, a progressive liberal who had battled long and hard for school integration in New Orleans, and a very demanding prelate. He soon lost the first two attributes. In early June 1970, while treasurer of the American Church he put $2 million into Penn Central stocks. A few days later the shares collapsed and the company went bankrupt. He had illegally invested the money during the administration of his duly elected successor, to whom Cody refused to hand over the account books until well after the loss. He survived the scandal.

Within weeks of his arrival in Chicago, he had demonstrated his own particular brand of progressive liberalism toward some of his priests. In the files of his predecessor, Cardinal Albert Meyer, he discovered a list of "problem" priests, men who were alcoholic, senile, or unable to cope. Cody began to make Sunday afternoon excursions to their rectories. He then personally dismissed the priests, giving them two weeks to leave their homes. There were no pension funds, no retirement schemes, no insurance policies for priests in Chicago in the mid-1960s. Many of these men were over seventy. Cody simply tossed them out into the street.

He began arbitrarily to move priests from one part of the city to another. He took similar action with regard to closing convents, rectories, and schools. On one occasion, by order of Cody, a wrecking crew began to demolish a rectory and a convent while the occupants were showering and having breakfast.

Cody apparently suffered from a profound inability to recognize the Second Vatican Council as a fact of life. At the council there had been endless talk of power-sharing, of a collegial style of decision-making. The news never reached the cardinal's mansion.

Among the clergy in Chicago, the battle lines began to be drawn between factions for and against Cody. Meanwhile, the majority of the 2.4 million Catholics in the diocese were wondering what was going on.

The priests formed a trade union of sorts, the Association of Chicago Priests (ACP). Cody basically ignored their requests. Letters asking for meetings were not answered. Phone calls found the cardinal constantly "unavailable." Some priests stayed on to continue the fight for a more democratically run Church. Many left. In a decade, one third of Chicago's clergy left the priesthood. Despite this evidence that something was very wrong, Cardinal Cody continued to insist that his opponents were "merely the highly vocal minority."

The cardinal also attacked the local media, claiming that they were hostile. In fact, the Chicago media were extraordinarily fair and tolerant during most of Cody's reign.

The man who fought for integration in New Orleans became known in Chicago as the man who closed Catholic schools in the inner city, claiming that the Church could no longer afford to run them; this in a diocese with an annual revenue approaching $300 million.

Like much else that Cody did, many of the school closures went into effect without anyone having been consulted, including the school boards. When the cry of "racist" went up, Cody defended himself by stating that many of the blacks were non-Catholics and that he did not feel the Church had a duty to educate middle-class black Protestants. But the label of racism was a hard one for him to throw off.

As the years passed, the charges and allegations against Cody increased tenfold. His conflict with large sections of his own clergy grew bitter. His paranoia blossomed.

He began to tell tales of how he had been employed on secret espionage work for the U.S. government. He spoke of his contributions to the FBI. He told priests that he had also undertaken special assignments on behalf of the CIA, which included flying into Saigon.

The details were always vague, but if Cody was telling the truth, he had been involved in secret activities on behalf of the government since the early 1940s. It would seem that John Patrick Cody, the son of a St. Louis fireman, had lived many lives.

The reputation for financial astuteness which he had brought to Chicago, a reputation that had suffered somewhat after the $2 million Penn Central debacle, took a further knock when some of Cody's opponents began to dig into his earlier, highly colorful career. In between his real or imaginary flights over enemy territories he had unwittingly succeeded in bringing some of the Church to a state of poverty, though not quite in the manner envisioned by Albino Luciani. Cody had left the diocese of Kansas City $30 million in debt. He had performed the same feat in New Orleans, which gave added significance to the *Te Deum* of thanks when he departed. At least he left a permanent memento of his stay in Kansas City, having spent substantial amounts of money to gild the dome of the downtown cathedral.

In Chicago he began to monitor the day-by-day movements of priests and nuns he suspected of disloyalty. Dossiers were assembled. Secret interrogations of friends of "suspects" became the norm. What all of this had to do with the Gospel of Christ is unclear.

When some of the activities described above led the Chicago clergy to complain to Rome, Pope Paul VI worried and agonized.

It seems abundantly clear that the most senior member of the Roman Catholic Church in Chicago had demonstrated by the early 1970s that he was unfit to preside over the diocese; yet the pope, with a strange sense of priorities, hesitated. Cody's peace of mind seemed to weigh more heavily than the fate of 2.4 million Catholics.

One of the most extraordinary aspects of the Cody affair is that the man controlled—apparently entirely on his own, without consulting anyone—the entire revenue of the Catholic Church in Chicago. A sane, highly intelligent man would have problems efficiently managing an annual sum of between $250 and $300 million. That it should be placed in the hands of a man like Cody defies explanation.

The total assets of the Roman Catholic Church in

Chicago were by 1970 over $1 billion. Because of Cardinal Cody's refusal to publish an annual certified account, priests in various parts of the city took to holding back sums of money, which in happier days would have been destined for control by the cardinal. Eventually, in 1971, six years after his despotic rule had begun, Cody deigned to publish what passed for a set of annual accounts. They were a curious affair. They did not reveal real-estate investments. They did not include portfolio investments. With regard to revenue from cemeteries they did give, at last, some evidence of life after death. The movement of the profit was very lively. Six months before the figures had been published, Cody had confided to an aide that the figure was $50 million. When the accounts were made public, this had dropped to $36 million. Perhaps for a man who could simultaneously be in Rome, Saigon, the White House, the Vatican, and the cardinal's mansion in Chicago, misplacing some $14 million of cemetery revenue was child's play.

There were $60 million of parish funds on deposit with the Chicago chancery. Cody declined to tell anyone where the money was invested or who was benefiting from the interest.

One of the cardinal's most notable personal assets was the large number of influential friends he assiduously acquired within the power structure of the Church. His prewar days in the Roman Curia, working initially in North American College in Rome and subsequently in the Secretariat of State, reaped rich dividends in times of need. Cody was from a very early age a man of single-minded ambition. Ingratiating himself with Pius XII and the future Paul VI, he established a formidable power base in Rome.

The Vatican's Chicago connection was by the early 1970s one of its most important links with the United States. The bulk of Vatican Incorporated's investment in the U.S. stock market was tunneled through Continental Illinois. On the board of the bank along with David Kennedy, a close friend of Michele Sindona, was a Jesuit priest, Raymond C. Baumhart. The large amounts of money that Cody funneled to Rome became an important factor in Vatican fiscal policy. Cody might not be able to handle his priests, but he did know how to make a buck. When the bishop controlling the diocese of Reno made some "unfortunate investments" and its finances totally collapsed, the Vatican asked Cody to bail him out. Cody telephoned his banking friends and the money was quickly found.

Over the years the Cody-Marcinkus friendship became particularly close. They had so much in common, so many vested interests. In Chicago, with its very large Polish population unwittingly aiding him, Cody began to divert hundreds of thousands of dollars via Continental Illinois to Marcinkus in the Vatican Bank. Marcinkus would then divert the money to the cardinals in Poland.

The cardinal took out further insurance by spreading Chicago's wealth around certain sections of the Roman Curia. When Cody was in town—and he made over one hundred trips to Rome—he distributed expensive presents wherever they would do him the most good. A gold cigarette lighter to this monsignor, a Patek Philippe watch to that bishop.

Complaints continued to flood into Rome even faster than Cody's expensive gifts. In the Sacred Congregation for the Doctrine of Faith, which acts as the Vatican's policeman on matters of doctrinal orthodoxy and clerical morality, the pile of letters grew. They came not only from priests and nuns in Chicago but also from men and women in many walks of life. Archbishop Jean Hamer, O.P., in charge of the Sacred Congregation, pondered the problem. Moving against a priest is a relatively easy matter. After due investigation, the congregation would merely put pressure on the relevant bishop, requesting that the priest be removed from the area of contention. But on whom do you put pressure when the man you want to move is a cardinal?

The Association of Chicago Priests publicly condemned Cody and stated that he had been lying to it. Eventually it passed a vote of censure on him. Despite this, Rome remained silent.

By early 1976, Archbishop Hamer was not the only senior member of the Roman Curia who knew the problems the Chicago connection was causing. Cardinals Benelli and Baggio had independently and then jointly decided that Cody must be replaced.

After long consultation with Pope Paul VI a plan

was developed. In the spring of 1976, when Cody made one of his many trips to Rome, Benelli offered him a post in the Roman Curia. He would have a wonderful title but absolutely no power. It was known that Cody was ambitious and that he believed he had the talent to climb higher than controlling Chicago. What the cardinal had in mind was to become pope. It is indicative of Cody's arrogance that having caused such mayhem in Chicago he could seriously think he had a chance of becoming pope. With this ambition in mind, he would have been happy to exchange Chicago for control of one of the Curia congregations that gave out money to needy dioceses throughout the world. Cody reasoned that he could buy enough bishops' votes to place himself on the throne of Rome when the opportunity arose. Benelli was aware of this, hence the job offer; but it was not the job Cody was seeking. He declined. Another solution was needed.

In January 1976, a few months before the Benelli-Cody confrontation, a delegation of priests and nuns from Chicago visited Jean Jadot, the apostolic delegate in Washington. Jadot had told them that Rome had the situation in hand. As the year progressed without any resolution, the battle in Chicago recommenced. Cody's public image was by now so bad that he hired a public-relations firm, at the Church's expense, in an attempt to obtain favorable media coverage.

The irate priests and nuns began to complain again to Jadot in Washington. He counseled patience. "Rome will find the solution," he promised. "You must stop this public attack. Let the issue calm down. Then Rome will handle the problem, quietly and discreetly."

The clergy understood. The public criticism abated, only to be provoked to new heights by Cody himself when he decided to close the aforementioned inner-city schools. Baggio seized this issue in yet another attempt to persuade Pope Paul VI to act decisively. The pope's concept of decisiveness was to write a stiff letter to Cody asking for an explanation of the school closures. Cody ignored the letter and boasted openly that he had ignored it.

In the face of the Vatican's inactivity, the letters from Chicago continued. Among them were new allega-

tions supported by depositions, affidavits, and financial
records. There was evidence indicating that Cody's behavior in yet another area left something to be desired.
These allegations concerned his friendship with a woman
named Helen Dolan Wilson.

Cody had told his staff in the chancery that Helen
Wilson was a relative. The exact nature of the relationship varied; usually he described her as a cousin. To
explain her very stylish mode of life, which included
fashionable clothes, frequent traveling, and a very expensive apartment, the cardinal let it be known that his
cousin had been left very "well fixed" by her late
husband. According to the allegations made to Rome,
Cody and Helen Wilson were not related; her husband,
whom she had divorced long ago, was still very much
alive at a time when Cody already had him in the next
world; and when he finally did die, in May 1969, he left
no will, and his only possession was an eight-year-old
car worth $150, which went to his second wife.

These allegations, made in the strictest confidence
to the Vatican, continued with proof that Cody's friendship with Helen Wilson had begun years ago, that he
had taken out a $100,000 life-insurance policy with Helen
Wilson as the beneficiary, and that the records of the
work she had done at the Chicago chancery had been
falsified by Cody to enable her to obtain a larger pension.
The pension was based on twenty-four years of work for
the archdiocese, which was demonstrably false. Evidence was also produced that showed that Cody gave
his woman friend $90,000 to enable her to buy a house
in Florida. The Vatican was reminded that Helen Wilson had accompanied Cody to Rome when he was made
cardinal. It is true that many other people had accompanied Cody. Unlike Helen Wilson, however, they did not
have the run of the Chicago chancery or decide on the
furnishings and fabrics for the cardinal's residence. It
was also alleged that Cody had diverted hundreds of
thousands of dollars of Church funds to this woman.

As if this were not enough, the allegations went on
to itemize the large amounts of diocesan insurance business that had gone to Helen's son David. David Wilson
had first benefited from "Uncle" John's largesse back in
St. Louis in 1963. As the cardinal had moved, so had the

insurance business. It was alleged that the commissions David Wilson had earned by monopolizing Church insurance business that Cody controlled were over $150,000.

Baggio carefully studied the long, detailed list. Inquiries were made. The Vatican is unrivaled in the business of espionage: consider how many priests and nuns there are in the world, each one owing allegiance to Rome. The answers came back to Cardinal Baggio, indicating that the allegations were accurate. It was now late June 1978.

In July 1978 Baggio again discussed the problem of Cody with Pope Paul VI, who eventually accepted that Cody should be replaced. Paul insisted, however, that it must be done with compassion, in a manner that would enable Cody to retain face. Above all, it must be done in a way that would minimize any possible scandalous publicity. It was agreed that Cody was to be told he must accept a coadjutor—a bishop who would for all practical purposes run the diocese. Officially it would be announced that this change was due to Cody's health, which in fact was not good. Cody would be permitted to stay on as titular head of the Chicago archdiocese until he reached the retirement age of seventy-five in 1982.

Armed with the papal edict, Cardinal Baggio quickly made his travel arrangements, packed his suitcase, and departed for the airport. At the airport, he was advised that the pope wished to speak to him before he flew to Chicago.

Paul had danced yet again, backward. He told Baggio that the plan for a coadjutor to strip Cody of power could proceed only if Cody agreed.

Dismayed, Baggio pleaded with the pope: "But Holy Father, may I not insist?"

"No, no, you must not order him. The plan is to go forward only if His Eminence agrees."

A very angry and frustrated Cardinal Baggio flew to Chicago.

Spy networks are a two-way conduit for information, and Cardinal Cody had his own sources within the Roman Curia. The element of surprise that Baggio had hoped would catch Cody off balance had, unknown to Baggio, been lost within a day of his crucial meeting with the pope. Cody was ready and waiting.

Most men in Cody's position would subject themselves to a little self-examination, a consideration, perhaps, of events over the years that had led this most sensitive of popes to the agonizing conclusion that the power Cody wielded must, in the interests of all, be handed to another. Ever considerate of the feelings of the man he wished to replace, the pope had arranged matters so that Baggio's stopover in Chicago would be a secret. Officially, he was flying direct to Mexico to finalize arrangements for the Puebla Conference. Such gestures were entirely lost on Cardinal Cody.

The confrontation took place at the cardinal's residence on the grounds of the seminary at Mundelein College. Baggio laid out the evidence. He established that in making gifts of money to Helen Wilson, the cardinal had intermingled money he was entitled to dispose of with Church funds. In addition, the pension he had awarded his friend was improper. The Vatican investigation had clearly established a wide variety of indiscretions that would bring the Roman Catholic Church into disrepute if they became public knowledge.

Cody was far from contrite as the confrontation rapidly developed into a shouting match. He began to rant about his massive contributions to Rome; about the vast amounts of money he had poured into the Vatican Bank to be used in Poland; about the gifts of money he had bestowed on the pope during his *ad limina* visits (periodic, obligatory visits to report on the diocese)—not the pitiful few thousand dollars that others brought but hundreds of thousands of dollars. The two princes of the Church could be heard shouting at each other all over the seminary grounds. Cody was adamant. Another bishop would come in and run his archdiocese "over my dead body." Eventually, like a broken record, Cody would only repeat a single phrase: "I will not relinquish power in Chicago."

Baggio departed in defeat. A defiant Cody who refused to accept a coadjutor was in total breach of canon law, but for it to become public knowledge that the cardinal of one of the most powerful archdioceses in the world was openly defying the pope was, for Pope Paul, unthinkable. The pope would tolerate Cody to the end of his days rather than face the alternative. His days of toleration were few, however. Within one week of receiving Baggio's report the pope was dead.

By mid-September, Albino Luciani had studied the Cody file in depth. He met Cardinal Baggio and discussed it. He went over the implications of the Cody affair with Villot, Benelli, Felici, and Casaroli. On September 23 he had another long meeting with Cardinal Baggio. At the end of it he told Baggio that he would notify him of his decision within the next few days.

In Chicago, for the first time in his long, turbulent history, Cardinal Cody began to feel vulnerable. After the conclave he had privately been dismissive of this quiet Italian who had followed Paul. "It's going to be more of the same," Cody had declared to one of his close curial friends. More of the same was what Cody wanted; it would enable him to go on ruling the roost in Chicago. Now the news from Rome indicated that he had seriously underrated Luciani. As September 1978 drew to an end, John Cody became convinced that Luciani would act where Paul had not. Cody's friends in Rome advised him that whatever course of action this new pope decided on, one thing was certain: he would see it through. They cited many examples from Luciani's life that indicated his unusual inner strength.

On Luciani's desk in his study was one of the few personal possessions he treasured. A photograph. Originally it had been contained within a battered old frame. During his time in Venice a grateful parishioner had had the photograph remounted in a new silver frame with semiprecious jewels. The photograph showed his parents against a background of the snow-covered Dolomites. In his mother's arms was the baby Pia, now a married woman with her own children. During September 1978 his secretaries observed the pope on a number of occasions lost in thought as he studied the photograph. It was a reminder of happier times, when such men as Cody, Marcinkus, Calvi, and the others did not disturb his tranquillity. There had been time for silence and small things then. Now it seemed to Luciani that there was never enough time for such important facets of his life. He was cut off from Canale and even from his family. There were the occasional telephone

conversations, with Edoardo, with Pia, but the impromptu visits were now gone forever. The Vatican machine saw to that.

Even Diego Lorenzi attempted to turn Pia away
when she telephoned. She had wanted to bring him
some little presents, reminders of the North. "Leave
them at the gate," Lorenzi said, "the pope is too busy to
see you." Overhearing this conversation, Luciani took
the telephone and told Pia, "Come and see me. I haven't
got time, but come all the same."

They lunched together. Uncle Albino was in excellent health and good spirits. As the meal progressed he
commented on his new role: "Had I known I was going
to become pope one day, I would have studied more."
Then in a superb understatement he remarked, "It's
very hard being pope."

Pia saw just how hard the job could be—made
harder by the inflexibility of the ever-watchful Curia.
Luciani wanted to treat Rome as his new parish, to
wander through the streets as he had in Venice and his
other dioceses. For a head of state to behave in such a
manner presented problems. The Curia flatly declared
the idea not only unthinkable but also unworkable. The
city would be thrown into constant chaos if the holy
father went out on walks. Luciani abandoned the idea
but only for a modified version. He told the Vatican
officials that he wished to visit every hospital, church,
and refuge center in Rome and gradually work his way
around what he regarded as his parish. For a man bent
on being a pastoral pope the reality on his own door-
step presented a powerful challenge.

Rome has a Catholic population of 2½ million. It
should have been producing at least seventy new priests
per year. When Luciani became pope it was producing
six a year. The religious life of Rome was being maintained by enormous importations of clergy from outside.
In many parts of the city church attendance had fallen
to less than 3 percent of the population. Here, in the
heart of the Faith, cynicism abounded.

The city that was now home to Luciani was also
home to a Communist mayor, Carlo Argan—a Communist mayor in a city whose major industry, religion, is
rivaled only by the crime rate. One of the new titles

Luciani had acquired was Bishop of Rome. Before that, the city had been without a bishop, in the sense that Milan, Venice, Florence, and Naples had a bishop, for over a century. It showed.

As Pia lunched with the pope, Don Diego was involved in a loud, lengthy argument with a curial official who refused even to consider the papal wish to visit various parts of Rome. Luciani interrupted his conversation with Pia.

"Don Diego. Tell him it must be done. Tell him the pope wishes it."

Lorenzi conveyed the papal instruction, only to be met with a refusal. He turned to the pope. "They say it can't be done, Holy Father, because it's never been done before."

Pia sat, fascinated, as the game of Vatican tennis continued. Eventually Luciani apologized to his niece for the interruption and told his secretary he would instruct Villot. Smiling at Pia, he observed, "If the Roman Curia permits, your uncle hopes to visit Lebanon before Christmas." He talked at length about that troubled country and his desire to intercede before the powder keg exploded.

After lunch, as she was leaving, he insisted on giving her a medal presented to him by the mother of the president of Mexico. A few days later, on September 15, his brother Edoardo came for dinner. These two family meetings were destined to be the last Albino Luciani would have.

As the papacy of Albino Luciani progressed, the gulf between the pope and the professional Vatican-watchers increased, in direct proportion to the growing closeness between the pope and the general public. The bewilderment of the professionals was understandable.

Confronted with a noncurial cardinal who apparently lacked an international reputation, the experts had concluded that they were observing the first of a new breed of pope, a man deliberately selected to ensure that there would be a reduction of power, a less significant role for the papacy. There can be little doubt that Luciani felt that his papacy should be less royal. And yet the very essence of Albino Luciani, his personality, intellect, and extraordinary gifts, meant that the general public promptly gave the new pope a position of greater importance, held what he had to say as being of deeper significance. The public reaction to Luciani clearly demonstrated a desire for an enlarged papal role, exactly the reverse of that intended by many cardinals. The more Luciani was self-dismissive, the more exalted he became for the faithful.

Many who had not known Luciani well were profoundly surprised by what they considered to be the change in the man. In Venice, Vittorio Veneto, Belluno, and Canale there was no surprise. This was the real Luciani. The simplicity, the sense of humor, the stress on catechism—these were integral elements within the man.

On September 26, Luciani could look back with satisfaction on his first month in the new job. He had been able to initiate some of the changes he hoped to make. His investigations into corrupt and dishonest practices had thrown the perpetrators into deep fear. His impatience with curial pomposity had caused outrage. Again and again he had abandoned officially written speeches, publicly complaining, "This is too curial in style" or "this is far too unctuous."

His verbatim words were rarely recorded by Vatican Radio or *L'Osservatore Romano*, but the other news media heard them and so did the public. Borrowing a phrase from Saint Gregory, the pope observed that in electing him, "The emperor has wanted a monkey to become a lion." Lips tightened within the Vatican as mouths parted in smiles among the public. Here was a "monkey" who during the course of his first month spoke to them in Latin, Italian, French, English, German, and Spanish.

On September 7, during a private audience, his friend Vittore Branca expressed concern about the weight of the papacy. Luciani responded:

Yes, certainly I am too small for great things. I can only repeat the truth and the call of the Gospel as I did in my little church at home. Basically men need this, and I am the keeper of souls above all. Between the parish priest at Canale and me there is a difference only in the number of faithful, but the task is the same, to remember Christ and his word.

Later the same day he met with all the priests of Rome. He spoke to them of the need for meditation in words that have a deeply poignant significance when one considers how little time and space a new pope has for meditation.

> I was touched at the Milan station to see a porter sleeping blissfully with his head on a bag of coal and his back against a pillar. Trains were whistling as they left and their wheels were screeching as they arrived. Loudspeakers constantly interrupted. People came and went noisily. But he, sleeping on, seemed to say, "Do what you must but I need some peace." We priests must do the same. Around us there is continual movement. People talking, newspapers, radio, and TV. With the discipline and moderation of priests we must say, "Beyond certain limits you do not exist for me. I am a priest of the Lord. I must have a little silence for my soul. I distance myself from you to be with my God for a while."

Although his speeches in general audiences on successive Wednesdays were recorded (he spoke on faith, hope, and charity), Luciani's pleas that these virtues be shown toward, for example, drug addicts went unreported by the Curia, which controlled the Vatican media. When on September 20 he uttered the memorable phrase that it is wrong to believe *Ubi Lenin ibi Jerusalem* (where Lenin is, there is Jerusalem), the Curia announced that the pope was rejecting "liberation theology." He was not. Further, Vatican Radio and *L'Osservatore Romano* neglected to record Luciani's important qualification that between the Church and religious salvation, and the world and human salvation, "There is some coincidence but we cannot make a perfect equation."

By Saturday, September 23, Luciani's investigation into Vatican Incorporated was well advanced. Villot,

Benelli, and others had provided him with reports that
he had had a chance to review. That day he left the
Vatican for the first time, to take possession of his
cathedral as bishop of Rome. He shook hands with
Mayor Argan and they exchanged speeches. After the
Mass that followed, with the majority of the Curia
present, the pope touched several times on the inner
problems with which he was grappling. Referring to the
poor, that section of society closest to his heart, he
remarked:

> These, the Roman deacon Lawrence said, are
> the true treasures of the Church. They must be
> helped, however, by those who can, to have
> more and to be more, without becoming humili-
> ated and offended by ostentatious riches, by
> money squandered on futile things and not
> invested, insofar as is possible, in enterprises of
> advantage to all.

Later in the same speech he turned and, looking
directly at the gentlemen of the Vatican Bank gathered
together, he began to talk of the difficulties of guiding
and governing:

> Although for twenty years I have been bishop
> of Vittorio Veneto and Venice, I admit that I
> have not yet learned the job well. In Rome I
> shall put myself in the school of Saint Gregory
> the Great, who writes, "[the pastor] should,
> with compassion, be close to each one who is
> subject to him: forgetful of his rank he should
> consider himself on a level with the good
> subjects, but he should not fear to exercise the
> rights of his authority against the wicked. . . ."

Without a knowledge of events within the Vatican,
the members of the public merely nodded wisely. The
Curia knew precisely to what the pope was alluding.
This was in Vatican style an elegant, oblique pronouncement of events to come.

Changes were in the air, and within the Vatican

village there was frenetic speculation. Bishop Marcinkus and at least two of his closest associates, Mennini and de Strobel, were going. That was known for a fact. The speculation concerned other possible changes.

When on Sunday, September 24, a private visitor to the papal apartments was identified by one sharp-eyed monsignor as Lino Marconato, excitement within the village reached new heights. Marconato was a director of Banco San Marco. Did his presence in the papal apartments indicate that a successor to Banco Ambrosiano had been found already?

In fact the meeting dealt with far less exotic banking matters. Banco San Marco had been made the official bank of the diocese in Venice by Luciani after he had angrily closed all accounts at Banca Cattolica del Veneto. Now Luciani needed to clear up his personal accounts at San Marco, knowing he would never return to live in Venice. Marconato found his soon-to-be former client in the best of health. They chatted happily about Venice as Luciani gave instructions that the money in his patriarch's account be passed on to his successor.

The preoccupation with the forthcoming changes was intense. In many cities. For many people.

Another with a direct vested interest in what Luciani might be about to do was Michele Sindona. Sindona's four-year battle to avoid extradition to Italy was moving to a climax in September 1978. Earlier that year, during May, a federal judge had ruled that the Sicilian who had become a citizen of Switzerland should now be returned to Milan to face the highly expensive music he had orchestrated. He had been sentenced to 3½ years *in absentia*, but Sindona was fully aware that *that* sentence would seem lenient when the Italian courts had finished with him. In the United States, despite the federal investigation, he still remained free of any charges. The Franklin National collapse had been followed by a number of arrests, but as of September 1978 the Shark himself remained untouched. His major problem at that time was in Italy.

Sindona's million-dollar battery of lawyers had persuaded the courts to withhold the extradition order until the United States prosecutors had proved that there was well-founded evidence against Sindona with regard to the charges he faced in Milan

Since the ruling in May, the prosecutors had been working hard to obtain that evidence. Sindona, with assistance from the Mafia and his P2 colleagues, had been working equally hard to make that evidence disappear. As September 1978 drew to a close, Sindona still had a number of outstanding problems.

The first was the evidence given at the extradition proceedings by a witness named Nicola Biase, a former employee of Sindona. Deeming his evidence to be dangerous, Sindona set about to make it "safe." After he had discussed the problem with the Mafia Gambino family, a small contract was put out. It was to be nothing particularly sinister: Biase, his wife, family, and lawyer were to have their lives threatened. If they succumbed to the threats and Biase withdrew his evidence, the matter would rest there. If Biase refused to cooperate with the Mafia, then the Gambino family and Sindona planned to "review" the situation. This review would not augur well for the continued good health of Biase. The contract for less than $1,000 would be amended to a more appropriate figure. The contract was given to Luigi Ronsisvalle and Bruce McDowall. Ronsisvalle is by profession a hired killer.

Another contract was also discussed with Ronsisvalle. The Mafia informed him that Michele Sindona required the death of Assistant U.S. District Attorney John Kenney.

Nothing so clearly illustrates the mentality of Michele Sindona as the act of putting out a contract on John Kenney. Kenney was the chief prosecutor in the extradition hearings, the man leading the U.S. government's attack on Sindona's continued presence within the United States. Sindona reasoned that if Kenney were eliminated, the problem would disappear. Kenney's death would serve as a warning to the government that he, Michele Sindona, was objecting to the heat. The investigation would then cease. There would be no more irritating court appearances, no more absurd attempts to get him sent back to Italy. The thought processes at work here are 100 percent Sicilian Mafia. It is a philosophy that works again and again in Italy. It is an essential part of the Italian Solution. The authorities can be cowed, and are. Investigators replacing a murdered colleague will move very slowly. Sindona reasoned that what was effective in Palermo would work in New York.

Luigi Ronsisvalle, although a professional murderer, was unwilling to accept the contract. The fee of $100,000 looked good, but Ronsisvalle, with a deeper appreciation of the American way of life than Sindona, did not foresee having much opportunity to spend it. If Kenney were murdered there would be waves, big ones. Ronsisvalle began to look for someone, on behalf of the Gambino family, who might feel more optimistic than he about the odds for survival after killing an assistant U.S. district attorney.

Sindona and his associates then turned to the next problem, Carlo Bordoni, former business associate and close friend of Sindona. Bordoni was facing a number of charges stemming from the collapse of the Franklin National, and Sindona was aware that he could give lethal testimony against the Shark as part of a deal to reduce his own punishment. It was decided that the treatment about to be given to Nicola Biase should be extended to Carlo Bordoni.

But the more serious problems lay in Italy, particularly within the Vatican. If Marcinkus fell, then Calvi would go. If Calvi went, then Sindona would be pulled down with him. The four-year fight to avoid extradition would be over. Might a man who believed he could solve his problems in the United States by murdering an assistant U.S. district attorney feel that the major threat facing him in Italy could be eliminated by the death of a pope?

Sindona, Calvi, Marcinkus, and Cody: by September 28, 1978, each of these men stood to lose much if Albino Luciani were to decide on certain specific courses of action. Others who stood to be directly affected were P2 leaders Licio Gelli and Umberto Ortolani: Calvi was the lodge's paymaster general and they could not afford to lose him. By September 28, another name was added to the growing list of people who could be seriously affected by actions Luciani might soon take. The new name was that of Cardinal Jean Villot, the pope's secretary of state.

On September 28, after a light breakfast of coffee, a

croissant, and some rolls, Luciani was at his desk before 8:00 A.M. There was much to be done.

The first problem he tackled was *L'Osservatore Romano*. During the previous month, he had been given cause to complain about the paper on numerous occasions. After the battle had been won about the use of the royal "we" and "our," which the paper had initially insisted on substituting for the pope's use of the humbler first person, each day's edition had produced further irritations for the pope. The paper had adhered rigidly to the Curia-written speeches and ignored his own personal comments. It even complained when Italian journalists had accurately reported what the pope had said rather than what *L'Osservatore Romano* deemed he should have said. Now there were new problems of a far more serious nature.

A number of curial cardinals had to their horror discovered a reply that Albino Luciani had made shortly before the conclave when asked for his opinion on the recent birth of Louise Brown, known as "the first test-tube baby." Although Luciani had been interviewed on the subject three days before the death of Pope Paul VI, the article had not appeared in the Rome newspaper *Prospettive nel Mondo* until after his election. The hard-liners on artificial birth control read with growing dismay the views of the man who was now pope.

Luciani had begun cautiously, making it clear that what he was expressing were his own personal views, because he, like everyone else, "waited to hear what the authentic teaching of the Church would be when the experts had been consulted." His surprise election had, of course, produced a situation where the authentic teaching of the Church on this as on any other subject was now totally within his own province.

In the interview Luciani expressed qualified enthusiasm about the birth. He indicated concern about the possibility of "baby factories," a prophetic concern in view of current events in California, where women are lining up to be impregnated with the sperm of Nobel Prize winners.

Speaking of the child and her parents, Luciani said:

Following the example of God, who desires and loves human life, I too send my best wishes to the baby. As for her parents, I have no right to condemn them; subjectively, if they acted with good intentions and in good faith, they may even have great merit before God for what they have decided and asked the doctors to do.

He went on to draw attention to a pronouncement by Pius XII that might put the act of artificial fertilization in conflict with the Church. Then, considering the view that every individual has the right to choose for himself or herself, he expressed an opinion that lay at the heart of his attitude toward many moral problems. "As for the individual conscience, I agree, it must always be followed, whether it commands or forbids; the individual, though, must seek always to develop a well-formed conscience."

The element within the Vatican who believed that the only well-formed conscience is one formed exclusively by them began to mutter. Discreet meetings were held. It was clear to those who attended these meetings that Luciani had to be stopped. They talked airily of "the betrayal of Paul," which was in essence an elegant way of saying, "I disagree."

When news of the cautious dialogue between the Secretariat of State's office and the U.S. State Department began to leak to this group, they determined on action. The subsequent information that a delegation of officials concerned with artificial birth control had been granted an audience with the pope gave an added sense of urgency to those within the Vatican who felt that *Humanae Vitae* should remain the last word on this subject.

On September 27, there appeared on the front page of *L'Osservatore Romano* a long article entitled "*Humanae Vitae* and Catholic Morality." It was written by Cardinal Luigi Ciappi, O.P., theologian to the papal household. Cardinal Ciappi had been personal theologian to Pius XII and Paul VI. Coming from such an authority, the article would appear to carry the personal imprimatur of the new pope. It had previously been published in *Laterano* to celebrate the tenth anniversary of *Humanae Vitae*. Its republication was a deliberate attempt to forestall any change on the issue of artificial birth control that Albino Luciani might wish to make.

The article in essence extols the virtues of *Humanae Vitae*. There are copious quotations from Paul VI, but from Luciani not a single word affirming he shared either Paul's or Ciappi's views. The reason for that is simple. Ciappi had not discussed the article with Luciani. Indeed, as of September 27, 1978, Cardinal Ciappi was still awaiting a private audience with the new pope.

The first Luciani knew of the article and the views it contained was when he read the front page of the paper on September 27. With rising anger he turned to page two to continue reading. There he was confronted with yet another of the Curia's efforts to undermine his position. Running over three entire columns was another article, entitled "The Risk of Manipulation in the Creation of Life." This was a blunt, dogmatic condemnation of the birth of test-tube baby Louise Brown and of all artificial fertilization.

Again, there had been no reference to Luciani. It was not necessary. The Curia knew full well that for all the *L'Osservatore Romano* claims to be only semiofficial, such an article would be clearly seen by the world as representing the views of the new pope. The battle was on.

On September 28, therefore, shortly after 8:00 A.M., the pope telephoned Villot and demanded a full explanation of how the two articles had appeared; then he phoned Cardinal Felici in Padua, where he was about to attend a spiritual retreat.

Luciani had taken to using Felici more and more as a sounding board for his ideas. Aware that their views on a wide range of subjects differed, Luciani was equally aware that Felici would respond with total honesty. He also realized that, as dean of the Sacred College, Felici knew his way through the machinations of the Curia better than most.

Luciani expressed his anger at the two articles. "You recall some days ago advising me that the Curia wished me to restrain my natural exuberance?"

"It was merely a suggestion, Holiness."

"Perhaps you would be kind enough to return the compliment on my behalf. Tell that little newspaper to restrain its views on such issues. Editors are like popes. Neither is indispensable."

Luciani now moved on to the next problem: the Dutch Church. Five of the seven Dutch bishops held moderate positions on the issues of abortion, homosexuality, and the employment of married priests. The five included Cardinal Willebrands, the man who had offered words of comfort to Luciani during the conclave. The five were opposed by two extremely conservative bishops, Gijsens of Roermond and Simonis of Rotterdam. A synod in Holland scheduled for November promised to be the battle arena that would expose the deep divisions to the Dutch public. There was a further problem, which was covered in a detailed report that had been submitted to the late pope, Paul VI.

Among the Dutch problems was the world-famous theologian and Dominican professor, Edward Schillebeeckx. His ideas, like those of his Swiss contemporary, Hans Küng, were considered by the conservatives to be radical and dangerous. Although the feared index of banned and prohibited books had been abolished by Paul VI, his death had left unresolved the problem of how the Church would control its forward thinkers. In the past Luciani had borrowed a phrase from Küng to condemn "sniper theologians," but men such as Küng and Schillebeeckx were not sniping. Rather, they articulated a deep desire to return the Church to its origins, something of which Albino Luciani wholeheartedly approved. At a few minutes to ten, Luciani placed the report to one side and immersed himself in one of the happier aspects of his job—a series of audiences.

First to be received was a group that included the man whom Luciani had promoted to the presidency of Cor Unum, Cardinal Bernardin Gantin. The pope beamed at the strong, youthful figure of Gantin, who for him represented the Church's future. During their conversation, Luciani remarked, "It is only Jesus Christ whom we must present to the world. Apart from this we would have no reason, no purpose, we would never be listened to."

Also in this first group was Henri de Riedmatten. When the news had flown around Rome shortly after the conclave that Luciani had written to Pope Paul before *Humanae Vitae*, urging him not to reaffirm the ban on artificial contraception, it had been Riedmatten who called such a report "a total fantasy." His discussion with the pope on September 28 concerned his work as secretary of Cor Unum, but Luciani gave Riedmatten a clear warning against any further "denials."

"I understand that my report on birth control passed you by?"

Riedmatten mumbled something about possible confusion.

"One should take care, Father Riedmatten, not to speak publicly until all confusion has cleared. Should you need a copy of my report I'm sure it can be found for you."

Riedmatten thanked the pope profusely. Thereafter Riedmatten maintained a wise silence while Luciani discussed the problems of Lebanon with Cardinal Gantin. Luciani advised Gantin that the previous day he had discussed his projected visit to Lebanon with Patriarch Hakim, whose Greek Melkite rite dioceses covered not only invaded Lebanon but invading Syria as well.

Also received in audience that morning was a group of bishops from the Philippines who were making their *ad limina* visit. Confronted with men who had to contend with the day-to-day reality of President Marcos, Luciani talked to them on a subject very close to his heart: evangelization. Aware of the difficulties facing these men if he spoke out directly against Marcos, the pope chose instead to make his points by stressing the importance of evangelization. He reminded them of Pope Paul's trip to the Philippines:

> At a moment when he chose to speak about the poor, about justice and peace, about human rights, about economic and social liberation, at a moment when he also effectively committed the Church to the alleviation of misery, he did not and could not remain silent about the "higher good," the fullness of life in the kingdom of Heaven.

The message was clearly understood, not only by the bishops but subsequently also by the Marcos family.

After the morning audiences Luciani had a meeting with Cardinal Baggio. Luciani had arrived at a number of decisions and was now about to impart two of them to Baggio.

The first was the problem of Cardinal John Cody of Chicago. After weighing every consideration Luciani had decided that Cody must be removed. It was to be done in a classic Vatican manner, he hoped without undue publicity. He told Baggio that Cody was to be given the opportunity to resign because of ill health. There should be little adverse press comment about this because Cody's health was indeed far from good. If Cody declined to resign, rather than suffer the uproar of publicly removing him against his will, a coadjutor was to be appointed. Another bishop would be brought in to take over all effective power and to run the diocese. Luciani felt sure that faced with the alternative, Cody would choose to go with dignity. If he insisted on staying, then so be it. He would be relieved of all responsibility. Luciani was crystal clear on all of this. There was to be no asking, no request. A coadjutor would be appointed.

Baggio was delighted; finally the situation had been resolved. He was less than pleased with the next decision at which Luciani had arrived. Venice was without a patriarch. Baggio was offered the job.

Many men would have felt honored at such an offer. Baggio was not; he was angry. He saw his future in the short term as dominating the Puebla Conference in Mexico. He believed that the Church's future lay in the Third World. In the long term he saw his place in Rome, at the heart of the action. In Venice he would be out of sight and, more important, out of mind when it came to formulating future plans. He turned down the offer point-blank.

Baggio's refusal astonished Luciani. Obedience to the pope and to the papacy had been instilled into Luciani from his earliest days in the seminary at Feltre, and the obedience that he had acquired had been of an unquestioning nature. Through the years, as his career had progressed, he had begun to question, most notably over the issues of Vatican Incorporated and *Humanae Vitae*, but it would have been unthinkable for Luciani to express his opposition publicly, even on issues as important as these. This was the man who at Paul's request had written article after article that supported the papal line, who, when writing such an article on divorce gave it to his secretary, Father Mario Senigaglia, with the wry comment, "This will bring me many headaches I am sure, when it is published, but the pope has requested it." To refuse a direct request from the pope in the arrogant way Baggio was now doing was beyond belief. The two men were functioning with two quite different sets of values. Luciani was considering what was best for the Roman Catholic Church. Baggio was considering what was best for Baggio.

There were several reasons why the pope had concluded that Baggio should move from Rome to Venice. Not least of these was one particular name on the list of Masons that Luciani had received—Baggio, Masonic name Seba, lodge number 85/2640; enrolled on August 14, 1957.

Luciani had made further inquiries after his conversation with Cardinal Felici. A remark of Felici's had nagged away at him. "Some on the list are Masons. Others are not." Luciani's problem was to distinguish the genuine from the false. The inquiries had helped by producing some clarifications.

The meeting between Baggio and Luciani has been described to me as "a very violent argument, with the violence and anger entirely deriving from His Eminence. The Holy Father remained calm."

Calm or otherwise, Luciani had an unresolved problem at lunchtime. Venice was still without a leader, and Baggio was insisting his place was in Rome. A thoughtful Luciani began his soup.

The Indian summer that Rome had been enjoying throughout the month gave way to cooler weather on that Thursday. After a short siesta Luciani decided to confine his exercise for the day to indoor walking. He began to stroll alone through the corridors. At 3:30 P.M. the pope returned to his study and made a number of telephone calls. He talked to Cardinal Felici in Padua and to Cardinal Benelli in Florence. He discussed the events of the morning, including the Baggio confrontation, and then went on to talk about his next appointment, which was with Villot. The various decisions Luciani had arrived at were about to be given to the secretary of state.

Luciani and Villot sat sipping their camomile tea. In an attempt to get closer to his secretary of state, the pope had from time to time during their numerous meetings spoken to Villot in his native French. It was a gesture the cardinal from St. Amant-Tallende appreciated. He had been deeply impressed at how quickly Luciani had settled into the papacy. The word had gone out from the Secretariat of State's office to a number of Luciani's friends and former colleagues. Monsignor Da Rif, still working at Vittorio Veneto, was one of many to be given a progress report:

> From Cardinal Villot down they all admired Papa Luciani's way of working. His ability to get to the root of problems, to make decisions quickly and firmly. They were very struck with his ability to carry out his tasks. It was clear that he was a man who made decisions and stuck to them. He did not give way to pressure. In my own personal experience this ability to stick to his own line was a very remarkable feature of Albino Luciani.

During the late afternoon of September 28 Jean Villot was given an extended demonstration of this ability that had so impressed him during the previous month. The first problem to be discussed was the Istituto per le Opere di Religione, the Vatican Bank. By now Luciani had a great deal of highly detailed information. Villot himself had submitted a preliminary report. Luciani had also obtained further information from Villot's deputy, Archbishop Giuseppe Caprio, and from Benelli and Felici.

Villot advised the pope that inevitably word of the investigation would leak and that the Italian press was already becoming very curious. Furthermore, a major story had just been published in America. *Newsweek* magazine clearly had some excellent Vatican sources. It had learned that before the conclave a considerable number of cardinals had requested a full report on the Vatican Bank from Villot. It had also, through its "knowledgeable source," picked up the fact that there were moves afoot to oust Marcinkus. The magazine quoted its curial source: "There's some movement to get him out of there. He'll probably be made an auxiliary bishop."

Luciani smiled. "Does *Newsweek* tell me with whom I am replacing Marcinkus?"

Villot shook his head.

As their conversation progressed, Luciani made it clear that he had no intention of leaving Marcinkus in Vatican City, let alone the Vatican Bank. Having personally assessed the man during a forty-five-minute interview earlier in the month, Luciani had concluded that Marcinkus might be more gainfully employed as an auxiliary bishop in Chicago. He had not indicated his thinking to Marcinkus, but the cool politeness he had shown had not gone unnoticed.

Returning to his bank offices after the interview, Marcinkus had confided to a friend, "I may not be around here much longer." To Calvi via the telephone and to his colleagues in the bank he now observed: "You would do well to remember that this pope has different ideas from the last one. There are going to be changes around here. Big changes."

Marcinkus was right. Luciani advised Villot that Marcinkus was to be removed immediately. Not in a week's or a month's time. The following day. He was to take a leave of absence. A suitable post in Chicago would be found for him once the problem of Cardinal Cody had been resolved.

Villot was told that Marcinkus was to be replaced by Monsignor Giovanni Angelo Abbo, secretary of the Prefecture of Economic Affairs of the Holy See. As a key figure in the financial tribunal of the Vatican, Monsignor Abbo would bring to his new job a great deal of financial expertise.

The inspiration of Pope John's first hundred days had clearly galvanized Albino Luciani. The claws of the lion that those who knew him had waited to see revealed were now on full display to Villot. Luciani, a man so unassuming and gentle, had, before his papacy, seemed much smaller than his five feet, nine inches. Because of his calm and quiet manner his presence had often gone unnoticed in large gatherings. Now Villot was left in no doubt of his presence. Luciani told him:

There are other changes within the Istituto per le Opere di Religione that I want to see implemented immediately. Mennini, de Strobel, and Monsignor de Bonis are to be removed. At once. De Bonis is to be replaced by Monsignor Antonetti. The other two vacancies I will discuss with Monsignor Abbo. I want all of our links with the Banco Ambrosiano group to be cut, and the cut must happen in the very near future. It will be impossible, in my view, to effect this step with the present people holding the reins.

In speaking to me about Luciani, Father Magee made the following general observation: "He knew what he wanted. He was very clear indeed about what he wanted. The manner in which he went about his aims was very delicate."

This "delicacy" was evident in Luciani's explanation to Villot. Both men knew that Marcinkus, Mennini, de Strobel, and de Bonis were all closely linked not only to Calvi but also to Sindona. What was not said could not be misquoted at a later date.

Cardinal Villot noted these changes without much comment. He had been aware of a great deal over the years. Many within the Vatican considered him ineffectual, but for Villot it had often been a case of deliberately looking the other way. In the Vatican village it was a survival technique.

Luciani moved to the problem of Chicago and his discussion with Baggio concerning the ultimatum that was to be given to Cardinal John Cody. Villot voiced approval. Like Baggio he regarded Cody as a running sore in the American Church. That the problem was finally to be resolved gave him deep gratification. Luciani stated that he wanted inquiries to be made through the papal nuncio in Washington about a possible successor to Cody. He was concerned that the choice be a good one: "There has been a betrayal of trust in Chicago. We must ensure that whoever replaces His Eminence has the ability to win the hearts and minds of all within the diocese."

Luciani discussed Baggio's refusal to accept the see of Venice and his own determination that Baggio should accept the offer. "Venice is not a tranquil bed of roses. It needs a man of Baggio's strength. I want you to talk with him. Tell him that we all have to make some sacrifice at this time. Perhaps you should remind him that I had no desire for *this* job." The argument would have limited value for Baggio, who himself had earnestly desired to be Paul's successor, but Villot diplomatically neglected to make this point.

Luciani then advised Villot of the other changes he planned to make. Cardinal Pericle Felici was to become vicar of Rome, replacing Cardinal Ugo Poletti, who would replace Benelli as archbishop of Florence. Benelli was to become secretary of state. He would take over Villot's own job.

Villot considered the proposed changes that included *his* "resignation." He was old and tired. Furthermore, he was seriously ill, an illness not helped by the two packs of cigarettes he smoked daily. In late August Villot had made it plain that he sought early retirement. Now it had come somewhat sooner than he had bargained for. There would be a transition period, of course, but for all intents and purposes his days of wielding power were now over. The fact that Luciani proposed to replace him with Benelli must have been particularly troubling to Villot. Benelli had been his number two in the past, and it had not been the happiest of relationships.

Villot studied the notes he had made of the proposed changes. Albino Luciani put his own notes to the side and poured some more tea for both of them. Villot said, "I thought you were considering Casaroli as my replacement."

"I did, for a considerable time. I think much of his work is brilliant, but I share Giovanni Benelli's reservations about some of the policy initiatives that have been made in the recent past toward Eastern Europe."

Luciani waited for some sign or word of encouragement. The silence grew longer. Never in the course of their relationship had Villot dropped his formality. Luciani had tried directly, and also through Felici and Benelli, to inject some warmth into his dealings with Villot, but his cold, professional aloofness remained. Eventually it was Luciani who broke the silence, "Well, Eminence?"

"You are the pope. You are free to decide."

"Yes, yes, but what do you think?"

Villot shrugged. "These decisions will please some and distress others. There are cardinals within the Roman Curia who worked hard to get you elected who will feel betrayed. They will consider these changes, these appointments contrary to the late Holy Father's wishes."

Luciani smiled. "Was the late Holy Father planning to make appointments in perpetuity? As for the cardinals who claim to have worked hard to make me pope—understand this—I have said it many times, but clearly it needs to be said yet again. I did not seek to become pope. I did not want to be pope. You cannot name one single cardinal to whom I proposed anything. Not one whom I persuaded in any form to vote for me. It was not my wish. It was not my doing. There are men here within Vatican City who have forgotten their purpose. They have reduced this to just another marketplace. That is why I am making these changes."

"It will be said that you have betrayed Paul."

"It will also be said that I have betrayed John. Betrayed Pius. Each will find his own guiding light according to his needs. My concern is that I do not betray our Lord, Jesus Christ."

The discussion continued for nearly two hours. At 7:30 P.M. Villot departed. He went back to his own offices nearby and, sitting at his desk, studied the list of changes. Then, reaching into a drawer, he pulled out another list—perhaps it was just coincidence. Each of the clerical personnel Luciani was removing was on the list of alleged Masons, the list that the disenchanted P2 member Pecorelli had published. Marcinkus. Villot. Poletti. Baggio. De Bonis. Each of the clerical replacements Luciani had so far nominated was absent from the list. Benelli. Felici. Abbo. Antonetti.

Cardinal Villot put the list aside and studied an other note on his desk. It was the final confirmation that the proposed meeting between Scheuer's group and Albino Luciani would take place on October 24. An American group that wanted to see a change in the Church's position on the Pill would in a few weeks be meeting with a pope who also wanted to make such a change. Villot rose from his desk, leaving the various papers carelessly in view. The lion had indeed revealed his claws.

At seven-thirty, immediately after his meeting with Villot, Albino Luciani had asked Father Diego Lorenzi to contact Cardinal Colombo in Milan. A few minutes later Lorenzi informed him that Colombo would not be available until about eight forty-five. While Lorenzi returned to his desk, the pope was joined by Father Magee. Together they recited the final part of the daily breviary in English. At ten minutes to eight Luciani sat down to dinner with Magee and Lorenzi and conversed with them amiably, totally unruffled by his long session with Villot. Sisters Vincenza and Assunta served a dinner of clear soup, veal, fresh beans, and salad. Luciani sipped a little from a glass of water while Lorenzi and Magee drank red wine.

Father Lorenzi was suddenly struck by the thought that Luciani's papacy must already have passed the shortest on record. He was about to voice this thought when the pope began to fuss with his new watch. It had been given to him by Paul's secretary, Monsignor Macchi, after Felici had told the pope that some of the Curia considered his old watch inadequate. Their concern was, as usual, with image. In such a manner did the Curia seek to reduce the pope to a used-car salesman who took care that his pants were always neatly pressed. The last time Luciani had seen his brother Edoardo he had offered him the old watch with the words, "Apparently the pope is not allowed to wear an old battered watch that needs to be constantly wound. Will you be offended if I give it to you?"

When the television news began, Luciani passed the new watch to Magee to reset. It was now one minute before eight.

Shortly after this pleasant, uneventful dinner, the pope went back to his study to look over the notes he had used during his discussions with Villot. At 8:45 P.M. Lorenzi connected him with Cardinal Colombo in Milan. They discussed the changes Luciani intended to make. Of the phone conversation, Cardinal Colombo has said, "He spoke to me for a long time in a completely normal tone from which no physical illness could be inferred. He was full of serenity and hope. His final greeting was 'Pray.'"

Lorenzi noted that the phone call finished at about 9:15 P.M. Luciani then glanced over the speech he planned to make to the Jesuits on September 30. Earlier he had telephoned the superior general of the Jesuits, Father Pedro Arrupe, and warned him that he would have a few things to say about discipline. He now underlined a part of the speech that was not without relevance to the changes he had made that day:

You may well know and justly concern your-selves with the great economic and social prob-lems that trouble humanity today and are so closely connected with the Christian life. But in finding a solution to these problems may you always distinguish the tasks of religious priests from those of the laymen. Priests must animate and inspire the laity to fulfill their duties, but they must not take their place, neglecting their own specific task of evangelization.

Putting the speech down, he again picked up the notes on the dramatic changes he had discussed with Villot. Luciani walked to the door of his study and opening it saw Father Magee and Father Lorenzi. He said good night to them both: *"Buona notte. A domani. Se Dio vuole."* ("Good night. Until tomorrow. If God wishes.")

It was a few minutes before 9:30 P.M. Albino Luciani closed his study door. He had spoken his last words. His dead body would be discovered the following morning. The circumstances surrounding that discovery make it abundantly clear that the Vatican perpetrated a cover-up. The Vatican began with a lie and then developed a tissue of lies. It lied about little things. It lied about big things. All of the lies had but one purpose: to suppress the fact that Albino Luciani, Pope John Paul I, was murdered sometime between 9:30 P.M. on September 28 and 4:30 A.M. on September 29, 1978.

Albino Luciani was the first pope to die alone for over one hundred years, but then it has been a great deal longer since a pope was murdered.

Cody. Marcinkus. Villot. Calvi. Gelli. Sindona. At least one of these men had decided on a course of action that was implemented during the late evening of the twenty-eighth or the early morning of the twenty-ninth. That course of action was derived from the conclusion that the Italian Solution must be applied. The pope must die.

WE ARE LEFT
FRIGHTENED

How and why did darkness fall on the Catholic Church on September 29, 1978?

The possible answers to "why" have already been established. There were many with motives. The "how" also has an alarming number of possibilities.

If Albino Luciani was murdered for any of the reasons discussed, then a number of factors had to apply.

1. The murder would have to be achieved by stealth. If the corruption that existed prior to Luciani's election were to continue, the act of murder had to be masked. There could be no dramatic shooting of the pope in the middle of St. Peter's Square. No public attack that would inevitably give rise to a full inquiry into why and how this quiet, holy man had been eliminated. The sudden death would have to be achieved in such a way that public questions and anxiety would be kept to a minimum.

2. The most efficient way to kill the pope was by poison—by a drug that when administered would leave no telltale signs. Research indicates that there are over two hundred such drugs. The drug digitalis is one example. It has no taste. No smell. It can be added to food, drink, or medication. It acts in such a way that the victim does not discover that he has taken a fatal dose.

3. Whoever planned to murder the pope in such a way would have to have an intimate knowledge of Vatican procedures. They would have to know that there would be no autopsy. Confident of that one fact, they could use any of the more than two hundred drugs available. On conducting an external examination of the body the Vatican doctors would simply conclude that death had been caused by a heart attack.

The conspirators, then, would have been fully aware that there was nothing within the apostolic laws requiring that an autopsy be carried out. Furthermore, they would have known that even if suspicions were aroused at the highest levels within the Vatican, it would be virtually certain that Vatican officials and examining doctors would content themselves with a cursory examination of the body. Given this knowledge, the conspirators could have confidently administered a drug such as digitalis to an unsuspecting Luciani in the late evening. In keeping with his routine, the pope would retire to his room for the night. He would go to bed—this time to his final sleep. Death would occur from two to six hours after consumption of the fatal dose. The pope kept beside his bed, on the small table with his battered alarm clock, a bottle of Effortil, a liquid medicine that he had been taking for some years to alleviate low blood pressure. A fatal dose of digitalis, half a teaspoonful, would be undetectable if added to the medicine.

The only other medicines the pope was taking were vitamin pills, which he took three times a day with his meals, and a series of injections for the adrenal cortex, drugs to stimulate the gland that secretes adrenaline. Again these were taken to alleviate low blood pressure. This series of injections was given twice a year, in the spring and in the autumn. The drugs used varied. One that was frequently used was Cortiplex. The injections were administered by Sister Vincenza. Luciani was now in the process of taking a series, hence the need for Vincenza in the papal apartments. The drugs used for the injections, like the Effortil by the bedside, could easily have been tampered with. No special precautions were taken in storing them. Access to these drugs would not have presented any problem to a person with murder in mind. Indeed, as will be demonstrated, access to any part of the papal apartments presented no problem to anyone determined to end the life of Albino Luciani.

At 4:30 A.M. Friday, September 29, Sister Vincenza carried a container of coffee to the study as usual. A few moments later she knocked on the pope's bedroom door and called out, "Good morning, Holy Father." For once there was no reply. Vincenza waited for a moment, then padded away quietly. At 4:45 A.M. she returned. The tray of coffee in the study was untouched. She had worked for Luciani since 1959 in Vittorio Veneto. Not once in eighteen years had he overslept. Anxiously she moved to the bedroom door and listened. There was no sound. She knocked on the door, timidly at first, then with greater force. Still nothing but silence. There was a light shining from under the door. She knocked again. Still there was no answer. Opening the door she saw Albino Luciani sitting up in bed. He was wearing his glasses, and gripped in his hands were some sheets of paper. His head was turned to the right, and the lips were parted, showing his teeth. It was not the smiling face that had so impressed the millions but an expression of agony. She felt his pulse. Recently she recounted that moment to me.

"It was a miracle that I survived, I have a bad heart. I pushed the bell to summon the secretaries, then I went out to find the other sisters and to awaken Don Diego."

The sisters resided on the far side of the papal apartments. Father Magee slept upstairs in the attic area. Father Lorenzi was temporarily installed near the pope's bedroom while his own room in the attic area, previously occupied by Paul's secretary, Monsignor Macchi, was being redecorated. Lorenzi was shaken out of his sleep by Sister Vincenza.

A number of early-rising Romans had already noted with quiet satisfaction the light shining from the pope's bedroom. It was good to know you were not the only one up at such an early hour. The light had remained unnoticed throughout the night by Vatican security guards.

A half-dazed Diego Lorenzi stared in shock at the lifeless body of Albino Luciani. Next to respond was Father Magee. For the second time within two months he looked on a dead pope, but under very different circumstances. When Paul VI had died on August 6, many were gathered around the deathbed in Castel Gandolfo, the papal summer residence just outside Rome. Medical bulletins gave a highly detailed account of the last twenty-four hours of Paul's life and an equally detailed account of the sequence of physical ailments that led to his death at 9:40 P.M.

Now, after a mere thirty-three days as pope, Albino Luciani had died alone. Cause of death? Time of death?

After one of the shortest conclaves in history had come one of the shortest reigns. It had been nearly four hundred years since a pope had died so soon after his election. To find a briefer papacy it is necessary to go back to 1605, when the Medici Leo XI served for seventeen days.

Father Magee's first action was to telephone Secretary of State Villot, residing two floors below. Less than twelve hours earlier, Albino Luciani had told Villot of his impending replacement by Benelli. Now, far from being a former secretary of state, Villot assumed the role of *camerlengo*, virtually the acting head of the Church. By 5:00 A.M. Villot was in the pope's bedroom and had seen for himself that Albino Luciani was dead.

If Luciani died naturally, Villot's actions and instructions are completely inexplicable. His behavior becomes understandable only when related to one specific conclusion: Either Cardinal Jean Villot was part of a conspiracy to murder the pope, or he saw clear evidence in the papal bedroom indicating the pope had been murdered, and he promptly determined that to protect the Church that evidence must be destroyed.

On the small bedside table was the medicine that Luciani had been taking for low blood pressure. Villot pocketed the medicine. From the dead pope's hands he took the notes on the papal transfers and appointments. These he pocketed as well. The pope's last will, which had been in the desk in his study, was removed. His glasses and slippers disappeared from the bedroom. None of these items has ever been seen again.

Villot then created for the shocked members of the pope's household a totally fictitious account of the circumstances leading to the finding of Luciani's body. He imposed a vow of silence concerning Sister Vincenza's discovery and instructed the household that news of the death was to be suppressed until he indicated otherwise. Then, sitting down in the pope's study, he began to make a series of telephone calls.

Based on the eyewitness accounts of people I have interviewed, the medicine, the glasses, the slippers, and the pope's will were all in the bedroom and the papal study before Villot entered the rooms. After his initial visit all the items had vanished.

News of the death was given to Cardinal Confalonieri, the eighty-six-year-old dean of the Sacred College. Then to Monsignor Casaroli, head of Vatican diplomacy. Villot instructed the nuns on the switchboard to locate Archbishop Giuseppe Caprio, his deputy and the number three man in the Church hierarchy, who was presently vacationing in Montecatini. Only then did he telephone Dr. Renato Buzzonetti, deputy head of the Vatican's health service. Next he phoned the Swiss Guard. Speaking to Sergeant Hans Roggan, Villot told him to come immediately to the papal apartments.

Father Diego Lorenzi, the only man to have accompanied Luciani from Venice, wandered shocked and bewildered through the apartments. He had lost a man who over the past two years had been a second father to him. In tears he attempted to understand, to find some meaning. When Villot eventually decided that the world could know, millions would share Lorenzi's grief and bewilderment.

Despite Villot's stricture that the news not leak out, Lorenzi telephoned Antonio Da Ros, who had been Luciani's physician for over twenty years. Lorenzi vividly remembers the doctor's reaction. "He was shocked. Stunned. Unable to believe it. He asked me the cause, but I didn't know. Doctor Da Ros was equally mystified. He said he would drive to Venice immediately and catch a plane to Rome."

Lorenzi's next phone call was to Luciani's niece Pia, who was probably closer to her uncle than any other member of the family. Diego Lorenzi appears to have been the only member of the Church to appreciate the fact that even popes have relatives. Lorenzi naturally felt that the family should get a personal phone call rather than hearing the news on the radio.

"We found him this morning. You need a great faith now." Many were going to be in need of a great faith. Many were going to have to suspend disbelief to swallow what Villot and his colleagues would say within the next few days.

The news was now starting to spread through the Vatican village. In the courtyard near the Vatican Bank, Sergeant Roggan met Bishop Paul Marcinkus. It was 6:45 A.M. What the president of the Vatican Bank, who lives in the Villa Stritch on Via della Nocetta in Rome and is not known as an early riser, was doing in the Vatican at that time of the morning remains a mystery. The Villa Stritch is a twenty-minute drive from the Vatican. Roggan blurted out the news: "The pope is dead." Marcinkus just stared at the sergeant of the Swiss Guard. Roggan moved closer to Marcinkus. "Papa Luciani. He's dead. They found him in his bed."

Marcinkus continued to stare at Roggan, without displaying any reaction. Eventually Roggan moved on, leaving Paul Marcinkus staring after him.

Some days later, during the pope's funeral, Marcinkus offered Roggan an explanation for his strange behavior. "Sorry, I thought you had gone mad."

Dr. Buzzonetti made a brief examination of the body. He informed Villot that the cause of death was acute myocardial infarction, a heart attack. The doctor set the time of death at about 11:00 P.M.

To establish that the time of death was 11:00 P.M. and the cause myocardial infarction on the basis of such a brief external examination is a medical impossibility.

Villot had already decided before Buzzonetti's examination, which took place at approximately 6:00 A.M., that the body of Albino Luciani should be immediately embalmed. Even before his phone call to Cardinal Confalonieri at 5:15 A.M., Villot had acted to ensure a rapid embalmment. The Signoracci brothers Ernesto and Renato had embalmed the last two popes. Now a dawn telephone call and a Vatican car that arrived at 5:00 A.M. were the beginning of what was to prove a long day for the Signoracci brothers. For them to have been contacted so early clearly establishes that the Vatican gave the relevant instructions to the Institute of Medicine, which employs the brothers, at some point between 4:45 and 5:00 A.M.

At 7:00 A.M., more than two hours after his body had been discovered by Sister Vincenza, the world at large still remained ignorant of the fact that Pope John Paul I was dead. The Vatican village, meanwhile, was totally ignoring Villot's edict. Cardinal Benelli in Florence heard the news by telephone at 6:30 A.M. Grief-stricken and openly crying, he immediately retired to his room and began to pray. All the hopes, dreams, aspirations were shattered. The plans Luciani had made, the changes, the new direction—all had come to nothing. When a pope dies, all decisions yet to be publicly announced die with him. *Unless his successor decides to carry them through.*

By 7:20 A.M. the bells in the parish church in Albino Luciani's birthplace, Canale D'Agordo, were tolling. Vatican Radio remained silent on the death. Finally at 7:27 A.M., some 2¾ hours after the death had been discovered by Sister Vincenza, Cardinal Villot felt sufficiently in control of events:

> This morning, September 29, 1978, about five-thirty, the private secretary of the pope, contrary to custom not having found the holy father in the chapel of his private apartment, looked for him in his room and found him dead in bed with the light on, like one who was intent on reading. The physician, Dr. Renato Buzzonetti, who hastened to the pope's room, verified the death, which took place presumably toward eleven o'clock yesterday evening, as "sudden death that could be related to acute myocardial infarction."

Later bulletins stated that the secretary in question was Father Magee, who according to the Vatican usually said Mass with the pope at 5:30 A.M., and that when he died the pope had been reading *The Imitation of Christ*, the fifteenth-century work usually attributed to Thomas a Kempis.

Along with the medicine, the papal notes, the will, the glasses, and the slippers, the fact of Sister Vincenza's discovery of the body at 4:45 A.M. had also vanished. Even with 2¾ hours in which to concoct a story, Villot and those who advised him had botched up the job. While every newspaper and radio and television station in the free world was carrying stories based on the Vatican bulletins, Villot was having difficulties making his story stick. The difficulties centered around *The Imitation of Christ*.

This embellishment, involving as it did a book that Luciani revered, might have seemed like inspired thinking to Villot. The problem was that there was not a copy in the pope's bedroom or for that matter in the entire papal apartments. Luciani's copy was still in Venice. A few days earlier when he had wanted to quote accurately from the book, he had sent Lorenzi to borrow a copy from his Vatican confessor. This copy had been returned before the pope's death. Now Lorenzi's complaints about an obvious fabrication could not be stilled. The Vatican finally dropped this particular lie, after having maintained it until October 2—for four days. Within those first four days the false information given out by the Vatican had become, in the minds of the people, the reality, the truth.

And people were deceived by other false information that came out of the Vatican. There was, for example, the tale of Father John Magee going to the pope's bedroom shortly before 10:00 P.M. on the twenty-eighth. According to this story, which emanated directly from the Roman Curia, Magee had told the pope about the murder of a student in Rome. "Are those young people shooting at each other again? Really, it is terrible." These were widely reported around the world as being the pope's last words. They provided the added bonus of giving a possible explanation for the unexpected death of Luciani: he died of shock after hearing such appalling news. The conversation between Magee and Luciani did not occur. It was a Vatican fabrication.

Another Vatican fabrication, which played a role in Villot's announcement, was that Luciani generally said Mass with Magee at 5:30 A.M. Mass in the papal apartments was not until 7:00 A.M. As previously noted, Albino Luciani spent the time between 5:30 and 7:00 A.M. in meditation and prayer, usually alone, sometimes joined at about 6:30 A.M. by Magee and Lorenzi. The image of Magee becoming alarmed by Luciani's nonappearance at five-thirty is simply Vatican fantasy.

The tragic, unexpected death shocked the entire world. The massive bronze doors to the Basilica of St. Peter were closed, the Vatican flag was flown at half mast—these were external indications—but news of Albino Luciani's death was so stunning that the disbelief expressed by his personal doctor was echoed by millions. He had delighted the world. How could God's duly elected candidate pass so quickly from them?

Cardinal Willebrands of Holland expressed the thoughts of many when he said, "It's a disaster. I cannot put into words how happy we were on that August day when we had chosen John Paul. We had such high hopes. It was such a beautiful feeling, a feeling that something fresh was going to happen to our Church."

Cardinal Baggio, one of the men whom Luciani had determined to move out of Rome, was considerably more restrained. "The Lord uses us but does not need us," he had said after viewing the dead body. He continued, "He was like a parish priest for the Church." Asked what would happen now, he responded calmly, "Now we will make another one."

Baggio, though, was one of the exceptions. Most people displayed deep shock and love. In Florence, when Cardinal Benelli finally emerged from his room at 9:00 A.M., he was immediately surrounded by reporters. With tears still running down his face, he said: "The Church has lost the right man for the right moment. We are very distressed. We are left frightened. Man cannot explain such a thing. It is a moment that limits and conditions us."

Back in the Vatican, Villot's plans for an immediate embalming had run into trouble. Cardinals Felici in Padua and Benelli in Florence, who knew very precisely the nature of the changes Luciani had been about to make, were particularly disturbed and indicated as much in telephone conversations with Villot. Already there were murmurs among the Italian public that an autopsy should be performed. It was a view that under the

circumstances Benelli and Felici were inclined at least
to consider. If the body were embalmed, then a subsequent autopsy would be far less likely to reveal that the
cause of death had been poison.

Officially, the Vatican created the impression that
the body of Pope John Paul I was embalmed before
being put on public display in the Sala Clementina at
noon on the twenty-ninth. In fact, this was not the case,
as Father Diego Lorenzi's comments make clear:

> The body was taken from the private apart-
> ment to the Clementina Hall in the papal
> apartments. At that time no embalming had
> been done. Papa Luciani was dressed by Father
> Magee, Monsignor Noe, and myself. I stayed
> with the body, as did Magee, until eleven in the
> morning. The Signoracci [brothers] came at that
> time and the body was taken to the Sala
> Clementina.

The contrast to Pope Paul's death was startling.
Then there had been little public emotion; now there
was a flood. On the first day a quarter of a million
people filed past the body. The public speculation that
this death was not natural grew by the minute. Men
and women were heard shouting as they passed the
body: "Who has done this to you? Who has murdered
you?"

Meanwhile, the cardinals who were gathering in
Rome debated about whether there should be an autopsy.
If Albino Luciani had been an ordinary citizen of Rome,
there would have been no debate. There would have
been an immediate autopsy. Italian law states that no
embalming can be undertaken until at least twenty-four
hours after death without dispensation from a magistrate.
If an Italian citizen had died under circumstances similar to those of Luciani, there would have been an immediate autopsy.

For men with nothing to hide, Villot and other
members of the Roman Curia continued to act in incom-
prehensible ways. When men conspire to cover up it is
inevitably because there is something to hide.

It was from a cardinal residing in Rome that I

learned of the most extraordinary reason given for the cover-up:

> He [Villot] told me that what had occurred was a tragic accident. That the pope had unwittingly taken an overdose of his medicine. The *camerlengo* pointed out that if an autopsy was performed it would obviously show this fatal overdose. No one would believe that His Holiness had taken it accidentally. Some would allege suicide, others murder. It was agreed that there would be no autopsy.

On two occasions I have interviewed Professor Giovanni Rama, the specialist who was responsible for prescribing the Effortil, Cortiplex, and other drugs to alleviate Albino Luciani's low blood pressure. Luciani had been a patient of Dr. Rama's since 1975. Rama's observations regarding a possible accidental overdose are illuminating:

> An accidental overdose is not credible. He was a very conscientious patient. He was very sensitive to drugs. He needed very little. In fact, he was on the minimum dose of Effortil. The normal dose is sixty drops a day, but twenty or thirty drops per day were enough for him. We were always very prudent in prescribing medicines.

Further discussion with my cardinal informant established that Villot had arrived at his deduction of an accidental overdose in those few moments in the pope's bedroom before he pocketed the medicine bottle. Villot was clearly a highly gifted man. The pope dies alone, having retired to his bedroom a well man who has just made a number of crucial decisions including one that directly affects Villot's future. Without any forensic tests, without any internal or external evidence whatsoever, the secretary of state deduces that the pope has accidentally killed himself. Perhaps in the rarefied atmosphere of the Vatican village such a story has credibility. In the real world outside, actual evidence would be essential.

Some of the key evidence that would have established the truth had already been destroyed by Villot—
the medicine and the notes Luciani had made that
detailed the vital changes. The extent of Villot's panic
can be gauged from the disappearance of Albino Luciani's
will. It contained nothing of significance with regard to
his death, yet it disappeared along with the other vital
pieces of evidence. Why the pope's glasses and slippers
also vanished remains a mystery.

Rumors swept through the Vatican village. It was
said that the alarm light on a panel in the papal apartments had glowed throughout the night but that no one
had responded to the call for help. It was said that signs
of vomiting had been found in the bedroom; various
items had been stained, and this was why the slippers
and glasses were now missing. Vomiting is frequently
one of the symptoms of a digitalis overdose. Behind
closed office doors, bishops and priests now speculated
about the sudden tragic death of the Russian Orthodox
archbishop of Leningrad, Nikodim. He had been received in a special audience by Albino Luciani on September 5. Suddenly, without warning, the forty-nine-
year-old Russian prelate had slumped forward in his
chair. Moments later he was dead. Now the word went
around the Vatican that Nikodim had drunk a cup of
coffee intended for Albino Luciani. Nikodim was in poor
health and had already had several heart attacks. In the
frightened Vatican village, though, these facts were swept
aside. His death was now seen in retrospect as a sign, a
warning of the awful events that had just occurred in
the papal apartments.

In the course of the day everything else within the
papal apartments belonging to Albino Luciani was
removed, including his letters, notes, books, and a small
handful of personal mementos such as the photograph
of his parents with Pia. Villot's colleagues from the
Secretariat of State removed all the confidential papers.
Soon all material evidence that Albino Luciani had ever
lived and worked there had been put into boxes and
carried away. By 6:00 P.M. the entire nineteen rooms of
the papal apartments were totally bereft of anything
remotely associated with the papacy of Luciani. It was
as if he had never been there, had never existed. At 6:00

P.M. the papal apartments were sealed by Cardinal Villot. They were to remain unopened until a successor had been elected.

Unobtrusively the nuns and the two secretaries left. Magee kept as a memento the cassettes used by Luciani to improve his English. Lorenzi took with him a jumble of images and memories. Carefully avoiding the waiting reporters, the group took up residence in a house run by the Sisters of Maria Bambina.

John Magee was destined to be a secretary to a pope for a third time, a unique and remarkable achievement. Diego Lorenzi, the intense young Italian, was totally devastated by the death of a man he loved. He would be sent back to northern Italy to work in a school. Vincenza would be sent even farther north, to an obscure convent. With this virtual banishment the Vatican machine would ensure that neither was easy to locate.

When the doors of the Clementina Hall closed to the public at 6:00 P.M. on Friday, September 29, Villot was presumably quite relieved. Finally the work of the embalmers could begin. Once the body had been embalmed it would be difficult during any subsequent autopsy to discover and establish the existence of poison within the body. If the pope had indeed died because of acute myocardial infarction, the embalming fluids would not destroy the naturally damaged blood vessels.

In what was presumably an ironic coincidence, the Rome Association of Pharmacy Owners chose this of all days to issue a press release stating that a number of medicines essential for the treatment of certain cases of poisoning and heart ailments were to be removed from the market. Of greater relevance, perhaps, was the statement that the Italian reporters had finally managed to extract from Cardinal Villot: "When I saw His Holiness yesterday evening, he was in perfectly good health, totally lucid, and he had given me full instructions for the next day."

Behind closed doors in the Clementina Hall the process of embalming continued for three hours. The care and preservation of the body were the responsibility of Professor Cesare Gerin, but the actual embalming was performed by Professor Marracino and Ernesto and Renato Signoracci.

When the two Signoracci brothers had examined the body before it had been moved to the Clementina, they had concluded from the lack of rigor mortis and the temperature of the body that death had taken place not at 11:00 P.M. on the twenty-eighth but between 4:00 and 5:00 A.M. on the twenty-ninth. They were given independent confirmation of their conclusion by Monsignor Noe, who told them that the pope had died shortly before 5:00 A.M. I have interviewed both brothers at length on three separate occasions. They insist that death occurred between 4:00 and 5:00 A.M. and that the pope's body was discovered within one hour of his death. If they are right, then either the pope was still alive when Sister Vincenza entered his bedroom, or he was barely dead. Only a full autopsy would have resolved this issue.

At the Vatican's insistence, no blood was drained from the body, nor were any organs removed. Formalin and other preservatives were injected into the body through the femoral arterial, and vein passages. The three hours the process took was considerably longer than the norm. The process took so long because of the Vatican's insistence that no blood be drawn off, contrary to normal practice in which the blood is drained or cleared with a solution of salt water that is circulated around the body. A small quantity of blood would, of course, have been more than sufficient for a forensic scientist to establish the presence of any poisonous substances.

The cosmetic treatment given to the body eliminated the expression of anguish on the face. The hands that had gripped the now missing sheets of paper were clasped around a rosary. Cardinal Villot finally retired to bed shortly before midnight.

Pope Paul VI, in keeping with Italian law, had not been embalmed until twenty-four hours after his death. Although there had been allegations of medical incompetence after Paul had died, there had not been a single suggestion of foul play. Now with both the general public and the news media urging an autopsy, the body of Albino Luciani had been embalmed some twelve hours after it had been discovered.

39. (*Above*) An ebullient and zestful Luciani with Cardinal Rosales of the Philippines. This last photograph was taken a few hours before the pope died.

40. (*Below, left*) Father Magee.

41. Within one month of rejoining Albino Luciani in the Vatican, Sister Vincenza was to discover his dead body.

42. Ernesto and Arnaldo Signoracci, papal embalmers.

43. Luciani, Pope John Paul I, lying in state.

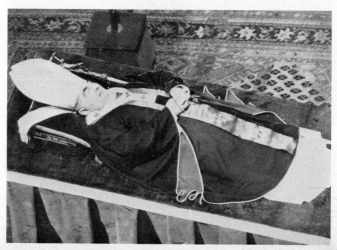

44. Prime Minister Andreotti (*third from left*) prays by the body.

45. The new pope with Cardinal Benelli, who was prevented by a mere handful of votes from succeeding Luciani.

46. On July 10, 1976, the murder of Italian magistrate Vittorio Occorsio halted the investigation into links between a neo-Fascist movement and the Masonic Order, P2.

(*Left*, 47) and (*below*, 48) Emilio Alessandrini, a Milan magistrate, was murdered on January 29, 1979, soon after he opened an investigation into Calvi's Banco Ambrosiano.

49. (*Opposite, above left*) Mino Pecorelli was a disenchanted P2 member who began to talk. He, too, was murdered.

50. (*Opposite, above right*) The deputy general manager of the Bank of Italy, Mario Sarcinelli, leaves jail after being falsely imprisoned on trumped-up charges arranged by Gelli.

(*Opposite, below left*, 51 and *right*, 52) Giorgio Ambrosoli was murdered hours after he gave vital evidence against Sindona.

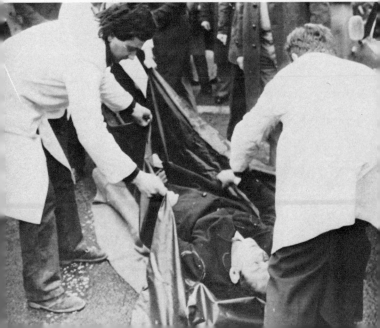

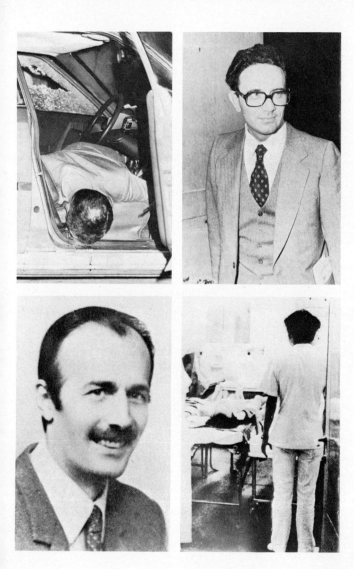

53. Two days before he was murdered Giorgio Ambrosoli had conferred with the Palermo police chief, Boris Giuliano. Within two weeks of Ambrosoli's death, Giuliano was also murdered, and laid to rest.

54. The Milan headquarters of Roberto Calvi.

55. Bologna railway station, 1980, where 85 people were killed and 182 injured in a bomb explosion masterminded by P2.

56. By 1980 Roberto Rosone (*left*), deputy chairman of Banco Ambrosiano, was becoming a threat to Calvi's activities. On April 27, 1980, Rosone was shot and seriously wounded.

57. The body of Rosone's assailant, Danilo Abbruciati, after he was shot dead by Banco Ambrosiano guards.

58. Flavio Carboni (*center, right*), friend of Roberto Calvi.

59. Roberto Calvi "suicided" in London on the night of June 17, 1982.

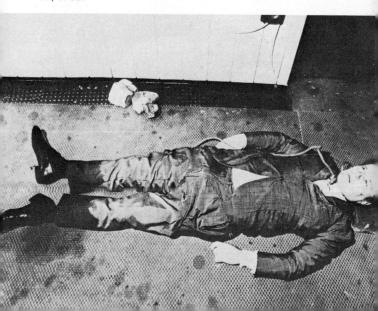

60. A few hours before Calvi's death his secretary, Graziella, also "suicided" from the fourth floor of the Banco Ambrosiano headquarters. An ambulance leaves with her body.

61. With all the other suspects dead, in prison, or fugitives from justice, Marcinkus (*foreground, center*) remains inside the Vatican.

62. "God's Banker" in his bank.

63. Umberto Ortolani, who could open any door within the Vatican.

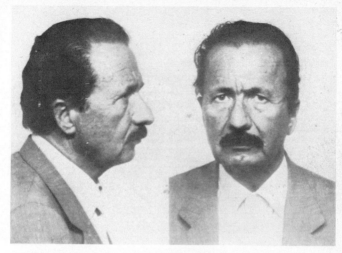

64. Swiss police photographs of Licio Gelli.

65. Michele Sindona is serving 25 years in prison in the United States.

By Saturday, September 30, one particular question was being asked with increasing urgency: "Why no autopsy?" The news media began to seek an explanation for such a sudden, unheralded death. The Curia had been very quick to remind inquiring reporters of an off-the-cuff remark that Albino Luciani had made during his last general audience on Wednesday, September 27. Turning to a group of sick and handicapped people in Nervi Hall, Luciani had said, "Remember, your pope has been in the hospital eight times and has had four operations."

The Vatican press office now responded to requests for details of Luciani's health by repeating the late pope's phrase. They used it so often that it began to sound like a recorded message, and it gave listeners just about as much satisfaction.

The media commented that Luciani had not appeared to be in ill health during his brief papacy. On the contrary, they observed, he appeared the picture of health, full of life and zest. Others, who had known Luciani for considerably longer, began to be contacted for their views.

When Monsignor Senigaglia, Luciani's secretary in Venice for over six years, revealed that the late pope had undergone a full medical checkup shortly before leaving Venice for the conclave and that the results had "been favorable in all respects," the demands for an autopsy grew louder.

When Italian medical experts began to state categorically the need for an autopsy to ascertain the precise cause of death, the panic within the Vatican reached new heights. It was clear that while doctors were prepared to put forward a variety of reasons that could have been contributory factors (the sudden stress of becoming pope was a popular one), they would not accept without an autopsy the Vatican's assertion that Albino Luciani died of acute myocardial infarction.

The Vatican countered by stating that it was against Vatican rules for an autopsy to be performed. This was yet another lie passed out to the world's press. Further questioning by Italian journalists established that the Vatican was referring to the apostolic constitution announced by Pope Paul VI in 1975. This was the docu-

ment that had laid down the procedures for electing his
successor—requiring a search for bugs in the conclave
area, specifying the size of voting cards, and so forth.
Careful reading of the document establishes that Paul
had failed to cover the possibility of any controversy
over the cause of his death. An autopsy was neither
banned nor approved. It was simply not referred to.

After Paul's death there had also been a great deal
of public debate, although over a different topic. It is
abundantly clear that Paul's life could have been
prolonged. The medical treatment he had been given
during his last days had in the opinion of many of the
world's experts left a great deal to be desired. From his
Cape Town hospital, Dr. Christiaan Barnard, when informed that Pope Paul had not been placed in an
intensive-care unit, said: "If this was to happen in South
Africa, the doctors responsible would have been denounced to their Medical Association for malpractice."

One of the principal doctors in control of Pope Paul's
treatment had been Dr. Renato Buzzonetti, the deputy
head of the Vatican medical services. Now this same
man, who in Dr. Barnard's view had acted negligently
in August, had performed a medical impossibility in
determining the cause of Albino Luciani's lonely death.
Without an autopsy his conclusion was totally without
meaning.

It was against this background that Cardinal Confalonieri presided over the first meeting of the Congregation of Cardinals, the group that watches over and controls Church affairs in the period following a pope's
death. This group comprises every cardinal—if they happen to be in Rome. When this initial meeting took
place, at 11:00 A.M. on Saturday, September 30, the vast
majority of cardinals were still scattered around the
world. Of the 127 cardinals only 29 were present, most
of them, of course, Italian. This minority made a number of decisions. They decided that Albino Luciani's
funeral would take place on the following Wednesday,
October 4. In the meantime, the massive number of
people who wanted to visit the pope's body was creating havoc for Vatican officials. They had anticipated a
degree of interest similar to that shown when Paul died—
yet another example of the Curia's failure to understand

the extent of Luciani's impact. The decision was made
to move the body that evening to St. Peter's Basilica.
The two most significant decisions made that morning,
however, were that the next conclave should take place
at the earliest possible date, October 14, and that there
would be no autopsy.

The doubts and concerns of men such as Benelli,
Felici, and Caprio about Luciani's death were overruled.
Acutely aware that the controversy would grow unless
public attention could be distracted, Villot and his colleagues totally reversed the way they had reasoned in
August. Then the conclave had been delayed until almost the last possible moment. Now the delay was to
be as short as possible. It was a shrewd ploy. Curial
cardinals, in particular, reasoned that after the funeral
the media would become preoccupied with Luciani's
possible successor. If they could hold out until the funeral took place in a few days' time, they would be safe.
Furthermore, any of the majority of the cardinals yet to
arrive who felt like insisting on an autopsy would be
confronted with decisions already made. To reverse such
decisions in the limited time before the funeral would
be a virtual impossibility. "Seek the truth and ye shall
know the truth and the truth shall make you free,"
Jesus tells us, an injunction that twenty-nine cardinals
chose to ignore on behalf of the Roman Catholic Church
on the morning of September 30, 1978.

After the meeting had adjourned, Cardinal Confalonieri offered his opinion as to why the pope had
suddenly died:

> He couldn't stand the solitude; all popes live in
> a kind of institutional solitude, but perhaps
> Luciani suffered from it more. He, who had
> always lived among the people, found himself
> living with two secretaries whom he did not
> know and two nuns who did not even raise
> their eyes in the presence of the pope. He did
> not even have the time to make any friends.

Father Diego Lorenzi had worked closely and inti-
mately with Luciani for over two years. Sister Vincenza
had worked with Luciani for nearly twenty years. Far

from casting her eyes upon the ground at his approach, she was a source of great comfort to him. Indeed, Luciani was cut off, but would a bevy of intimates have been able to prevent a solitary, mysterious death?

There can be no doubt that the curial hostility and arrogance displayed during his last thirty-three days had not made for the happiest of experiences, but Albino Luciani had fought clerical hostility and arrogance for nearly a decade in Venice.

At 6:00 P.M. on Saturday, September 30, the embalmed body was moved, uncovered, to the Basilica of St. Peter. Much of the world watched on television as the procession, including twenty-four of the cardinals and one hundred bishops and archbishops, passed through the First Loggia, the Ducal Hall, the Hall and Stairway of the Kings, and through the bronze doorway and out into St. Peter's Square. At that point the singing of the *Magnificat* was unexpectedly drowned by one of those gestures that is so peculiarly Italian. The massive crowds broke into loud, sustained applause, the Latin counterpart of Anglo-Saxon silence.

Throughout the world informed and uninformed opinion attempted to assess the life and death of Albino Luciani. Much of what was written tells a great deal more about the writers than about the man. The belief expressed in the Curia that minds could be readily diverted from the death to the succession soon began to prove accurate. *The Times* of London neatly mirrored the transitory nature of life with an editorial entitled, "The Year of the Three Popes."

Some observers talked perceptively of a great promise unfulfilled, others of a pontificate that had promised to be joyful. With regard to an explanation for the sudden death, the Roman Curia disinformation service had achieved a remarkable coup. Writer after writer talked about a long record of illness. That someone as experienced as Patrick O'Donovan of the *Observer* could be deceived into writing the following indicates just how successful the lies were: "It is only now generally known that Cardinal Luciani had a long record of all but mortal illness."

Exactly what these illnesses were was not stated. It is clear that O'Donovan and the other reporters, fighting to meet deadlines, had no time for personal research but relied on Vatican contacts. Some talked of Luciani's heavy smoking, of the fact that he had only one lung, of his several bouts of tuberculosis. Since his death others have been told by Vatican sources about his four heart attacks, about the fact that he suffered from phlebitis, a painful circulatory disease, and about his struggle with emphysema, a chronic illness of the lungs. There is not a word of truth in any of it.

The overkill of Vatican lies is self-defeating. Would 111 cardinals gather in Rome in August 1978 and elect a man suffering from all of the above? And then permit him to die alone? Along with the lies about Luciani's medical history the Vatican disinformation service was busy in other areas. The Curia was pushing the non-attributable, off-the-record view that Luciani was no good as a pope anyway. Why mourn what was worthless? I discussed this smear campaign with Cardinal Benelli, who remarked:

> It seemed to me that their [the Roman Curia's] aim was twofold. To minimize Luciani's abilities would reduce the sense of loss and consequently reduce the demands for an autopsy. Second, the Curia was preparing for the next conclave. They wanted a curial pope.

When Luciani had lunched with his niece Pia, one of the subjects they discussed had been press distortion. Now in death Luciani became a victim of such distortion. The negative comments were mainly inspired by insignificant priests or monsignors who were normally busy writing irrelevant Vatican memos. They found it highly flattering to be asked for their opinion of the late pope. The fact that none of them was near the corridors of power or had ever been within the papal apartments was obscured by that all-encompassing description, "a highly placed Vatican source said today." What they said was part of the great injustice done to the memory of the dead pope. It enabled writers who before the August conclave had been dismissive of Luciani to put behind them the uncomfortable fact that Luciani's election had been a major demonstration of how ill in-

formed they were. Their thinking appears to have been:
"Well, yes, we discounted him, but you see, he should
have been discounted." Thus:

> The audiences attracted the immediate sympa-
> thy of the public but had disappointed and
> sometimes worried Church officials. The pope
> expressed a philosophy of existence that on oc-
> casion resembled the *Reader's Digest*: common
> sense, a little simple at that, which broke the
> grand theological flights of oratory of Paul VI.
> Clearly he did not have the culture and the
> intellectual training of his predecessor.
>
>   Vatican correspondent Robert Sole for
>   *Le Monde*

> We followed first with eagerness, then with a
> growing sense of the ridiculous, his generous
> efforts to discover who he was. He smiled, his
> father was a Socialist, he rejected the tiara for
> a simple stole, he spoke informally at audiences.
>
>   *Commonweal*

Newsweek expressed the opinion that Luciani's rejection of the philosophy *Ubi Lenin, ibi Jerusalem* was a
betrayal of the Latin American cardinals who had played
such a key role in his election. It also wrote that in
making this observation Luciani had rejected the theology of liberation. Because of Curia censorship, *Newsweek*
missed the fact that he had added an important qualification—"There is some coincidence but we cannot
make a perfect equation"—and in doing so, it missed
the point.

Peter Nichols, the very experienced *Times* of London correspondent but writing on this occasion in the
Spectator, compared Luciani to a popular Italian come-
dian of yesteryear who had but to stand there in sight of
the populace to be given an ovation. He failed to explain why Paul VI had not received ovations on each
appearance.

Others criticized the fact that Luciani had reconfirmed all the Curia heads in office. They neglected to

point out that this had also been done by the last three
popes before Luciani and that he retained the power
and authority to move any of them at any time.

Much of the world's news media had, in the days
following the pope's death, carried stories about the
Vatican ritual that surrounds this moment. The newspapers were full of accounts of how Cardinal Villot had
approached the body and asked three times, "Albino,
are you dead?" each question being followed by the
symbolic striking on the pope's forehead with a small
silver hammer. The press also gave dramatic descrip-
tions of how Villot had then taken the Fisherman's ring
from Luciani's hand and subsequently smashed the ring
to pieces.

With the death of Albino Luciani there was, in fact,
no head-tapping, no calling of names. These ceremonies
had been abolished in Paul's lifetime. As to the papal
ring, Luciani's reign was so brief that the Vatican had
not even created the ring. The only ring on Luciani's
hand throughout his entire papacy was the one given to
all bishops who had attended the Second Vatican Council.

What makes this highly inaccurate journalism worth
considering, when one is aware not only of how much
Luciani did achieve in such a brief span, but also of the
high regard in which he was held by men such as
Casaroli, Benelli, Lorscheider, Garrone, Felici, and many
others, is the fact that it is evidence for an orchestrated
campaign. Not one single editorial or article carried
any of the facts recorded in the previous chapter. One of
the many expressions that residents of Vatican City are
fond of quoting is, "Nothing is leaked from the Vatican
without a very specific purpose."

On October 1, the pressure for an autopsy increased.
Italy's most respected newspaper, *Corriere della Sera*,
carried a front-page article entitled, "Why Say No to an
Autopsy?" It was by Carlo Bo, a highly talented writer
with considerable knowledge of the Vatican. That the
article appeared at all is significant. In Italy, thanks to
the Lateran Treaty and subsequent agreements between
the Italian government and the Vatican, the press is
seriously muzzled when writing on the Catholic Church.
The libel laws are very stringent. Critical comment, let

alone an outright attack, can rapidly result in the newspaper concerned being brought to court.

Carlo Bo cleverly avoided any such risk. In a style reminiscent of Mark Antony's speech to the Roman populace, Bo talked of the suspicions and allegations that had surfaced after the sudden death. He told his readers that he felt confident that the palaces and cellars of the Vatican had been free from such criminal actions for centuries. Precisely because of his confidence, he said, he simply could not understand why the Vatican had decided not to perform any scientific checks, "in humble words, why was there no autopsy?" He continued:

> The Church has nothing to fear, therefore nothing to lose. On the contrary, it would have much to gain.
>   ... Now, to know what the pope died of is a legitimate historical fact, it is part of our visible history and does not in any way affect the spiritual mystery of his death. The body that we leave behind when we die can be understood with our poor instruments, it is a leftover: the soul is already, or rather it always has been, dependent on other laws which are not human and so remain inscrutable. Let us not make out of a mystery a secret to guard for earthly reasons and let us recognize the smallness of our secrets. Let us not declare sacred what is not.

The fifteen doctors on the staff of the Vatican's health services steadfastly refused to comment on the desirability of performing autopsies on dead popes. Edoardo Luciani, however, failed to help the Vatican's position when he was asked about his brother's health:

> The day after the enthronement ceremony, I asked his personal doctor how he had found him, bearing in mind all the pressures he was now subjected to. The doctor reassured me, telling me that my brother was in excellent health and that his heart was in good condition.

Asked if his brother had ever had any heart trouble, Edoardo replied, "As far as I know, absolutely none." It did not fit very well with the Vatican-orchestrated fantasy.

By Monday, October 2, the controversy surrounding the pope's death had become worldwide. In France at Avignon, Cardinal Silvio Oddi found himself the object of many questions. As an Italian cardinal surely he could tell his French questioners the true facts? What Oddi told them was that the College of Cardinals "will not examine the possibility of an inquiry at all and will not accept any supervision from anyone and it will not even discuss the subject." Oddi concluded: "We know in fact, in all certainty, that the death of John Paul the First was due to the fact that his heart stopped beating from perfectly natural causes." Clearly Cardinal Oddi had achieved a major medical breakthrough—the ability to diagnose without an autopsy what is diagnosable only with an autopsy.

Meanwhile, the protests of Father Lorenzi and other members of the papal apartments about one particular lie had finally borne fruit. The Vatican announced:

> After the necessary inquiries, we are now in a position to state that the pope, when he was found dead on the morning of September 29, was holding in his hands certain sheets of paper containing his personal writings such as homilies, speeches, reflections, and various notes.

When the Vatican had previously announced that Luciani had been holding *The Imitation of Christ*, Father Andrew Greeley records in his book *The Making of the Popes,* "some reporters openly laughed."

These papers, detailing the crucial changes that Albino Luciani was about to make, have undergone some extraordinary metamorphoses over the years: report on the Church in Argentina; notes for his next *Angelus* speech; sermons made in Belluno/Vittorio Veneto/Venice; a parish magazine; the speech he was about to deliver to the Jesuits (in fact, this was found on his study desk); a report written by Pope Paul. When a head of state dies in apparently normal circumstances his last actions are of more than academic interest. When a head of state dies in circumstances such as those surrounding Albino Luciani's death, the need to know becomes a vital matter of public interest. The fact that Luciani was holding his personal notes on the various crucial changes he was proposing to make has been confirmed to me by five different sources. Two are direct Vatican sources; the other three are external to the Vatican. With the Vatican officially retracting *The Imitation of Christ* version, the curial machine was beginning to show signs of strain.

The strain grew greater when the world's press began to comment on a number of disturbing aspects. For a pope to have no one monitoring his welfare from midevening until the following day struck many observers as wrong. The fact that Dr. Renato Buzzonetti worked mainly at a Rome hospital and consequently would not necessarily be available if needed seemed outrageous. If the observers had known the full extent of Vatican inefficiency, their outrage would have been even greater. Vatican inefficiency was such that there was a potential not only for premature natural death but also for murder.

In Spain as in other countries, the controversy broke into public debate. Professor Rafael Gambra of the University of Madrid was one of a number who complained of the Vatican "doing things in the Italian manner or in the Florentine manner as in the Renaissance." Urging that an autopsy be performed, Gambra voiced fears that a pope who was manifestly going to bring a much-needed discipline back into the Church might have been murdered.

In Mexico City, the bishop of Cuernavaca, Sergio Arceo, publicly demanded an autopsy, declaring, "To Cardinal Miguel Miranda [of Mexico City] and me it seems that it would be useful." The bishop ordered a detailed statement to be read out in all churches in his diocese. The Vatican machine moved fast. The detailed statement, like much else in this affair, vanished from the face of the earth, and by the time the Vatican had finished with Cardinal Miranda he was able to declare on his subsequent arrival in Rome that he had no doubts whatsoever with regard to the death of the pope.

As people continued to file past the pope's body at

the rate of twelve thousand per hour, the controversy roared on. The will of Albino Luciani had vanished, but by its extraordinary behavior the Vatican was ensuring a bitter legacy. A pope with an ability to speak openly, directly, and simply was surrounded in death by deviousness and deceit. It was clear that the loss felt by ordinary people was immense. From the Vatican there was scant acknowledgment of that widespread feeling. Rather, there was a bitter rearguard action to protect not the memory of Albino Luciani but those to whom the evidence of complicity in his murder clearly pointed.

Noncurial priests were now debating in newspapers the pros and cons of an autopsy. Pundits and Vatican observers were castigating the Vatican for its stubbornness. What had become abundantly clear, as Vittorio Zucconi observed in *Corriere della Sera*, was that "behind the doubts about the pope's death lies a vast dissatisfaction with 'official versions.' "

The organization of traditionalist Catholics known as Civiltà Christiana indicated just how deeply dissatisfied they were. Secretary Franco Antico revealed that he had sent an official appeal for a full judicial inquiry into the death of Pope John Paul I to Vatican City's chief justice.

The decision to appeal and the reasons for it made headlines around the world. Antico cited a number of the inconsistencies that had emerged from the Vatican. What his group wanted was not merely an autopsy but a full judicial inquiry. Antico said: "If President Carter had died under such circumstances, you can be sure the American people would have demanded an explanation."

Antico told the press that his organization had initially considered making a formal allegation that the pope had been killed by a person or persons unknown. Displaying a wonderful example of the complexity of the Italian mind, he said that the organization had refrained from such a step because "we are not seeking a scandal." Civiltà Christiana had also sent the appeal to Cardinal Confalonieri, dean of the Sacred College. Some of the issues it raised were the gap between the discovery of the body and public announcement of death, the fact that the pope had apparently been working in

bed without anyone checking on his welfare,* and the
fact that no death certificate had been issued. No Vatican doctor had, via an official death certificate, taken
public responsibility with regard to the diagnosis of the
cause of Albino Luciani's death.

The rebel Archbishop Marcel Lefebvre's supporters,
who had previously announced that Luciani had died
because God did not want him to be pope, now announced through Abbot Ducaud-Bourget, Lefebvre's right-
hand man, a different theory: "It's difficult to believe
that the death was natural considering all the creatures
of the devil who inhabit the Vatican."

Having already been obliged to retract the statement that papal autopsies were specifically banned, the
Vatican was confronted on Tuesday, October 3, with the
results of some tenacious probing on the part of the
Italian press. As the press pointed out, an autopsy had
in fact been performed on another pope. Pius VIII had
died on November 30, 1830; the diary of Prince Don
Agostini Chigi recorded that the following evening an
autopsy had been performed. The result of the autopsy
is officially unknown, because officially the Vatican has
never admitted that it took place. However, what the
autopsy had revealed was that apart from some weakness in the lungs all the organs appeared to be healthy.
It was suspected that the pope had been poisoned.

On October 3 at 7:00 P.M. a curious event occurred.
The gates of St. Peter's were closed to the public for the
day. The church was deserted except for the four Swiss
Guard members posted at the corners of the catafalque,
the traditional twenty-four-hour protection accorded to
the body of a dead pope. At 7:45 P.M. a group of about
150 pilgrims from Canale d'Agordo, Albino Luciani's
birthplace, accompanied by the Bishop of Belluno, were
quietly let into the church through a side entrance. The
group had only just arrived in Rome and had been
granted special permission by the Vatican to pay their
last respects to a man many of them knew personally,
after the official closure for the day. Clearly someone in

---

*It has been alleged but not confirmed that the pope had
pressed a bedside alarm and that the alarm light was ignored
throughout the night.

Vatican City with plans of his own with regard to the body of the pope had not been advised. Within a few minutes of their arrival the pilgrims found themselves being bundled out unceremoniously into St. Peter's Square.

Vatican officials had appeared together with a group of doctors. Everyone else was ordered to leave. The four Swiss Guard members were also dispensed with. Large crimson screens were placed all around the body, preventing anyone who might still be in St. Peter's from seeing what the doctors were doing. This sudden unannounced medical examination continued until 9:30 P.M. When it was concluded, a number of the pilgrims from Canale d'Agordo who had remained outside asked if they could finally pay their last respects to the corpse. The request was refused.

Why less than twenty-four hours before the funeral did this examination take place? Many in the news media were convinced that an eve-of-funeral autopsy had indeed been performed. Did the Vatican finally make a move to allay public anxiety? If it did, then the subsequent Vatican statements concerning this medical examination lead inevitably to the conclusion that the examination confirmed all those fears and anxieties that the pope had been murdered.

There was no announcement after the examination and, despite being deluged with questions by the news media, the Vatican press office continued to maintain a total silence on what had occurred in St. Peter's until after the pope was buried. Only then did it give its version. Previously, off the record, it had told the Italian news agency ANSA that the medical examination was a normal check on the state of preservation of the body and that it was carried out by Professor Gerin and Ernesto and Renato Signoracci, among others. It had also told ANSA that several more injections of the embalming fluid were made.

When the Vatican press office finally spoke officially, it reduced the ninety-minute examination to twenty minutes. It also stated that everything was found to be in order and that subsequently the pilgrims from Canale d'Agordo were allowed back in. Apart from the errors or deliberate lies inherently contained within the press statement there are a number of other disquieting facts. Professor Cesare Gerin, contrary to the Vatican informants questioned by ANSA, was not present. Furthermore, when I interviewed the Signoracci brothers, they also insisted that they had not been present during this bizarre event. It was clearly a conservation check without the conservationists.

If, as many believe, an autopsy was indeed performed, even a partial autopsy—for in ninety minutes it could not have been the full standard postmortem—then the results, if negative, would have been announced loudly and clearly. What better way to silence the tongues? *Corriere della Sera* stated that "at the last minute a famous doctor from the Catholic University joined the special team." Since then the "famous doctor" seems to have vanished in the morning mists rising from the Tiber.

Catholic psychologist Rosario Mocciaro, commenting on the behavior of the men entrusted with controlling the Roman Catholic Church during this period of the empty throne, described it thus: "A sort of Mafialike *omertá* [silence] disguised as Christian charity and protocol."

The dialogue of love that Albino Luciani had inspired between himself and the people continued until the bitter end. Ignoring the continuous rain, nearly a hundred thousand people were in St. Peter's Square for the open-air Requiem Mass on October 4. Nearly one million people had filed past the body during the previous four days. The first of the three readings, taken from the Apocalypse of St. John, ended with the words, "I am Alpha and Omega, the beginning and the end. I will give water from the well of life free to anybody who is thirsty."

The body of Albino Luciani, hermetically sealed in three coffins of cypress, lead, and ebony, went to its final resting place inside a marble sarcophagus in the crypt of St. Peter's. Even as his mortal remains went into the cold Roman dusk to take their place between those of John XXIII and Paul VI, the discussion continued as to whether before his death Albino Luciani had been given something other than water from the well of life.

A great many people remained disturbed about the sudden death, among them Albino Luciani's own doctor, Antonio Da Ros.

With the pope buried within three coffins, it was clearly going to be virtually impossible to persuade the Vatican to change its mind. The formal request by Civiltá Christiana to the Vatican tribunal rested with a single judge, Giuseppe Spinelli. Even if Spinelli had earnestly desired that there be an autopsy and a full investigation, it is difficult to see how he would have overcome the power of Vatican City and the men who ran it.

It was all very well for the Jesuits to compare Luciani's death to a flower in a field that closes at night, or for the Franciscans to talk of death being like a thief in the night. Others continued to seek a more practical explanation. Skeptics could be found on both sides of the Tiber. Among those who were most disturbed within the Vatican was the group who knew the truth about the discovery of the pope's body by Sister Vincenza. As more and more official lies were told, their concern mounted. Eventually, with the pope buried, several of them talked. They spoke initially to the news agency ANSA and more recently to me. Indeed, several members of this group convinced me that I should investigate the death of Albino Luciani.

On October 5 they gave ANSA the factual details of Sister Vincenza's discovery. Their information even correctly identified that the notes Luciani was holding in death concerned "certain nominations in the Roman Curia and in the Italian episcopate." The group also revealed that the pope had discussed the problem of Baggio's refusal to accept the patriarchate of Venice. When the story exploded on the public, the Vatican response was very reminiscent of Monsignor Henri de Riedmatten's when confronted with questions about the Luciani document on artificial birth control. Riedmatten had dismissed that document as "a fantasy." Now, confronted by literally hundreds of reporters demanding a Vatican comment on the latest leaks, the director of the Vatican press office, Father Panciroli, issued a one-line laconic denial. "These are reports devoid of all foundation."

Among those unimpressed by this denial were a

number of the cardinals still arriving in Rome for the next conclave. At the meeting of the Congregation of Cardinals on October 9, their unease surfaced. Cardinal Villot in particular found himself under attack. As *camerlengo* he had made the decisions and authorized the statements that clearly indicated that the death of Luciani had been followed by a cover-up. Many of the non-Italian princes of the Church demanded to know exactly what was being covered up. They wanted to know why the cause of death had not been precisely ascertained and why it had merely been presumed. They wanted to know why there was not greater clarification about the time of death and why a doctor had not taken official responsibility by putting his name to a death certificate that could be made public.

They were unsuccessful in their efforts to obtain these facts. The next conclave was fast approaching, thanks to the decision made by a minority the day after the discovery of the pope's body. The minds of the cardinals began to concentrate on the lobbying and the intrigues surrounding the problem of who should succeed Albino Luciani, an indication that the men of the Roman Curia, with an inherited experience of nearly two thousand years, have indeed learned a great deal from their predecessors.

On October 12, less than forty-eight hours before the next conclave, the Vatican made its final public statement concerning the furor over the death of Albino Luciani. It was issued by the Vatican press secretary, Father Romeo Panciroli:

> At the end of the *Novemdiales* [the mourning period], when we enter a new phase of the *sede vacante*, the director of the press office of the Holy See expresses words of firm disapproval for those who in recent days have indulged in the spreading of strange rumors, unchecked, often false, and sometimes reaching the level of grave insinuations, all the more grave for the repercussions they may have had in those countries where people are not accustomed to excessively casual forms of expression. In these

moments of mourning and sorrow for the Church
one expected greater control and greater respect.

He repeated that "what happened has been faithfully reported in the communiqué of Friday morning,
September 29, which maintains its full validity and
which reflected the death certificate signed by Professor
Mario Fontana and Dr. Renato Buzzonetti so faithfully
as to render its publication unnecessary."

He also noted with satisfaction "the rectitude of
many professionals who in such a difficult moment for
the Church, showed loyal participation in the events
and informed public opinion with considered and objective reports."

Wishing to avoid "grave insinuations" I will make
instead a categorical statement: I am completely convinced that Pope John Paul I was murdered.

To this date no death certificate has ever been made
public. Despite my repeated requests, the Vatican refused to make one available to me. Undoubtedly it would
state that the cause of death was acute myocardial
infarction. The continued refusal to make the death
certificate available means that no doctor is prepared
to accept publicly the legal responsibility for diagnosing the cause of Albino Luciani's death. The fact that
the diagnosis was based on an *external* examination,
which is unacceptable medically, may have something
to do with that Vatican refusal.

The fact that a full autopsy or postmortem was not
performed despite international unease and concern cannot but suggest Vatican concern that the pope *was*
murdered. If Luciani's death was natural, then why not
have an autopsy and allay that concern?

It is clear that, officially at least, the Vatican does
not know when Luciani died or what killed him. "Presumably toward eleven o'clock" and "sudden death that
could be related to" are statements that clearly demonstrate a high degree of ignorance, of presumptions and
assumptions. The body of a beggar found in the gutters
of Rome would be accorded a greater degree of professional care and attention. The scandal is all the greater
when one is aware that these examining doctors had
never treated Albino Luciani while he was alive. When I

spoke to Dr. Renato Buzzonetti in Rome I asked what medicines the pope had been taking in the weeks before his death. He replied, "I don't know what medicines he was taking. I was not his doctor. The first time I saw him in a doctor-patient relationship he was dead."

Dr. Seamus Banim is a heart specialist with over twenty years' professional experience. He is the senior consultant at St. Bartholomew's Hospital, London, and Nuffield Hospital, North London. During my interview with him he said:

> For a doctor, any doctor, to diagnose myocardial infarction as the cause of death is wrong. I would not be satisfied. If he had known the patient before, had treated him for a period of time, had cared for him during a previous heart attack, had observed the living man after what was to prove to be a fatal heart attack, then the diagnosis might just be permissible. But if he had not known the patient before he is not entitled to make that diagnosis. He is taking a very grave risk, and he certainly would not be entitled to take such a risk and make such a diagnosis in this country. Such a diagnosis can only be given after an autopsy.

We have, therefore, an unacceptable conclusion about the cause of death. The conclusion we have about the time of death turns out to be equally unacceptable.

The Vatican told the world that it happened "presumably toward eleven o'clock" on the evening of September 28. Dr. Derek Barrowcliff, a former British Home Office pathologist with over fifty years' experience, advised me:

> Unless there were a graded series of temperature readings in the rectum it is a very, very brave man who will say that death occurred at such and such a time. A very brave man indeed.
>
> Rigor mortis tends to be detectable after five or six hours depending on a number of factors, including the heat of the room. A hot room brings it on quicker—a cold room, slower.

It may take twelve hours to develop, then remain firmly fixed for twelve hours, then start to weaken during a further twelve hours. This is very, very approximate. If rigor mortis is present, it is reasonable to assume that death occurred some six hours or more before. Certainly a liver temperature reading [which was not taken] would have helped. If one is examining a body very, very carefully in a medicolegal sense, then one does detect slight degrees of rigor. It comes on very gently. Hence if the body were stiff at six o'clock in the morning it would be reasonable to say death occurred at eleven o'clock the previous evening. But it could equally have been nine o'clock the previous evening.

So two facts have been indisputably established:
1. We do not know what caused the death of Albino Luciani.
2. We do not know with any degree of certainty what time he died.

When Pope Paul VI died in August 1978 he was surrounded by doctors, secretaries, and priests. Consider the detail contained in the official bulletin that was published and signed by doctors Mario Fontana and Renato Buzzonetti.

During the course of the past week, the Holy Father, Paul VI, suffered a serious accentuation of the painful symptoms related to the arthritic illness with which he has been affected for many years. On the afternoon of Saturday, August 5, he suffered from fever due to the sudden resurgence of an acute cystitis. Following consultation with Professor Fabio Prosperi, chief urologist of the United Hospitals of Rome, the appropriate curative measures were begun. During the night of August 5–6 and all through Sunday, August 6, the Holy Father was suffering from high fever. About 6:15 P.M. on Sunday, August 6, sudden, serious, and progressive heightening of arterial pressure was observed. There followed rapidly the typical symptoms of insufficiency of the left ventricle with the clinical picture of acute pulmonary edema.

Despite all the precise attentions that were at once applied, His Holiness Paul VI died at 9:40 P.M.

At the time of Paul's death, the doctors in attendance indicated the following general clinical picture: cardiopathic arteriosclerotic polyarthritis, chronic pyelonephritis, and acute cystitis. Immediate cause of death: hypertensive crisis, insufficiency of the left ventricle, acute pulmonary edema. Less than two months later, Paul's successor dies "like a flower in a field that closes at night" with not a single member of the medical profession in sight.

In contrast to the plethora of lies that poured from Vatican City about the medical history of Luciani, the following are the facts:

In his infancy he had shown signs of a tubercular illness, the symptom being enlarged neck glands. At the age of eleven his tonsils were removed; at the age of fifteen, his adenoids. Both these operations were performed in the general hospital in Padua. In 1945 and again in 1947 he was admitted to a sanatorium with suspected tuberculosis. Tests on both occasions produced negative results, and the pulmonary illnesses were diagnosed as bronchitis. He made a complete recovery, and every subsequent chest X ray was negative. In 1964 he was operated on in April for gallstones and a blocked colon and in August for hemorrhoids. Professor Amedeo Alexandre performed both operations at the Pordenone hospital. After checking the medical records he informed me that Albino Luciani suffered from no other ailments at that time and that all his pre- and postoperative medical tests confirmed that he was in perfect health. These tests included X rays and a number of ECGs, a test specifically designed to record heart abnormalities. Professor Alexandre stated that his patient's recovery from both of these minor operations was total and complete. "I reexamined him in the summer after the second operation. Then too he was in excellent health."

Albino Luciani's excellent health during this period

is reflected in his daily routine, which was described to me by his former colleague Monsignor Taferal. It is virtually identical to his routine in Venice and subsequently in the Vatican. He awoke between 4:30 and 4:45 A.M. and retired for the night some sixteen hours later, between 9:00 and 10:00 P.M. Monsignor Taferal advised me that Luciani, apart from his many other functions, made pastoral visits to every one of his 180 parishes and was two thirds of the way through a second round of pastoral visits when he was promoted to go to Venice.

In December 1975, Luciani suffered a blood clot in the central vein of the retina of the left eye. No operation was required and his specialist, Professor Rama, told me:

> The treatment was only general and was based on hemokinetic medicine, anticoagulants, and mild medicines to dilate the blood vessels and, above all, a few days' rest in the hospital. The result was almost immediate, with a complete recovery of vision and general recovery. He was never what one would call a physical colossus, but he was fundamentally healthy and the tests carried out on several occasions never revealed heart troubles.

Professor Rama noted that Luciani had low blood pressure, which under normal conditions oscillated around 120/80. Low blood pressure was considered by the twenty-three members of the medical profession whom I consulted to be "the best possible condition for increased life expectancy."

During his time in Venice, Luciani occasionally had slight swelling in the ankles. His doctors thought this attributable to the low blood pressure and the need for more exercise. In July 1978 he spent ten days at the Stella Maris Institute on the Lido to counteract a possible reoccurrence of gallstones. He was put on a bland diet and took extensive walks in the morning and in the evening to alleviate the slight swelling in the ankles. A medical checkup after this stay concluded that he was in excellent health. The checkup included an ECG.

The above is the sum total of Albino Luciani's medical history. It is based on interviews with the doctors who treated him, relatives, friends, and colleagues. It should be closely compared with the assortment of lies concerning his health that poured out of Vatican City. The overriding question that springs immediately to mind is, why all the lies? The more one probes into Luciani's life, the more one becomes convinced that this man was murdered. For nearly six years the Vatican lies concerning the late pope have gone unchecked and unchallenged. The Roman Curia would have the world believe that Albino Luciani was an invalid and a simple, rather foolish man, a man whose election was an aberration and whose natural death was a merciful release for the Church. In this way they hoped to conceal murder. It is as if the past four hundred years never were: we are back with the Borgias.

While the news media of the world carried details of the Vatican fantasy about Luciani's health, there were many who, if they had been asked, would have provided a different picture:

> I knew him from 1936 onward. Apart from the two periods of confinement for suspected tuberculosis, he was perfectly healthy. He made a complete recovery after the second confinement. Certainly up to 1958, when he became bishop of Vittorio Veneto, there were no major illnesses. [Monsignor Da Rif, to author]

> His health while in Vittorio Veneto was excellent. He had the two operations in 1964 for gallstones and hemorrhoids and made a complete recovery. His workload remained exactly the same. I have heard about the low blood pressure and the swollen legs. Neither occurred while he was here, and subsequently, after he had gone to Venice, I saw him many times. He was always in excellent health. Between 1958 and 1970 apart from those two operations his health was perfect. [Monsignor Taferal, to author]

In the eight years he was in Venice I only once saw Cardinal Luciani in bed because he was unwell, that was for simple influenza. For the rest, the patriarch of Venice was very healthy and he did not suffer from any illness. [Monsignor Giuseppe Bosa, apostolic administrator of Venice]

He had absolutely no cardiopathic characteristics; besides, his low blood pressure should, at least in theory, have made him safe from acute cardiovascular attacks. The only time I needed to give him treatment was for the influenza attack. [Dr. Carlo Frizzerio, Venice physician]

Albino Luciani did not have a bad heart. Someone with a bad heart does not, as the patriarch did every year with me from 1972 to 1977, climb mountains. We would go to Pietralba, near Bolzano, and we would climb the Corno Bianco, from fifteen hundred to twenty-four hundred meters, at a good speed. . . . There was never a sign of cardiac insufficiency. On the contrary, at my insistence in 1974 an electrocardiogram was carried out, which recorded nothing irregular. Immediately before leaving for the conclave in August 1978 and after his visit to the Stella Maris Institute he had a full medical checkup. The results were favorable in all respects. As for the theory of stress or exhaustion, it's nonsense. His working day in the Vatican was no longer than here in Venice; and in the Vatican he had many more assistants, a great deal more help, and goodness knows how many more advisers. Mountain men do not die of heart attacks. [Monsignor Mario Senigaglia, secretary to Albino Luciani, 1970–76, to author]

Doctor Da Ros said to me, "Do you have a secret medicine? Albino Luciani is in perfect

health and he is so much more relaxed. What
magic drugs do you have?" [Father Diego
Lorenzi, secretary to Albino Luciani, 1976 to
his death, to author]

All of these people plus more than twenty others
who knew Albino Luciani since he was a child confirmed that he had never smoked, drank alcohol only
rarely, and ate sparingly. This life-style together with
his low blood pressure would make him a highly unlikely candidate for coronary disease.

In addition to the doctors already referred to, there
was Luciani's regular physician, Dr. Giuseppe Da Ros.
It was through Dr. Da Ros that Luciani's health was
constantly and regularly monitored over the last twenty
years of his life.

Dr. Da Ros was also a friend and in Vittorio Veneto
visited Luciani every week. In Venice Da Ros came once
every two weeks at 6:30 A.M. and stayed for a minimum
of ninety minutes. They would have breakfast together,
but the visits were professional as well as social.

The visits continued after Luciani's election as pope.
Da Ros gave Luciani three full medical examinations
during his thirty-three day papacy. The last was on
Saturday, September 23, immediately before Luciani
left the Vatican for his first public engagement in Rome,
meeting Mayor Argan and officially accepting the Church
of St. John Lateran—a public ordeal that presumably
would have highlighted any physical ailment from which
Luciani might have been suffering. Dr. Da Ros found
his patient in such good health that he told Luciani that
instead of seeing him two weeks hence, as usual, he
would not come for three weeks. When Father Lorenzi
asked the doctor about the pope's health on that
Saturday, Dr. Da Ros declared, *"Non sta bene ma
benone."*—"He is not well, but *very* well."

Da Ros consulted Dr. Buzzonetti of the Vatican the
same day, and they discussed Luciani's medical history.
Obviously the pope would eventually need a regular
general practitioner based in Rome, but the doctors
agreed that there was no immediate urgency. Da Ros
would continue for the time being to travel down from

Vittorio Veneto regularly. That the doctor who had cared for him for over twenty years and the Vatican medical staff were content with an arrangement whereby the pope's physician lived 350 miles away is perhaps the most illuminating evidence possible. That such an arrangement was satisfactory to all leads to only two conclusions. Either Dr. Da Ros and the Vatican medical staff were guilty of the most appalling negligence and are unfit to practice medicine, or Albino Luciani was a perfectly healthy man without any illness whatsoever at the time of his death. In view of the care and attention Dr. Da Ros provided, not to mention the very real affection he felt for his patient, clearly the latter conclusion must be drawn. Da Ros, you will recall, was "shocked, stunned, and mystified" when told of the death.

> Dr. Da Ros stated that he found the pope in such good health that in the future he would come every third Saturday rather than every second because the pope was so well. On the last evening he was perfectly fit. During his papacy this business of leg swelling did not occur. He took daily exercise either in the Vatican garden or in the big hall. [Father John Magee, secretary to Pope John Paul I from late August 1978 until his death, to author]

Largely because of his personal friendship with Dr. Da Ros, few men could claim to have received greater medical attention than Luciani—weekly, then biweekly visits for over twenty years. Medical attention of a remarkable consistency was followed by a sudden, unexpected death, which was in turn followed by a false diagnosis and the failure to publish a death certificate.

How then do we explain the inexplicable? A popular theory at the time of the pope's death was that it was caused by stress. It is not a theory given any credence by the many doctors I have interviewed. Many were scathing about what they termed "the stress business," an industry where fortunes are made by playing on popular fears. Too much sexual intercourse causes stress. Too little sexual intercourse causes stress.

Playing video games causes stress. Watching sports events causes stress. Too much exercise causes stress. Too little exercise causes stress.

> I see an awful lot of people with stress symptoms, but they don't have coronary disease. They are a pain in the neck. They are all working long hours, overworked, six, seven days a week, totally involved in their work, they lose perspective. My impression is that, after a while, they build up this tremendous negative balance if they don't relax. They see a neurologist about headaches, a specialist about stomach disorders such as ulcers, they come to me with chest pains. It is never heart disease they are actually suffering from. Here in St. Bartholomew's we have a very busy coronary unit. It's not the whiz kids from the city we have as patients, it's the porters and the messengers. If the myth of stress had any validity we would not see the change in mortality that we are seeing. What we are seeing are the upper classes reducing their coronary attacks and the lower classes increasing theirs. Your risk factors if you are poor are much higher than if you are middle or upper class. The vast amount of people with stress symptoms are not turning up coronary problems, they are turning up funny chest pains, they are turning up funny breathlessness, they are turning up feeling funny. It's never the heart. They merely need a great deal of reassurance. You dare not tell them what the real heart symptoms are or otherwise they will be back with them.   [Dr. Seamus Banim, to author]

Research indicates that stress sometimes can lead to heart disease and, indeed, to a fatal heart attack; but the heart disease caused by stress does not occur overnight. Symptoms manifest themselves for months or even years. No such symptoms were ever noted by any of the doctors who cared for Albino Luciani in the course of his life.

The Vatican lied when it stated that an autopsy on the pope was forbidden under Vatican rules.

The Vatican lied when it stated an autopsy on a pope had never been performed.

The trickle of lies became a flood.

The pope's will. The pope's health. The time of his embalming. The exact nature of the medical examinations that took place on the body before the funeral. The Vatican lied about each and every one of these aspects.

Consider the will of Albino Luciani. No will has ever been produced or made public. Luciani's family has been told that no will exists. And yet:

It certainly exists. I don't know its length, much less what it says. I remember that the pope spoke about it at the dinner table a couple of weeks before he died. Edoardo, his brother, spoke with great enthusiasm about Paul VI's will. "My will is of another tone and less weighty," he said. Then, indicating a small gap between his index finger and thumb, Papa Luciani said, "Mine is like this." [Father Diego Lorenzi, to author]

When cardinal of Venice he drew up a three-line will that left everything to his seminary in Venice and appointed his auxiliary bishop as executor. When the auxiliary bishop died, Luciani crossed out the bishop's name and put in mine and showed me the will. [Father Mario Senigaglia, to author]

When he died his will was never found, although I am sure he made one. Some money that he had on account in Venice was sent to my family because he had in theory died intestate. We sent it back to the Venice diocese, knowing that was his intention. Part went to his successor and part to nominated charities. I know there was a will. When he went from Belluno to Vittorio Veneto he destroyed his will and made a new one; similarly, when he went to Venice he destroyed that will and made a new one.

Equally when he became pope, Father Carlo, one of his secretaries in Venice, was asked to bring that will down. Don Carlo took it to the Vatican. Either there should be a will dating from the thirty-three days or the Venice will. He was always very meticulous about this. I do not know why they were unable to find it.   [Pia Luciani, to author]

As has already been established, worldly goods held no interest for Luciani, but a papal will invariably includes more than instructions on material assets. There is always a spiritual message—comments and reflections on the state of the Church. Was the will of Albino Luciani destroyed because it accurately reflected the pope's feelings and views on what he had discovered in those thirty-three days? Luciani, an accomplished writer, one of the most literary popes in modern times, failing to leave a final written observation? Were there no last reflections from the revolutionary pope?

It may be considered shocking that so much false information emanates directly from the Vatican, a place considered by millions to be the spiritual home of Christianity. Is it any less shocking that men who have dedicated their lives to Christ destroyed so much vital evidence? Is it any less shocking that the secretary of state, Cardinal Villot, imposed a vow of silence on members of the papal household? Is it any less shocking that Villot, acting in his capacity as virtual caretaker pope, took from the papal bedroom medicine, reading glasses, and slippers? That he removed and destroyed the papers clutched in the dead pope's hands—papers that detailed the important changes Albino Luciani was about to make and that he had discussed with Villot a short time before his totally unexpected death? Was Villot party to a conspiracy to murder the pope? Certainly his subsequent actions were those of a man determined to cover up the truth of that death. Doubtless he took the will as he sat at Luciani's desk in his study and made his series of early-morning phone calls. Having removed the papers from Luciani's hands, Cardinal Villot was clearly determined that no trace of those changes that had so concerned him on the last evening of the pope's life should remain. God alone knows what else was stolen from the papal apartments. We know beyond all doubt that the items already mentioned vanished.

> Father Magee and the sisters and I searched everywhere in the apartment for these things. We could not find them. We searched during the morning of the twenty-ninth of September. [Father Diego Lorenzi, to author]

We know beyond any doubt that these items were in the apartment before Villot was summoned. Indeed, the glasses were on Albino Luciani's face. When Villot left, the items had vanished.

The Vatican lied when it stated that the initial discovery of the dead body was made by Father Magee at "about 5:30 A.M. on the morning of September 29." Sister Vincenza recounted directly to me the moment when she discovered the dead pope. Previously she had used virtually the same words to Monsignor Mario Senigaglia, to Luciani's niece Pia, and to his sister Nina. "It was a miracle that I survived. I have a bad heart. I pushed the bell to summon the secretaries, then I went out to find the other sisters and to awaken Don Diego." She also told me that as she stood for a moment looking transfixed at the body of the dead pope, the alarm clock began to ring. Instinctively she reached out and turned it off.

There is a strange fact that confirms the veracity of Sister Vincenza's statements. Conan Doyle had his fictional creation Sherlock Holmes observe, on one occasion, that there was an odd and significant fact about a dog. It did not bark. In the papal apartments there was beside the pope's bed an alarm clock that did not ring. I have questioned both of the papal secretaries as well as other members of the papal apartments very closely about this. All of them are certain that on the morning Albino Luciani was found dead, the alarm clock he had set every day for many years did not ring. It was set for 4:45 A.M. His body was not officially found until after 5:30 A.M. Diego Lorenzi, who slept so near the pope's bedroom that he could usually even hear the pope moving around, heard no alarm.

When Pope Paul VI died in August 1978 a full twenty-four hours elapsed before his body was embalmed, in accordance with Italian law. When Albino Luciani died in September 1978 Italian law was thrown out the window.

The body of Albino Luciani was embalmed within fourteen hours of his death. Why the hurry? Evidence suggests that Villot wanted an even quicker embalming— that the embalmers were in fact summoned even before the body was "officially" found. If Magee found the body at "shortly after 5:30 A.M." why were the Vatican morticians, the Signoracci brothers, summoned forty-five minutes earlier? Prudence carried to unusual lengths.

On September 29, the Italian news agency ANSA, a highly reputable organization comparable to the Associated Press or Reuters, carried on its wire service, as one of the many news items it ran that day on the pope's death, the following: "The two Signoracci brothers, Ernesto and Renato (the others are Cesare and Arnaldo) were awoken this morning at dawn and at five were collected from their homes by a Vatican car that took them to the mortuary of the little state where they began the operation."

I have traced and interviewed the journalist responsible for that news item, Mario de Francesco. He confirmed the accuracy of his story, which was based on an interview with the Signoracci brothers the same day. I have interviewed the Signoracci brothers on a number of occasions. With regard to the time that they were first contacted they are now, some five years later, uncertain. They confirmed that it was early on the morning of September 29. If Francesco's story is accurate, then we have a Mafia-like situation: morticians ordered before a body is found.

Embalmers were summoned before the cause of death had even been guessed at. Why would the Vatican wish to destroy the most valuable evidence before the official cause of death had been determined?

Was there a secret autopsy on the eve of the pope's funeral? The evidence clearly established a long and detailed examination. What was the purpose? A routine embalming check would have taken only minutes. What were the examining doctors doing behind screens in a locked church for nearly 1½ hours?

It must be recorded that Albino Luciani's personal doctor flew from Venice to Rome on September 29 and agreed with the Vatican doctors that the cause of death was an acute myocardial infarction. But it must also be recorded that in view of the fact that he observed a body that had been dead for hours and contented himself with an external examination, his medical opinion on this was worthless.

If there was one man in Italy who was in a position to confirm that Albino Luciani did in fact die of an acute myocardial infarction, that man was Professor Giovanni Rama, the eye specialist who had been treating Luciani since 1975 for a blood clot in his left eye. He said that this vascular complaint may have led ultimately to Luciani's death, but he added that as a medical opinion it was worthless without an autopsy. If Cardinal Villot and his senior Vatican colleagues really did believe that Albino Luciani had died naturally of an acute myocardial infarction, Professor Rama, with over three years' experience of treating Luciani, was *the* man to call to the Vatican. He told me that he had not been contacted by the Vatican after Albino Luciani's death, and he remarked, "I was very surprised that they did not ask me to come and examine the pope's body."

Easily the most significant observation from a member of the medical profession was the comment attributed to Professor Mario Fontana. Apparently he gave his opinion privately shortly after the pope's death, but it did not become public knowledge until after his own death in 1980.

"If I had to certify, under the same circumstances, the death of an ordinary unimportant citizen, I would quite simply have refused to allow him to be buried."

Professor Mario Fontana was the head of the Vatican medical service.

How and why did darkness fall on the Roman Catholic Church on September 28, 1978?

To establish that a murder has taken place it is not essential to establish a motive. But it helps, as any experienced police officer can confirm. With regard to

the death of Albino Luciani, there is no shortage of
motives. I have clearly identified a number of them in
this book. I have also identified the men with those
motives.

The fact that three of those men—Villot, Cody, and
Marcinkus—are priests does not rule them out as
suspects. Men of the cloth should in theory be above
suspicion. They *should* be. Unfortunately, in the course
of history, many have demonstrated the ability to commit appalling crimes.

Villot, Cody, Marcinkus, Calvi, Sindona, Gelli—each
had a powerful motive. Might Cardinal Villot have murdered to protect his position as secretary of state, to
protect other men who were about to be moved, and
most of all to avoid the furor that undoubtedly would
have ensued when Albino Luciani took a public stance
on the issue of artificial birth control?

Might Cardinal Cody, aided by some of his many
friends within the Vatican, have silenced a pope who
was about to remove him?

Might Bishop Marcinkus, sitting at the head of a
demonstrably corrupt bank, have acted to ensure he
remained president of the IOR?

It is possible that one of these three men is guilty.
Certainly Villot's actions after the pope's death were
criminal: destruction of evidence, a false story, the im-
position of silence. It is conduct that leaves much to be
desired.

Why was Bishop Paul Marcinkus wandering in the
Vatican at such an early hour on September 29? A
normal police investigation would have demanded many
answers from these three men, but at this point such an
interrogation would be impossible. Villot and Cody are
dead, and Marcinkus is hiding from the Italian police
inside the Vatican.

The strongest evidence in defense of these three
men is not the fact that they would have claimed they
were innocent. It is the very fact that they were men of
the cloth; men of the Roman Catholic Church. Two
thousand years has taught such men to take the long
view. The history of the Vatican is the history of countless popes eager to make reforms and yet hemmed in
and neutralized by the system. If the Church in general

and Vatican City in particular so wishes it can and does dramatically influence and affect papal decisions. It has already been recorded how a minority of men imposed their will on Paul VI on the issue of artificial birth control. It has also been recorded how Baggio flatly refused to replace Luciani in Venice.

As for the changes Luciani was about to make, even those within the Vatican who were most deeply opposed to these changes were more likely to react in a manner less dramatic than murder. This does not rule out Villot, Cody, and Marcinkus. Rather, it places them at the bottom of the list of suspects and moves Calvi, Sindona, and Gelli to the top. Did any of these men have the capacity for the deed? The answer, quite simply, is yes.

Whoever murdered Albino Luciani was clearly gambling that the next conclave and the next pope would not hold to Luciani's instructions. All six men stood to gain if the "right" man were elected. Would any kill merely to buy a month's grace? If the "right" man was elected, that month would be extended indefinitely. Two of these men, Villot and Cody, were in the perfect position to influence the next conclave. Marcinkus was not without influence. Neither were Calvi, Sindona, and Gelli.

Recall that it was at the villa of Umberto Ortolani that a group of cardinals had made the final plans that resulted in the election of Pope Paul VI. Gelli and Ortolani as the rulers of P2 had access to each and every part of Vatican City, just as they had access to the inner sanctum of the Italian government, the banks, and the judiciary.

But how could the murder of Albino Luciani have been carried out? Surely Vatican security could not be penetrated? The truth is that Vatican security at the time of Luciani's death could be penetrated with consummate ease—with the same ease that a man named Michael Fagin calmly entered Buckingham Palace in the middle of the night and, after wandering around, sat in Her Majesty's bedroom and asked the Queen of England for a cigarette.

Vatican security in 1978 could be penetrated as easily as the security surrounding President Reagan was

penetrated when John Hinckley wounded the president
and members of his staff. Or as easily as it was on
Wednesday, May 13, 1981, when Mehmet Ali Agca fired
three bullets into Pope John Paul II.

John XXIII had abolished the practice of the Swiss
Guard maintaining an all-night vigil outside his apartment. Nevertheless, Albino Luciani deserved better protection than he was accorded. Vatican City, on an area
of slightly more than a hundred acres, with six entrances,
presented no serious problem to anyone intent on
penetration.

The conclave that had elected Luciani was in theory one of the most stringently guarded places on earth.
The reader may recall the extraordinary lengths that
Pope Paul VI had gone to to ensure that no one could
get in or out during the sessions that chose the new
pope. After his election, Luciani kept the conclave in
session on Saturday, August 26. Father Diego Lorenzi
has graphically described to me how, anxious to join
Luciani, he had wandered unchallenged into the very
heart of the conclave. Only when he was within sight of
the 110 cardinals and his newly elected pope did someone ask him who he was and what he was doing. By
then he could have blown the entire building into the
next world if he had so chosen.

At the time of the August conclave, many writers
commented on the total lack of security. To quote just
two:

> There was too, on this occasion, the unceasing
> if unspoken threat of terrorism. In my view,
> security around the Vatican has not been im-
> pressive over the past week, and the rambling
> place, which opens on to the streets in many
> places, poses perhaps insuperable problems. All
> the more reason for getting the conclave over
> quickly.
>
> Paul Johnson, *London Sunday Telegraph*, Au-
> gust 27, 1978

> As far as I can see, the security cops are mostly
> interested in talking to pretty girls in sidewalk

cafes. I hope the Red Brigades don't have anything in mind for the evening [the day of Paul
VI's funeral]. They could arrive and knock out
many of the world's leaders in one fell swoop.

Father Andrew Greeley, *The Making of the Popes*

Then, suddenly, less than two months later, at the
funeral of Albino Luciani, "the security precautions are
enormous" (Greeley).

It seems strange that after his death the security
that had been nonexistent during Albino Luciani's lifetime should suddenly appear. "There were no security
guards in the area of the papal apartments when I was
there with Albino Luciani," Father Diego Lorenzi has
told me.

I interviewed Sergeant Hans Roggan of the Swiss
Guard. He was the officer in charge on the night Luciani
died. He told me how earlier in the evening he had been
out in Rome for a meal with his mother. They saw the
light on in the papal bedroom when they returned at
10:30 P.M. Roggan's mother left, and he went on duty.
He told me:

For some reason that was a terrible night for
me. That night I was the officer in charge of the
palace. *I simply could not get to sleep.* Eventually I got up and went to the office and worked
on a couple of ledgers. Normally I sleep well.

This is the officer in charge of palace security on
the night of Luciani's sudden death, tossing and turning
in his bed as he tries to *sleep*. To add that no one saw fit
to look into why the pope's bedroom light continued to
shine throughout the night seems almost superfluous.
Much criticism was made at the time of the assassination of President Kennedy about the security, or lack of
it, in Dallas. By comparison with what passed for security around Luciani, the president was extremely well
protected.

Further research has established that at the time of
Luciani's papacy, there was a Swiss Guard member at
the top of the stairs on the Third Loggia. His function

was merely ceremonial, as few people ever entered the papal apartments by this route. Access to the apartments was usually by the elevator—for which many had the key. The elevator entrance was not guarded. Any man dressed as a priest could enter and leave the papal apartments unchallenged.

Further instances of the chaotic security within Vatican City abound. Recently, since the death of Albino Luciani, a staircase near the papal apartments has been rediscovered. It was not hidden by later construction. Quite simply, no one knew of its existence. Or did they? Did someone perhaps know of it in September 1978?

Swiss Guard members who officially sleep on duty. Swiss Guard members who guard an entrance no one uses. A staircase that no one knew about. Even an amateur assassin would not have experienced any great difficulty, and whoever killed Albino Luciani was no amateur. To assist any would-be murderer, *L'Osservatore della Domenica* published a detailed plan, complete with photographs, of the papal apartments. Date of publication: September 3, 1978.

If Mehmet Ali Agca had done his homework, Pope John Paul II would now be dead, murdered as his predecessor was. The more I investigated, the more apparent it became that anyone determined to murder Albino Luciani had a relatively simple task. To obtain access to the papal apartments in September 1978 and to tamper with either the medicines or food or drink of the pope with any of two hundred lethal drugs would have been simple.

The virtual certainty that there would not be an official autopsy merely makes the deed that much easier. There was not even a doctor on twenty-four-hour duty. The Vatican health service did not have at that time the standard equipment of an ordinary modern hospital. There was no emergency medical structure. And in the center of this shambles was an honest man who by the various courses of action he had embarked on had given at least six men very powerful motives for murder.

Despite the appalling attack on Luciani's successor, little has changed with regard to security within the Vatican. During my research I walked in the gardens of the Augustinian residence where Luciani had walked before the August conclave. It was a Sunday in September 1982. Across St. Peter's Square, His Holiness came out onto the balcony to deliver the midday *Angelus*. From where I stood he was in a direct firing line of less than two thousand yards, the top half of his body entirely unprotected. If Agca or one of his kind had been standing there, the pope would have been dead and the assassin back in the heart of Rome within minutes. I had walked into the gardens unchallenged.

A few days after this I walked unchallenged through the St. Anne Gate of the Vatican. Carrying a case large enough to contain several bombs, I went unchecked to the Vatican Bank. The following week I returned to the Vatican in the company of two researchers, all three of us carrying cases and bags. We walked unsearched through the very heart of the Vatican on our way to see Cardinal Ciappi. These events took place only sixteen months after Pope John Paul II had nearly been murdered in St. Peter's Square.

Is it possible that in a country with one of the lowest death rates for coronary heart disease in Europe, a perfectly fit man, whose one unusual physical characteristic, that of low blood pressure, mitigates against a death from heart disease, did in fact die of an acute myocardial infarction? Is it possible that the nonsmoking, moderately eating, abstemious Luciani, who was doing everything that heart specialists would have had him do, was merely unfortunate? Unfortunate in that he died of an acute myocardial infarction despite taking every conceivable health precaution? Unfortunate in that he died despite constant medical checkups, including numerous ECGs, which had never indicated any heart weakness? Unfortunate in that his death was so sudden, so immediate that he did not even have time to press the alarm bell a few inches from his hand? In the words of Professors Rulli and Masini, two of the experts I consulted in Rome, "It is very, very unlikely that death is so quick that the individual does not take any action. Very, very rare."

Indeed, the evidence is all against Luciani's death being natural. The evidence very strongly suggests murder. For myself I have no doubt. I am totally convinced that Albino Luciani was murdered and that at least one of the six suspects I have already identified holds the key.

At sixty-five years of age, Albino Luciani was considered by the conclave that elected him to be exactly the right age for the papacy. Paul VI had been sixty-six when elected and had ruled for fifteen years. John XXIII had been seventy-seven when elected as a stopgap pope, yet he ruled for five years. The conclave had felt that Luciani would rule for at least a decade. Conclaves are expensive affairs. The death of Paul VI and the election of his successor cost over $5 million. The Church is not disposed toward frequent conclaves or short papacies. As a result of Luciani's sudden and unexpected death there were two conclaves in less than two months.

It is not, of course, my contention that the plot to murder Luciani was conceived on September 28, 1978. Obviously the final act was carried out on that day, but the decision had been made earlier. How much earlier is a moot point.

It could have been within days of Luciani's election when the new pope initiated his investigations into Vatican Incorporated. It could have been within the first two weeks of September when the fact that Luciani was investigating Freemasonry within the Vatican became known to some members of the Vatican village. It could have been mid-September when the attitudes of the new pope on artificial birth control and his plans to implement a liberal position on the issue were causing deep concern within the Vatican. It could have been the third week of September when the removal of Marcinkus and others at the Vatican Bank became a certainty. Or the decision may have been made within a few days of its being carried out, days during which Albino Luciani arrived at other far-reaching and crucial decisions. Whenever the plan originated, for the suspects already identified, its implementation came not a moment too soon. For each of these suspects, a few more days might have been too late.

Doubtless it will be observed by some that much of the evidence is circumstantial. But when one is dealing with murder the evidence often is entirely circumstantial. Men and women who plan murder are not given to announcing their intentions on the front page of *The*

Times of London or *Le Monde* or *The Washington Post*. It is relatively rare for independent observers to be present and in a position to offer incontrovertible evidence. Circumstantial evidence has been deemed sufficient to send many a man and woman to the gallows, the electric chair, the firing squad, or the gas chamber. One fact is of overriding importance when considering the murder of Albino Luciani. If it was to succeed in its aim, it had to be committed in such a way that the death could appear to be natural. For nearly six years the perpetrators of the murder of Albino Luciani have succeeded in what must rank as one of the crimes of the century.

To identify correctly who was responsible for the murder of Albino Luciani it is necessary to consider what happened at the conclave following his death and what has happened since then. An examination of certain events should establish which of the six men was at the heart of the conspiracy to murder "God's candidate."

BY BENEFIT OF MURDER—BUSINESS AS USUAL

When voting in the conclave to select a successor to Albino Luciani began on Sunday, October 15, 1978, the Holy Spirit was noticeably absent. A long, bitter struggle, primarily between the supporters of Siri and Benelli, was the predominant theme of the first day's voting. Whoever had been responsible for the murder of Luciani very nearly found themselves faced with the task of ensuring that a second pope should suddenly die. During the course of eight ballots over two days, Cardinal Giovanni Benelli came very close to winning. If Benelli had been elected there is no doubt whatsoever that many of the courses of action Luciani had decided on would have been carried out. Cody would have been removed. Villot would have been replaced. Marcinkus, de Strobel, and Mennini would have been thrown out of the Vatican Bank.

But Benelli fell nine votes short, and the eventual winner, a compromise candidate, Cardinal Karol Wojtyla, bears little resemblance to Albino Luciani. Wojtyla has given countless demonstrations that all he has in common with his predecessor is the papal name John Paul. Despite the efforts of Benelli, Felici, and others, the papacy of John Paul II has been a case of business as usual. The business has benefited immeasurably not only from the murder of Albino Luciani but also from the murders that have followed that strange, lonely death in the Vatican in September 1978.

On being elected, the current pope learned of the changes that Luciani had proposed making. He was advised of the various meetings and discussions that his predecessor had had on a variety of problems. The fiscal information collected by Benelli, Felici, members of APSA, and others on behalf of Luciani was made available to Wojtyla. He was shown the evidence that had led Luciani to conclude that Cardinal Cody of Chicago should be replaced. He was shown the evidence that indicated that Freemasonry had infiltrated the Vatican. He was told of Luciani's dialogue with the U.S. State Department and of the meeting scheduled with the congressional subcommittee on population and birth control. Villot made the new pope fully aware of Albino Luciani's general position on birth control. In short, Pope John Paul II was in the position to bring all Luciani's plans to fruition. Not one of Luciani's proposed changes became a reality. Whoever had murdered the pope had not murdered in vain.

Villot was again appointed secretary of state. Cody remained in control of Chicago. Marcinkus, aided by Mennini, de Strobel, and Monsignor de Bonis, continued to control the Vatican Bank and continued to ensure that the criminal activities with Banco Ambrosiano flourished. Calvi and his P2 masters Gelli and Ortolani were free to continue their massive thefts and frauds under the protection of the Vatican Bank. Sindona was able, at least in the short term, to maintain his freedom in New York. Baggio did not go to Venice. The corrupt Poletti remained cardinal vicar of Rome.

Many millions of words have been written since the election of Karol Wojtyla in attempts to analyze and understand what kind of man he is. As can be seen, he is the kind of man who could allow men like Villot, Cody, Marcinkus, Mennini, de Strobel, de Bonis, and Poletti to

remain in office. There can be no defense on the grounds
of ignorance. Marcinkus is directly answerable to the
pope, and it is inconceivable that the pope could be
unaware of the degree of guilt that clings to Marcinkus.
With regard to Cody, His Holiness was made aware of
the full facts in October 1978 by Cardinals Benelli and
Baggio. Wojtyla did nothing. We have a pope who publicly berates Nicaraguan priests for their involvement
in politics and simultaneously gives his blessing for
large quantities of dollars to be made available, secretly
and illegally, to Solidarity in Poland. It is a papacy of
double standards: one for the pope and another for the
rest of mankind. The papacy of John Paul II has been a
triumph for the wheeler-dealers, for the corrupt, for the
international thieves such as Calvi, Gelli, and Sindona.
While His Holiness has maintained a very highly publi-
cized image, not unlike some endless rock 'n' roll tour,
the men backstage are ensuring that it is business as
usual. It is to be regretted that the severely moralizing
speeches of His Holiness cannot, apparently, be heard
backstage.

As I have recorded earlier, after the election of
Luciani, Bishop Paul Marcinkus cautioned his colleagues
in the Vatican Bank and Roberto Calvi in Buenos Aires:
"Remember that this pope has different ideas from the
previous one and that many things will be changing
here."

With the election of Wojtyla it was straight back to
the values of Paul VI, with interest. With regard to the
infiltration of the Vatican by Freemasons, for example,
the Vatican, through the current pope, has now not only
taken on board various Masons from various lodges but
it has also acquired its own in-house version. Its name
is Opus Dei (God's Work).

On July 25, Albino Luciani had written on Opus Dei
in *Il Gazzettino*, the Venetian newspaper. His remarks
were confined to a short history of the movement and a
discussion of some of the organization's aspirations toward lay spirituality. As to the more controversial aspects of Opus Dei, Luciani was either ignorant of them,
which is unlikely, or was yet again displaying his sense
of quiet discretion.

With the election of Karol Wojtyla quiet discretion

has become a rare commodity. His espousal of Opus Dei is well documented. In view of the fact that this Catholic sect shares many views and values with the corrupt P2 and that Opus Dei is now a force to be reckoned with inside Vatican City, a few basic details are in order.

Opus Dei is a Roman Catholic organization of international scope. Though its actual membership is relatively small (estimates vary between sixty thousand and eighty thousand), its influence is vast. It is a secret society, something that is strictly forbidden by the Church. Opus Dei denies that it is a secret organization but refuses to make its membership list available. It was founded by a Spanish priest, Monsignor Josemaría Escrivá de Balagner, in 1928. It is part of the extreme right wing of the Catholic Church, a political fact that has ensured that the organization has attracted enemies as well as members. About 5 percent of its members are priests; the remainder are laypersons of both sexes. Although Opus Dei has members from many walks of life, it seeks especially to attract those from the upper classes, including young professionals with potential to rise to positions of power. Dr. John Roche, an Oxford University lecturer and former member of Opus Dei, describes it as "sinister, secretive, and Orwellian." It may be that its members' preoccupation with self-mortification is the cause for much of the news media hostility that has been directed toward the sect. Certainly the idea of flogging yourself on your bare back and wearing strips of metal with inward-pointing prongs around the thigh for the greater glory of God might prove difficult for the majority of people in the latter part of the twentieth century to accept. No one, however, should doubt the total sincerity of the Opus Dei membership. They are equally devoted to a task of wider significance: the take-over of the Roman Catholic Church. That should be a cause of the greatest concern not only to Roman Catholics but also to everybody else. Under Pope John Paul II, Opus Dei has flourished. If the present pope is not a member of Opus Dei, he is to its adherents everything they could wish a pope to be. One of his first acts after his election was to go to the tomb of the founder of Opus Dei and pray. Subsequently he has granted the sect the status of a personal prelature, a significant step on the journey to Cardinal Cody land, where one becomes answerable only to Rome and God.

This organization has, according to its own claims, members working on over six hundred newspapers, journals, and scientific publications scattered around the world. It has members in over fifty radio and television stations. In the 1960s three of its members were in the cabinet of Spanish dictator Francisco Franco, helping to create Spain's "economic miracle." The head of the huge Rumasa conglomerate in Spain, José Mateos, is a member of Opus Dei; he is also currently on the run after disclosures concerning the network of corruption he built, a network not unlike that of Calvi.*

Opus Dei is massively wealthy. José Mateos alone has funneled millions into the organization. A considerable amount of the money from Mateos came from illegal deals with Calvi perpetrated in both Spain and Argentina. P2 paymaster and Opus Dei paymaster: could this be what the Church means when it talks of God moving in mysterious ways?

Since the death of Albino Luciani and his succession by Karol Wojtyla, the Italian Solution that was applied to the problem of an honest pope has been frequently applied to other problems that have confronted Marcinkus, Sindona, Calvi, and Gelli. The litany of murder and mayhem perpetrated to mask plundering on an unimaginable scale makes grim reading. It also serves as powerful evidence after the deed to confirm that Albino Luciani was murdered.

Roberto Calvi, Licio Gelli, and Umberto Ortolani did not return to Italy while Luciani reigned as pope. Calvi eventually returned in late October after the election of Karol Wojtyla. Gelli and Ortolani continued to monitor events from Uruguay. Was the fact that the three men were in various South American cities together just mere coincidence? Did their business discussions really need to continue throughout August and September into October? Was it really necessary for either Gelli or Ortolani to insist on staying close to Calvi throughout September 1978? Did it really take

---

*In late April 1984 Mateos was arrested in West Germany. The Spanish authorities have begun extradition proceedings.

Calvi all that time to meet important officials to discuss opening new branches of Banco Ambrosiano?

The breathing space that Calvi had gained because of Luciani's death looked as if it might come to an end when, on October 30, Calvi met in Milan with Bank of Italy inspector Giulio Padalino. Again Calvi, with his eyes focused firmly on his shoes, declined to give straight answers to the questions he was asked. On November 17, the Bank of Italy inspection of Banco Ambrosiano was completed.

Despite the fraudulent letter from Marcinkus and his Vatican Bank colleagues concerning the ownership of Suprafin, despite the lies and evasions of Roberto Calvi, despite the help of his protector Licio Gelli, the central bank inspectors concluded in a very lengthy report that a great deal was rotten in the state of Calvi's empire.

From South America and using his own special code name, Gelli telephoned Calvi at his private residence. For Calvi, wallowing ever deeper in a mire of Mafia/Vatican/P2 dealings, the news was bad.

Within days of Inspector Giulio Padalino handing in his report to Mario Sarcinelli, head of vigilance of the Bank of Italy, a copy of the full report was in Gelli's hands in Buenos Aires, courtesy of the P2 network. Gelli advised Calvi that the report was about to be sent from the Bank of Italy to the Milan magistrates and specifically to a man Gelli feared would receive it, Judge Emilio Alessandrini.

Again Calvi was teetering on the edge of exposure and total ruin. Emilio Alessandrini could not be bought. Highly talented and courageous, he represented for Calvi, Marcinkus, Gelli, and also Sindona a very serious threat. If he pursued this investigation with his customary vigor, then Calvi was certainly finished, Marcinkus would be exposed, Gelli would have lost the crucial assets that the continuing thefts from Ambrosiano brought him, and Sindona would be confronted with the most powerful argument yet for his immediate extradition from the United States.

By early January 1979 the financial circles of Milan were yet again buzzing with rumors about the Knight, Roberto Calvi. Judge Emilio Alessandrini, having carefully studied a summary of the five-hundred-page report compiled by the Bank of Italy, ordered Lieutenant Colonel Cresta, the commander of the Milan tax police, to send his men into the "priests' bank." His men were to check point by point the many criminal irregularities that were detailed in the report. No one outside official circles had access to the report—no one, that is, except Calvi and Gelli.

On January 21 *L'Espresso* commented on the rumors that were flying around the city, including the rumor that Calvi and his entire board of directors were about to be arrested and that Calvi's passport would be withdrawn. Something had to be done quickly before the general public created a run on Banco Ambrosiano.

On the morning of January 29 Alessandrini kissed his wife good-bye, then drove his young son to school. Having dropped off the boy, he began to drive to his office. A few seconds before 8:30 A.M. he stopped for a red light on Via Muratori. He was still gazing at the red light when five men approached his car and began firing bullets into his body.

Later in the day a group of left-wing terrorists called Prima Linea claimed responsibility for the murder. The group also left a leaflet about the murder in a telephone booth in Milan Central Station. Neither the phone call nor the leaflet gave any clear reason for the murder.

Why would an extreme left-wing group cold-bloodedly murder a judge who was nationally known for his investigations into right-wing terrorism? Emilio Alessandrini was one of the leading investigators into the Piazza Fontana bombing, a right-wing atrocity. Why would Prima Linea murder a man who was clearly attempting, through legal and proper channels, what the terrorists would in theory most applaud—to bring right-wing criminal elements to task for their acts?

Groups such as Prima Linea and the Red Brigades do not kill and maim merely for political and ideological motives. They are also guns for hire. The links, for example, between the Red Brigades and the Naples Camorra (local Mafia) are well documented.

At the time of writing, five men who have already confessed to the murder of Alessandrini are standing trial. Their evidence concerning the actual murder is full of detail, but when it comes to the motive their evidence raises more questions than it answers.

Marco Donat Cattin, the second man who opened fire on the trapped, unarmed, and helpless judge, observed: "We waited for the newspapers to come out with reports of the attack and we found in the magistrate's obituaries the motives to justify the attack."

Three days after the murder, on the afternoon of February 1, Roberto Calvi was enjoying a drink at a Milan cocktail party. The conversation inevitably turned to the recent outrage. Calvi promptly attempted to elicit sympathy, not for Signora Alessandrini and her children, but for himself: "It really is such a shame. Only the day before this happened Alessandrini had told me that he was taking no further action and that he was going to have the case filed."

The murder of Luciani had given Marcinkus, Calvi, Sindona, and their P2 friends breathing space. Now the murder of Emilio Alessandrini bought them further time. The investigation initiated by Judge Alessandrini continued, but at a snail's pace.

In the Bank of Italy, Mario Sarcinelli was acutely aware of the lack of momentum. Sarcinelli and the director of the Bank, Paolo Baffi, were determined that the long, complex investigation that had been carried out during the previous year would not be a wasted exercise.

In February 1979 Mario Sarcinelli summoned Calvi to the Bank of Italy. Calvi was questioned closely about Suprafin, about the Ambrosiano relationship with the IOR, about the Nassau branch, and about who precisely owned Banco Ambrosiano. With Alessandrini dead, Calvi was a new man, or rather his old self. The eyes were again ice cold. Licio Gelli's protection had inspired in him an even greater degree of arrogance than usual. He flatly refused to answer Sarcinelli's questions, but the encounter left Calvi in no doubt that the Bank of Italy investigation had not been brought to an end by the latest murder.

Again he discussed his problems with Gelli, who reassured him the matter would be dealt with. Before that problem was resolved there was, however, another matter causing the Masons of P2 considerable concern.

This was the problem posed by lawyer and journalist Mino Pecorelli. Among Pecorelli's many activities was that of editing an unusual weekly emanating from the agency referred to earlier, OP.

OP, the name of the weekly, has been described as "muckraking" and "scandalistic." It was both. It was also accurate. Throughout the 1970s it acquired and subsequently printed an astonishing number of exposés and allegations on Italian corruption. It became required reading for anyone who was interested in knowing exactly who was robbing whom. Despite Italy's stringent libel laws, it led a charmed life. Pecorelli clearly had access to highly sensitive information. Italian journalists frequently went into print with OP-inspired articles. Privately they tried to ascertain who was behind this weekly, which was clearly above the law, but OP remained a mystery. Pecorelli's sister Rosita alleged during a television interview that the news agency OP was financed by Prime Minister Andreotti.

In the early 1970s the name of Michele Sindona was frequently linked with OP. Pecorelli obviously had sources working within the Italian secret service, but his major contacts were inside an organization more powerful and, indeed, more secret than such official government agencies. Mino Pecorelli was a member of P2, and it was from this illegal Masonic lodge that he derived much of the information that set the Italian news media buzzing. At one lodge meeting Licio Gelli invited members to contribute documents and information that would be passed on to OP. The primary function of OP during this period was, therefore, to further Gelli's ambitions and the aims of P2. In mid-1978, however, Pecorelli decided on a little private enterprise. Blackmail. He obtained information about one of the biggest thefts in Italian financial history. The mastermind behind the theft was Licio Gelli. The scheme was responsible for robbing Italy of $2.5 billion in oil tax revenues.

In Italy, the same petroleum product is used to heat buildings as to drive diesel trucks. The oil for heating is dyed to distinguish it from that used for vehicles and is taxed at a rate fifty times lower than the diesel fuel. It was a situation ready-made for a criminal such as Gelli.

Under his guidance, oil magnate Bruno Musselli, a P2 member, doctored the dyes. The head of the finance police, General Raffaele Giudice, a P2 member, falsified the paperwork to ensure that all the fuel was taxed at the lower rate. The fuel was then sold to petroleum outlets, which paid the conspirators at the higher rate.

The profits were then transferred, thanks to P2 member Michele Sindona, through the Vatican Bank to a series of secret accounts at Sindona's Swiss bank, Finabank. Licio Gelli became a familiar sight walking through the St. Anne Gate with large suitcases containing billions of stolen lire.

General Giudice had been appointed head of the finance police by Prime Minister Giulio Andreotti, a close friend of Licio Gelli. This particular appointment had been made after Cardinal Poletti, cardinal vicar of Rome, had written to the prime minister strongly recommending Giudice for the post. Poletti, it will be recalled, was one of the men Albino Luciani had planned to remove from Rome. The Vatican link with this scandal was unknown to Pecorelli, but he knew enough about this gigantic theft of government revenue to begin publishing small tidbits of information. A deputation that included Christian Democrat Senator Claudio Vitalone, Judge Carlo Testi, and General Donato lo Prete of the finance police bought his silence. The articles on the scandal ceased.

Realizing that more money could be obtained by such dubious techniques, Pecorelli began to write about the Freemasons. His issue of early September 1978, containing, incredibly, the names of over one hundred Vatican Freemasons,* had been a warning shot across Gelli's bows. The fact that a copy arrived on the desk of Albino Luciani who, having carefully checked it, began to act upon the information, was the supreme irony for Gelli, who was already acutely aware of the threat Luciani posed to his paymaster, Roberto Calvi.

With Luciani dead, Gelli attempted to deal with Pecorelli. Gelli bribed him. Inevitably Pecorelli demanded more money for his silence. Gelli refused to pay. Pecorelli published the first of what he promised would be a

*The Vatican Freemasons were, by and large, not P2 members.

series of articles. It revealed that Gelli, the pillar of extreme right-wing fascism, had spied for the Communists during the war and had continued to work for them afterward. Pecorelli, having now embraced the mantle of a fearless investigative journalist, promised his readers he would reveal everything about P2. For good measure he revealed that Licio Gelli, former Nazi, ex-Fascist, and late Communist, also had very strong links with the CIA. Pecorelli had revealed so much of the truth that his colleagues in P2 concluded that he had betrayed them.

On March 20, 1979, Gelli telephoned Pecorelli at his Rome office. He suggested a peace talk over dinner the following day "if that is convenient." It was. During the course of the conversation Pecorelli mentioned that he would be working late at the office that evening, but dinner on the following day would be possible. It was a dinner that Pecorelli never ate.

Mino Pecorelli left his office on Via Orazio at 9:15 P.M. and headed toward his car parked a short distance away. The two bullets that killed him as he sat in his car were fired from within his mouth, a classic Sicilian Mafia gesture of *sasso in bocca*, a rock in the mouth of a dead man to demonstrate that he will talk no more.

Unable to have dinner with his old friend, Licio Gelli used the time to open his secret files of P2 members and write "deceased" alongside the entry for Mino Pecorelli.

No one has ever "claimed" responsibility for Pecorelli's murder, but in 1983 Antonio Viezzer, at one time a high-ranking officer in SID, Italy's secret service, was arrested and charged on suspicion of involvement in the killing of Pecorelli. Antonio Viezzer was a member of P2.

A few days before Pecorelli was silenced forever, one of the men he had named on the list of Vatican Masons, Cardinal Jean Villot, preceded him to the grave. He died still holding the vast array of official titles that had been his during Luciani's brief reign. For a man who, if not a party to the criminal conspiracy to murder Albino Luciani, most certainly gave that conspiracy vital aid, Villot's own death, which, as we shall see, was described in a series of well-documented medical reports, serves as a curious contrast to that of Luciani, who "died like a flower in the night."

While the Vatican buried its late secretary of state, the battle for a little secular purification continued across the Tiber. The head of vigilance of the Bank of Italy, Mario Sarcinelli, and his director, Paolo Baffi, were by now demanding swift action on the Calvi investigation. They insisted that there was more than enough evidence to justify immediate arrest. Clearly Gelli and Calvi agreed with them.

On March 25, 1979, arrests were made—but not of Roberto Calvi and his colleagues. The men arrested were Sarcinelli and Baffi. Rome magistrate Judge Mario Alibrandi, a man of known right-wing sympathies, released Baffi on bail because of his age, sixty-seven years. Sarcinelli was less fortunate and was thrown into prison. The charges against the two men of failing to disclose knowledge of a crime were clearly false, and after two weeks Sarcinelli was also freed on bail. The charges, however, would hang over the two men until January 1980, when their spuriousness was finally admitted. In the interim, the magistrate refused to lift his order that barred Sarcinelli from returning to his position as head of vigilance at the bank for a year. With this action P2 had effectively neutralized the investigation. Paolo Baffi, the shocked and distressed director of the bank, resigned in September 1979. The demonstration of the power of Calvi and his criminal associates had convinced Baffi that he and his men were fighting a force far greater than any wielded by the Bank of Italy. After the false arrests in March there had been a second, even greater demonstration of the power of these forces. This demonstration occurred in Milan. It was organized and paid for by Michele Sindona.

While Calvi and his friends were coping in their own particular way with their problems in Italy, their fellow P2 member, Michele Sindona, was getting his fair share in New York. Sindona had finally beaten the attempts to have him extradited to Italy, but the manner of his victory brought him little comfort.

On March 9, 1979, the Justice Department had indicted Sindona and charged him with ninety-nine counts of fraud, perjury, and misappropriation of bank funds.

The charges stemmed directly from the collapse of the Franklin National. Sindona, having posted a $3 million bond, had been released on the condition that he present himself daily to the U.S. marshal's office.

In the first week of July 1979 a federal court judge ruled that Sindona could not be extradited to Italy to face bank fraud charges because he was soon to face similar charges in the United States. The extradition treaty between Italy and the United States has a double-jeopardy clause. Assistant U.S. Attorney John Kenney commented that the U.S. government intended to send Sindona back to Italy after the case against him in the United States had been completed.

Kenney, still alive despite the $100,000 contract that had been put out by Sindona's colleagues, owed his continuing survival to one fact alone. In Italy, to kill a judge or a prosecutor is often an effective ploy in persuading the authorities to slow down a prosecution. The Alessandrini murder is an excellent example. In the United States, such a murder would have precisely the opposite effect. A $100,000 fee was very tempting, but the professionals knew that Kenney's murder would result not only in a ruthless pursuit of the killer but also in a vigorous acceleration of the prosecution against Sindona.

While confronting the reality of a New York trial with the tenacious Kenney prosecuting, Sindona decided to use the Italian Solution on another man who was causing him an even greater degree of discomfort: Giorgio Ambrosoli.

On September 29, 1974, the attorney Giorgio Ambrosoli was appointed the liquidator of Sindona's Banca Privata Italiana. As stated earlier, Banca Privata had been created by Sindona in July 1974 when he merged two of his banks, Banca Unione and Banca Privata Finanziaria—one large crooked bank to replace two medium-sized crooked banks. By 1979 no man knew more about Sindona's crooked dealings than Giorgio Ambrosoli. Appointed liquidator jointly by the Treasury Ministry and the director of the Bank of Italy, Ambrosoli had begun the nightmarish task of unraveling the affairs of a modern Machiavelli. As early as March 21, 1975, the cautious and careful Ambrosoli, in a secret report to Italy's attorney general, showed he was convinced of the criminality of Sindona's activities. The evidence he had studied at that date satisfied him that far from the bankruptcy being caused merely by bad business practices, Sindona and the management running his banks in early 1974 "wanted to create the circumstances for bankruptcy." It had been a coldly planned looting.

Giorgio Ambrosoli was a courageous man. At about the same time that he was informing the attorney general of his preliminary findings, he confided some of his inner feelings to his wife. "Whatever happens, I'll certainly pay a high price for taking this job. But I knew that before taking it on, and I'm not complaining. It has been a unique chance for me to do something for the country. . . . Obviously I'm making enemies for myself."

Slowly and methodically Ambrosoli began to make sense of what Sindona had deliberately made senseless. The parking of shares, the buy-backs, the dazzling transfers through the myriad companies. While Sindona was lecturing American students on his dreams of cosmic capitalism, the quiet, circumspect Milanese lawyer was establishing beyond all doubt that Sindona was corrupt to his well-manicured fingertips.

In 1977, Ambrosoli was approached by Rome lawyer Rodolfo Guzzi with a complicated offer to buy Banca Privata out of bankruptcy. Ambrosoli discovered that Guzzi was working on behalf of Michele Sindona. He declined the offer despite the fact that at least two Christian Democrat ministers supported it.

The power Sindona still wielded can be gauged from this ministerial support. Ambrosoli was given a further illustration of that power when Baffi, the director of the Bank of Italy, told him of the pressure being exerted by Franco Evangelisti, Prime Minister Andreotti's right-hand man, who was urging the Bank of Italy to arrive at a variation of the Italian Solution. He wanted Baffi to authorize the central bank to cover Sindona's debts. Baffi refused. The Ambrosoli investigation continued.

In the mountain of papers he was diligently working his way through, Ambrosoli kept coming across references to "the five hundred"; other references made it clear that these five hundred people were the super exporters on the black market, the men and women who, with the aid of Sindona and the Vatican Bank, had poured currency out of Italy illegally. The actual list of names might continue to elude Ambrosoli, but very little else did. He ascertained that a large number of public organizations, respectable institutions such as the insurance giant INPDAI, placed their funds at Sindona's banks for a lower rate of interest than was generally current—8 percent rather than 13 percent. They received, however, a secret interest rate that went straight into the pockets of the directors of these companies.

Ambrosoli identified many of the devices that Sindona had used to export money illegally, including buying dollars at higher than the market rate with the balance paid to a foreign account in London, Switzerland, or the United States.

Ambrosoli began to compile his own list of guilty names. It never reached five hundred—Michele Sindona saw to that—but it did reach seventy-seven names, including the Vatican's Massimo Spada and Luigi Mennini. The liquidator obtained irrefutable evidence of Vatican Bank complicity in many of Sindona's crimes. Throughout the entire period of his work on behalf of the Bank of Italy this man, working virtually single-handedly, was subjected to the range of Sindona behavior. Sindona brought actions alleging embezzlement against Ambrosoli. Then the actions would be dropped to be replaced by a different approach from Sindona's son-in-law, Pier Sandro Magnoni, inviting Ambrosoli to become president of Sindona's new bank "once you have settled this tiring business of the bankruptcies."

Sindona's P2 infiltration was so total that Magnoni was able to quote verbatim a passage from a secret report compiled by Ambrosoli that had been officially seen by only a handful of bank officials.

By March 1979 Ambrosoli was able to put a figure on the size of Il Crack Sindona as far as Banca Privata was concerned. The loss was 257 billion lire (about $300 million). Also by March 1979 Ambrosoli had been subjected to a series of threatening phone calls. The callers always had American accents.

The threats and the insults had grown in intensity since late 1978. The callers varied their tactics—sometimes tempting Ambrosoli with offers of vast amounts of money, other times making outright threats. It was made quite clear on whose behalf the calls were being made. "Why don't you go and see Sindona in the States? As a friend," said one caller with a heavy American accent. Ambrosoli declined the invitation and began taping the phone calls. He told his friends and colleagues of the calls. Eventually he played one of the tape recordings to one of Sindona's lawyers. A few days later the next call came. "You dirty bastard. Think you've been clever taping the calls, eh?" The Sindona lawyer was later to admit that after hearing the tape he had immediately called Sindona in New York.

On April 10, 1979, Sindona confronted another man he considered an enemy, Enrico Cuccia, managing director of Mediobanca, a publicly owned investment bank. Sindona's assessment was accurate. Cuccia had thwarted the Sindona take-over of Bastogi in 1972. He had arrived at the conclusion long before many others that Sindona was a megalomaniacal crook. During their April 1979 meeting Cuccia was given ample evidence to justify the conclusion he had arrived at nearly eight years earlier. What had prompted Cuccia's visit to New York was a series of phone calls that *he* had been receiving from men with American accents. These calls, like those to Ambrosoli, were of a threatening nature. While Ambrosoli chose to stay with his work in Milan, Cuccia elected to confront Sindona.

Sindona made a number of demands. One was that Cuccia should have the Italian arrest warrant withdrawn—the fact that in his absence he had been sentenced to 3½ years' imprisonment Sindona brushed aside as a trivial point. Sindona further demanded that Cuccia find 257 billion lire and bail out Banca Privata. For good measure he also demanded that Cuccia find even more money to provide for the Sindona family. Apart from making the gracious gesture of allowing Signor Cuccia to continue to live, it is unclear what Sindona was offering in return.

During the course of this highly unusual conversation Sindona, perhaps by way of demonstrating Cuccia's very real danger, introduced the subject of Giorgio Ambrosoli. "That damned liquidator of my bank is harming me, and therefore I want to have him killed. I will make him disappear in such a way that he leaves no trace." This is the reality of the Mafia mentality. Al Pacino and well-cut suits, lovable children, and doting fathers is the fantasy world of the Mafia. The reality is men such as Michele Sindona.

These threats were uttered less than one month after Sindona had been indicted on ninety-nine counts. The same mentality that had concluded that the extradition proceedings would vanish if Assistant U.S. Attorney John Kenney were murdered was at work again. If Ambrosoli could be silenced, presumably the criminal charges would vanish like the morning mist. A mind that reasons along such lines would not have much difficulty planning to kill a pope.

Enrico Cuccia left the meeting unimpressed. In October 1979 a bomb exploded under the front door of Cuccia's apartment in Milan. Luckily no one was injured. Giorgio Ambrosoli was to prove less fortunate.

It was apparent to all parties concerned with the forthcoming trial of Sindona that the evidence of Giorgio Ambrosoli was of paramount importance. On June 9, 1979, the judge who had been appointed to try the Sindona case, Thomas Griesa, arranged for Ambrosoli to swear a deposition in Milan.

By that date the man who was given a $100,000 contract to kill Giorgio Ambrosoli had been in the Hotel Splendido, Milan, for twenty-four hours. He had checked in as Robert McGovern. He was also known as "Billy the Exterminator." His real name is William Arico. At his first-class hotel near Milan Central Station, Arico dined with the five men who were to assist him with the murder. His two main accomplices were Charles Arico, his son, and Rocky Messina. Their weapons included an M-11 machine gun specially fitted with a silencer, and five P-38 revolvers. Arico hired a Fiat and began to stalk Ambrosoli.

The request for a detailed statement from Ambrosoli had initially been made by Sindona's lawyers. They had hoped to demonstrate the absurdity of the charges with which their client stood accused in New York. Their

awakening, which began on the morning of July 9, was
rude in the extreme. Drawing on his four years of work
and over a hundred thousand sheets of meticulously
prepared notes, Ambrosoli quietly began to reveal the
appalling truth in front of a cluster of American lawyers,
two special marshals representing Judge Griesa, and
the Italian judge Giovanni Galati.

When the court adjourned after the first day's
hearing, Sindona's lawyers could easily be identified as
they left. They were the men with worried faces.

Oblivious of the fact that he was being followed,
Ambrosoli went on to another meeting. This was with
Boris Giuliano, the deputy superintendent of the Palermo
police force and head of that city's CID. The subject was
the same as the one on which Ambrosoli had been
testifying all day—Michele Sindona. Giuseppe Di Cristina,
a Mafia enforcer employed by the families Gambino,
Inzerillo, and Spatola, had been murdered in Palermo
in May 1978. On his body Giuliano had discovered checks
and other documents that indicated that Sindona had
been recycling the proceeds from heroin sales through
the Vatican Bank to his Amincor Bank in Switzerland.
Having compared notes on their separate investigations,
the two men agreed to have a fuller meeting once
Ambrosoli had finished his testimony to the American
lawyers.

Later that day, Ambrosoli was again involved in
business concerning Sindona. Ambrosoli had a long telephone conversation with Lieutenant Colonel Antonio
Varisco, head of the security service in Rome. They
discussed the object of Varisco's current investigation,
P2.

On July 10, as his deposition continued, Ambrosoli
dropped one of a large number of bombshells. Detailing
how Banca Cattolica del Veneto had changed hands and
how Pacchetti had been unloaded by Sindona to Calvi,
Ambrosoli stated that Sindona had paid a "brokerage
fee of $6.5 million to a Milanese banker and an Ameri-
can bishop."

On July 11 Ambrosoli completed his deposition. It
was agreed that he would return the following day and
sign the record of his testimony and that the week after
he would be available for questioning and clarification

of his evidence by the U.S. prosecutors and Sindona's
lawyers.

Ambrosoli had a long day; by the time he got back
to his apartment it was nearly midnight. From the window his wife waved. They were about to have a belated
dinner. As Ambrosoli moved toward his door Arico and
two of his aides appeared from the shadows. The question came out of the darkness.

"Giorgio Ambrosoli?"

"Sì."

Arico aimed at point-blank range, and at least four
bullets from a P-38 entered the lawyer's chest. He died
instantly.

By 6:00 A.M. Arico was in Switzerland. A $100,000
sum had been transferred from a Sindona account at
Calvi's Banca del Gottardo into an account Arico had
under the name of Robert McGovern at the Crédit Suisse
in Geneva. The account number is 415851-22-1.

On July 13, 1979, less than forty-eight hours after
the murder of Giorgio Ambrosoli, Lieutenant Colonel
Antonio Varisco was being driven in a white BMW along
the Lungotevere Arnaldo da Brescia in Rome. It was
8:30 A.M. A white Fiat 128 pulled alongside. A sawed-off
shotgun appeared through its window. Four shots were
fired, and the lieutenant colonel and his chauffeur were
dead. One hour later the Red Brigades "claimed"
responsibility.

On July 21, 1979, Boris Giuliano went into the Lux
Bar on Via Francesco Paolo Di Biasi in Palermo for a
morning coffee. The time was 8:05 A.M. Having drunk
his coffee, he moved toward the cash register to pay. A
man approached and fired six shots into Giuliano. The
cafe was crowded at the time. Subsequent police questioning established that no one had seen anything. No
one had heard anything. Boris Giuliano's position was
taken by Giuseppe Impallomeni, a member of P2.

Not even the members of the Red Brigades "claimed,"
falsely or otherwise, the responsibility for the murders
of Giorgio Ambrosoli and Boris Giuliano. When the news
of the murder of Ambrosoli was flashed to New York,
Michele Sindona, the man who had paid to have the
liquidator taken care of by an exterminator, responded
in typical fashion. "No one must link me with this act

of cowardice, and I will take decisive legal action against anyone who does."

Two years earlier, during an interview with *Il Fiorino*, Sindona had made a far more significant statement. He spoke of the "plot that exists against me" and listed men he thought were its "leaders," including Giorgio Ambrosoli. Sindona observed: "There are many who should be afraid. . . . I repeat, there are very many."

Giorgio Ambrosoli did not die in vain. His many years of work plus the unsigned deposition were to prove powerful weapons for the prosecution during the forthcoming trial of Michele Sindona.

The Milanese banker and the American bishop referred to in Ambrosoli's sworn deposition were quickly identified as Calvi and Bishop Paul Marcinkus. Marcinkus was to deny flatly receiving such a commission. Ambrosoli was most certainly not the kind of man to make such an accusation without overwhelming proof. With regard to the veracity of statements made by Bishop Marcinkus, it will be recalled that shortly after the Sindona crash he denied ever having met Sindona.

Who were the main beneficiaries of this series of appalling and inhuman crimes? The list begins to have a familiar ring: Marcinkus, Calvi, Sindona, Gelli, and Ortolani.

In Milan the terror after the series of murders was most discernible in the Palace of Justice. Men who had worked alongside Ambrosoli suddenly had trouble remembering that they had assisted him during his investigation of Sindona's affairs. Judge Luca Mucci, who had taken over the criminal investigation after Alessandrini's murder, was proceeding so slowly that spectators might have thought he had been turned to stone. An initial evaluation of the Bank of Italy's investigation into Banco Ambrosiano arrived at the astounding conclusion that Calvi's explanations were perfectly acceptable. This at least was the view of the finance police.

Padalino, the Bank of Italy official who had actually headed the 1978 probe, found himself frequently summoned to Milan, where he was confronted by doubting magistrates. As the summer of 1979 wore on, Padalino was threatened and harassed by elements of the Milan judiciary. He was warned that his report on Ambrosiano amounted to libel. Gelli's P2 and Sindona's Mafia were reducing the concept of justice to a depravity.

An example of just how powerful the Calvi-Gelli axis was can be gauged from events in Nicaragua at about the time of Emilio Alessandrini's murder in January 1979. Calvi had opened a branch of his empire in Managua in September 1977. The bank was called Ambrosiano Group Banco Comercial. Its official function was "conducting international commercial transactions." Its actual function was to move from the Nassau branch, with director Bishop Paul Marcinkus's approval, a large amount of the evidence that would reveal the fraudulent and criminal devices used in the share-pushing/acquisition of the Milan parent bank. In this way, the evidence would be hidden even more securely from the Bank of Italy. As always there was a price to be paid. Gelli had smoothed the way with introductions to Nicaragua's dictator, Anastasio Somoza. After several million dollars had been dropped into the dictator's pocket, he announced that it would be an excellent idea for Calvi to open a branch in his country. One of the side benefits for Calvi was the acquisition of a Nicaraguan diplomatic passport, something he retained to the end of his life.

Calvi and Gelli were aware of the possibility of a Sandinista take-over in the not too distant future. These men, who had carried both Fascist and Partisan papers during the Second World War, had not changed a lifetime's habit of being double-faced or, in banking terms, prudent. Calvi gave equally large amounts of money to the rebels—some went to buy grain, some went to buy arms.

Early in 1979 the left-wing take-over of Nicaragua became a reality. Like many left-wing take-overs before, this one promptly nationalized all foreign banks—with one exception: the Ambrosiano Group Banco Comercial continued to trade under Roberto Calvi. Even left-wing idealists, it would seem, have a price.

In New York, with a large array of his Italian enemies silenced either permanently or temporarily, Michele Sindona decided toward the end of July 1979 that he would after all return to Italy. Illegally. The fact that he was on $3 million bail in New York and had to report daily to the marshal's office and that he had already been sentenced to 3½ years' imprisonment in Italy and was wanted on further charges might seem like good reasons not to return. Sindona's solution was simplicity itself. With the aid of his Mafia associates in New York and Sicily he arranged his own "kidnap."

Among Sindona's reasons for returning to Italy was his need to marshal support for his forthcoming trial in New York. Sindona took the view that a great many people owed him favors. He now wished to collect. To persuade his Italian friends and colleagues to repay him, Sindona was prepared to play the one ace he still held. He would name the five hundred.

The list of five hundred major Italian exporters of illegal currency has proved elusive to Italian authorities during the past ten years. A number of investigators apart from Giorgio Ambrosoli were continually stumbling over references to the list of five hundred, which allegedly includes the names of many of the most powerful men in Italy. It has become the Holy Grail of Italian finance, but the list is not merely legendary. It exists. Sindona and Gelli certainly have copies of it, and Calvi had one, too. Sindona believed that the threat to make the mysterious names public would effect his complete rehabilitation in Italian society. The prison sentence would be quashed, all other outstanding charges against him would be dropped, he would reacquire his Italian banks, and the New York court would be confronted by a man who would claim that he was the victim of wicked conspiracies, probably Communist-inspired. An array of very respectable people would testify that Michele Sindona was not only a man who had been wronged, but also the world's most brilliant banker, a man who personified good, clean, healthy capitalism. All of this would be achieved by a technique of which Sindona had frequently boasted he was a master— blackmail.

Later Sindona would claim there was another reason for his trip. To the present day he will still insist to anyone who cares to listen to him that its purpose was to overthrow the Italian government in Sicily and declare the island an independent state. According to Sindona, he would then offer Sicily to the United States as the fifty-first state of the union in exchange for all criminal charges he faced in the United States being dropped. Sindona asserts that the plan would have succeeded except for the fact that after the Mafia had arranged a fake kidnap, they proceeded to carry out a real one. Fantasies and delusions such as this are laughable until one remembers that good, honest men such as Giorgio Ambrosoli did not die laughing.

The madness of Michele Sindona is perhaps nowhere more clearly revealed than in the fine detail of this plan. Sindona asserts that the Gambino family was fully prepared to give up its heroin factories in Sicily, a murderous industry that was bringing in profits to the Gambino, Inzerillo, and Spatola families estimated by the Italian authorities at $600 million minimum a year. In exchange for this public-spirited action, the Gambino family would be given control of the trade in oranges, and Rosario Spatola would be allowed to build a casino in Palermo.

Sindona duly vanished from the streets of New York during the afternoon of August 2, 1979. He was clearly going to be extremely busy if Sicily was to be annexed and a deal with the president of the United States was to be effected before the trial, which was scheduled to begin on September 10. Carrying a false passport in the name of Joseph Bonamico (Italian for good friend) and accompanied by Anthony Caruso, Sindona, wearing glasses, a white wig, and a false moustache and beard, boarded TWA flight 740 to Vienna at Kennedy International Airport. The farce, complete with ransom demands to a variety of people from "kidnappers" calling themselves the "Proletarian Committee for the Eversion [sic] of an Improved Justice," continued until October 16, when an "emotionally exhausted and physically weak" Sindona, with a healing bullet wound in the thigh, telephoned one of his New York lawyers from a phone booth on the corner of Forty-second Street and Tenth Avenue in Manhattan.

By any standards his trip had been less than an overwhelming success. Sicily had not become part of the union. Many of Sindona's former friends remained just that, former friends. The list of five hundred, despite all the threats, had not been revealed, and Sindona

would in the near future face additional charges of
perjury, bail-jumping, and arranging a false kidnap.
The main gain for Sindona appears to have been 30
billion lire (more than $36.5 million). This sum was
paid by Roberto Calvi after the kindly Licio Gelli had
interceded yet again on Sindona's behalf. It was paid to
Sindona's "kidnappers" from a Calvi-owned bank, the
Banca del Gottardo, in Switzerland. In theory the sum
was paid to Mafioso Rosario Spatola for the "release"
of Sindona—an Italian version of the three-card trick.

The main conspirators, apart from Sindona himself,
were Anthony Caruso, Joseph Macaluso, Johnny Gambino, Rosario Spatola, Vincenzo Spatola, and Joseph
Miceli Crimi. The Italian authorities established that
Rosario Spatola, who could normally be found wandering around the lines of cement mixers at the large construction company he owned in Palermo, had been in
New York at precisely the time Sindona had vanished.
Asked the reason for his visit he replied, "Family
business."

Sindona's trial on the massive array of charges aris-
ing from the collapse of the Franklin National finally
began in early February 1980. Right before it started,
the Vatican gave clear indication that the Roman Catholic Church at least was going to stand by its former
financial adviser.

Cardinal Giuseppe Caprio, Cardinal Sergio Guerri,
and Bishop Paul Marcinkus had agreed to a defense
counsel request that they help Sindona's case by swear-
ing depositions on videotape. Intrigued by what these
devout men might say about Sindona, the prosecution
had raised no objection to this unusual gambit. It is
normal for witnesses to have their statements tested on
oath, in a courtroom, in front of judge and jury. For the
men from the Vatican, trial judge Thomas Griesa waived
this consideration, and he instructed Sindona's lawyers
to fly to Rome on Friday, February 1. The understanding was that the deposition would be taken the following day, and the lawyers would report back to the judge
on the following Monday. Their report, contained within
the trial transcripts of *United States* v. *Michele Sindona*,
makes extraordinary reading.

At the last minute—or more exactly, four hours

before the depositions were to be sworn—the secretary of state, Cardinal Casaroli, intervened. There would be no depositions. "They would create a disruptive precedent. There has been so much unfortunate publicity about these depositions. We are very unhappy about the fact that the American government does not give diplomatic recognition to the Vatican."

The sophisticated New York lawyers were still in a state of disbelief when they reported to Judge Griesa. At 11:00 A.M. on the Saturday morning, Cardinal Guerri's secretary, Monsignor Blanchard, had telephoned the American embassy to confirm that the cardinals and Marcinkus would be there at 4:00 P.M. A few minutes later he had called back to say Casaroli had withdrawn from the arena. He was asked about his earlier call. The monsignor promptly denied making any earlier call. He compounded that lie with another when he told the embassy the "American judge knows all about this."

The bemused embassy official, unaccustomed to such a graphic display of Vatican dishonesty, set about contacting Cardinal Guerri directly. When she eventually located His Eminence, he confessed that he did not know if he was coming to swear a deposition or not. As it turned out, he did not. Guerri, Caprio, and Marcinkus all assured the American lawyers that their depositions would have been full of praise for Michele Sindona— that was not their difficulty. The problem had arisen when Cardinal Casaroli realized the full range of the implications. If the jury found Sindona guilty, then three high prelates of the Roman Catholic Church would, in effect, be branded liars. Further, to allow the three to testify, even through voluntary depositions, would open a Vatican gate through which would come pouring every Italian magistrate demanding the same cooperation. That would lead to a breach of the Lateran Treaty, which granted a cardinal complete immunity from arrest in Italy. The next step would be a very unwelcome light shining on Vatican Incorporated.

Casaroli had shrewdly saved the Vatican at the eleventh hour. What the American lawyers did not know was that in doing so he had actually overridden a decision taken by the pope. John Paul II had readily ac-

ceded to the request that Marcinkus and the others tell
the world how highly they regarded Michele Sindona.

On March 27, 1980, Michele Sindona was found
guilty on sixty-five counts, including fraud, conspiracy,
perjury, false bank statements, and misappropriation of
bank funds. He was sent to the Metropolitan Correctional Center in New York City to await sentence.

On May 13, two days before he was due to be
sentenced, Sindona attempted to commit suicide. He
slashed his wrists, but, more significantly, he took a
dose of digitalis. Acting on Grand Master Gelli's advice,
Sindona had carried with him everywhere, for many
years, a lethal dose of digitalis. Gelli had advised not
only Sindona but also other top P2 members always to
carry the drug. It was P2's insurance against a member
being forced to reveal details of the organization.

How the digitalis got into the prison remains a
mystery. Sindona has apparently claimed to have had it
sewn into the lining of a suit for years. To smuggle
digitalis into his prison would have been a far more
difficult feat than to get it into the papal apartments in
September 1978.

Initially it appeared that Sindona would die, particularly as the doctors were at a loss as to what drug he
had taken, but the dose was inadequate. Having eventually established that it was digitalis, they were able to
administer an antidote. Sindona made a full recovery,
and on June 13, 1980, he was sentenced to twenty-five
years' imprisonment and fined over $200,000. Carlo
Bordoni, who had been the main prosecution witness
against Sindona, received a seven-year prison sentence
and a $20,000 fine. Sindona was subsequently found
guilty of arranging his own false kidnap and sentenced
to a further 2½ years. Also found guilty of conspiring
with him and assisting him in bail-jumping were Anthony Caruso and Joseph Macaluso. Both were sentenced
to five years' imprisonment.

While these events were unfolding in New York,
Sindona's P2 comrades Calvi and Gelli were continuing
business as usual on the other side of the Atlantic. By
1979, Roberto Calvi was seeking protection in all
directions: a private army of eight bodyguards; twenty-
four-hour guards for Calvi, his family, and his Milan,

Rome, and Drezzo homes; armor-plated Alfa Romeos with bulletproof tires. These manifestations of the master thief's personal fears were costing the shareholders of Ambrosiano over $1 million a year. No one in Italy, including the president or the prime minister, was as well protected. He sought protection from a broad spectrum of political parties—the Christian Democrats, the Socialists, the Communists, all were illegally bankrolled by Calvi. He had the protection of Gelli's P2 and his Mafia associates, but both of these were double-edged swords that could be used against him.

The illegally purchased shares in Banco Ambrosiano were concealed in Panamanian companies beyond the jurisdiction of the Bank of Italy, but Calvi was always afraid that officialdom would discover this aspect of his many criminal activities. First the Nassau branch had been used to bury the illegal transactions. When the Bank of Italy came within an ace of proving what they suspected, Calvi had moved the axis of the fraud to Nicaragua. Then, in 1979, he moved much of the activity that governed the fraud even farther away, to Peru. On October 11, 1979, Banco Ambrosiano Andino opened its doors in Lima. Shortly afterward the majority of the loans that had been extended to the shell Panamanian and Liechtenstein companies were transferred to Peru. These small shell companies, many with a nominal capital of a mere $10,000 continued to proliferate. Eventually there would be seventeen. The majority were owned by a Luxembourg company, aptly named Manic S.A., which in turn was owned by the Vatican Bank.

If the international banks lining up over the years to lend Calvi millions upon millions of dollars had done any research at all, Calvi would have been exposed years before he suffered his ultimate fate. It is true that the 1978 Bank of Italy report on Banco Ambrosiano was highly confidential and not freely available. That was still the case when I obtained it in 1981. If one author can obtain such a report, so presumably can any of the 250 banks scattered throughout the world that lent Calvi money. These bankers have a much-vaunted reputation for shrewdness and astuteness, yet they believed the doctored accounts Calvi showed them. The statements he made assuring them that the vast loans were to finance Italian exports were accepted. Did no one check? Did no one subsequently monitor? That over $450 million should be loaned by the international banks, not to another bank, but to a mere holding company called Banco Ambrosiano Holdings, based in Luxembourg—a company manifestly unsupported by any central bank—is a strong condemnation of the lending practices of the interbank market. Those who sit on the boards of these lending banks should be made to answer to their shareholders and to all who have accounts with them.

It is not pleasant to reflect that patriotic British citizens undoubtedly financed the purchase of Exocet missiles for Argentina, missiles that killed many British soldiers during the Falklands war. Yet there is no doubt that this evil chain of events did occur. Calvi diverted millions of dollars, some of it from British banks, to Licio Gelli, who in turn used some of that money to purchase Exocets for Argentina. Doubtless the men who negotiated these huge loans to Calvi would claim that at the time it looked like very good business.

Just how obscene this particular transaction was can only be appreciated when one is aware that this money was diverted to Gelli and Ortolani through a Panamanian company owned by the Vatican.

The company in question, Bellatrix, was controlled by Marcinkus at the Vatican Bank but created by a trinity of P2 members—Gelli, Ortolani, and Bruno Tassan Din, managing director and financial strategist to the giant Rizzoli publishing group. These Masons milked the Ambrosiano cow of $184 million. The capital of Bellatrix?—$10,000. The vast, nonreturnable loan was secured on paper against a large number of Rizzoli shares. Rizzoli was jointly owned by P2 and the Vatican. The value placed on the Rizzoli shares far exceeded their real worth.

Astolfine, yet another of the Panamanian companies owned by the Vatican, was able, on a capital of $10,000, to run up debts of $486 million. Its security? A large helping of grossly overvalued Banco Ambrosiano shares.

With business practices such as these, capitalism need have no fear that ultimately it will be destroyed

328 IN GOD'S NAME

by Marxism. All Marxists have to do is sit back and wait for capitalism to self-destruct automatically.

It is understandable that ENI, one of the biggest conglomerates in the world, should suddenly start lending Calvi money; that this huge government-owned oil company should suddenly start functioning as a bank and lend to, instead of borrow from, Banco Ambrosiano Holdings in Luxembourg: the chairman of ENI, Giorgio Mazzanti, and the head of its financial department, Leonardo di Donna, are both members of P2. But to date no P2 members have been discovered in the higher reaches of the many international banks that continuously poured millions of dollars down Calvi's throat between 1978 and 1980.

When the man in the street in London, Paris, New York, Copenhagen, Tokyo, Ottawa, and Sydney curses the high rate of his bank charges, he should tilt his hat at the ghost of Roberto Calvi and at the ever elusive Licio Gelli and Umberto Ortolani. He should also spare a thought for Vatican City. When we pay our high bank charges we are helping to pick up their tab.

Incontrovertible evidence that the Vatican owns these mysterious Panamanian companies reaches back to 1971, to the time when Calvi and Sindona put Bishop Paul Marcinkus on the board of Calvi's section in Nassau.

In Milan during 1979, the magistrate Luca Mucci attempted to question Calvi. Calvi would study his shoes or the floor intently, mutter about his need to preserve banking secrecy, discuss Inter Milan's chances of winning its next game, and leave an outmaneuvered judge.

By the end of 1979 the financial exposure of the Vatican-owned front companies that Calvi controlled was over $500 million. Fortunately, the cosmic banking fantasies of Sindona had not yet become a reality. There were still financial situations Calvi could not control. The dollar began to rise against the lira. Ambrosiano's assets, such as they were, consisted very largely of lira-denominated shares. The game became frenetic. Just to keep up with the fraud required an insane juggling act, particularly when the operating costs included 30 billion lire (about $36.5 million) for buying the Venice newspaper *Il Gazzettino* to keep the Christian Democrats happy and "lending" the Rome daily *Paese Sera* 20 billion lire (about $24 million) to keep the Communists content. Everyone had his hands out, and it always seemed that the man with the biggest hands was Licio Gelli.

In January 1980 Banco Ambrosiano de America del Sud opened its doors in Buenos Aires. There was practically no banking activity, but this arm of the Calvi empire helped finance Argentinian purchases of Exocet missiles. It also provided funds for arms purchases by other South American regimes.

In July 1980 Judge Luca Mucci felt sufficiently impressed by the investigation that the Guardia di Finanza, the financial police, had carried out in the wake of the 1978 inquiry by the Bank of Italy to order Calvi to surrender his passport and to warn the banker that he would be facing criminal charges. It was a small step forward in the name of justice.

One step forward, two steps back. Within a few months Calvi's passport was restored, again through the good offices of Gelli. The grand master was less inclined to intercede, however, when Massimo Spada, formerly of the Vatican bank and currently chairman of Banca Cattolica del Veneto, was arrested and charged with involvement of a criminal nature in Il Crack Sindona. Next to feel the handcuffs, at least momentarily, was Luigi Mennini, still active in the Vatican Bank, on similar charges.

As the net began to draw tighter around Calvi, despite the valiant efforts of Gelli to corrupt all and sundry, the Milanese banker's hopes of continuing to plunder hinged primarily on Marcinkus. The game was becoming much rougher, and without the constant cooperation of the Vatican Bank, concealment of Calvi's crimes would no longer be possible. This had always been the case, but in the past the pressure on the Vatican had been minimal; now, with the arrest of Mennini, the pressure intensified. Calvi began to fear that, despite the massive amounts of money he had channeled into the hands of Bishop Paul Marcinkus, the time might be fast approaching when the man across the Tiber might withdraw his active support and leave Calvi alone and highly vulnerable.

Early in 1981 the Italian Treasury minister, Beni-

amino Andreatta, who had been promoted to the post
the previous October, concluded that the Vatican should
withdraw its support immediately. He had studied the
1978 Bank of Italy report at length and felt compelled
to make an attempt to protect the Church. He went to
the Vatican and spoke at length to the foreign minister,
Cardinal Casaroli. Andreatta outlined the entire situation.
He urged the Vatican to break all links with Banco
Ambrosiano before it was too late. The advice was
ignored. Marcinkus would claim later that he had no
knowledge of this meeting. In any event, if the devout
Catholic Andreatta had been aware of the full facts,
he would have known that it was impossible for the
Vatican to sever the links. It actually owned Banco
Ambrosiano. Through the array of Panamanian and
Liechtenstein companies, it had acquired control of over
16 percent of Banco Ambrosiano. With the rest of the
shares in the bank so widely scattered among small
shareholders, that gave the Vatican a controlling interest.

At noon on March 2, 1981, the Vatican press office
released a document that puzzled many. Issued without
explanation, it reminded all Catholics of the canon laws
covering Freemasons and stressed the fact that the present
code "forbids Catholics under pain of excommunication from joining Masonic or similar associations." No
one could understand the timing. Roman Catholics had
been subjected to automatic excommunication on these
grounds since 1738. Why remind them in early March
1981? The answer was not long in coming and indicates
that the intelligence-gathering network of the Church is
at least as efficient as Licio Gelli's. The Vatican statement did not explain how all the good Catholics who
appeared on the membership list of P2 could have their
names expunged from the records before the Italian
authorities discovered them. For P2 member Calvi, this
apparently insurmountable problem was to have disastrous consequences.

When public exposure of P2 finally came, it came,
ironically, through Calvi's association with his protector Licio Gelli. Italian magistrates in 1981 were still
attempting to clarify the facts concerning Sindona's
self-arranged kidnap. On March 17 police raided Gelli's
palatial villa in Arezzo and his office at the Gio-Le

textile factory. They were merely looking for evidence of Gelli's involvement in Sindona's surprise trip to his homeland. What they found was a Pandora's box of scandal. In Gelli's safe they discovered a list of the 962 members of P2. They also found dossiers and secret government reports.

The list of P2 members was a veritable Who's Who of Italy. The armed forces were heavily represented, with over fifty generals and admirals. The government of the day was there, with two cabinet ministers, as were businessmen, journalists (including the editor of *Corriere della Sera* and several of his senior staff), members of Parliament, rock stars, pundits, police officers, and many others. It was a state within a state. Many have said that Gelli was planning to take over Italy. They are wrong. He *had* taken over Italy. Of the grand master himself there was no sign. The arrangements for the police raid had been top secret, which translated meant: tell only trusted police officers and Licio Gelli. He had fled to South America.

The ensuing scandal brought down the Italian government and gave considerable momentum to the Milan magistrate's investigation of Calvi. Judge Mucci was replaced by Gerardo d'Ambrosio. It had been over two years since the murder of Judge Emilio Alessandrini, two years of procrastination. Now with a new investigating judge, helped by the compromising documents found in Gelli's safe, within two months Calvi was arrested and in a prison cell in Lodi.

Now was the time for all good friends to come to the aid of the man who had so often helped other parties. In the weeks following Calvi's arrest, Bettino Craxi, the leader of the Socialist party, and Flaminio Piccoli, the president of the Christian Democrats, stood up in Parliament and made pleasant remarks about Calvi and his bank. The Vatican stayed silent. Its attention was focused on a far graver situation. Seven days before Calvi's arrest, Pope John Paul II was shot in St. Peter's Square by Mehmet Ali Agca.

While much of the world prayed that the pope would survive, Roberto Calvi in his prison cell was totally preoccupied with his own survival. Through his family he began to press Marcinkus to admit publicly that over the years he had been standing side by side with Calvi in the kitchen as they cooked the books.

After many futile telephone calls, Calvi's son Carlo finally got through to Marcinkus. He pleaded with the bishop, saying that the gravity of his father's position would be greatly reduced if the Vatican Bank admitted its involvement. The deals had been channeled through Calvi's Banca del Gottardo in Lugano, which could not reveal the truth because of the very stringent Swiss banking regulations, but the Vatican Bank was its own master. It could volunteer information. Marcinkus, however, had no intention of publicly accepting responsibility. He told Calvi's son: "If we do, it's not only the IOR and the Vatican's image that will suffer. You'll lose as well, for our problems are your problems, too."

Indeed they were. The two banks were completely interlocked. They had been for years. Bishop Marcinkus was in a bind. To tell the truth would bring down on the Vatican the wrath of Italy. The alternative was to leave Calvi unsupported in the hope that the Vatican's deep and continuing involvement would remain secret and that after Calvi's trial, business could proceed as usual. Bishop Marcinkus took the latter course. Undoubtedly this decision was based on the fact that of all the crimes perpetrated by Calvi, the charges he now faced involved only two of his illegal transactions, namely his having sold himself shares in Toro and Credito Varesino that he happened already to own, at vastly inflated prices. This had involved illegally exporting currency out of Italy, and that was the offense the Milan magistrates were hoping would enable them to convict Calvi. Marcinkus reasoned that if everyone kept calm, the game could continue. Calvi, sitting in Lodi prison, was unimpressed by the messages from his sanguine partner in the Vatican. International bankers shook their heads in disbelief as Calvi continued to run Banco Ambrosiano from inside prison.

On July 7, the Italian government charged Michele Sindona with ordering the murder of Giorgio Ambrosoli. Calvi's reaction to the news was particularly interesting. He tried to commit suicide the following evening. He took an overdose of barbiturates and slashed his wrists. He later explained his reasons: "Because of a kind of lucid desperation. Because there was not a trace of justice in all that was being done against me. And I am not talking about the trial." If, of course, he had really wanted to end his life, he could have obtained the digitalis recommended by Gelli by having it smuggled into prison. His trial judges were unimpressed.

On July 20 he was sentenced to four years' imprisonment and was fined 16 billion lire. His lawyers immediately filed an appeal, and he was freed on bail. Within a week of his release, the board of Banco Ambrosiano unanimously reconfirmed him as chairman and gave him a standing ovation. The international bankers again shook their heads in disbelief. As Marcinkus had predicted, it was indeed business as usual. P2 was a continuing power. The Bank of Italy allowed Calvi to return. The Italian government made no move to end the extraordinary spectacle of a man convicted of banking offenses running one of the country's biggest banks.

One banker did raise objections. Ambrosiano's general manager, Roberto Rosone, pleaded with the Bank of Italy to approve the removal of Calvi and replace him with the previous chairman, Ruggiero Mozzana. The Bank of Italy, with its eyes still firmly fixed on the power of P2 and the political muscle that Calvi had bought over the years, declined to intervene.

A second threat to Calvi's banking empire came from Peru and Nicaragua. To counter it, Calvi enlisted the help of Marcinkus. The bishop had declined to give Calvi any support, public or private, during his trial, but he was now about to help him in every way possible to ensure that the criminal fraud perpetrated by both men remained secret.

During the time of Calvi's trial the Vatican announced that Pope John Paul II had appointed a commission of fifteen cardinals to study the finances of the Roman Catholic Church. The function of the commission was to recommend improvements that would increase Vatican revenue.

Bishop Paul Marcinkus was not included as a member of the commission, but he obviously felt that as head of the Vatican Bank he could nevertheless make a crucial contribution to the troublesome question of Vatican finances. He held a number of secret meetings with the convicted Calvi, which resulted in the Vatican Bank officially admitting an increase in its outstanding debts of nearly $1 billion. This was the sum that was owed to the Calvi banks in Peru and Nicaragua as a result of their having loaned, on Calvi's instructions, hundreds of millions of dollars to Bellatrix, Astolfine, etc. Peru and Nicaragua, despite being Calvi subsidiaries, were finally displaying a little independence. The securities backing these enormous loans were negligible.

Peru and Nicaragua wanted greater cover. Who picked up the bill in the event of a default? Who exactly owned these mysterious Panamanian companies? Who had borrowed so much with so little? The gentlemen from Peru were particularly anxious, having loaned some $900 million.

At this stage, in August 1981, Calvi and Marcinkus perpetrated their biggest fraud. The documents would become known as "letters of comfort." They offer no comfort to any Roman Catholic, no reassurance to any who believe in the moral integrity of the Vatican. The letters were written on IOR letterhead and were dated September 1, 1981. They were addressed to Banco Ambrosiano Andino in Lima, Peru, and Ambrosiano Group Banco Comercial in Managua, Nicaragua. On the instructions of Bishop Paul Marcinkus, they were signed by Luigi Mennini and Pellegrino de Strobel. They read:

> Gentlemen:
> This is to confirm that we directly or indirectly control the following entries:
> Manic S.A., Luxembourg
> Astolfine S.A., Panama
> Nordeurop Establishment, Liechtenstein
> United Trading Corporation, Panama
> Erin S.A., Panama
> Bellatrix S.A., Panama
> Belrose S.A., Panama
> Starfield S.A., Panama
> We also confirm our awareness of their indebtedness toward yourselves as of June 10, 1981, as per attached statement of accounts.

The attached accounts showed that the "indebtedness" to the Lima branch alone was $907 million.

The directors in Nicaragua and Peru relaxed. They had now clear admission that the massive debts were the responsibility of the Vatican Bank. The Holy Roman Catholic Church was the guarantor. No banker could wish for a better security. There was just one small problem. The directors in Peru and Nicaragua knew only half of the story. There was another letter. This one was from Roberto Calvi to the Vatican Bank, dated August 27, 1981. It was safely in Marcinkus's hands before he acknowledged that the Vatican Bank was liable for the debts of $1 billion. Calvi's letter made a formal request for the letters of comfort in which the Vatican would admit that it owned the Luxembourg, Liechtenstein, and Panamanian companies. This admission, Calvi assured the Vatican, "would entail no liabilities for the IOR." His letter concluded with a paragraph confirming that whatever happened, the Vatican Bank would "suffer no future damage or loss." Hence the Vatican Bank was secretly absolved from debts to which it was about to admit.

For Calvi's secret letter to Marcinkus to have any legal validity, its existence and precise contents would have had to have been revealed to the directors in Peru and Nicaragua. Further, the arrangement between Calvi and Marcinkus would have had to have been agreed on by the majority of the directors in Milan. Moreover, to have been a legal agreement, it would have been essential for the contents of both letters to have been public knowledge to all the shareholders of Banco Ambrosiano, including the many small shareholders in the Milan area.

The two letters and the agreement between Calvi and Marcinkus constitute a clear case of criminal fraud by both men. That all of this should have transpired on the third anniversary of the election of Albino Luciani adds to the obscenity. Luciani, a man committed and dedicated to the elimination of corruption within the Vatican, had been succeeded by Pope John Paul II, a man who wholeheartedly approved of Bishop Paul Marcinkus.

This appalling effrontery grew when on September

28, 1981, the third anniversary of Luciani's death, Marcinkus was promoted by the pope. It was announced that he had been appointed pro-president of the Pontifical Commission for the State of Vatican City. This virtually made him governor of Vatican City. He still retained his position as head of the Vatican Bank, and the new post meant that he was automatically elevated to archbishop.

Through his Lithuanian origins, his continual espousal, in fiscal terms, of Poland's needs, and his close proximity to the pope because of his role as personal bodyguard and overseer of all security on foreign trips, Marcinkus had discovered in the person of Karol Wojtyla the most powerful protector a Vatican employee could have. Sindona, Calvi, and others like them are, according to the Vatican, wicked men who have deceived naïve, trusting priests. Either Marcinkus has misled, lied to, and suppressed the truth from Pope John Paul II since October 1978, or the present pope also stands indicted.

While Karol Wojtyla displays remarkable charisma and tells the world that a man who looks at his wife with desire could well be committing adultery of the heart, Marcinkus has continued to seduce many of the world's bankers. While the pope from Cracow demonstrates his preoccupation with maintaining the Roman Catholic status quo by his declaration that divorced Roman Catholics who have remarried can be given holy communion only if they totally abstain from sexual relationships with their married partners, the pope's bankers have shown themselves to be less fastidious about whom they sleep with. While Pope John Paul II has justified the Roman Catholic Church's continuing treatment of women as second-class citizens with assertions such as "Mary, the mother of God, was not among the apostles at the Last Supper," the men from Vatican Incorporated have continued to display a more liberated attitude: they will steal and embezzle from either sex.

In the years since the election of Wojtyla, Licio Gelli, the unbeliever, has continued to demonstrate his own power and charisma. None would call him God's representative, but many would continue to jump when the puppetmaster tugged the string.

From the sanctuary of his home in the Uruguayan capital of Montevideo, Licio Gelli remained in contact with Calvi. Still pulling that particular string, still extorting huge amounts of money from the banker, he would frequently telephone when Calvi was at his villa in Drezzo. Calvi's wife, Clara, and his daughter Anna have confirmed that the number was known only to Gelli and Umberto Ortolani—a P2 hot line. Gelli would never give his name when the Calvi family would ask who was calling. It was always the special code name: Luciani.

Why would the grand master of P2 choose for himself Albino Luciani's name—a name Gelli had used since 1978 when contacting Calvi? Was it a constant reminder of a certain event? A constant threat that this master blackmailer might reveal details of that event unless the money kept pouring into Gelli's bank accounts? Undoubtedly the money did continue to flow to Gelli. Right until the end, Calvi was still paying Gelli off. With the grand master disgraced and in hiding in South America, wanted by the Italian authorities on a variety of charges, his protection of Calvi was limited. Why, then, the millions of dollars that each mention of the name "Luciani" sent pouring into Gelli's pocket? Calvi personally estimated that Gelli and Ortolani eventually were worth over $500 million each.

Months before the P2 scandal broke, when the grand master was still in Italy, Calvi was clearly attempting to break all links with Gelli. Why did Calvi avoid the phone calls? Tell his family to say he was ill or was not there? From the accounts of the Calvi family, Gelli, the insatiable collector of secrets and information, had a frightening hold over Roberto Calvi. What was the ultimate secret Gelli knew that sent Calvi into fits of perspiring terror at the mere mention of Gelli's name?

Gelli's hold on Calvi continued until the end of the banker's life. When he whistled, Calvi danced. Late in 1981 Carlo De Benedetti, chief executive of Olivetti, became deputy chairman of Banco Ambrosiano at Calvi's request. It gave his bank's tattered public image a healthy injection of respectability. In Uruguay Gelli and Ortolani heard the news with alarm. An honest deputy chairman was not consistent with their plans to continue the plunder of Banco Ambrosiano. "Luciani" picked up his telephone and dialed the private number at the Drezzo villa. Having persuaded De Benedetti to join his bank, Calvi proceeded to make life impossible for him. "You must take the greatest care," he said to De Benedetti, "the P2 is preparing a dossier on you. I advise you to take care, because I know." Little more than a month later, De Benedetti had left.

A long letter of complaint, complete with highly detailed appendices, was sent by a group of Milanese shareholders in Banco Ambrosiano to John Paul II. The letter, dated January 12, 1981, was a slashing attack on the bank. It set out the links among Marcinkus, Calvi, Gelli, and Ortolani. The shareholders were particularly distressed that the previously staid Catholic bank, Ambrosiano, and the Vatican Bank had bred such an unholy alliance. As these troubled Catholics of Milan observed:

> The IOR is not only a shareholder in the Banco Ambrosiano. It is an associate and partner of Roberto Calvi. It is revealed by a growing number of court cases that Calvi stands today astride one of the main crossroads of the most degenerate Freemasonry [P2] and of Mafia circles, as a result of inheriting Sindona's mantle. This has been done once again with the involvement of people generously nurtured and cared for by the Vatican, such as Ortolani, who move between the Vatican and powerful groups in the international underworld.
>
> Being a partner of Calvi means being a partner of Gelli and Ortolani, given that both guide and influence him strongly. The Vatican is therefore, whether it likes it or not, through its association with Calvi also an active partner of Gelli and Ortolani.

The letter contained an appeal to Pope John Paul II for help and guidance. Though the pope speaks many languages, including Italian, the Milanese thoughtfully had the letter translated into Polish and also took steps to ensure that neither the Curia in general nor Villot's replacement, Casaroli, should prevent the letter from reaching the pope. In any event, the letter was ignored. The Milanese shareholders were not even graced with a formal acknowledgment.

Calvi was aware that the letter had been sent and was equally aware that it had the approval of his general manager and deputy chairman, Roberto Rosone. He discussed with his friend and fellow P2 member, Flavio Carboni, the threat that Rosone's attempts to clean up the bank were posing.

The range of Carboni's friends and contacts was wide. It included such men as the two rulers of Rome's underworld, Danilo Abbruciati and Ernesto Diotallevi.

On the morning of April 27, 1982, Rosone left his apartment at a few minutes before 8:00 A.M. Fortunately for Rosone, he happened to live directly above a branch of Ambrosiano, which, like all Italian banks, is protected around the clock by armed guards. As Rosone emerged into the street, a man approached and began firing. Wounded in the legs, Rosone collapsed to the ground. The armed bank guards retaliated. Moments later the assailant was also laid out on the pavement. Dead. His name was Danilo Abbruciati.

The day after the attempted murder of Rosone, April 28, Flavio Carboni paid the surviving leader of the Rome underworld $530,000. The job had been botched, but Calvi was a man who honored his debts—with other people's money.

Calvi, who undoubtedly had ordered the assassination of his own deputy chairman, now rushed to his bedside, complete with the requisite bunch of flowers. "Madonna! What a world of madmen. They want to frighten us, Roberto, so that they can get their hands on a group worth twenty thousand billion lire."

In May 1982 the screws began to tighten on Calvi. Consob, the Milan Stock Exchange regulatory agency, finally forced him to list his shares publicly on the exchange. Such a listing would necessitate an independent audit of the bank's books.

Roberto Calvi's wife, Clara, has stated under oath that earlier that year in a private audience with Pope John Paul II, Calvi had discussed the problem of the $1 billion debt the Vatican had incurred very largely through

the efforts of Calvi, Gelli, Ortolani, and Marcinkus. The
pope allegedly made Calvi a promise. "If you can extricate the Vatican from this debt you can have full control of rebuilding our finances."

If this offer was indeed made, then His Holiness
was obviously seeking more of the same. It was to be
business as usual for ever and ever with no amen.

The pope and Calvi were only two of many beginning to show real concern about the fortune in dollars
that had poured into the Vatican-owned offshore companies. On May 31, 1982, the Bank of Italy wrote to
Calvi and his board of directors in Milan. They demanded that the board give a full accounting of foreign
lending by the Banco Ambrosiano Group. The board of
directors, in a pitifully late show of resistance to Calvi,
voted 11 to 3 to comply with the central bank's demand.

Licio Gelli, who on May 10 had secretly returned to
Europe from Argentina, was another making demands
on Calvi. Gelli was in the market for more Exocet missiles to help his adopted country in its Falklands war
with Great Britain. With the bulk of Argentina's foreign
assets frozen and an official arms embargo in force,
Gelli was obliged to turn to the black-market arms
dealers, who displayed some skepticism about Gelli's
ability to pay what he was offering for the deadly
missiles. He was offering $4 million per missile, with a
minimum order of twenty. Since this figure was six
times the official price, there was considerable interest
in the order, subject to Gelli raising the necessary money.
He was well known to the arms dealers as a man who in
the past had purchased radar equipment, planes, guns,
tanks, and the original Exocets on behalf of Argentina.
Now he needed at least $80 million, and the need was
urgent. The war in the Falklands hung in the balance.

Thus Calvi, already juggling the needs of Pope John
Paul II, his Mafia clientele, his irate shareholders, the
Consob watchdogs on the Milan Stock Exchange, a re-
calcitrant board of directors, and an incompetent assassin who had succeeded in getting himself killed, yet
again found Gelli with his hand out.

Calvi saw only two ways out. Either the Vatican
had to help him fill the ever-growing hole in the bank's
assets, or Gelli, the puppetmaster, must yet again dem-

onstrate that he still controlled the Italian power structure and save his P2 paymaster from ruin.

Calvi discussed the options with Flavio Carboni,
who continued secretly to tape their conversations.

It is clear from Calvi's remarks that he felt the Vatican Bank should fill the huge hole in Banco Ambrosiano
if for no other reason than that it was the main beneficiary of the missing millions and further that it was
legally obligated. Calvi observed: "The Vatican should
honor its commitments by selling part of the wealth
controlled by the IOR. It is an enormous patrimony.
I estimate it to be ten billion dollars. To help the
Ambrosiano the IOR could start to sell in chunks of a
billion at a time."

If any layman in the world should have known the
worth of the Vatican, that man should have been Roberto Calvi. He was privy to virtually all its financial
secrets. For over a decade he had been *the* man to
whom the Vatican had turned in financial matters. I
have previously noted that at the time Albino Luciani
became pope in 1978 the wealth controlled by both
sections of APSA and the Vatican Bank was conserva-
tively in the region of $3 billion. Now in early 1982 the
highly conservative Roberto Calvi placed the patrimony
of the IOR alone at $10 billion.

It is clear that as 1982 progressed the man who is
mistakenly known to the world as "God's banker" had a
multitude of problems, the majority of them self-created.
"God's thief" would be a more appropriate name for
this man who stole millions on behalf of the Vatican
and P2. Since the late 1960s there has been only one
man who deserves the sobriquet of "God's banker," and
that is Archbishop Paul Marcinkus.

In spite of the formidable range of problems confronting him at the time, problems that were only partly
known to me, Roberto Calvi was initially calm when I
interviewed him by telephone on the evening of June 9,
1982. The interview had been arranged by an intermediary whom Calvi trusted. It covered a wide range of
subjects. Through my interpreter, I began to question
Calvi closely about the Banca Cattolica del Veneto
transaction. He had been told that I was writing a book
about the Vatican, and when I mentioned the bank in

Venice he asked what the central subject of the book was. I told him, "It's a book on the life of Pope John Paul I, Papa Luciani."

Calvi's manner suddenly underwent a complete change. The calmness and control gave way to a torrent of loud remarks. His voice became excited and very emotional. My interpreter began to translate the stream of words for me.

"Who has sent you against me? Who has told you to do this thing? Always I pay. Always I pay. How do you know Gelli? What do you want? How much do you want?"

I protested that I had never met Licio Gelli. Calvi had barely stopped to listen to me before he began again.

"Whoever you are, you will not write this book. I can tell you nothing. Do not call me again. Ever."

Eight days later, the body of Roberto Calvi was found hanging under Blackfriars Bridge in the City of London.

Within days a hole was discovered in Banco Ambrosiano Milan. A $1.3 billion hole.

The focus of my investigation has been the death of another man, Albino Luciani. Villot, Calvi, Marcinkus, Sindona, Gelli, Cody—one of these men was at the very heart of the conspiracy that resulted in the murder of Luciani. Before you, the reader, arrive at your verdict, let us take one final look at these men.

Cardinal Jean Villot, whom Albino Luciani had decided to remove from office, retained his position as secretary of state with the election of Karol Wojtyla. Villot also retained his many other posts, including the control of the vital financial section, the Administration of the Patrimony of the Holy See, APSA. It was APSA that had played the Vatican role in the marriage with Sindona. Archbishop Marcinkus has frequently been castigated for bringing Sindona inside Vatican City. Marcinkus bears no responsibility for that act. The decision was made by Pope Paul, Monsignor Macchi, Umberto Ortolani, and the gentlemen of the APSA, including, naturally, its head, Cardinal Villot. If Luciani had lived, then Villot's removal from the Secretariat of State would also have meant his automatic removal from APSA. It is this organization, with its immense portfolio of investments, not Marcinkus's Vatican Bank, that is recognized as a central bank by the World Bank, the International Monetary Fund, and the Bank of International Settlement in Basel. It is a section that has much to hide, dating back to its deep involvement with Sindona.

At the time of Luciani's election, Villot had only a short while to live. He was a sick, tired man who by September 1978 knew he was seriously ill. He died less than six months after Luciani, on March 9, 1979. His death, according to the Vatican, was due to "bilateral bronchial pneumonia attacks with complications, circulatory collapse, renal and hepatic insufficiency." It was known that he had wanted to retire, but it was also known he wanted to pick his successor, and the man he had in mind was not Benelli. If Benelli discovered the scandal of the APSA section he would undoubtedly alert the new pope. This, combined with the other changes that Villot knew Luciani was about to make, created a powerful motive. If Villot was at the heart of a conspiracy to murder Luciani, the motive would have been the future direction of the Church. On the testimony of three Vatican witnesses, Villot considered the changes that were about to be implemented "a betrayal of Paul's will. A triumph for the restoration." He feared that they would take the Church back to pre-Vatican Council II. That his fear was unfounded is not relevant. Villot felt it and felt it profoundly. He was also bitterly opposed to Luciani's plan to modify the Roman Catholic Church's position on artificial birth control, which would have permitted Catholics throughout the world to use the contraceptive pill. With Paul VI, the creator of *Humanae Vitae*, barely dead, Villot was watching at close range the destruction of an edict he had many times publicly supported. Did Villot conclude that the greater good of the Church would be served with Luciani's death?

Villot's behavior after the pope's death was either that of a man who was responsible for or deeply involved in that death, or of a man suffering a severe moral crisis. He destroyed evidence. He lied. He imposed a vow of silence on members of the papal household. He rushed through an embalming before a majority of the cardinals had arrived in Rome, let alone been consulted. If Villot is blameless with regard to Luciani's death, then after the fact he most certainly materially assisted whoever was responsible. His actions and statements ensured that someone got away with murder. He himself clearly had a motive; it is also clear he had opportunity. In addition, by dint of his position as *camerlengo*, he had virtually total control over immediate subsequent events or, as in the refusal to perform an official autopsy, nonevents.

It may well be that Villot's various illegal actions after the discovery of Albino Luciani's body were motivated by what Villot considered the paramount factor, the greater good of the Catholic Church. That is, if he saw clear evidence of murder, clear proof that Albino Luciani did not die a natural death, he may have acted to protect the Church. Many believe that this was the case. Even given that rationale, however, I would still contend that at the very least, morally Villot appears to have been in need of help.

Cardinal John Cody, another of the men Luciani had been determined to remove from office, retained his position as cardinal of Chicago with the election of Albino Luciani's successor, Karol Wojtyla. In his book *The Making of the Popes*, Father Andrew Greeley observes:

> Cardinal Cody parlayed his past financial contributions to Poland (and some new contributions, according to Chicago sources), the size of the Polish population in Chicago, and his alleged friendship with the Pope into a successful counter offensive against his enemies. John Paul II, according to what the Cardinal told visitors in early December [1978] offered him a job in Rome, which he declined. The Pope, the Cardinal intimated, indicated the matter was closed.

My own research confirms this account. Further, the financial contributions Cody subsequently made to the Vatican, which were secretly funneled into Poland, were part of a much larger operation that Marcinkus and Calvi undertook on behalf of Pope John Paul II.

Cardinal Cody continued to be lavish with his gifts. In October 1979 Pope John Paul II visited the United

States. When he arrived at O'Hare International Airport in Chicago he was met by Cardinal Cody, who thrust a small wooden box into his hands as "a personal gift." Inside the box was $50,000. No one would deny the cardinal the right to give the pope a gift but, apart from the crassness of the gesture, the question this act raises is, where did the money come from? Was it from diocesan funds? Was it from funds exclusively controlled by Cody? From exactly what source had $50,000 so mysteriously appeared?

Within a year of this incident, the United States government had mounted an official but secret investigation into Cody. Government attorneys began to probe allegations that Cardinal Cody had illegally diverted up to $1 million of Church funds to his lifelong friend Helen Wilson. They also began to investigate a number of other allegations, including the following: that he had commingled personal and Church funds, that he had paid Helen Wilson a secret salary over many years, that he had improperly awarded her pension benefits, that he had bought for her a $90,000 home in Florida. The fact that all of this had allegedly been done with Church funds, which are tax-exempt, made it a government issue. In view of the highly sensitive political implications of such an investigation, the fact that the government initiated the inquiry is indicative of the very strong *prima facie* case that existed. The investigation began in September 1980.

In January 1981 a federal grand jury served Cody with a number of subpoenas, demanding to see his financial records. If Cody was as pure as the driven snow, his subsequent behavior is inexplicable. Only the cardinal, his lawyers, and one or two very close confidants knew of the investigation and subpoenas. Cody kept these developments hidden from the people of Chicago, from the apostolic delegate in Washington, and from the Vatican. He also refused to comply with the government demands to hand over the diocesan financial records. For an ordinary citizen to decline to cooperate would have meant prison, but Cody, who is on record as declaring, "I don't run the country but I do run Chicago," demonstrated that the boast was not empty.

In September 1981, when the *Chicago Sun-Times*
broke the story, Cody still had not complied with the
subpoenas. The *Sun-Times* had been conducting its own
investigation of the cardinal for nearly two years. It
proceeded to give its readers chapter and verse on a
large array of serious crimes that Cody had allegedly
committed.

The cardinal refused to produce a shred of evidence
to rebut the charges and attempted instead to rally
behind him the 2,440,000 Catholics of the city with the
assertion, "This is not an attack on me. It is an attack
on the entire Church."

Many responded to this totally fallacious statement.
Many did not. The massive damage to the image and
reputation of the Roman Catholic Church that Albino
Luciani had rightly foreseen was now a reality. The city
was divided. Initially the majority supported Cody but,
as the months dragged on, one fundamental fact began
to sink in. Cody had still not complied with the government subpoenas. His own supporters began to demand
that he comply. His initial response through his lawyers
had been, "I am only answerable to God and Rome." It
was a view that he took to the grave. In April 1982, with
the government still waiting for answers, Cardinal Cody
died. Notwithstanding that he had a long history of
illness, Cody's body, unlike Albino Luciani's, was subjected to an autopsy. His death had been caused by
"severe coronary artery disease."

Cody had left a final message to be read after his
death. It contained no proof of his innocence with regard to the very serious charges that he had faced. It
contained, instead, that arrogance that had characterized his entire life: "I forgive my enemies but God will
not."

With the despotic Cody dead, there was immediate
speculation about his successor. A name frequently mentioned was that of Archbishop Paul Marcinkus, citizen
of Cicero, Illinois, who was currently drowning in scandal in Italy. The American Church hierarchy demurred,
telling the Vatican that to give Chicago to Marcinkus
"would be more of the same." Instead, the position
went to Archbishop Joseph Bernardin of Cincinnati, who

promised an immediate Church investigation into *l'affaire* Cody.

The government announced that it was closing its own inquiry, and the federal grand jury investigation was terminated without any charges being brought. In view of the fact that the man who had been accused was dead, there was little alternative.

In December 1982, Bernardin issued a two-page pastoral letter to Chicago's Catholics. The conclusions in the letter were not supported with any documentary evidence. Bernardin concluded that a probe of Cody's finances showed no wrongdoing, that he may have unfairly awarded a pension to Helen Wilson, that he "did not always follow preferred accounting procedures." More significantly, the accountants Bernardin had employed refused to certify the "accuracy of the estimated receipt and expenditure figures," though they found the figures "within an acceptable range of reasonableness for the purposes of the inquiry." The reason the accountants refused to certify the records was because, as Bernardin admitted, some of the financial records of the archdiocese could not be located, and "if they were subsequently to become available, then the conclusions might require reevaluation." Nearly two years later, those financial records are still missing.

The despotic, arrogant Cody clearly had a motive, and a powerful one, to involve himself in a conspiracy to murder Albino Luciani. Some question may remain with regard to his financial corruption. There can be no doubt, however, that Cody suffered from acute paranoia. If he was a paranoid psychotic, it is entirely plausible that he would have sought to solve his problems, real or imagined, in a violent manner. Clearly, if any pope was going to remove Cody from Chicago it would be over his dead body—either Cody's or the pope's. During his early years in Rome and then during his numerous visits, Cody had succeeded in ingratiating himself with two future popes, Pacelli and Montini, and had built up a large network of friends and informants. That this man could put one finger in the air to Pope Paul VI is an indication of his power. The many cash gifts, not only to Poland but also to favored members of the Roman Curia, also served to consolidate loyalty. Cody had his

own Mafia or P2 planted deep within Vatican City—
men with constant access to the papal apartments.

Archbishop Paul Marcinkus, the third of the men
Albino Luciani had been determined to remove from
office, retained his position as head of the Vatican Bank
with the election of Karol Wojtyla. Indeed, as already
mentioned, he had been promoted to archbishop and
given even greater power. For a man who on his initial
appointment to the Vatican Bank observed, "my only
previous financial experience is handling the Sunday
collection," Marcinkus has come a long way. He has far
greater claim to the title of "God's banker" than either
of his two former close friends and business associates,
Roberto Calvi and Michele Sindona. Marcinkus can also
justly claim to have done more than any other priest in
modern times to bring the Roman Catholic Church into
disrepute.

It is abundantly clear that in the mid-1970s Calvi
and Marcinkus devised a scheme that spawned a multitude of crimes. It is equally clear that the Panamanian
and other offshore companies the Vatican owned, and
still owns, were run for the mutual benefit of Banco
Ambrosiano and the Vatican Bank.

The Vatican has claimed since Calvi's death that
the first it knew of the offshore companies and its ownership of them was in August 1981. This is yet another
Vatican lie. Documentary evidence established that as
early as 1978 Bishop Marcinkus was actively working to
suppress the fact that these companies were owned by
the Vatican. As for the Vatican's lack of knowledge of
the companies it owned, one example will suffice. United
Trading Corporation of Panama (UTC) is one of the
companies referred to in the letters of comfort, a company that the Vatican now claims it knew nothing about
until shortly before the notorious letters were written
by Marcinkus. Documentation dated November 21, 1974,
and duly signed by Vatican Bank officials requests that
Calvi's Banca del Gottardo arrange on behalf of the
Vatican Bank the formation of a company called United
Trading Corporation.

For Calvi the illegal scheme had many virtues. And
what did the Vatican Bank gain? It gained money. Vast
amounts of it. Calvi bought his own shares, from himself,

at greatly inflated prices, but on paper these shares
were legally owned *and still are legally owned* by the
Panamanian companies, which, in turn, are owned by
the Vatican. Calvi duly turned over the annual dividend
on the huge block of shares to its rightful owner, the
Vatican Bank. The sum involved varied over the years
but averages out annually at $2 million.

That was but the tip of the iceberg. More substantial gains can be traced. For example, in 1980 the Vatican Bank sold two million shares in a Rome-based
international construction company called Vianini. The
shares were sold to a small Panamanian company called
Laramie. This was the first stage of a deal in which it
was planned that the Vatican would sell to Laramie six
million shares in Vianini. The price of the shares was
grossly inflated. The first two million cost Laramie $20
million. Laramie is yet another of the companies owned
by the Vatican. It might be considered a futile exercise
to sell yourself your own shares at an inflated figure. It
becomes less futile, however, if you are using someone
else's money, as Calvi had demonstrated over the years.
The $20 million to pay for the shares came from Ro-
berto Calvi. And the Vatican Bank kept the shares it
already owned and the $20 million as well. Further, it
did not own and never has owned six million shares in
Vianini. Its maximum stake in the company has never
been more than three million shares. It was with schemes
like this that Calvi paid off Marcinkus.

In March 1982, Archbishop Marcinkus granted a
rare interview to the Italian weekly *Panorama*. His comments about Roberto Calvi are particularly illuminating,
coming as they did just eight months after Calvi had
been fined $13.7 million and sentenced to four years'
imprisonment, and only seven months after the Vatican
and Marcinkus discovered (if we believe the Vatican
version) that Calvi had stolen over $1 billion and left
the Vatican to pay the bill.

> Calvi merits our trust. This I have no reason to
> doubt. We have no intention of ceding the Banco
> Ambrosiano shares in our possession; and fur-
> thermore, we have other investments in this

group, for example in the Banca Cattolica, which
are going very well.

These comments are on a par with Marcinkus's
words of praise for another man on another occasion—
namely, on the occasion of his meeting, in April 1983,
with American officials who were investigating his alleged involvement in a $1 billion counterfeit bond
swindle. During that meeting, it may be remembered,
Marcinkus extolled the virtues of a man he now claims
to have hardly ever met, a man who, for his part, insists,
"We met many, many times over the course of the years
in which we did business together. Marcinkus was my
partner in two banks." That man is Michele Sindona,
who, apart from his many other crimes, is responsible
for the biggest single banking disaster in United States
history, a man whom Marcinkus considered to be
"well ahead of his time as far as banking matters are
concerned."

It may be argued on behalf of Marcinkus that his
observation was made a year before Il Crack Sindona.
In 1980, six years after the Sindona crash, Marcinkus
was ready to testify on behalf of Sindona and was stopped
only by the intervention of Cardinal Casaroli, who felt
obliged to overrule Pope John Paul II.

Today there is only one reason why Marcinkus has
not been further elevated to cardinal. Despite the massive worldwide disgrace that his activities have brought
on the Vatican and Roman Catholicism, Karol Wojtyla
was still going ahead with plans to make Marcinkus a
cardinal. Again, only the insistence of Casaroli saved
the day. It would seem the pope takes a more tolerant
view of sins perpetrated behind a bank counter than he
does of sins perpetrated in bed.

With regard to the murder of Albino Luciani,
Marcinkus had the motive and the opportunity. Among
the many functions he performed for Paul VI was that
of personal papal bodyguard and security adviser. His
knowledge of the security arrangements, such as they
were, was unsurpassed. Exactly why the president of
the IOR was wandering around Vatican City shortly
after six-thirty on the morning on which Albino Luciani
was discovered dead has yet to be established. Research

indicates that Marcinkus was not, as a rule, near the bank premises at such an early hour. Unlike Villot, he did not live inside the Vatican walls but at the Villa Stritch in Rome. Marcinkus brought many facets to his work in the Vatican Bank; not the least of these were elements of his early childhood in Al Capone's Cicero. "How are your gangster friends in Chicago, Paul?" was a running joke in the early 1970s. It was heard less after Sindona's trial. It is not heard at all since the Calvi debacle.

If not actively involved in the conspiracy to murder Albino Luciani, Marcinkus may have acted as a catalyst, wittingly or unwittingly. Many years ago an English king cried out, "Will no one rid me of this meddlesome priest?" and soon after, the Roman Catholic Church had a martyr in the person of Thomas à Becket. There is no doubt that Marcinkus conveyed in full to Roberto Calvi his fears concerning the new papacy. There is also no doubt that Albino Luciani was about to remove Marcinkus from the Vatican Bank and cut off all links with Banco Ambrosiano. Did the fears that Marcinkus expressed not only to Calvi but also to others about this new pope provoke a course of events that, on the morning of September 29, left Bishop Marcinkus open-mouthed and stunned when a Swiss Guard member told him the pope was dead?

Michele Sindona is often incorrectly referred to as "God's banker." A more accurate label would be "God's speculator." At the time of Albino Luciani's murder, Sindona was fighting an extradition order served by the Italian government. He was also wanted for questioning in connection with a wide variety of financial crimes in a number of other countries. By September 1978 the possibility that the United States authorities would initiate criminal proceedings against him with regard to the Franklin National collapse was becoming a virtual certainty. These proceedings would save him from extradition but would place him in immediate jeopardy in the United States. The one remaining ace he could hope to play depended on Vatican cooperation. Sindona reasoned that if three such august people as Bishop Marcinkus, Cardinal Guerri, and Cardinal Caprio gave evidence on his behalf, a jury would be heavily influenced. With Albino Luciani as pope, however, the possibility of any Vatican testimony, let alone favorable testimony, did not exist.

Sindona, as a member of both the Mafia and P2, had not only the motive and opportunity for murder but also, as has been amply demonstrated, the capacity. He was a man deranged enough to believe that if an assistant U.S. attorney were murdered, his troubles in the United States would be at an end, a man deranged enough to believe that if he ordered the murder of Giorgio Ambrosoli his Italian problems would vanish. Such a man clearly had the capacity to murder an honest, reforming pope.

Sindona remains a man very much in demand. There is the 3½-year prison sentence already passed on him in Italy. There is the July 1981 Italian government indictment charging him with having ordered the murder of Giorgio Ambrosoli. Also named in that arrest warrant are his son Nino Sindona and his son-in-law Pier Sandro Magnoni. There is the January 1982 indictment from Palermo, Sicily, in which he and sixty-five members of the Gambino, Inzerillo, and Spatola Mafia families were charged with operating a $600 million per year heroin trade between Sicily and the United States. There are the further Sicilian indictments, which charge Sindona with illegal possession of arms, fraud, using a false passport, and violating currency regulations. Then there are the further indictments issued by the Italian government in July 1982, charging Sindona and others, including the Vatican's Massimo Spada and Luigi Mennini, with a long list of criminal offenses connected with the fraudulent bankruptcy of Banca Privata Italiana. The prosecution's case with regard to these last alleged offenses is based, very largely, on the valiant work of the murdered Giorgio Ambrosoli. But no words of mine could convey so exactly the kind of man Sindona is (and the kind of family he has spawned) as those uttered by his son Nino Sindona. The following is taken from a tape-recorded interview with Nino Sindona, conducted by writer Luigi di Fonzo. (The tape is now with the New York prosecutor's office.) The long interview took place during the evening of March 18 and the early morning of March 19, 1983.

My father admitted to me that it was Arico . . . who committed the murder.* They was threatening Ambrosoli and it was effective for a while. Billy Arico was sent to Milan by Venetucci [a heroin smuggler and alleged member of the Gambino family] at my father's request and was supposed to shoot at Ambrosoli but not kill him. Arico committed the murder. . . . Ambrosoli's family do not deserve any pity. I have no compassion for the fucking guy and this is not enough for a son-of-a-bitch like him. I'm sorry he died without suffering. Let's make sure on this point. I'm never going to condemn my father because Ambrosoli doesn't deserve to be on this earth. . . . My father has gone through enough. Now it's time our enemies go through something. Griesa, Kenney, it's their turn to suffer. Not my father again, not us. We have done nothing. . . . To obtain justice there would be no crime that I would be afraid of committing. People like Kenney, Griesa, they could die of the worst pain, and for me it would be only a case for a big champagne celebration. I believe in justifiable homicide.

Thomas Griesa was the trial judge in *United States* v. *Michele Sindona*. John Kenney was the chief prosecutor. Luigi di Fonzo asked Nino Sindona how he could justify murder.

I could justify it in about a second and a half. Like I could justify political murder in a second and a half. Let's assume I want to kill Judge Griesa. For me it's self-defense . . . because he committed the enormous crime of putting my father in jail for life. And there is no chance of a

*On February 19, 1984, William Arico fell to his death while trying to escape from the Metropolitan Correctional Center in New York City. Arico and Michele Sindona were due to face an extradition hearing two days later. The Italian authorities wanted to put both men on trial for the murder of Giorgio Ambrosoli.

retrial as long as Judge Griesa is alive. So by
killing him we will obtain a chance for a retrial.
So self-defense.

Clearly for people such as Michele Sindona and his
son to murder a pope who stood in their way would be
a matter of "self-defense."

Roberto Calvi. It was once said by Lenin: "Give a
capitalist enough rope and he will hang himself." Clearly
the first coroner's jury that considered the death of
Calvi agreed with Lenin. It returned a verdict of suicide.
The fact that the hearing was compressed into a single
day, that witnesses were missing, that witnesses who
were present constantly committed perjury, and that
very little of the highly relevant background evidence
was presented did not appear to disturb the coroner. In
Italy the verdict was greeted with incredulity. In 1983 a
second coroner's jury got nearer to the truth when it
returned an open verdict on the man who had been
found hanging, appropriately enough, next to a sewer
outlet.

I have no doubt that Calvi was "suicided" by his P2
friends—yet another example of the very high risks involved if one pursues a career in Italian banking. Hours
before Calvi died, his secretary in Milan, Graziella
Corrocher, was "suicided" from a fourth-floor window
at the Banco Ambrosiano headquarters in Milan. Her
"death note," which showered curses on Roberto Calvi,
was discovered by Roberto Rosone, still getting around
on crutches after the attempt on his life. A few months
later, on October 2, 1982, Giuseppe Dellacha, an executive at the bank, was also "suicided" from a window in
the Milan headquarters. Calvi's widow, Clara, is on record as laying the blame for her husband's death at the
bronze doors of the Vatican: "The Vatican had my husband killed to hide the bankruptcy of the Vatican Bank."

If it did, and it is not a view I share, then it would
perhaps be poetic justice. The case against Roberto Calvi
with regard to his direct involvement in the death of
Albino Luciani is strong. Very strong.

Calvi was engaged in the ongoing theft of over $1
billion, a theft that would have been completely exposed if Luciani had lived. That exposure would have

occurred in 1978. With Luciani dead, Calvi was free to continue his colossal and frightening array of crimes. Over $400 million of the money that has apparently vanished in a Panamanian version of the Bermuda Triangle was borrowed by Calvi from the world's banks *after* the death of Albino Luciani.

Calvi advised everyone to read *The Godfather* because, as he used to say, "Then you will understand the ways of the world." It was certainly the way of the world he inhabited.

Until the end of his life he was laundering money for the Mafia, the role he had inherited from Michele Sindona. Calvi was also recycling money for P2. These functions were carried out with the assistance of the Vatican Bank, with money moving from Banco Ambrosiano into a Vatican account in Italy, then on to Banca del Gottardo or Union de Banques Suisses (UBS) in Switzerland. He laundered money from kidnappings, drug sales, arms deals, bank raids, holdups, and thefts of jewelry and works of art. His criminal contacts ran the gamut, including what is sometimes known as High Mafia, ordinary run-of-the-mill murderers and members of right-wing terrorist organizations.

The $1.3 billion hole in Banco Ambrosiano was not only created by the fraudulent purchase of shares in Calvi's own bank. Many millions went to sustain Gelli and Ortolani. For example, Calvi diverted $65 million from Peru to a numbered account at UBS Zurich. The owner of that account is Licio Gelli. Another $30 million was diverted into Swiss accounts owned by Calvi's close friend Flavio Carboni.

In early 1982 Calvi transferred direct from the mother bank in Milan $470 million to the bank in Peru. He then gave his secretary a plane ticket to Monte Carlo and a pile of telex messages. The messages, duly sent from Monte Carlo, moved the money into a variety of Swiss numbered accounts.

The Italian Christian Democrats, Communists, and Socialists were not the only political groups to receive money from Calvi. At Gelli's instructions, millions were given to the military regimes that then controlled Argentina and still control Uruguay and Paraguay. Money stolen by Calvi was used by the Argentinian military junta to purchase Exocet missiles from the French; Calvi's bank in Peru assisted in that deal. Millions went secretly and illegally to aid Solidarity in Poland. This particular transaction was a mix of money that Calvi had stolen and Vatican Bank funds collected from the Catholic faithful. Calvi often talked about these transactions to trusted friends. They included Carboni who, like all good Masons, was secretly running a tape recorder:

> Marcinkus must watch out for Casaroli, who is head of the group that opposes him. If Casaroli should meet one of those financiers in New York who are working for Marcinkus, sending money to Solidarity, the Vatican would collapse. Or even if Casaroli should find just one of those pieces of paper that I know of—good-bye, Marcinkus. Good-bye, Wojtyla. Good-bye, Solidarity. The last operation would be enough, the one for twenty million dollars. I've also told Andreotti, but it's not clear which side he is on. If things in Italy go a certain way, the Vatican will have to hire a building in Washington behind the Pentagon. A far cry from St. Peter's.

The total amount that was secretly and illegally funneled on behalf of the Vatican to Solidarity was over $100 million. Many who sympathize with Solidarity's aims might applaud such action. To interfere in such a manner, however, with the affairs of another country creates a dangerous precedent. Why not $100 million funneled secretly to the IRA to kill and maim on the British mainland? A billion dollars to the Sandinistas to blow up a few skyscrapers in New York? Playing God, even for a pope, can be a dangerous occupation. For Karol Wojtyla publicly to upbraid Nicaraguan priests for participating in politics while he interferes in the affairs of Poland is breathtaking hypocrisy.

> We have no temporal goods to exchange, no economic interests to discuss. Our possibilities for intervention are specific and limited and of a special character. They do not interfere with

the purely temporal, technical and political affairs, which are matters for your governments.

Thus spoke Albino Luciani to the diplomatic corps accredited to the Vatican. It is clear that the man who has succeeded him takes precisely the opposite point of view.

With regard to the murder of Albino Luciani, Roberto Calvi had the motive, the opportunity, and undoubtedly, like Michele Sindona, the capacity.

Before Luciani's murder, Calvi associates in P2 had demonstrated their capacity to kill with a series of terrorist bombings. Their ability to kill a specific individual was demonstrated with the murder of Vittorio Occorsio. After the death of the pope, murder and mayhem proceeded at the same tempo as the gigantic thefts in which Calvi was indulging. The fact that Emilio Alessandrini, Mino Pecorelli, Giorgio Ambrosoli, Antonio Varisco, and Boris Giuliano are all dead is the most telling evidence of the kind of company that Roberto Calvi kept. The fact that the director of the Bank of Italy and one of his most trusted colleagues could be falsely charged, that Sarcinelli was forced to endure two weeks of imprisonment, that for years men who knew the truth were frightened to act on it, all demonstrate the terrifying power at the command of Calvi: power that came from many sources, including Licio Gelli, grand master of P2.

Licio Gelli was the puppetmaster with a few thousand strings from which to select. Strings appear to have led everywhere: to the heart of the Vatican, to the White House, to presidential palaces in a wide range of countries. It was Gelli who advised senior P2 members always to carry a fatal dose of digitalis. Such a dose will cause, to use a lay term, a heart attack. Any subsequent medical examination that is merely external will confirm that death has been caused by acute myocardial infarction. The drug is odorless and is impossible to trace unless an autopsy is performed.

Why did Licio Gelli use such a strange code name, "Luciani," whenever he called his P2 paymaster on the special hot line? Was mere mention of the name enough to send the million on millions flowing from Calvi into Gelli's various bank accounts?

According to the members of his family, Calvi attributed all his problems to "the priests." He made it clear which priests he had in mind—those in the Vatican. In September 1978 one priest in particular represented the greatest threat Roberto Calvi had ever been confronted with. Calvi was with Gelli and Ortolani in South America in August 1978, planning new schemes. Can anyone really believe that Gelli and Ortolani would have merely shrugged their shoulders when Calvi told them that Albino Luciani was about to take a course of action that would mean the party was over?

The murder of a magistrate or a judge or a policeman could be carried out openly. The death would remain a mystery or be blamed on one of the many terrorist organizations then rampaging throughout Italy. But the murder of a pope to cover up what was ultimately a $1 billion theft would have to be achieved by stealth. It would have to arouse as little concern as possible. For the murder to succeed in its aim, the death would have to appear natural.

The cost, no matter how high, in bribes, contracts, fees or commissions, was irrelevant. If the object of the pope's death was to protect and sustain Roberto Calvi while he continued to steal millions, then there was a vitual well of Ruth to draw upon. The problem of Deputy Chairman Roberto Rosone, which Calvi discussed at great length with fellow Mason Carboni, was intended to be resolved with the contract murder of Rosone. He lived, but Carboni still paid $530,000, the day after the attack, to the surviving gangster, Ernesto Diotallevi. Half a million for a deputy chairman. How much for a pope when you have an entire bank at your disposal?

After the death of Roberto Calvi, perhaps the most relevant obituary came from Marco Sarcinelli, one of the many who had personal experience of the powers on which Calvi could call: "He began as a servant, then became a master, only to become the servant of other masters later on." Calvi's ultimate master was the man I believe to be at the very heart of the conspiracy to murder Albino Luciani: Licio Gelli.

This book has already recorded many instances of

the power and influence that Gelli has exerted. At the time of Albino Luciani's death in September 1978, Licio Gelli, for all practical purposes, ran Italy. His access to any person or any place within the State of Vatican City was unrivaled, thanks to Umberto Ortolani. The fact that these two men were in South America at the time of Luciani's death is no alibi in the conventional legal sense. Sindona was enjoying an early-evening dry martini in New York at the precise moment that Giorgio Ambrosoli was murdered by William Arico in Milan. That arrangement will not save Sindona now that the Italian authorities have managed to have him extradited from the United States.

The puppetmaster who uses the secret code name Luciani continues to give impressive demonstrations of the fact that he is a man of extraordinary influence. In 1979 Gelli and Ortolani began working to bring about a political reconciliation among Christian Democrat leader and former prime minister Giulio Andreotti and the Socialist leader, Bettino Craxi. The exposure of nearly one thousand P2 members in 1981 slowed down these delicate negotiations. They have now flowered. At the time of this writing the prime minister of Italy is Bettino Craxi; the foreign minister is Giulio Andreotti. Both men have much for which to thank Licio Gelli.

On April 8, 1980, Gelli wrote from Italy to Phillip Guarino, a senior member of the Republican National Committee, which at the time was concentrating all its efforts on getting Ronald Reagan elected president. Gelli wrote: "If you think it might be useful for something favorable to your presidential candidate to be published in Italy, send me some material and I'll get it published in one of the papers here."

Without any knowledge of the power that Gelli wielded, one might find this a very strange offer. How could a man who officially owned no newspapers guarantee sympathetic coverage for Reagan? The answer lies in a consortium of P2 members plus the Vatican-controlled Rizzoli, the massive publishing group, with interests stretching as far as Buenos Aires. Among the many magazines and newspapers was *Corriere della Sera*, Italy's most prestigious newspaper. Other P2 members were planted throughout the television, radio, and

newspaper media of the country. The favorable comments about Ronald Reagan, carefully placed by Licio
Gelli, duly appeared in Italy.

In January 1981, Licio Gelli was an honored guest
at the presidential inauguration. Guarino later ruefully
observed, "He had a better seat than I did."

In May 1981, after the discovery of the list of nearly
one thousand members of P2, including several current
cabinet ministers, had led to the collapse of the Italian
government, Gelli continued his exercise of power from
a variety of South American bases. An indication that
Gelli was far from being a spent force can be seen in
the movement of $95 million by Calvi from Banco
Ambrosiano to the Panamanian company of Bellatrix,
one of the P2-controlled shell companies. This transfer,
via a number of exotic routes, including Rothschild in
Zurich, Rothschild in Guernsey, and the Banque Nation-
ale de Paris in Panama, sprayed money in the most
unlikely directions, including some $20 million into
Ansbacher & Co., a small merchant bank in Dublin.

One year later, in May 1982, with the Falklands
war at its height, Licio Gelli, a man in hiding, on the
run, wanted on countless charges, calmly showed up in
Europe to help his Argentinian friends. The original
Exocet missiles that Gelli had purchased for the junta
had proven to be highly successful, and as previously
described, Gelli now planned to buy more. He stayed
with Ortolani at a villa on Cape Ferrat and began secret
negotiations not only with a number of arms dealers
but also with Aerospatiale, the makers of the missile.
British intelligence became aware of these negotiations
and alerted their counterparts in the Italian secret service,
who promptly began to descend on the Cape Ferrat
villa. They were stopped, however, by the DST, the
French secret service, which blatantly prevented all attempts to arrest Gelli. That is an example of the power
of Licio Gelli.

While negotiating with a variety of potential Exocet
suppliers, Gelli was also in daily contact with Calvi.
The two Freemasons still had much in common. By the
second week of June 1982 Calvi, like Gelli, was a man
on the run. With his Ambrosiano empire on the verge of
collapse, he had illegally left Italy, traveling first to

Austria and then to London. Once again he and Gelli
needed each other. Calvi needed protection from the
Italian authorities, Gelli needed many millions for the
Exocet purchase. My research indicates that the French
were planning to find a way around the embargo of
arms sales to Argentina. The missiles would find their
way to Argentina via Peru. French technicians were
standing by to be flown out to modify the Exocets for
the Argentinian air force.

This time Gelli and Calvi's priorities clashed fatally.
The war would not wait while the puppetmaster pulled
his Italian strings. Calvi, at Gelli's suggestion, traveled
to London and to his death. He was "suicided" on June
17, 1982, the same day that General Galtieri was replaced as president of Argentina by General Bignone.
Argentina had lost the war. Calvi's P2 colleagues considered that by failing to divert money promptly for the
Exocets he had contributed to that defeat.

In August 1982, the Argentinian junta secretly decided to recommence hostilities against the British forces
guarding the Falklands. They felt that with more Exocets
they could win the war and the islands. This time Gelli
dealt with a former officer of the Italian secret service,
Colonel Massimo Pugliese, a member of P2. Again British intelligence learned of the proposed deal. The British took steps to ensure that the deal fell through.

During the same month, August 1982, Gelli was
encountering a problem with one of his secret bank
accounts in Switzerland. It was not performing to order.
Every time that Gelli, in South America, attempted to
transfer money, the UBS in Geneva declined to comply
with the instructions. Gelli was told that he would have
to appear at the bank in person.

Using a fake Argentinian passport, Gelli flew to
Madrid and then to Geneva on September 13, 1982. At
the bank he presented his false documentation and was
told there would be a short delay. Minutes later, he was
arrested. He had walked into a carefully prepared trap.
The account had been frozen at the request of the Italian
government, which had been informed by the Swiss of
the real identity of the accountholder.

The account had been created for Gelli by Roberto
Calvi. Into it the Milanese banker had poured over $100

million. At the time of his arrest Gelli was attempting
to have the $55 million remaining in the account trans-
ferred to Uruguay.

Extradition proceedings began immediately, with
Gelli singing the same song that had earlier been heard
from Sindona and Calvi: "I am a victim of political
persecution. It is a plot of the left." While Swiss magistrates considered the issues, Licio Gelli was held in one
of Switzerland's maximum-security prisons, Champ
Dollon. Extradition proceedings involving any member
of P2, as this book has already established, tend to be
protracted. Gelli was still in Champ Dollon in the summer of 1983.

With Italy about to face another general election in
June, the parliamentary commission that had been investigating P2 was suspended. At least five of the Christian Democrats running for office were members of P2.
Tina Anselmi, who had chaired the commission, was
asked what her views were on P2 after two years of
intensive study. She responded:

> P2 is by no means dead. It still has power. It is
> working in the institutions. It is moving in
> society. It has money, means, and instruments
> still at its disposal. It still has fully operative
> power centers in South America. It is also still
> able to condition, at least in part, Italian politi-
> cal life.

The evidence overwhelmingly supports Tina Anselmi's conclusions. When Gelli's arrest became known in
Argentina, Admiral Emilio Massera, a member of the
ruling junta, remarked, "Signor Gelli has rendered invaluable service to Argentina. This country has much to
thank him for and will forever be in his debt."

Admiral Massera, like General Carlos Suarez Mason,
the First Army commander, like the organizer of the
Argentinian death squads, José Lope Rega, is a member
of the Argentinian section of P2. In Uruguay P2 membership includes the former commander in chief of the
armed forces, General Gregorio Alvarez.

If anyone in Italy or elsewhere thought that Tina
Anselmi was merely attempting to score political points

before an election, they must have received a jolt on
August 10, 1983. Champ Dollon had one prisoner fewer
than the day before. Licio Gelli had escaped. The Swiss
authorities, attempting to cover their deep embarrassment, are now in the process of laying the entire blame
at the feet of one corrupt guard, Umberto Cerdana,
who, they claim, helped Gelli escape for a bribe of less
than $10,000.* If any reader of this book believes that
Gelli escaped from Switzerland with the help of only
one prison guard, they also probably believe that Albino Luciani died a natural death. A guard takes the
equivalent of four months' salary for an act for which
he now has been sentenced to eighteen months?

Nine days after Gelli's escape, the Swiss authorities
approved the extradition request from Italy. The trouble was that there was now no Gelli to extradite. Gelli
had been driven to France by his son in a hired BMW.
From there, the pair had been transported by an unwit-
ting helicopter pilot to Monte Carlo. The excuse given
to the pilot for diverting from Nice and landing at
Monte Carlo was that Gelli urgently needed dental
treatment. Via a yacht belonging to Francesco Pazienza,
a man who claims to have been a good friend of the late
Roberto Calvi, Gelli continued his search for a good
dentist in Uruguay. As of this writing he is still in
Uruguay, pulling his strings from a ranch a few miles
north of Montevideo. He is wanted in many countries
for many crimes, but the mass of information that he
has so diligently acquired over the years ensures that he
continues to be protected.

The Italian election in June 1983 had resulted in
Bettino Craxi, one of the many beneficiaries of Calvi's
largess, becoming prime minister. Told of Gelli's escape,
he said: "The flight of Gelli confirms that the grand
master has a network of powerful friends."

If (and it is indeed a very large if) Licio Gelli ever is
handed over alive to the Italian government, he faces a

---

*Early in 1984, Cerdana was sentenced to eighteen months in
prison. The sentence was suspended. The court received a
letter from Gelli in which the puppetmaster recommended
leniency. He also apologized for escaping, and he stated that
he was a victim of political persecution.

variety of criminal charges. They include the following:
extortion, blackmail, drug smuggling, arms smuggling,
conspiracy to overthrow the legal government, political
espionage, military espionage, illegal possession of state
secrets, and involvement in a series of bombings, including the Bologna station attack in which eighty-four people died.

The chain that link by link leads from a murdered
pope to Bishop Paul Marcinkus to Roberto Calvi to
Umberto Ortolani to Licio Gelli is strong. For circumstantial evidence to succeed, it must be strong; it must
be able to withstand the closest scrutiny before a jury
can bring in a verdict of "guilty." No jury confronted
with the evidence contained in this book could return in
Albino Luciani's case a verdict of "death by natural
causes." No judge, no coroner in the world would accept such a verdict on this evidence. That is beyond all
argument. No evidence exists to indicate that Albino
Luciani's death was the result of an accident. We are
left with murder—not, in my view, by a person or persons unknown, but by persons all too well known, with,
at the heart of the conspiracy, Licio Gelli.

Gelli's P2 members included the brother of Cardinal Sebastiano Baggio, Francesco. Gelli's meetings with
the powerful and famous included audiences with Pope
Paul VI. Gelli was a man whose close friends included
Cardinal Paolo Bertoli. Gelli's closest P2 adviser, Umberto
Ortolani, knew his way around Vatican City better than
many cardinals. Ortolani, with his drawer full of Vatican honors and awards, was so close to the nerve center
of Vatican power that he had been the one to host the
preconclave secret meeting that had finalized strategy
for and brought about the election of Paul VI. Ortolani
conceived the idea of the multimillion-dollar sale of the
Vatican interests in Società Generale Immobiliare,
Ceramiche Pozzi, and Condotte. Ortolani was the P2
marriage broker, joining as partners the Mafioso and
fellow P2 member Michele Sindona with His Holiness
Pope Paul VI. Ortolani had collected vast commissions
from one and papal honors from the other. Through
Ortolani, no room in the State of Vatican City could
deny access to the puppetmaster or to the men and
women he controlled. Gelli was also a collector of inter-

esting bits of knowledge and information, including, for example, photographs of Pope John Paul II completely nude next to his swimming pool. When Gelli showed these snapshots to senior Socialist Party politician Vanni Nistico he remarked, "Look at the problems the secret services have. If it's possible to take these pictures of the pope, imagine how easy it is to shoot him." Indeed. Or poison his predecessor.

> And Jesus went into the temple of God, and cast out all them that sold and bought in the temple, and overthrew the tables of the money-changers, and the seats of them that sold doves.
> And said unto them, It is written, My house shall be called the house of prayer; but ye have made it a den of thieves.
>
> Matt. 21:12–13

Albino Luciani had a dream. He dreamed of a Roman Catholic Church that would truly respond to the needs of its people on vital issues such as artificial birth control. He dreamed of a Church that would dispense with the wealth, power, and prestige it had acquired through Vatican Incorporated; of a Church that would get out of the marketplace, where the message of Christ had become tainted; of a Church that would once again rely on what has always been its greatest asset, its source of true power, its greatest claim to a unique prestige: the Gospel.

By the evening of September 28, 1978, Albino Luciani had taken the first steps toward the realization of his extraordinary dream. At 9:30 P.M. he closed his bedroom door, and the dream ended.

In Italy now there is talk of declaring Albino Luciani a saint. Already petitions with many thousands of signatures have been collected. Ultimately if this man, who was "a poor man, accustomed to small things and silence" is canonized, it would be more than fitting. On September 28, 1978, he was martyred for his beliefs. Confronted with a man such as Albino Luciani, with the problems his continuing presence would pose, the Italian Solution was applied. The decision was made that the pope must die, and thus "God's candidate" was murdered.

EPILOGUE

If the good that Albino Luciani represented was interred with his bones, the evil perpetrated by Roberto Calvi has most certainly lived after him.

Within hours of his body being identified in London, the alarm had been sounded throughout Italy. On the first day the banks were opened after the Knight had been found hanging not far from where monks had offered sanctuary to embezzlers, swindlers, and thieves in the Middle Ages, the Banco Ambrosiano began to experience a heavy run of withdrawals. What is not public knowledge until now is that the Vatican Bank suffered the same fate. Many millions of dollars were withdrawn by those members of the Italian establishment who, privy to the facts, were aware that a $1.3 billion hole in the Ambrosiano group would soon be public knowledge and that the hole was not unconnected with Calvi's long-standing business and personal relationship with Paul Marcinkus and the IOR.

By September 1982, Marcinkus, who had never left the pope's side during his visit to Britain in May and June, had become a virtual prisoner within the Vatican. He was replaced as organizer and advance guard of international papal trips—to have ventured out of Vatican City would have been to invite immediate arrest by the Italian authorities.

Marcinkus continued to function as head of the Vatican Bank and he declared that the Vatican did not and would not accept any responsibility for the $1.3 billion that had disappeared.

The Roman Curia refused to accept judicial papers that the Italian government attempted to serve on Marcinkus and others at the Vatican Bank. Protocol must be observed at all times, the Curia insisted, even when the theft of over $1 billion is involved. The papers would have to be handed to the Italian ambassador to the Vatican.

Vatican City did establish a commission of inquiry after a great deal of prodding from the Italian government. Simultaneously, the Vatican Bank's own lawyers busied themselves with an inquiry. The Italian government had also created a commission of inquiry. By now there were jobs for nearly everyone. The lawyers working for Marcinkus came up with their conclusions first:

1. The Institute for the Works of Religion has not received either from the Ambrosiano group or from Roberto Calvi any monies, and, therefore, does not have to refund anything.

2. The foreign companies indebted to the Ambrosiano group have never been run by the IOR, which has no knowledge of the operations carried out by the same.

3. It is established that all the payments made by the Ambrosiano group to the aforementioned companies were made prior to the so-called letters of comfort.

4. These latter, by their date of issue, have not exercised any influence on the same payments.

5. In any future checking of the facts, all the above will be proved to be true.

I have already established that these Vatican "facts" are very far from the truth.

The commission of inquiry set up by the Vatican has yet to report. Its conclusions were due at the end of March 1983, then the end of April 1983, then August 1983, then October, then November.

The commission comprises "four wise men." Two of them, by their presence on a commission of inquiry that Cardinal Casaroli has predictably called "objective," completely invalidate any findings that may eventually be reached. One is Philippe de Weck, the former chairman of UBS (Union des Banques Suisses) Zurich. De Weck still maintains very close links with the UBS. This is the bank that holds on behalf of Licio Gelli $55 million of the stolen money. It is the bank that holds on behalf of the late Roberto Calvi and Flavio Carboni over $30 million of the stolen money. It is the bank that holds on behalf of Carboni's Austrian mistress, Manuela Kleinszig, $2 million of the stolen money.

Philippe de Weck is also the man at the center of what the French call "the sniffer planes affair." This involved a wonderful invention, the brainchild of an Italian technician, Aldo Bonassoli, and Count Alain de Villegas, an elderly Belgian. The invention came in two parts, one housed in a plane that beamed back information to the second part on earth. Cross sections of the geological strata many thousands of feet below the earth's surface were then seen as technical data on a computer screen.

The potential was limitless. Along with instant mineral and oil prospecting at a fraction of the traditional cost, there were also military implications—any eye that could locate oil thousands of feet below the earth's surface could also pinpoint a submerged nuclear submarine. Encouraged by President Giscard d'Estaing, the French oil giant Elf poured about $120 million into the count's Panamanian company Fisalma. Villegas was the sole shareholder, and the company was administered by Philippe de Weck. By the time the French realized that "le Sting" had been played on them, $60 million had vanished. De Weck told the French that the money had gone to research and "charitable works." One of the men acting for UBS Zurich who had been keeping an eye on this pioneering work in the art of international theft was Ernst Keller, who at the same time was also a shareholder of Ultrafin AG, a Calvi-owned company linked to Ambrosiano Holding Luxembourg. Ultrafin was the conduit by which the count's Panamanian company received its initial payments.

Another member of the Vatican commission is Herman Abs, who was head of the Deutsche Bank from 1940 to 1945. The Deutsche Bank was the Nazis' bank throughout the Second World War. Abs was in effect Hitler's paymaster. During this period Abs was also on the board of I. G. Farben, the chemical and industrial conglomerate that gave such wholehearted assistance to Hitler's war efforts. Abs participated in board meetings of I. G. Farben at which members discussed the use of slave labor at a Farben rubber plant located in the Auschwitz concentration camp.

No matter how many ex-bank chairmen or Nazi paymasters the Vatican employs, the truth will not go away. At least $1 billion of the monies owed to the various banks is the Vatican's responsibility. Perhaps the greatest irony of all is that no matter how much or how little the Vatican benefited from the phantom companies littered in Panama and elsewhere, it owned the companies when the debts were incurred. In fact it has benefited vastly, but if the banks that are owed money are really determined to get it back, then they have only one logical course of action: sue the Vatican. More specifically, sue the Vatican Bank and Pope John Paul II, for 85 percent of the profits from the bank go directly to the pope.

At the time of Calvi's death he was, according to subsequent sworn statements made by members of his family, negotiating with Opus Dei, which had agreed to buy the 16 percent of Banco Ambrosiano that the Vatican owned. If this deal had been completed, the $1.3 billion hole would have been filled, Calvi's empire would have remained intact, and Archbishop Paul Marcinkus would have been removed from office. Many, including Marcinkus, objected to that eleventh-hour deliverance from such a quarter.

Now, with Calvi dead, the Vatican has been wrangling with the Italian government and a consortium representing international banking for nearly two years. Eventually in February 1984 news that agreement had finally been reached began to filter out of the Geneva conference rooms. By mid-May 1984 the details were clear. The international banks will get back approximately two thirds of the $600 million they had loaned

Calvi's Luxembourg holding company. *Of that, some $250 million will be paid by the Vatican Bank.* The Vatican is due to hand over this sum on June 30, 1984. This payment is being made by the Vatican "on the basis of non-culpability" but "in recognition of a moral involvement." The reader may care to reexamine the Vatican denials of any involvement, recorded on page 367, in light of this impending repayment. This amount represents a loan made to the Vatican by Calvi's Peruvian bank, where there can be no possible dispute of the debt.

The faithful should ignore the appeals that will undoubtedly be made in Roman Catholic churches throughout the world. All the Vatican Bank is doing is repaying a part of the vast amount of money it acquired through the activities of Calvi and Marcinkus. And still, the Vatican Bank has walked away from the entire affair with millions upon millions of dollars that represent a substantial amount of the still missing monies.

At the time of this writing, Archbishop Paul Marcinkus still clings to office. He has been written off many times, yet he still survives. He still hides in the Vatican, afraid of being arrested by the Italian authorities in the event that he emerges. Word has reached me that Marcinkus recently appealed to the Italian courts asking for immunity from prosecution. I hope that before the Italian judiciary considers Marcinkus' plea they obtain access to a still-secret report of negotiations between Italy and the Vatican City State on the Ambrosiano bank failure. Possibly the most extraordinary information the report contains is the revelation that the secret, and criminal, agreement between Marcinkus and Calvi made in August 1981 was not, as the Vatican would have the world believe, a singular abberation by a kindly archbishop toward a devout Catholic banker. Rather, the report will show that other similar agreements were made by the two men, dating back as far as November 1976. The criminal conspiracy, therefore, began during the reign of Pope Paul VI. These facts serve to underline powerfully what would have occurred if Albino Luciani had lived. Also hiding within the Vatican are the archbishop's colleagues and partners in so many crimes, Luigi Mennini and Pellegrino de Strobel. In such a man-

ner does Pope John Paul II preside over his Vatican
Bank in May 1984.

While all three men remain fugitives from Italian
justice, the authorities have sequestered all Italian property belonging to Mennini and de Strobel. All three are
wanted by a wide range of Italian authorities in a number of cities. Yet another colleague who would also have
been promptly removed by Luciani if he had lived,
Monsignor Donato de Bonis, the secretary of the IOR, is
hiding within the Vatican walls from Turin magistrates
who are investigating a $1 billion tax-evasion scandal.
De Bonis, who has had his passport withdrawn by the
magistrates, continues, like his three colleagues, to work
at the Vatican Bank. In such a manner does Pope John
Paul II, to whom these men are answerable, preside
over his Vatican Bank in May 1984.

Cardinal Ugo Poletti, the cardinal vicar of Rome, is
another man that Luciani had decided to remove. In his
case, too, there is ample evidence to illustrate the wisdom of Luciani's decision. Poletti was responsible for
recommending to Andreotti, then prime minister, that
General Raffaele Giudice should be placed in command
of the finance police. In this capacity P2 member Giudice
organized the $1 billion tax-evasion scandal, diverting
massive amounts of money to Licio Gelli. In 1983 Cardinal Poletti indignantly denied using any influence to get
Giudice his job. The Turin magistrates then showed the
cardinal vicar of Rome a copy of his letter to Andreotti.
Poletti remains cardinal vicar of Rome. In such a manner does Pope John Paul II preside over the Roman
Catholic Church in May 1984.

The new concordat recently signed between the Vatican and the Italian government makes a fitting epitaph
for the current pope's reign. Italy, for nearly two thousand years regarded by Catholics as the home of their
faith, no longer has Roman Catholicism as "the religion
of the state." The Church's privileged position in Italy is
ending.

Another change must be bringing a warm smile to
the face of Licio Gelli. The new canon law that took
effect on November 27, 1983, has dropped the ruling
that Freemasons are subject to automatic excommunication. The survivors on the list of Vatican Masons that

Albino Luciani considered are now safe. The purge he
had planned will not be reactivated by his successor.

As has been shown here, none of Luciani's proposed
changes have been implemented. Vatican Incorporated
is still functioning. In all markets.

INDEX

373

ABOUT THE AUTHOR

DAVID A. YALLOP is the author of four previous investigative works: *To Encourage The Others* (which caused the British government to reopen a murder case which had been closed for over twenty years); *The Day The Laughter Stopped* (the definitive biography of Fatty Arbuckle); *Beyond Reasonable Doubt?* (which led directly to the freeing of a man serving a life sentence for murder); and most recently, *Deliver Us From Evil*, an investigation into the identity of the Yorkshire Ripper. It was during that investigation that Mr. Yallop's work came to the attention of the high-placed, secret sources within the Vatican who first convinced the author of the need for an examination of the circumstances surrounding the death of Albino Luciani. Three years of intensive investigation followed and led the author from Rome to New York, South America to London and to sources as diverse as cardinals and criminals. Mafiosi, monsignors and government agents; from private, confidential interviews to the exhaustive search through thousands of pages of previously overlooked public documents. The result is *In God's Name*—a work of monumental research and importance.